Graphical User Interfaces and Graphic Standards

Jon Peddie

McGraw-Hill, Inc.

New York St. Louis San Francisco Auckland Bogotá Caracas
Lisbon London Madrid Mexico City Milan Montreal New Delhi
Paris San Juan São Paulo Singapore Sydney Tokyo Toronto

FIRST EDITION
FIRST PRINTING

Library of Congress Cataloging-in-Publication Data

Peddie, Jon.
Graphical user interfaces and graphic standards / by Jon Peddie.
p. cm.
Includes index.
ISBN 0-8306-2505-4
1. Computer graphics—Standards. 2. User interfaces (Computer systems)—Standards. I. Title.
T385.P44 1991
006.6—dc20 91-18110
CIP

For information about other McGraw-Hill materials, call 1-800-2-MCGRAW in the U.S.
In other countries call your nearest McGraw-Hill office.

Acquisitions Editor: Larry Hager
Book Editor: Sally Anne Glover
Production: Katherine G. Brown
Book Design: Jaclyn J. Boone

Contents

Abbreviations

APA	all points addressable
bps	bits per second
CGA	Color Graphics Adapter
cps	characters per second
DOS	Disk Operating System
DPI	dots per inch
EGA	Enhanced Graphics Adapter
EIA	Electronic Industries Association
Hz	hertz
in	inch
I/O	input/output
Kbyte	kilobytes
KHz	kilohertz
LAN	local area networks
Mbytes	megabytes
MDA	Monochrome Display Adapter
MHz	megahertz
MSB	most significant bit
ns	nanosecond
POST	Power-On Self-Test
PS/2	Personal System/2
RAM	random-access memory
ROM	read-only memory
s	second
VGA	Video Graphics Array
W	watt

Acknowledgments

The author wishes to thank the following members of Jon Peddie Associates. Without them, this book would have not been possible.

Fred Dunn

Cynthia Peddie

R. Sterling Stites

Catherine Higgins Mee

The following companies were exceptionally helpful: HP, IBM, NeXT, Nuron Data, XVT.

Foreword

Forewords are a bit like motherhood and apple pie. The author of the foreword very often knows the author of the book, has been involved in the field, and has responded to the author's request to provide a brief introduction to the book. I have written several forewords myself, and I have had other people write them for me. The foreword's contents are usually the result of general observations about the need for the book, and the expectation that this particular author has done a superb job of fulfilling those expectations.

This is certainly the case with Jon Peddie in *Graphical User Interfaces*. But, beyond that, this foreword is being written by someone (me) who has had a chance to not only read the manuscript, but also to make immediate use of its enormously useful contents in conjunction with some recent consulting assignments.

As a computer graphics consultant, I have been carefully following (and admittedly somewhat confused about) the details of graphical user interfaces (GUIs) and graphics standards. Certainly there is a general agreement that they are needed, but they have appeared in such profusion that it has been difficult to get a clear picture of the overall situation and to obtain details of individual offerings.

Although it is possible to scramble through much of the current periodical literature and put a moderately complete picture together, it turns out to be a lot more convenient to make use of Jon Peddie's excellent book. He has brought together an extraordinarily useful overview, detailed information about each of the offerings, and knowledgeable comments about tradeoffs in the decision-making process. I can attest first hand that the availability of this information in one volume has been extraordinarily useful to me in my work. So, while I can enthusiastically commend the book to you on a "motherhood and apple pie" basis, I can even more enthusiastically commend it to you because it is a good, solid, working document that will help you in your day-to-day trek through the intricacies of GUIs and standards. Jon Peddie is to be congratulated on an extraordinary job that needed to be done and has been done with great skill.

Carl Machover
President, Machover Associates Corporation
Past-President, National Computer Graphics Association
June 10, 1991

Preface

The purpose of this book is to identify issues affecting the choice of a graphical user interface (GUI) for the individual user and company-wide installations. The first step for most organizations that are considering adopting a GUI approach to computing is to conduct a feasibility study. This book is your feasibility study. GUIs are available for almost every type of computer and operating system on the market. This book will help you understand the choices and recognize the obstacles.

GUIs for a large organization must function in an environment of PCs, microcomputers, and mainframes. Choosing a GUI for a single platform, such as for a single user or department, is easier, but not without tradeoffs. Furthermore, you should choose a GUI that users will feel comfortable with and welcome, not one that they will rebel against or not use.

Graphics standards

After many years of frustrated experience with device-dependent software, computer users identified portability of programs from one computer system to another as the single most important objective of a graphics standard. The second objective was to have a clear-cut division between the modeling of graphics objects and the viewing of graphics images based on those objects.

A review of standards

A significant development that started in the mid 1970s was a general awareness of the need for standards in device-independent graphics packages. That emerged into a widely known specification called the Core Graphic System (Core for short). Another standard, GKS, is a 2D vector-based graphic interface with no support for bit-maps (raster operations available on modern workstations today). GKS was popular mostly in Europe. The Programmer's Hierarchical Interactive Graphics Standard (PHIGS) defines a sophisticated graphics support system that controls the definition, modification, and display of hierarchical graphics data. Additional systems such as the X Window System are being considered by standards committees.

Graphical user interface

A GUI is distinguished by its window appearance and the way an operator's actions and input options are handled. Input options to computer programs can be designed as a set of *icons*, which are graphic symbols that look like the processing option they are meant to represent. Users select processing options by pointing, with a mouse or stylus, to the appropriate icon on the screen. The advantage of these systems is that the icons can take up less screen space than the corresponding text description of the functions, can be understood more quickly if well designed, and can initiate a whole series of operations or activities. The truly unique benefit provided by a windowing system is the ability to have multiple views of different objects on the screen at the same time.

Benefits of a GUI

Recent studies have shown that users in a GUI environment work faster, more accurately and with lower frustration and fatigue levels than users in a character-based environment. Productivity has increased 35 percent, and the accuracy of completed work has improved as much as 74 percent in some environments.

Graphical user interface development

Graphical user interface systems are not a new idea. They were first envisioned by Vannevar Bush in an article he wrote in 1945. Xerox was researching graphical user interface tools at the Palo Alto Research Center throughout the 1970s. By 1983, every major workstation vendor had a proprietary windowing system. It wasn't until 1984, when Apple introduced the Macintosh, that a truly robust windowing environment reached the average consumer.

Also in 1984, out of an MIT project called Athena, arose the X Window System. Athena investigated the use of networked graphics workstations as a teaching aid for students in various disciplines. They attempted to develop a windowing system that would allow students to run local tools like word processors and spreadsheets while simultaneously being able to call up library pictures and documents from remote sources.

X Window Systems

The X Window System is a nonvendor-specific windowing system developed at the Massachusetts Institute of Technology in the 1980s. It was specifically developed to provide a common windowing system across networks connecting machines from different vendors. The X Window System (commonly referred to as *X-Windows*, or *X*) is not a GUI. It is a portable, network-transparent windowing system that acts as a foundation on which to build GUIs (such as OSF/Motif and DECwindows). The X Window System provides a standard means of communicating between dissimilar machines on a network and can be viewed in a window. Any number of windows can be open simultaneously, each potentially showing a different process on a different machine. Typically, the communication is via TCP/IP protocol over an Ethernet network. As it is with Microsoft Windows, development of the X-based GUI is ahead of application software for it.

Since the X Window System is in the public domain and not specific to any platform or operating system, it has a good chance of becoming the *de facto* windowing system of the 1990s in heterogeneous environments from PCs to mainframes. The industry trend is to adopt a fully overlapping windows system that treats the screen in an all-points-addressable (APA) or bit-mapped graphics image with soft typefonts and a mouse-driven pointer that can move around by single-pixel increments. This is clearly an idea whose time has come.

The state of things

Both operating systems and GUIs are in a tremendous state of flux. Microsoft Windows will become the dominant GUI of IBM PCs for the first half of this decade. After that, it is feasible that OS/2 will have gained enough momentum to overtake Windows in mainstream applications. Presentation Manager (PM), the GUI of OS/2, has much the same look and feel as Windows, and programs written for Windows will run under OS/2 without modification (binary compatibility). Over the long term, it seems that Microsoft Windows will continue to be more popular for 286 or 386 computers because of its relationship to DOS.

Hardware classes

Computer hardware systems can be classified into 5 general environments used to display graphic and textual information: alphanumeric terminals, personal computers, graphic terminals, graphic visualization workstations and X-Terminals. The individual characteristics are discussed in detail in this book.

How to use this book

This book is organized in as logical a fashion as possible, given the range of topics and their interrelationships. The following points should aid the reader with the organization and conventions.

Glossary The topic of standards and GUIs makes use of many new and unusual words and terms. I have made great effort to avoid arcane computer terms. In some cases it just couldn't be avoided. In all cases uncommon words and terms are explained in the glossary. The reader is advised to refer to it during reading, as some terms have come to acquire ambiguous and antonymic meanings.

Terms and conventions Even within the normal limits of grammar, protocol and laws, each book and author has a certain style. This book and author are no different. The following are the conventions used in this book.

- *Client* and *Server* are the names of specific devices or systems and will be capitalized. A person who is the client of some organization will be lower case.
- *Windows* (with a capital W) refers to Microsoft's Windows. If necessary or appropriate a version number (e.g., 2.1, 3.1, etc.) will follow.
- The word *window* (with a lower case w) refers to a window that is displayed on a computer screen.

- *Clicking* a mouse refers to pressing and quickly releasing the button on the side or top of the mouse.
- *Buttons* or *dials* on a screen refer to the symbolic representation of such items and not actually physical buttons or dials.
- Versions of programs that represent a family are designated with a small *x*, as in 3.x, or 1.x.
- Versions of a processor that refer to a family are designated with a small x, as in 808x or 80xx6, or 680x0.

Organizations mentioned All organizations mentioned in this book can be found in the Appendix. The organizations name, address and phone number are included.

Trademarks The author makes no claim to trademarked names and relies on the fair use doctrine in the use of trademarked names throughout this book.

Introduction

Graphical user interfaces and graphics standards are probably one of the most important and exciting developments of this decade. Having been in an evolutionary state since the late 1960s, thirty years later the convergence of technological and human development has made computers easier to use and more productive. This book is designed to show the choices available and guide the reader in the selection of a graphical user interface (GUI) and graphics standard.

A common user interface

The goal of many organizations is to have a company-wide computing environment that will allow any experienced computer user (regardless of skill level) to go to any available computer and use it. This is sometimes referred to as a *common user interface* (CUI). Sounds simple enough, but in practice it is seldom realized. The establishment of local area networks (LANs) made possible, among other things, access to common applications; it was a great liberator. Depending upon an individual's local setup, the computers on a LAN are often similar enough that you can access your application and/or files in another person's office or workspace. In this example the CUI is often a simple character-based menu system, or a command-line prompt that is well known.

A graphical user interface

A common graphical user interface (GUI) is another way of reaching the same goal with several added benefits. It provides a friendlier, less intimidating, and less confusing environment. A GUI environment offers familiar symbols or icons that resemble commonly known functions or items such as files and trash cans so that complicated, arcane command-line sequences do not have to be memorized. GUIs may look a bit different, but they all contain the same basic desktop metaphor of iconic symbolism. This is often referred to as the same *look and feel.*

Arguments still take place between various pedantic groups about the efficiency or speed of using a command line versus a GUI. These are much like the tavern discussions of why a stick shift in a car is better than an automatic. For those power users who need the "feel of the machine" and don't mind wasting time trying to figure out the subdirectory structure, path, config.sys, trustee rights and/or setup on an alien machine, I say, "Have at it—may the operating system be with you." For the rest of us mere mortals who just want to get to an application, do a little work and go home or back to our own office, a GUI is a godsend.

In the 1950s, 1960s, and 1970s, scientists at the MIT Stanford Research Institute (SRI) and Xerox's Palo Alto Research Centre (PARC) investigated the interactive user interface. Their research showed that people could learn to use applications with a GUI more quickly than learning commands. So why use a GUI? Productivity, plain and simple. You can get more out of the computer in less time. You spend your time doing a job, not addressing the needs of the computer.

In the past, one of the arguments against using a GUI was the amount of power (often referred to as *cycles*) needed to make a graphic interface functional in a commercial environment. However, with the cost per MIPS (cost of cycles) steadily declining, the power argument is no longer valid.

Users are definitely attracted to GUIs. They were popularized by Macintosh, but the concept of a GUI has almost taken on a life of its own. Why is that? There is no single reason. It's due to a number of factors: a perceived ease of use (often based on hearsay), the promise of common interfaces across programs and ultimately across platforms, and an expectation that the user will have more control over the computer.

The early developers at Xerox started with a specific application area, the office. They identified problems in this domain and then applied the technology to solve them. Windows were used to expand the virtual screen and enable rapid movement among tasks. Icons were used as a reminder of what's available, and the mouse for direct manipulation to implement a simple *visual language*—where the icons are the nouns, and simple manipulations with the mouse are the verbs. Of equal importance was the need to provide the user with immediate, visual feedback about the effect of each action.

But does that mean GUIs provide the standard way of accessing computer resources, or that they're desired by every right-minded user and information systems manager? No, of course not. However, there are additional benefits that come with a GUI. According to surveys, a common quote from users and managers on GUIs versus text-based systems is that a typical GUI-based user works with six applications, while a character-based user (with a character user interface or CUI) works with no more than three or four applications. Why? Because of the more complex learning curve associated with the CUI. Users gain greater proficiency more quickly with a GUI, as shown in FIG. I-1.

For a wide range of applications, the graphical user interface style of windows and desktop metaphor is a tremendous improvement over the textual interface style that preceded it. However, although enjoying tremendous popularity now, the GUI with its icons and mouse has been around for over 15 years. The technology to support this style of interface is now maturing. Today major efforts are focused on standardizing the look and feel of these interfaces and ensuring they run in today's open system world. It's well known that the human short-term memory is limited to six (plus or minus two) items, and this constraint has a strong effect on a person's problem-solving perfor-

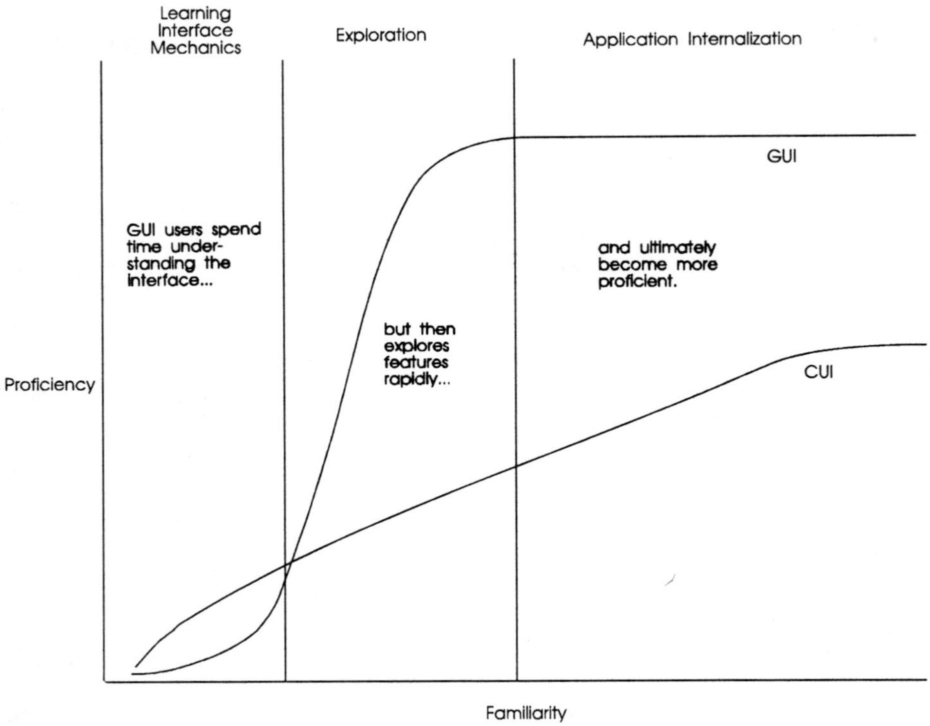

Fig. I-1. User proficiency.

mance. Visual displays act as an external short-term memory, effectively expanding the capacity beyond just six items. Visual displays also augment long-term memory as well. Icons on a screen are reminders that programs or files are available.

However, one of the real benefits isn't even graphical—it's that a GUI provides the resource to pull data from different sources and use it in a variety of applications. It would seem then that even beyond their concrete functions, GUIs seem to offer more. Some observers have pointed out that GUIs imply the future. People believe they will be more powerful and have more control with GUIs.

Enterprise vs. individual

A GUI will enhance the productivity of an individual. Equipping a user with a system that has a GUI is not very expensive relative to an organization's overall costs. As the user gets familiar with the GUI, his or her productivity will rise rapidly and then taper off. This is known as the asymptote of productivity. Put another way, for a relatively small investment an organization can see a rapid but limited gain in productivity or return on investment (ROI).

If an entire department is equipped with GUIs and true workgroup activities are employed, there will be a greater, but again limited, gain in productivity or ROI. However, the gain does not come as quickly. It takes longer to get the department working smoothly together. The training, hardware and software costs are obviously greater for a department than for an individual. However, the ROI per employee is greater than for just the single employee. Also, the ROI curve continues to go up over a longer period of time; but, it too has an asymptote.

When an organization invests in an enterprise-wide implementation of GUIs, it takes even more time and money to see any return. However, the return is almost twice as much per employee, and it continues to increase (albeit at a slower rate) for a much longer time, as FIG. I-2 shows.

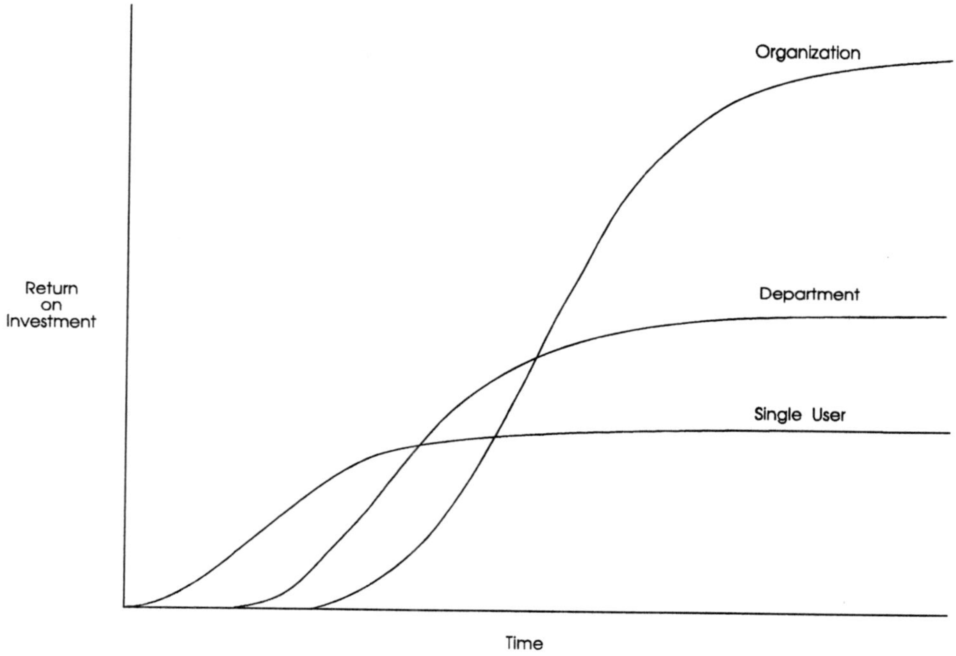

Fig. I-2. ROI for GUI.

With such tremendous ROI potential, shouldn't every organization invest immediately in an enterprise-wide GUI? Of course the answer is no. If the organization has no experience whatsoever with GUIs, all it would do is suffer an embarrassing loss and have almost nothing to show for it by plunging full force into GUIs. The logical course is to set up a test with one or two individuals. While that is in process, generate a plan, based on the empirical data gained from the test. Make no mistake, implementing an enterprise-wide GUI strategy is not a quick or easy process. The president or department manager can't simply go out and buy a dozen copies of some GUI package and expect magical results and spectacular ROI.

Enter GUI land with caution. There are riches there, but like any reward, it won't come for free.

Which one is best?

In a multivendor environment that may or may not be completely linked or networked, a GUI still offers a better chance for a new user to have some success with a machine (assuming the chosen application is not too dissimilar). However, it is still not possible to log on to a Sun workstation and call up WordPerfect, then go to an X-terminal and do some work in Excel and finish the day in front of a Macintosh and do a dBII search. The applications simply don't run across platforms (like they should), which would provide true enterprise-wide computing. Nonetheless, the day is coming, and GUIs are the vanguard of that desirable situation. Therefore, the question of which GUI is the best one is again like a discussion about automobiles—which one is the best one?

Charm

A GUI needs computer cycles (MIPS) to operate. In the past, when computers were not as fast as they are today and when memory was more expensive, a GUI would not have been possible, or it would have operated very slowly. However, a GUI, if designed properly, brings *charm* and user friendliness to a computer. Charm uses (some say squanders) computing horsepower because it takes a lot of computer cycles and memory to make a system convenient and easy to use. Nonetheless, charm will be the deciding factor of success for computer companies and software suppliers. User charm can be translated as meaning *cheap bits* or *cheap cycles*. It takes a lot of bits and a lot of CPU cycles to meet the challenge. If those things are expensive, then they won't be available to the masses and therefore they won't deliver the promise of productivity.

A GUI that has been designed for people will have a certain feel about it, the charm factor. Although difficult to describe, you know it when you experience it. (If it were easier to describe, there would be no problem in meeting the charm specifications, and every GUI would be so endowed.) While the graphical user interface may make computing easier for users, making one work well and exhibit the charm factor creates some problems for developers—problems that did not often arise in the creation of a purely character-based application.

The developer, often not versed in the nuances of user friendliness and charm, has to make decisions on various issues concerning the design of a GUI. For example, should applications be designed with pull-down or pop-up menus? In some GUI environments, that decision is made for the developer. In others, Motif, for example, the developer has the choice of either. There are also two schools of thought on iconic representation; should they represent real objects or be a symbolic representation of their main use, suggesting the key point of the application? The symbolic icon, for example, is very popular in Japan, while in the U.S., users prefer (in general) the real objects approach—so charm has a cultural aspect as well. Those are the unresolved and somewhat difficult to define issues of charm in a GUI.

The dark side of a GUI

There are some drawbacks and precautions to take in using a GUI.

Cost "For nothing you get nothing," or put another way, "There ain't no free lunch." GUIs come with a cost, and they are far from a panacea. Because of the cost, many users will not invest in GUIs unless they can see an immediate benefit or are already using graphics-oriented programs.

Training The use of a GUI is not as intuitive or obvious as people think. The need for clear, easy-to-understand instructions will not go away just because you have a GUI.

Stress In his book, *Technostress: The Human Cost of the Computer Revolution*, Dr. Craig Brod comments on a type of stress experienced by users and programmers of computers. "We are all being socialized to be more at ease with the computer than we are with people," according to Brod. He believes those who have become used to working with computers and technology find interaction with other people stress producing.

Sociologists and psychologists are concerned about what computers are teaching us about the rest of the world. "The machine is a socialization agent that teaches you a style of interaction that is then generalized and carried over to other situations," says Dr. Tim Lynch, President of New Wave Consultants in North Quincy, Massachusetts. "Because the computer gives immediate feedback, people begin to expect immediate feedback from other people within the company," Lynch says. "They want things and they want them now." Brod says this intense man-machine relationship is both draining and addictive at the same time. "By the end of a day working with computers, you feel exhausted. There is no time for reflection. You just want to be left alone to recuperate."

Initially, a computer user is very interested in finding out about the machine and the system. As stress sets in, there is much less obsessive curiosity about what new things you can do with the computer. Some psychologists think the reason some computer users may be so stressed is that they were born with a personality prone to be stressed—a trait that may have drawn them into a career in the computer field.

Psychologists suggest setting up the work area in such a way that there is direct human interaction. Also, schedules should be arranged so that computer users have to get up, move around, and talk to their fellow employees. They also suggest more social gatherings either during or after work. They advise doing anything that brings you back to that bodily sense you have lost. If you feel the need for faster responses from the computer, some psychologists suggest that you count to 10 or get up and walk around.

The possibility of technostress is something to consider. GUIs are supposed to free us from drudgery and make our jobs easier, but often they just give us more time to do more work.

Summary

In spite (or maybe because) of the size of it, there are only three points to make in this book:

No best solution There are over a dozen GUI possibilities. Not a single one of them is the ultimate or best solution. If you think you have found the best GUI, you are lucky. But you may as well keep it to yourself, because it will only be the best one for your situation and will misdirect others.

Why use a GUI? There is one, and only one reason—productivity.

Charm If you choose to use a GUI, and it is designed right and uses the right hardware, you will know it almost instantly and benefit from its charm.

Running a computer still takes a certain amount of brain power. If you don't have or won't use that brain power, a GUI, regardless of its charm factor, won't do it for you.

References

Brod, Craig. 1982. *Technostress: The human cost of the computer revolution*. Reading, Mass.: Addison-Wesley.

Temple, Barker, & Sloane. Inc. 1990. *The benefits of the graphical user interface*. Microsoft, Zenith Data Systems: Lexington, Mass.

1

Standards

Ever since computer graphics became a viable technological solution, an ambivalent attitude toward standards has been exhibited by both users and suppliers. Standards have been criticized for being too far behind current technology to be used and for adding overhead that diminishes performance. However, users have also complained that without standards they are at the mercy of vendors' proprietary systems.

Importance of standards

Standards for programming languages and graphic tools have many benefits. The important issues of standards will be discussed in this chapter. The graphics software burden and the need for standards will also be examined.

After many years of frustrated experience with device-dependent software, programmers and users formed standards committees to address the problems. Two major decisions were made by those committees that have influenced all subsequent work on the development of graphics standards:

- Portability. Portability of programs from one computer system to another was identified as the single most important objective of a graphics standard.
- Viewing modeling. Standard committees decided that a clear-cut division between the modeling of graphics objects and the viewing of graphics images based on those objects was necessary. The most urgent needs were considered to be standardization of the viewing, image manipulation, and user interaction functions.

Programming practices

It has now been demonstrated that common programming practices can be taught, refined, and reapplied to subsequent projects if standards are exercised. As a result, having a device-independent standard allows programmers to concentrate their primary efforts on developing applications. Many mundane tasks previously included in applications programs, such as data storage and manipulation, are handled by the support system defined in such a standard.

Software maintenance

The use of such standards creates an educated group of users and developers, and they become a long-term resource. This makes the maintenance of software more manageable, and new projects can be estimated, scheduled, and monitored with more accuracy due to relevant experience.

Developing a technology standard is similar to defining, building, delivering, and supporting a successful commercial product. Graphics standardization has been an ongoing activity on a national and international level since the early 1970s. The first proposal to achieve a graphics standard originated in April, 1974. It was an outgrowth of a workshop on Machine Independent Graphics sponsored by the Association for Computing Machinery Special Interest Group on Graphics (ACM-SIGGRAPH). This workshop later became the SIGGRAPH Graphics Standard Planning Committee (GSPC).

The American National Standards Institute (ANSI) and the International Standards Organization (ISO) founded specialized subcommittees whose charter was to develop the specifications for various functional levels of computer graphics. Obviously, standards have to continuously grow to keep pace with the graphics-hardware capabilities of the future. However, by necessity, standards always lag behind technological developments.

Benefit of standards

Building software tools today is more than just implementing a good idea. Today's software lives in a complex world populated by multiple versions and types of operating systems, different graphical user interfaces (GUIs) and various software subsystems. Software development for computer systems is a business proposition, and the business demands that the product be continually enhanced and continuously maintained.

Open systems, a foreign concept just a few years ago, are gaining ground as the hardware vendor community shifts to such open standards as Posix/UNIX, X-window, TCP/IP and Ethernet as a base. Today's software developers are learning to operate in the open-system world, porting products across platforms and developing methodologies and techniques for portable software.

Today, mainline software tools and products are no longer directed at a single hardware and software platform, as in the bygone days when the platforms of Digital Equipment, IBM and a few others dominated. Now, successful packages must run on a number of hardware/software platforms. And that means developers must cope with different processor architectures, different graphics subsystems and different software environments, including operating systems, compilers, and database software. Coming to the rescue is a rising body of software standards—Posix, ANSI C, X-window, common GUIs (OPEN LOOK, Motif, Windows), and TCP/IP.

Graphical standards and GUIs are a major part of this development. If today the benefit of viewing 3D-like data is not obvious, consider what the graphic display demand will be as we move into the 21st century. Today the casual novice is already being exposed to such technical images through commercial television. As we approach the next century, this novice, as well as others, will come to expect such graphic potential as standard operating procedure or capability.

Compare the information provided today by a premier computer display system with 3-dimensional visualizations to that of just a graphics terminal using display technology developed in the early to mid eighties. Which will be the most impressive to the viewer—to the potential customer or investor?

However, there is the danger that a company will adopt nonstandard graphics or GUI technology that will be outdated before the project is finished and online. If that is allowed to happen, the company will have to reinvest development dollars in rewriting software for its products and/or projects in order to accommodate the improved hardware and software performance that will be introduced in the coming years.

Hardware will be increasingly improved in performance capabilities while prices will drastically drop during the next 20 years. This suggests that as we begin to use these new high-performance, less costly hardware devices, the users will force multi-windowing and 3D-viewing environments as the *de facto* standard for interactive computer operation in the 1990s.

The risk is—you can either invest in the right graphics now (i.e., Standards), or take a quick hardware or software-dependent solution now and then have to redo it later.

The drawbacks and risks of standards

The current development time for an ANSI/ISO standard is five to seven years. Therefore, vendors have to decide early in the development process whether they should commit resources to produce products based on a standard. If a vendor comes to the market with a poor implementation of the standard, it can severely damage the product's chances for success. On a larger scale, if several vendors market products with poor implementations of a standard, it can kill use of the standard before it gets off the ground.

Standards-making organizations are not insensitive to these issues. Over the years, they have heard all the criticisms regarding slow development. Nevertheless, they say, it is difficult to make changes in the development process without compromising the consensus that needs to be established in order to produce a true international standard.

Graphic standards available today

Standards are permutating the entire computer business, and the graphics segment is no exception. The problem is the same. Users do not want to make large investments in software for specialized hardware only to find they can't afford to change suppliers. Graphic standards are contributing to stability in the industry and helping to answer the user's needs.

Software developments

What are graphic software standards? There are several actual standards and many more industry standards. This chapter will examine the actual standards—those approved by an independent body such as American National Standards Institute (ANSI), International Electrical and Electronics Engineers (IEEE), International Organization for Standardization (ISO), or the Association of Computing Machinery (ACM).

In the late seventies and early eighties, high-end workstations and a few PCs were optimized for particular graphics applications. Since graphics performance is typically computationally bound, hardware and software developers have been reluctant to incorporate standards. However, as applications and needs accelerated faster than equipment and software could be developed, both users and developers sought a way out of the specialization path. Several approaches were tried, and few succeeded. It should be noted that these early efforts were really the genesis of the concepts for a graphical user interface.

CORE-3D

CORE was the first attempt at an international graphic standard. It was a significant development that started in the mid-seventies when a general awareness was expressed for device-independent graphics packages. This emerged into a widely known specification called the Core Graphic System (CORE). This first standard, the CORE system, is defined as a portable hardware-independent application interface for 2D and 3D graphics output and interactive input. The first draft was presented at SIGGRAPH '77 and an expanded version at SIGGRAPH '79. This proposed standard was based on years of experience with device-dependent graphics packages and, in essence, embodied common concepts and practices in graphics programming of the era.

CORE specifies a graphics system model that simulates the capabilities of the 2D graphics terminals and pen plotters that characterized the late 1970s. Like 1970's style terminals, the CORE model has many built-in features that simplify developing applications programs, including input devices that allow the operator to interact with the application program and manipulate the graphics data. CORE's functions include 2D and 3D drawing primitives, such as polylines, polymarkers, and area fills. CORE also translates the primitive coordinates from the application's world coordinate space to a normalized device coordinate space and then to a coordinate space of a particular display device. This enables the CORE application to vary primitive attributes, such as color, fill pattern, and marker shapes.

Many graphic devices in the mid 1970s supported more powerful drawing primitives, such as circles and ellipses, which CORE did not specify in its standard. To enable applications programs to use such drawing primitives, CORE provided an escape mechanism whereby applications could call an escape subroutine to access device-specific functions. By using the escape mechanism, an application program loses its portability, but it gains the particular graphics device drawing capabilities. This benefit, also described at the time as richness, actually cost CORE the standardization platform so badly needed.

The most powerful feature in CORE is *segmentation*. Primitives are grouped into data structures, called segments, and stored in memory for later recall and display. In this way, the application does not have to recreate picture elements, such as menus that do not change. Once the application creates segments, further manipulation of this data is possible. CORE can *transform* (scale, rotate, and translate) segments, highlight segments, change color, make segments visible or invisible, and make them pickable/selectable from a pointing device such as a mouse or digitizer. These capabilities greatly facilitate interactive program design.

However, CORE has several drawbacks. One is that the CORE standard supports only one output device, even though many graphics applications require multiple output devices. CORE also does not specify a standard interface between an applications program and the subroutine library that implements the standard. As a result, CORE-based applications may require extensive modification to run on another CORE-based hardware and software platform.

GKS-2D

The *Graphical Kernel System* (GKS) is a 2D vector-based graphic interface with no support for bit-maps (raster operations available on modern workstations). GKS was initially European market driven. Today, the 2D capabilities of GKS are heavily used in U.S. military flight simulation and Command, Control, Communications, and Intelligence (CCCI) applications.

GKS is a basic graphic standard for programming 2D computer graphics applications. It was developed jointly by ANSI and ISO and formally adopted by these organizations as a U.S. and International standard in 1985. Today, GKS is a viewing system with functions for a display list, picture generation, picture presentation, segmentation, transformation, immediate-mode, input/output, and storage. Workstation transformation is a key feature of GKS; it allows an application program to define a rectangular region, called a *window*, in the normalized device coordinate space which maps the information onto another rectangular region, called a *viewport*, in the actual device display space. GKS then automatically clips and transforms primitives to fit into the viewport. This feature simplifies implementation of panning and zooming operations. GKS defines standard language bindings for major high-level languages, including FORTRAN and C. This procedure assures that an application program written with a GKS-compatible library will run with any other library that also supports GKS, with little modification (in theory). GKS also includes a specification for *metafiles* (a picture file stored on disk for later retrieval or transfer to another system). One image created on one GKS-based library should, in theory, be readable by any other GKS library.

The Computer Graphics Interface (CGI) is a subroutine library that can be stored and operated (interrupted) on either the host computer or a graphics controller board. The Computer Graphics Metafile (CGM) is actually a subset of CGI. It defines a standard file content and format for storing and retrieving pictures. Figure 1-1 shows the organization of GKS, CGM and CGI.

An application uses subroutine calls from the GKS library to manipulate 2D graphics. These graphics may be line graphs, bar charts, strip charts, maps, integrated circuit layouts, or any other picture that can be described in 2D by GKS. GKS is widely used in earth resources, mapping, CCCI, and distribution network applications today. It

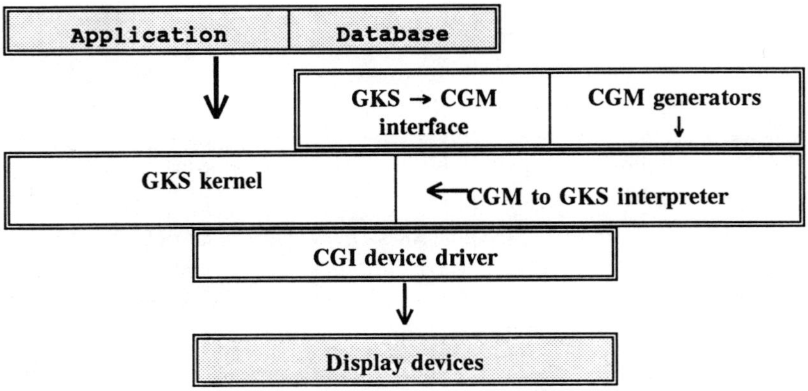

Fig. 1-1. GKS architecture.

supports operator input and interaction by supplying basic functions for graphical input and picture segmentation and provides the programmer with the ability to create graphic output on a wide variety of graphical devices. GKS was the first true standard for graphic applications programming to be adopted as an American and International Graphics Standard.

PHIGS

The Programmers Hierarchical Interactive Graphics Standard (PHIGS) defines a sophisticated graphics support system that controls the definition, modification, and display of hierarchical graphics data. PHIGS specifies functional description of system capabilities, including the definition of internal data structures, editing capabilities, display operations, and workstation control functions. By providing advanced graphics tools and support for high-performance workstations, PHIGS frees the application programmer to concentrate available resources on solving a particular application's problem. PHIGS manages the organization and display of data in a centralized database. This allows the application programmer to define and organize graphical data in a manner most convenient to the application.

At the same time, PHIGS specifies functional description of systems capabilities, including the definition of internal data structures, editing capabilities, display operations, and device control functions. Objects are defined in a PHIGS graphical database by a sequence of elements, including output primitives, attributes, transformations, and invocations of other objects and object part definitions. Because of the increased performance and complexity of implementing PHIGS, more powerful and, therefore, more costly workstations are required by the end users.

Performance is a key concept designed into PHIGS to allow smooth, dynamic motion of 3D graphical data. This is achieved by the application's control of the display updates and interactive modification of the display structure. Graphics data is stored and organized using a hierarchical model, also referred to as a display list. This differs from the segmentation-of-data approach used in CORE and GKS. In addition, PHIGS offers a rich set of graphics primitives, viewing and modeling transformations, and

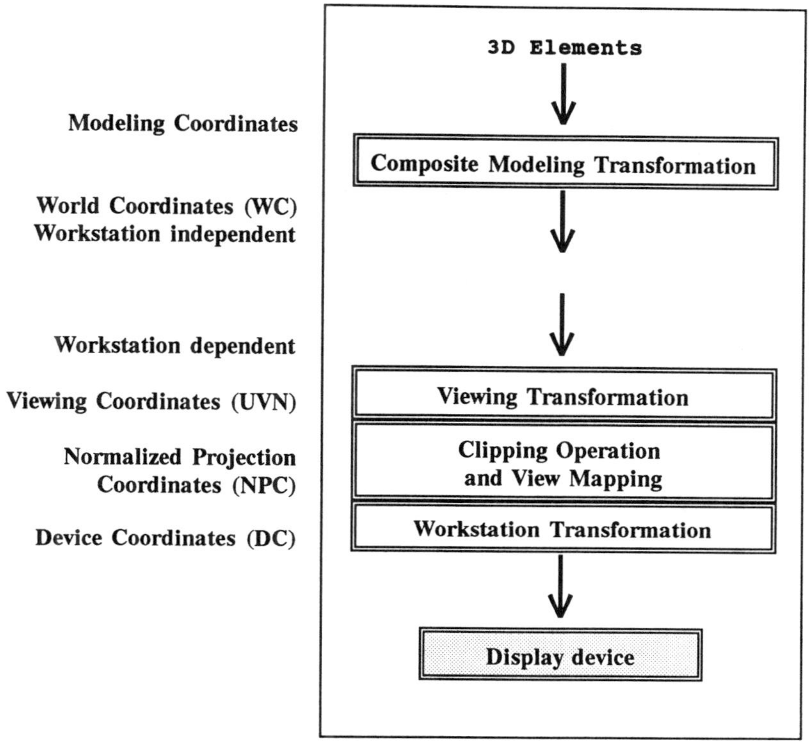

Fig. 1-2. PHIGS pipeline architecture.

interactive input/output for use with data models. Due to this comprehensive set of functions, the PHIGS standard is being widely adopted as an international graphics standard. PHIGS uses a pipeline architecture, as shown in FIG. 1-2.

PHIGS is now an ANSI standard, having been approved in July, 1988. When the ANSI/ISO committees were finalizing the specification for PHIGS, many new features were proposed for inclusion in the standard. Rather than delaying the approval process, a new group began work to specify the extensions known as PHIGS+. This work was scheduled to be completed in 1989. However, it is still in the process of being approved.

PHIGS is specifically designed for applications such as Mechanical Computer Aided Design (MCAD), Mechanical Computer Aided Engineering (MCAE), mapping, simulation, molecular modeling, and 3D end-user applications. Graphics software written with PHIGS can be ported easily across a variety of vendor's hardware platforms supporting PHIGS, thus preserving the developer's software investment.

Future graphic standards

In addition to the previously discussed standards, there are the currently proposed graphic standards being considered by the ANSI/ISO committees as future international graphic standards.

GKS-3D

As it name implies, GKS-3D specifies extensions for GKS for defining and viewing 3D wire-frame objects. It allows the operator to obtain information from 3D input devices and to perform hidden-line, hidden-surface removal at the workstation. However, it does not provide specific functions for controlling rendering techniques such as light source, shading, texturing, and shadow computations, which must be done locally at the workstation.

Currently, GKS-3D has not been accepted as a National or International standard. Nonetheless, numerous vendors have already implemented 3D extensions to their GKS graphics library. Also, third-party developers like IMSL have used GKS as the basis for graphics display programs that can generate images from FORTRAN data sets. Such programs are used for creating data renderings and graphs from numerically intensive applications to aid in visualizing the results.

PHIGS+

PHIGS+ extends PHIGS functionality in the area of realistic rendering. Functions are provided for using multiple-colored light sources, sophisticated shading, depth cueing, trimmed nonuniform rational b-splines (NURB), curves and surfaces, true color (RGB color), and complex geometric primitives.

PIK

The ANSI X3H3 Committee is working on a software standards for electronics imaging. Specifically, they are working on the Programmer's Imaging Kernel (PIK) standard that is an Application Programmer's Interface (API) software standard for applications in electronic imaging and image processing.

PIK defines a set of functions, a set of data objects, and operators that define how the functions operate on the data objects. Various operators include geometric transforms, spatial filters, and shape analysis. The X3H3.8 Task Group is also working with ISO in an attempt to internationalize their work.

X Window System

The X Window System is not a graphics system, although it is closely associated with graphics. It does not have an image model and does not offer any rules or guidelines on how to handle graphics functions. Nonetheless, the X Window System will be a standard. The National Institute of Standards and Technology (NIST) has published a Federal Information Processing Standard (FIPS) that references the base standard of the X Window System. The American National Standards Institute (ANSI) has a standards group, X3H3.6 that is also working on developing a standard for the X Window System. Extensions to the X-Window that address the different image model and graphics issues have been proposed.

PEX

The PHIGS (and PHIGS-PLUS) Extension to the X11 Window System, or simply *PEX*, is the emerging multivendor-supported protocol extension to the X11 Window

System for the rendering of PHIGS and PHIGS-PLUS-3-D graphics within windows in a distributed environment. PEX also allows developers to take advantage of advanced graphics capability by using a standard applications programming interface such as PHIGS (and PHIGS-PLUS).

PEX was designed to allow high-level graphics to be utilized in a distributed environment. PEX allows for support of a wide range of display devices and allows for acceleration to be done where available, and invisibly to the application or user. PEX is simply a protocol definition, it is NOT an application programming interface (API). In December 1988, the X Consortium issued a contract to Sun Microsystems for the development of a sample implementation of PEX, referred to as PEX-SI. The PEX-SI was completed and delivered to the X Consortium in February, 1991.

XIE

The X Window System Imaging Extension or *XIE*, is an extension that provides applications with support for visually interactive image enhancement and display operations. Intended applications for this extension include document storage and retrieval and image retrieval and display. Images are stored in CCITT compressed format and sent to the X-server for decompression and display. The goal of XIE is to maximize channel bandwidth and provide a core of primitives for manipulation and display of image data. Color mapping functions, scaling, image sharpening via Laplacian filters, gamma correction and dithering are some of the functions provided. XIE has been tested at a number of companies and government agencies.

VEX

The video complement to XIE (or *VEX*) is an extension for the transfer and display of real-time video images in an X-window. It also contains mechanisms for controlling external video devices such as video switches, laser disk players and tape recorders. Tektronix and Parallax have been very active in formulating and developing this extension. It is in the final stages of formalization and has been submitted to the X Consortium for approval.

SIE

Network Computing Devices, Inc., a supplier of X Window System terminals has developed software to support image compression and manipulation and has made the specification for the software available to application developers.

The NCD imaging software consists of six additional calls to the X Window System library (Xlib). Called the Simple Imaging Extension (SIE), it is a standard, free-of-charge feature of the X server software shipped with NCD products.

Without integral imaging support, X has lacked the ability to send compressed bit maps, or to manipulate those bit maps on the local display. Instead, the host computer has had to perform these functions—a heavy drain on disk and network resources. This has driven the need for extensions to X that enable compressed images to be shipped across the network and manipulated locally by the X terminal.

SIE supports compression of images using Group III and Group IV fax techniques, as well as the image-manipulation functions of rotation, scaling and panning. Fax images can be received and stored in compressed form on a UNIX host, for example, and then decompressed and manipulated on a networked NCD X terminal. SIE is a complementary solution to the X Imaging Extension (XIE) developed by Digital Equipment Corp. and submitted to the X Consortium as a proposed industry standard. DEC's XIE is a very large, comprehensive imaging capability that supports color, all imaging functions and a complex programming interface. SIE, on the other hand, is designed to support processing of simple monochrome document images. It is smaller and has an easy-to-program interface.

XIM

One of the most significant international proposals has been the development of the X Input Method (or *XIM*). XIM incorporates standard procedures for handling international character sets and keyboards for use by X programmers. Japanese XView, which developers can use to create OPEN LOOK applications, is based on the X Input Method (XIM) specification. XIM is under consideration by the X Consortium as a proposed vehicle for internationalizing the X Window System. XView is a very portable toolkit, thus the new Japanese version enables developers to create applications in Japanese for any high-performance computer system that uses the X Window System.

Extensions to the extensions

Either as a part of the proposed XIE extension, or perhaps in an extension of its own, Tektronix has submitted a color model to the committee. It is for a color matching system (CMS) that provides a method for color selection, editing and screen-to-printer color matching. It is based on the hue-value-chroma color model. Users haven't been able to obtain true color WYSIWYG because of the difficulty of matching the cyan-magenta-blue characteristics of the screen with the red-yellow-blue properties of print.

What is available today?

Most of the minicomputers and workstation companies have adopted two application-related standards for their systems: GKS and PHIGS. Because these standards have to be specifically ported to a platform, the manufacturers generally add their name to the front of the standard.

The following is an example of Digital's implementation of graphic standards. It is typical of most manufacturers, and the reader could substitute Digital's name with that of several other companies and have a good appreciation for available products. Digital named its products:

- DEC PHIGS version 2.0.
- DEC GKS.

With DEC GKS and DEC PHIGS graphics software, the user gains portability across operating systems and graphical operating devices. This produces portable, device-independent graphics applications, from a VMS subroutine library.

Digital, like Hewlett-Packard, Sun Microsystems and others, employs the ANSI/ISO Graphical Kernel System (GKS) standard in its DEC GKS two-dimensional, device-independent graphic system. For three-dimensional device-independent graphics, Digital Programmer's Hierarchical Graphics System (PHIGS) utilizes the ANSI/ISO PHIGS standard as well. DEC GKS and DEC PHIGS can also control multiple simultaneous views of the same picture on separate display surfaces. And the user can control the position of each view on the display surface.

DEC GKS and DEC PHIGS support the entire family of VAX workstations and DECstations and run on either the VMS or ULTRIX operating system. Two-dimensional support is based on DECwindows (X-11) and three-dimensional support is based on PEX (PHIGS extension for X-11).

DEC GKS and DEC PHIGS support industry-wide standards and architectures, including Compound Document Architecture (CDA) through the Digital Document Interchange Format (DDIF). They also support a variety of strictly compatible hardcopy output devices, including Hewlett-Packard Graphics Language (HPGL) devices, film recorders, ink-jet plotters, and PostScript devices.

The Digital product offering is a typical example. Simulation types of products that support such standards are also available from Hewlett-Packard, IBM, Sun Microsystems, Silicon Graphics, and many others.

Vendor-developed *de facto* standards

While standards committees were trying to set standards, several vendors decided not to wait and developed their own graphics software libraries. Their motivation was a combination of impatience, desire for added functionality and the drive for product differentiation. The following is a list of vendors' graphic software libraries, interfaces, APIs and toolkits. These graphics tools are not official industry-wide standards. However, they are used widely enough to be considered as vendor implemented standards.

TABLE 1-1 contains a list of the most popular vendor-created software libraries, interfaces, APIs and toolkits. The list is not meant to include every proprietary library or interface offered, only the most commonly used. TABLE 1-2 shows a matrix that compares the capabilities and applications of all the current and proposed graphic standards.

Display PostScript Display Postscript (DPS) is a screen-description language developed and marketed by Adobe Systems. Currently, DPS is integrated into the DEC windows system. Sun Microsystems offers a DPS-compatible product called XPS as part of the X11/NeWS (Network Extensible Window System) windowing system.

DPS uses the same language and techniques as Adobe's *de facto* industry standard PostScript page-description language, which can effectively turn displays into laser-printer emulators. However, unlike PostScript, the acceptance of DPS has not been fast or widespread. One of the reasons for the hesitation has been that it is not an open product. Certain parts of DPS, such as the Bezier curve algorithms and the font generation hints, or fudge factors, remain proprietary to Adobe. Yet, with Digital's commitment to DPS, X-window terminals that are also DEC windows terminals will have to support DPS to be DEC windows-compatabile.

DPS is not a substitute for the X Window System. However, several portions of it

Table 1-1. De facto *and vendor standards.*

Name	Supplier	Description
ADI	Autodesk	A device interface to several Autodesk programs.
GL	Silicon Graphics	The graphic library used by applications that run on the Silicon Graphics workstation. There is also a Distributed GL. IBM has licensed DGL for all its workstation products.
GSS/CGI	GSS	The Graphic Software System/Computer Graphics Interface was proposed as an ANSI standard in 1985; it was never approved, but has been widely used.
DGIS	GSS	Graphic Software Systems' implementation of their Direct Graphic Interface Standard for various graphic co-processors and controllers.
HALO	Media Cybernetics	The graphic library and device interface developed by Media Cybernetics was one of the early libraries and has been used in many PC-based applications.
HOOPS	Ithaca Software	A 3D-based graphics database and library.
HPGL	Hewlett-Packard	The HP Graphic Language used by plotters and laser printers.
Metafile		ANSI/ISO picture file format.
RenderMan	PIXAR	A file interface for photorealistic image interchange.
sunGKS	Sun Micro	Sun's popular version of the GKS library
sunPHIGS	Sun Micro	Sun's popular version of the PHIGS library
Figaro	Template	An expanded version of PHIGS from Template Graphics. The company also offers, Dimension - GKS.
TIGA	TI	The Texas Instruments Graphics Architecture for the TI TMS340x0-based graphics controllers.
Various	IBM	The company has introduced several hardware-related standards for graphics displays: CGA, EGA, VGA, 8514/a and XGA.

have the same functions as those found in the X Window System. For example, both the X Window System and DPS support graphics functions such as line drawing and the display of various fonts.

Unlike the X Window System with its xlib (the X Window System library), DPS is not in the public domain, nor is it vendor-independent. Vendors that want to include

Table 1-2. Graphic standards implementation.

Standard/capability	Application	Vendors/products	Standards
CORE 3D, linear display list,input/output,viewing system and Gouraud/Phong shading.	General 3D applications	DecCore, Hewlett-Packard/Apollo, IBM	ANSI/ISO standard 1979
GKS 2D, linear display list,input/output, viewing system and flat shading.	2D mapping	DecGKS IBM graGKS SunGKS	ANSI/ISO standard 1985
GKS-3D 3D, hidden line removal,input/Output, no shading/no rendering.	Flight simulation, CCCI	DecGKS IBM graGKS	Proposed standard
PHIGS 2D and 3D hierarchical display list, wireframe viewing application data, name sets, modeling systems & input/output.	Simulation, MCAD	DecPHIGS, SunPHIGS, IBM graPHIGS, Template - Figaro	ANSI/ISO standard 1988
PHIGS+ 2D and 3D, Gouraud & Phong shading, complex lighting models, digitizing multiple/spot/diffuse, NURBS, meshes, RGB color models and depth cueing.	Medical, simulation, animation, MCAD, solid rendering	SunPHIGS Stardent Hewlett-Packard/Apollo	Proposed standard
X-PEX X-Windows 11, graphic networking and transparent 3D networked images.	X-Windows, networked applications	SGI-distributed GL	proposed with X Windows System
RenderMan Complete geometric primitives, antialiasing dithering, viewing, multiple light sources, RGB file content, photorealistic rendering & ray tracing.	Medical, simulation, animation	PIXAR Autodesk NeXT	Industry accepted standard
CGI 2D, no display list, Orthographics and perspective viewing, flat shading.		GSS/CGI	ANSI pro-posed standard 1985, not accepted
CGM 2D picture storage format, output from GKS & PHIGS.	2D general charts	Archive file output from PHIGS and GKS	ANSI/OSI archive file
PostScript Text, lines, arcs, Bezier splines 2D transformations stencil/paint imaging models.	Hardcopy raster images and archives WYSIWYG applications, CASE, office automation,	Sun NeWS Digital IBM Adobe Systems	Industry-wide de facto standard

DPS in their windowing system must pay Adobe a royalty for each system sold. If DPS were offered, it would replace or augment portions of the X Window System library of routines. However, for an X Window System Server to support DPS, it would need to incorporate a DPS interpreter as part of its Server program. The DPS interpreter receives DPS command strings from the Client and executes them.

Differences between DPS and X There are two major differences between the way DPS and the X Window System deals with graphics issues.

- Fonts. The X Window System uses bit-mapped fonts, where an actual bit image of the character to be displayed is either stored locally on the Server or transmitted to the Server by the Client when needed. These bit-mapped fonts can be rotated at 90-degree increments and are not easily scalable to any random size. DPS uses an outline font technique, where the outline of the character is defined mathematically and is interpreted by the DPS interpreter. Once the outline of the character is calculated, it can be filled in by the DPS interpreter, or left open. One of the advantages of this method is that fonts can be rotated easily and scaled by any random increment and still look right.
- The graphics imaging model. The X Window System uses a basic pixel-oriented imaging model. The DPS imaging model uses a math-based model. If a diagonal line is drawn in the X Window System, the beginning and end points of the line are communicated as display coordinates (i.e., pixel addresses). In DPS, a real-world description of the line is sent to the DPS interpreter. An example of a real-world description is to give a starting position (relative to some coordinate system) and an instruction to draw a line at a 45 degree angle, 3 inches long. This is easier for programmers and developers to execute graphics functions; however, it places a significant burden on the Server processor.

Standards have been developed to satisfy the needs of applications, as well as portability. As is shown in FIG. 1-3, some standards are better suited for different applications than others. Because the requirements of applications often overlap somewhat, it is impossible to draw a perfect distinction between the applicability of standards and applications.

How much portability today?

With graphics software libraries, you gain portability across operating systems and graphical operating devices if development tools that have multiplatform/processor

	CASE	OA	DTP	ECAD	AEC	GIS	MCAD	Vis	Med
GKS					●	●		●	
PHIGS					●		●	●	
Xlib	●	●	●	●					
Postscript	●	●	●						
3D mode				●	●	●	●	●	●

OA = Office Automation
Vis = Scientific Visualization

Fig. 1-3. Applications and standards.

versions are used. This produces portable, device-independent graphics applications, from a processor-dependent subroutine library.

Graphic standards were developed primarily by software developers and interested end users demanding methods that would provide them processor-independence and operating system-independent software development techniques. Even so, with any software migration to other hardware platforms, the best that can be guaranteed is 85%-95% portability with any standard. No matter what standard is implemented, there will always be certain caveats that have to be taken into consideration for any application. In the best case, if you stick to an industry-wide standards library, portability should be relatively easy; it will most likely just require recompilation.

References

Bono, Peter R., 1985. A survey of graphics standards and their role in information interchange, *Computer Magazine*, October, 1985. Page 63.

Card, Stuart K. and Justin D. Henderson, Jr. 1987. *A multiple, virtual-workspace interface to support user task switching*. Palo Alto, CA: Xerox Palo Alto Research Center.

McEwan, Richard. 1987. Current status of graphics standards for the digital environment indicates different standards for different applications. *Hardcopy Magazine*, May, 1987, Page 111.

PostScript language reference manual. 1986. Menlo Park, CA: Adobe Systems, Addison-Wesley.

Salmon, Rod and Mel Slater. 1989. *Computer graphics systems & concepts*. Workingham, England: Addison-Wesley.

Williams, Tom. 1989. Software protocols smooth the path to a standard graphics interface. *Computer Design*, April 1, 1989. Page 70.

2

Portability

There are various opinions about what defines portability. This chapter will examine some of those viewpoints and arrive at a definition that will be used throughout the remainder of the book.

History

In the early days of computer deployment and usage during the late 1950s, there was no discussion about the division of functions, i.e., hardware and software. A computer system was a turnkey product that was delivered to the user fully functional with all the necessary parts to do a job. The jobs were usually very specific, such as payroll or inventory control. As users became more sophisticated and demand for computer systems began to develop, natural segmentation also developed. Existing computers (they were all mainframes at that time) were expanded. Additional terminals and printers were added. Memory and disks were increased and the functionality of the software was modified. Users and vendors began to create departments for various functions and services.

In the early 1960s, new companies entered the market, offering only components of a system such as a disk drive or a terminal. To be successful, these new vendors had to find out how to connect to the computer; they had to learn about its interface. The computer manufacturers knew that the new vendors needed this information, and they also knew that these new vendors were potential competition, so they were very guarded with their information. Nonetheless, the information on how an I/O port or the operating system worked became known. The computer manufacturers couldn't keep such information completely secret, or they would not be able to service the equipment. Also, by this time the users were beginning to develop their own applications, applications that were specific to their business, and they had to have information on the inner workings of the operating system and its I/O devices. In short, the computer manufacturers were being dragged into a partial opening of their systems.

As the users became more knowledgable, they also became more demanding on computer functionality. Competitors seeing this would exploit the weakness in one company's machine by offering a missing feature in their newest machine; thus began the leap-frogging phenomenon of the late sixties and early seventies. IBM was always the biggest, and so they were the target of most competitors. If Burroughs (now Unisys) or NCR could take a customer away from IBM, they considered that not only an economic victory but also a moral victory. However, it was never a victory for the user who was faced with a new operating system and new hardware characteristics. It meant all the programs the user had developed over the years had to be either rewritten or thrown out.

The revolution is started

The first glimmers of hope appeared when standard programming languages became available. FORTRAN, COBOL and BASIC were introduced, and most of the computer manufacturers had a version for their machine. In theory, a program written in FORTRAN on a Honeywell or Control Data computer could be recompiled and made to run on a Univac, IBM, or Burroughs machine—in theory.

During this same period, minicomputers were introduced by new start-up companies like Digital Equipment Corporation and Data General. In the mid sixties there were over two dozen minicomputer companies. These upstart machines used BASIC at first, and then FORTRAN. The talk of the time was about "bringing down applications" to the minicomputer. However, Digital's FORTRAN wasn't exactly the same as IBM's. So although they had the same basic construction (FOR loops and IF statements), there were still many little special features in each company's version.

Into this lion's den came the society of American Computing Machinery (ACM). Various members proposed setting up a standard for FORTRAN and COBOL, and in 1966 they did that. Computer manufacturers and the first few independent software companies then began adopting their compilers to comply with Fortran 66. However, all of the manufacturers, hardware and software, always had extensions to their compilers. Extensions were special features that some users found useful. Since a plurality didn't demand special features, they were not put into the standard. That allowed the standard to be finished, and kept it from being too big and unwieldy.

The problem of moving an application from one platform to another had improved a little, but there wasn't any no-cost solution. Typically, what would happen is a COBOL or FORTRAN program written on one machine (with its compiler and operating system) would have to be recompiled under the other system. When the compiler was run, the code would not compile (that was referred to as *blowing up*), and the reason was because the programmer had used some of the extensions of the other company's version of the language. If the new (called the *target*) system didn't have those features, then a rewrite of the code was necessary. That added cost and delayed the conversion process. This became a competitive tool of the hardware manufacturers, and they added as many special features to their operating systems and as many versions of the standard languages as possible.

Phase two of the revolution, the PC

In the late seventies, microcomputers began to appear. The first ones were just kits, but soon fully assembled models from Commodore and Tandy appeared. These machines offered a simple operating system and a BASIC interpreter. However, BASIC on one machine was not fully compatible with BASIC on another. Because of the limited memory space and the relatively slow operation of these early computers, most of the applications were written in machine code which made them totally unportable.

In the early eighties IBM introduced the PC. It was the biggest microcomputer available and had a more powerful CPU. Because IBM was the developer, many prospects who were interested in microcomputers now felt safe in investing in one. The rest of the story is well known; everybody in the universe got a PC.

The PC opened up a new chapter in computing in several ways. The main thing was it became a widespread standard. The technology was not difficult, and dozens of companies copied the design. (Today the number is hundreds.) As the PC infiltrated the offices, laboratories, manufacturing shops and homes of the world, it brought with it a stable operating system. That gave software developers something they never had before—a stable binary interface.

The ability to take an application from an IBM PC and run it on a Compaq without recompiling was immediately embraced by the users. It brought millions of new computer users into the market, and with them came an intolerance for difficulty. They didn't want to know about DOS (although some parts of it did have to be learned). They didn't want to know about megabytes or compilers or anything other than the operation of their application. There existed at this point true portability, albeit only within one machine category. Nonetheless, it showed the way, and it armed the users with an example to hold up to the refusals of the computer manufacturers.

Phase three, the Macintosh

In the mid eighties Apple introduced the Macintosh computer—the computer for the rest of us. The people at Apple correctly sensed the mood and needs of the average user and the desires of the potential user. Granted, a lot of pioneering work was done at other places, most notably Xerox PARC; however, it was Apple that popularized the notion of a computer that could be used by noncomputer people.

The Macintosh gave us an affordable, simple user interface. At that time it wasn't called a graphical user interface or GUI. That term came later. As with any new development, people derided the product. It was called easy to learn but not very fast or powerful. The hard core PC users said it took too long to work your way through the various menus, and they were generally right. Still, the revolution had started, and there would be no turning back.

Phase four, the workstation

Also in the early eighties, a college professor and some friends of his started a company to build a special computer primarily for software developers. This computer, which became known as a workstation, used a new operating system called UNIX, which had been developed at AT&T. The company named itself Sun Microsystems.

UNIX was a programmer's delight. It had or still has features that couldn't be found elsewhere, and it was affordable. Soon, workstations began to spread and were found in the software shops of all major companies and every university. Exciting things were being done on these workstations. New computational applications were being developed, and new graphical visualization programs were introduced. However, the workstation remained the tool (some would say toy) of the scientific elite and the programmers.

With the workstation, multiple applications being available to several users at the same time became popular. No longer would a programmer need two or more computers, or be given an opportunity to read when a program was being compiled. Now a programmer could open up another application at the same time. When such an application was opened up, it was done so with a window. It was (and still is) a common sight to go into the software developer's pit (polite people call them offices or labs, but the programmers know them as their den) and see a screen with three or four windows on it and applications running in them at the same time. The age of inexpensive and effective multitasking had arrived with the workstation, and its interface to the user was through windows.

A windowing environment does not come for free. Extra layers of software must be put between the user and the operating system, as the block diagram in FIG. 2-1 shows. Nonetheless, with the increased computing power of workstations, and the promise of more to come, the minor loss of performance due to the extra layers was a welcomed trade-off.

Developers discovered in the mid-1980s that writing code was extremely resource-intensive, requiring reams of code to manage windowing. Because as much as 80 percent of a program's code might be dedicated to those tasks, developers began to shift toward object-oriented programming (OOP) with hopes of gaining more code reusability among applications.

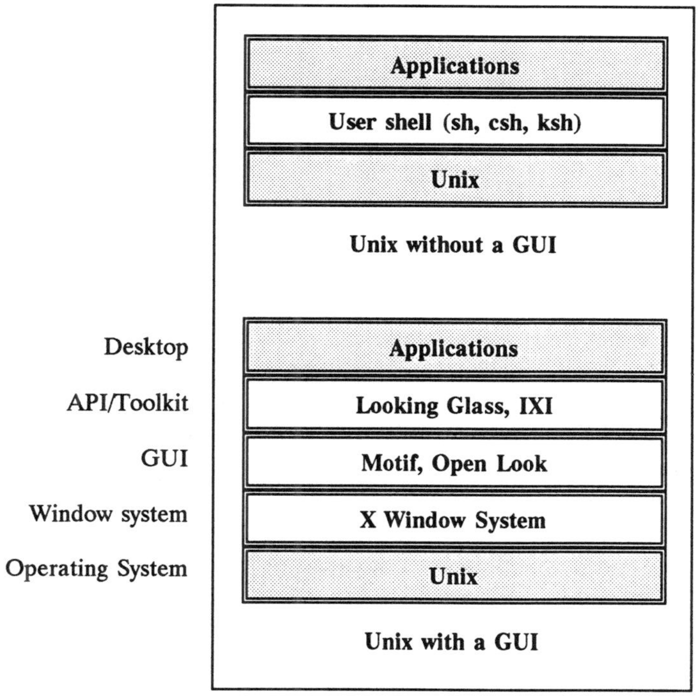

Fig. 2-1. GUI layers.

Phase five, interconnectivity

As PCs, Macintoshes, workstations, and minicomputers began to spread, users wanted to be able to access other systems. They also wanted access to some of the data that was stored in the huge disks of the mainframes. The workstations were the first to share data with a local area network (LAN) using a protocol developed by the Defense Advanced Research Projects Agency (DARPA) called Transmission Connect Protocol and Internet Protocol (TCP/IP). TCP/IP fit nicely into UNIX, and it became a standard feature of workstations almost immediately.

The concept of LANs was another development whose time had come, and they were quickly adopted to other platforms and systems. Mainframes, with their terminal services and multiplexers, didn't need LANs, but minicomputers, workstations and PCs made great use of them. Soon offices and labs had various workstation vendors connected together through a LAN using what became known as the Ethernet backbone.

Another early developer of a workstation was Datapoint. Datapoint actually pioneered the concept of workstations and LANs. They just didn't use those terms or share their ideas with very many people. Datapoint enjoyed great success from the late seventies up until the mid-to-late eighties. By then the rest of the world had caught up with them, and because Datapoint had been following the closed system approach of the mainframe companies, they were passed by. However, Datapoint's Arcnet LAN protocol has survived and is widely used in PC LANs.

In the mid-to-late eighties, almost all computers were being interconnected to one or more other computers. People were connecting Macintoshs to VAXes and Crays, big IBM 3090s to VAXes, PCs to everything, and workstations to almost everything. However, application and file compatibility in these networks was far from perfect. If a user on a Macintosh with Microsoft Word wanted to use a file from a user on a PC with WordPerfect, the best the user could do was to import an ASCII file. There was absolutely no way a PC program could be run on a Sun system or a Macintosh. And quite frankly, that's the way the manufacturers wanted it. There was little incentive, as far as they could see, in making their applications available to a competing platform. Arguments about lack of power or features were most often heard when such questions were raised.

However, the users were much smarter. They knew they had lots of unused computing power sitting in their offices and labs. They also knew they couldn't afford to go on buying new computers every time a new application was developed or when more power was needed. The users wanted to be able to tie together the various machines and make them work cooperatively.

It's unclear where the idea of sharing computer power across an enterprise came from. The manufacturers say they thought of it first, and the universities (with their advanced research and the need of invention due to the lack of necessities, i.e., no money) say they had the idea first. It hardly matters. What happened is a project called Athena was started at MIT with the support (and funding) of Digital, IBM and several others.

Athena's goal was simple—connect every computer together, let any machine run any application (or perhaps some specialized computer/application) and let anyone on the network use the application without having to run it on their local machine. The idea was good and it was right. It was within the means of the technology available at the time and it was needed. The project was renamed in 1987 to the X Window System. Soon, all workstation manufacturers declared their machines as X-compatible. Software for PCs was developed that made them compatible. Mainframes were a little more difficult, but they too are now compatible.

The revolution is complete.
The declaration of independence has been written.

With the X Window System, portability can be realized. However, it is not yet a perfect world. What the X Window System does for portability is to create a common interface between applications and users. For example, it is possible with the X Window System to start an application on a Hewlett-Packard workstation (which could be in another building) and have a user at a PC work with it. The user wouldn't know, or care, where the application was running; he or she would only know it was responding to his or her commands.

A perfect solution, right? Wrong. A very good solution, but not yet perfect. For the above scenario to work, the user needed a Hewlett-Packard workstation and a PC. That's close, but it's not real portability. Real portability would be if the user at the PC could load and run the application without having to own a workstation. Will we ever live in a perfect world where that can happen? Probably not. Furthermore, I'm not sure it's even a good idea at this point. To have total portability everyone would have to have a machine that was almost the same. That means everyone would have to have the maximum power available, and that's not practical or possible.

"But wait a minute," the revolutionists yell. "Aren't telephones all the same and aren't cars all basically the same?" they ask. The answer is no. That is a silly oversimplification. Yes, cars are very similar, but you wouldn't expect a seventy-year-old grandmother to have to drive a Corvette would you? And you don't see furniture being delivered in a Honda. Also, you can't plug a U.S. phone into a jack in England or use a U.S. touch-tone auto-dialer in Germany.

So there will always be a limitation to total standardization. Therefore, there will be a limit to portability. However, the limits should be based on realistic and practical reasons, not arbitrary product differentiation imposed by manufacturers or politically created specifications designed to protect a local industry.

The X Window System is a very comprehensive package. It solves a lot of portability problems for us. Initially it is difficult to work with, but it pays off in portability.

Life without X

As mentioned, the mainframe suppliers have not fully embraced or adopted the X Window System. One of the reasons is that it is based (today) on the UNIX operating system. The mainframe computers will not use UNIX as the primary operating system for a long time, and some say never. There are a host of technical and political reasons for this, which are beyond the scope of this book.

The mainframe computer companies have come up with their own architectures for interoperability between platforms. IBM's is called System Application Architecture (SAA), Digital has Network Application Support, Unisys has CTOS, Hewlett-Packard has NewWave Office, and NCR has Cooperation. These are all schemes to allow applications to migrate across platforms, albeit their platforms. These schemes are also being opened up to allow interconnection from alien platforms.

Furthermore, they are adopting windowing techniques and GUIs as a common user interface. In the near future it will be possible to walk up to almost any computer and recognize its functionality, log-on, search for public applications (or private ones if you have the right security access) and go to work. Today users familiar with a particular type of computer can do that, but even then it is sometimes difficult as you navigate through the environment trying to find utilities, programs and files.

GUIs to the rescue

The best hope the user community has for platform-independence and ease of use is the common user interface. Today that common user interface is the GUI. GUIs, combined with interconnectivity and a network-wide computing model like the X Window System will be the way to user portability, if not total application portability.

The computer industry is getting to user interface standards, but there is still no single solution for graphic use. The problem with all the user interfaces is they are not going to solve all of the problems for all of the users. Graphics software has become a commodity on most platforms, but because vendors think their products need differentiation, each company puts in an extra dialog box or radio button. Standards are supposed to make everybody play by the same rules, yet everybody tries to cheat a little bit. That creates several slightly different graphical user interfaces, and the result is there is no standard.

One of the problems with GUIs is the dilemma they create for programmers. GUIs give the user fancy pop-up dialogs and windows and other initially attractive features. The problem for software developers is providing a functional product that is useful and unique. How does a developer do that in an easy-to-use GUI?

This problem doesn't occur when dealing with a dedicated or proprietary system. However, under a GUI, if a user pulls up a dialog box, it may point to another 25, and it is no longer easy to use. Yet, the user wants to have all 25 because they may be needed at one time or another. So there has been a major dilemma between the development of an easy-to-use system and a system for an expert. That isn't to say that because a system is designed for experts, it should be hard to use. There is simply more to it—more to choose from.

One idea is to have two types of systems, and there are still a lot of people talking about how to do that—but it's difficult and complicated. The expert version tends to clutter up the screens. So the major dilemma for the GUI software developers now is how to represent the functionality of the product and resolve the conflict between *easy-to-use* and *advanced users*.

The main goal for GUIs was to make things the same. For example, you know that in a car the gas pedal is on the right and the brake is on the left. That was the goal of GUIs. The user gets into the system, and it operates the same. That is, the radio button works the same on every application. If there was a push-button widget, it operated the same. It wasn't that it made the application easier to use, although that certainly is a desirable by-product.

GUIs do not help in learning one application or another. What they do is help you understand that you can go from a Macintosh to a SPARC to a PC. You will know that you can use them all, but you may have to learn the minor differences of each.

Therefore, because the gas pedal is always on the right and the brake is always on the left, the winner of the GUI market is really going to be the best marketer. If GM insisted on saying their gas pedal is more functional than Ford's gas pedal, but the gas pedal is still on the right side, is the user really going to be able to understand what advantages GM (allegedly) gave them? Therefore, car companies don't talk about how their brake pedal is more ergonomic than another's. The reason is a user cannot perceive the differences, and that is a major problem for all these different standards. All the different vendors are pushing their GUIs, but if the goal is to standardize, a manufacturer can't really push his technology differentiation—it defeats the goal.

It is no longer reasonable to suggest that users must have special knowledge or skills. People are not going to accept that because it is contradictory to the goal, which is to have standards. The organizations that are going to win are not necessarily the technology experts, but those companies that market the best, and that is really the key to the impending GUI wars.

Therefore, the first rule for companies that want to be successful at developing new GUIs is they must be confined to the standards. The other important elements are common sense logic and common sense terminology. The style guides of GUIs only define certain features (such as the gas pedal is on the right and the brake is on the left) and it lets the software developer use his own judgment in the logic and terminology. If a developer doesn't use common sense, he or she will make the GUI more difficult to use.

There have been too many examples of products that are very hard to use. That is because the developers didn't go through the correct and logical thought process of how a typical user does a job. That will be the key differentiating factor.

Portability and common APIs

As will be discussed in detail in subsequent chapters, there are literally dozens of GUIs available. Furthermore, it is possible to have one or more of them on a workstation or PC. All of these GUIs have a toolkit associated with them, and sometimes there are several toolkits. The toolkits allow programmers to develop applications that comply with a particular GUI's style. It has proven more difficult for programmers to write programs in a GUI environment than in the old-fashioned character-based environment. This is not only because windowing systems and toolkits are complicated to use, but also because programmers must strive for the highest level of performance possible. Furthermore, with the GUI comes a new responsibility for quality, not only in the operation of the program, but also in its appearance and user interaction. The programmers are confronted with the need for charm in their programs. Because of the complexity of working in a GUI environment, programmers have had to (initially at least) commit to a single environment or system. The dream of portability had evolved to that, a dream. (See FIG. 2-2.)

A popular proposal that has been put forth several times has been that of a common

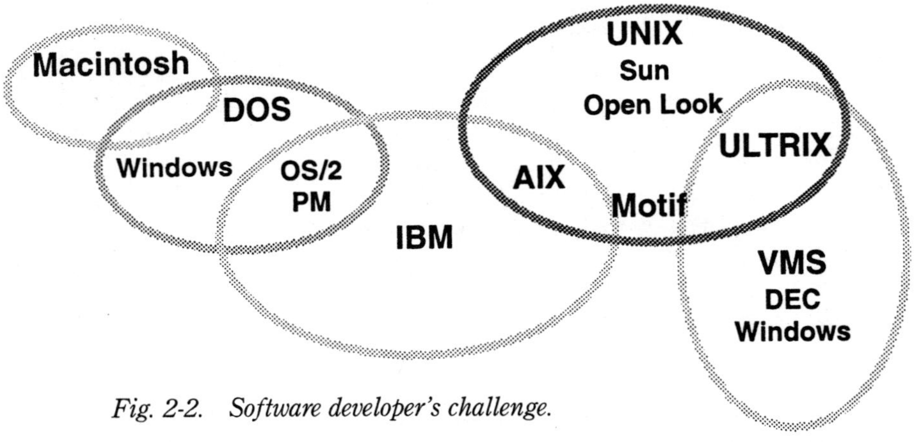

Fig. 2-2. Software developer's challenge.

toolkit, one that could translate the programmer's intentions to any environment desired. Typically, this concept has been given up as being too difficult, due to the eccentricities of the various systems and the costs of the translation stage. The concept is referred to as a common interface or an API (application program interface). APIs exist for operating systems like UNIX and DOS, and for the X Window System.

The IEEE effort

The IEEE has empowered a working group on standards, the IEEE P1201.1. The goal of this group has been to define a standard X Window System-based toolkit. However, because of the conflict between OSF/Motif and OPEN LOOK, the committee has been unable to achieve its goal. Also, many members wanted the standard API to work with non-X Window Systems, such as character displays, Macintosh, Microsoft Windows and Presentation Manager.

In June 1990 the committee held a (nonbinding) vote to base its proposed standard for a virtual API on a product from XVT Software, Inc. However, some members of the committee later decided that the vote was hasty (although not necessarily wrong), so they decided to be a little more methodical. The committee has drawn up a list of requirements and changed the name from virtual API to Layered API. When the committee completes their list of requirements, they will submit a request to the IEEE for a project authorization. If granted, that will give the committee permission to work on a standard. Then the committee will evaluate various approaches, which will include XVT's approach.

The concept behind XVT's approach and the goal of the members of the IEEE committee are the same—develop a common API and a set of libraries for each environment. A schematic of the concept is shown in FIG. 2-3.

Portability approaches

There are basically three ways to achieve portability: Least Common Denominator (LCD), Emulation, and Abstraction.

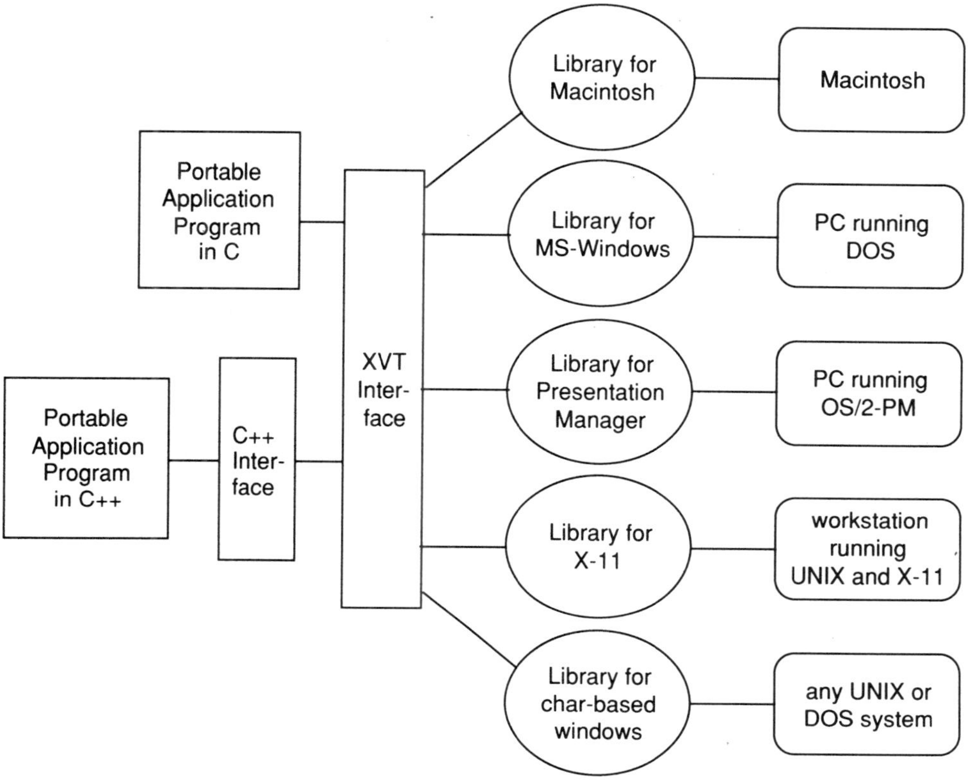

Fig. 2-3. Typical API architecture. XVT Corp

LCD The danger of the least common denominator approach (which many consider the obvious way to achieve portability) is that the interface will be too weak to be useful, or that the resulting applications will look clumsy and foreign. You cannot simply take the intersection of (for example) Motif and Windows functions or libraries and arrive at the common features. Of course, there are some common overlaying functions that map conveniently into each other but do not map into all of the functions. However, portability across user interface toolkits and platforms is possible if the right abstractions are chosen.

Emulation In the case of different processor types, LCDs do not work at all. Therefore, emulations are used. Emulations usually carry an overhead that keeps them from being widely used. A classic example is a PC emulating a Macintosh or vice versa. The most widely used application for emulation in GUIs has been character-based GUIs, with Tandy's DeskMate and Interactive Technology's Skylite being good examples.

Abstraction The greatest success has been achieved with abstractions. This allows an interface (for example) to be described and then duplicated in another environment. Sometimes this is referred to as *reverse-engineering*. Abstractions between GUIs and style-guides can be found in most products. The Mac-toolbox on DOS is another example.

Interapplication communication

The other obstacle in achieving total portability is that software developers think users want every feature possible in every product. Obviously, if that were taken to its logical conclusion, every application would be identical. What users really want is not necessarily more features in every program, but the ability to have communication between their word processors, spreadsheets, and databases. This capability is referred to as *interapplication communication*, or IAC.

It is not a new idea. The pioneers at Xerox PARC invented the concept, and the original Macintosh was shipped with the ability to cut, copy, and paste between applications. Today, DOS and UNIX allow connections between applications, which have been designed to work together, and Apple's System 7 has a very sophisticated data-sharing feature.

Hoping to capitalize on this need and potential opportunity, Userland Software introduced the IAC Toolkit. It provides the connections that let disparate applications access and use each other's features. IAC is a version of object-oriented programming where programmers use building blocks of data to build their applications from the ground up. Success depends on whether developers actually build this version of IAC into their products.

Object linking

Several approaches have been developed for the concept of hot links and various subsets of the concept. Software technologies under development at Apple Computer, Microsoft, and other firms will change the way users perceive, buy, and use applications. The goal is a more structured object-oriented approach with a greater emphasis on applications as smaller, coordinated building blocks instead of single, large programs.

Apple offers Interapplication Communications in System 7.0 of the Macintosh operating system and permits applications to cooperate with each other by exchanging a series of messages. Digital has developed LiveLink, a mechanism for allowing applications to share different types of data. Hewlett-Packard has NewWave, with linking and embedding capabilities. Microsoft uses Object Linking and Embedding (OLE).

If the process is done right, applications will fit together more smoothly than in the past. The industry is moving away from each application having its own environment and developers are investing a tremendous amount of energy reinventing what's already been done by someone else. However, the number of different object-oriented approaches may be a problem. Nonetheless, the goal of a more structured object-oriented approach that will result in applications being smaller building blocks instead of single, large programs remains.

However, making the transition to using metaphors could be a struggle for some users. One problem is the new approaches will have to coexist with existing programs for quite a while. Users will also have to deal with new user interface elements and different procedures for efficient operation.

Also, in practice, system administration may have to worry about compatibility issues and version control. If users work with a much larger number of smaller applications, not only does the risk of incompatibilities go up, but so does the difficulty of finding the offending or conflicting elements. In addition, keeping track of more licenses and updates could also become a more exasperating task if the average user wants to keep current with these applications.

Not revolutionary

The object-oriented approach, building blocks, and messages are all elements of Smalltalk, the quintessential object-oriented programming system. Versions for DOS-based PCs and Macintoshes are offered by Digitalk and ParcPlace Systems.

Apple Events and the Apple Script language can find close parallels in IBM's Rexx scripting language, used to integrate applications on mainframes, and even more parallels to a third-party implementation on OS/2 and Commodore's ARexx implementation on the Amiga. Several Amiga applications, including Commodore's flagship Amiga Vision authoring system, already include ARexx hooks for sharing information and coordinating work between applications running under that machine's multitasking operating system.

Since 1983 Metaphor Computer Systems has offered a self-contained object-oriented system that lets users construct capsules out of building-block object elements. Its version for OS/2 allows Metaphor software to access outside objects and applications as well.

It is well known that user interfaces change. The need for change becomes acute when the application designed for one type of user ends up being used by many more. ParcPlace Systems developed Objectworks for Smalltalk-80 to simplify the task of changing the user interface. Their Model-View-Controller (MVC) user-interface architecture establishes a communication protocol for the three different components of a user interface. Using MVC, a programmer can apply multiple views to the same piece of information, or reuse an interaction mechanism in different parts of the interface. The "pluggability" of MVC allows these changes to be made efficiently by allowing any one component to be replaced without affecting the rest.

In most programming systems, the application structure clumps together the components of an interactive application, creating difficult-to-manage interdependencies. The Smalltalk-80 user interface architecture called MVC separates the graphical application component (View), the data component (Model), and the interaction component (Controller). This enables a programmer to "plug" together graphical applications. The potential for reuse is substantially increased, while the impact of changes is significantly reduced. Applications are binary-code portable to any machine that supports Objectworks for Smalltalk-80. Write on one, deliver on many (i.e., portability) is possible when the architecture of a programming system is designed with that goal.

More than one approach

Users will gravitate toward the object-oriented approach, once it stabilizes. However, there are too many approaches and conflicting claims. Apple has taken a two-stage approach. The live link facility between documents to existing applications is an extension of the cut and paste metaphor. The Edition Manager allows applications to publish elements or sections of data, to which other applications can subscribe. The second step allows applications to increase the number of events (external messages) they respond to from the very limited set now provided by the operating system to an open-ended set that could include messages from other programs. With an events approach, applications could work cooperatively, passing not only data, but also instructions, requests, and status messages.

Microsoft has a different view. The company sees today's users working with an application-centered view. The user loads an application and uses it to operate on one or more documents. Microsoft wants to turn that relationship inside out and make documents the center of each work session instead of the applications. Microsoft's view is that the user won't think of the outermost window as belonging to some application, but rather as a document. There won't be a primary application. As users move through a document, they will use one or more tools as viewers. Hiding the application and starting with the document is a reasonable concept. People are used to working with documents and spend the majority of their time that way, not with the tools or storage devices for the documents. It's a familiar metaphor. Microsoft's Object Linking and Embedding (OLE) is a first step in this document approach (refer to Chapter 11 for more information on OLE). OLE also has many similarities to the "Active Documents" approach announced last year by Interleaf of Cambridge, Massachusetts.

The Object Management Group

While various firms develop proprietary paths, a coalition of over 100 manufacturers and developers has initiated an ambitious three-year effort to promote generic interfaces and standards that include many of the same capabilities.

The Object Management Group (OMG), based in Framingham, Massachusetts, was formed to develop standards to interoperability. Rather than construct its own software, the group's intention is to work with software vendors to provide standards based on commercial products.

Although OMG has so far avoided the polarization that has beset the UNIX-oriented Open Software Foundation, the group still faces political, as well as technical, challenges. Apple signed up with OMG, joining early members such as Hewlett-Packard, Digital Equipment Corp., and AT&T. However, Microsoft has so far declined an invitation, and IBM has endorsed a parallel private effort called Patriot Partners. Although IBM's effort is oriented toward 32-bit systems starting with OS/2, the goal of the OMG group is to maintain compatibility with current popular desktop operating systems.

The group's first step has been to develop an overall object management architecture guide as an overall architecture defining objects and terminology. This will be used as a basis for defining specific interfaces. The second step was to invite proposals for an *object request broker* that defines how a linking mechanism is to pass objects between applications and across networks, addressing all the necessary questions such as naming, addressing, parameter encoding, and security, with the ultimate goal being platform-independence. The next step will be to define class libraries, data models, a standard query language, and other related issues.

However, not everyone in the development or user community is convinced these new approaches are the right ones. As pointed out earlier, an ambivalent attitude toward standards continues to be exhibited by both the users and suppliers. In even the most optimistic of scenarios, the transition will be a lengthy one.

References

Andriole, Stephen J. 1985. *The future of information processing technology*. Princeton, NJ: Petrocelli Books.

Rosenthal, Steve. Altogether now. *Infoworld*. January 7, 1991. Page 44.

3

Graphical user interfaces—GUIs

Graphical user interfaces (GUIs) have been used since the late 1960s; however, the idea of graphical user interfaces really didn't start to become popular until 1981, when Xerox introduced the 8100Star workstation. Although it was not a great commercial success, it awoke the senses of many users and developers about the possibilities of a GUI.

The first truly commercial success of a GUI-based system was the Macintosh. It put the first system with charm into the hands of the masses, and the masses loved it. The Macintosh, which was patterned after the Xerox Star, showed the world that a computer could be friendly, easy-to-use, and even fun. GUIs were soon developed for UNIX workstations by Sun Microsystems and for PCs by Microsoft.

History of GUIs

Graphical user interface systems are not a new idea. They were first envisioned by Vannevar Bush in an article he wrote in 1945. Ivan Sutherland designed Sketchpad in the early 1960s for his graduate thesis.

Xerox was researching graphical user interface tools at the Palo Alto Research Center (Xerox PARC) throughout the 1970s. The historical roots of GUIs at Xerox go back to early work done in Smalltalk and the Star. Nearly all of the features that are now expected on a windowing system were available on the Xerox Star, which was introduced in April, 1981. It was a closed architecture and it only ran on Xerox proprietary architecture. Users bought the entire package, the hardware and the software, from Xerox. Smalltalk was an approximation of what is now considered a GUI. Star was the first fairly complete implementation of what is now considered a GUI.

The Star was one of the systems that Apple's Steve Jobs saw during his now-famous visit to Xerox that led to the development of Apple's Lisa, and then the popular

Apple Macintosh. However, even though the Xerox Star is generally recognized as the main introduction of the GUI, Xerox's own developers cite 14 earlier computer systems that influenced their work.

The inventor of the mouse was Douglas Englebark at Xerox PARC. Englebark's vision of the user interface included not only nonconventional I/O to the computer (i.e., the mouse and special function keys), but also interactive video to remote groups of users. Because of the inaccuracy of Englebark's early analog mouse, his design did not include what is known today as modeless interactivity, in which the user indicates the object first and then gives the command. In this early user interface, the schema was: move word, then click the mouse to indicate which word, then pick the object, and then do a command accept. There were four actions involved.

One of the first systems to offer intimacy between the computer and the user (i.e., the threshold of charm) was the RAND system developed at the RAND Laboratories in 1967. Initially done as an interface system for financial analysts who couldn't type, it employed the world's first data tablet. It had automatic sizing and object linking capabilities and character recognition. The user could draw symbolic boxes, interconnect them for their relationships, and label them (using hand-printed characters), as well as erase and other logical, normal day-to-day functions.

This system also had automatic geometry correction so that the user could draw an approximation of a box and the computer would automatically square it up and make it look like a box. The system had the first resizable capabilities, which were the inspiration for resizable windows on the Macintosh. The RAND system is literally where the Macintosh Window control capability came from, according to Alan Kay, one of the inventors of the GUI at Xerox PARC.

It is the degree of intimacy that largely contributes to the sense of charm in the user interface. Users often get frustrated when they first encounter computers because they appear to only offer typing, sorting and search functions or word-processing capabilities. What is preferred is the capability of finding and manipulating ideas rather than just words. The ability to manipulate ideas gives a user machine assistance in obtaining insight from raw text. The problem with the concept of computers is that it creates a belief that they can do anything and the user only needs to be smart enough to know how to use them.

By 1983, every major workstation vendor had a proprietary windowing system. For example, Sun Microsystems had SunView; Apollo had DM. It wasn't until 1984, when Apple introduced the Macintosh, that a truly robust windowing environment reached the average consumer. The Macintosh GUI has changed the user's entire expectations of a computer interface forever.

In 1985 Microsoft had Microsoft Windows for PC-compatible systems; Digital Research had GEM, used on the Atari ST and some PC compatibles; the Commodore Amiga had the Intuition interface; and Apple had Lisa.

In 1984, out of an MIT project called Athena, arose the X Window System. Athena investigated the use of networked graphics workstations as a teaching aid for students in various disciplines. They attempted to develop a windowing system that would allow students to run local tools like word processors and spreadsheets while simultaneously being able to call up library pictures and documents from remote sources. The X Window System progressed during the next 4 years from version 4 up to the current release.

In the PC area, character-based window-like user interface and operating system shells began to appear. IBM brought out TopView as a multitasking environment. Because it was IBM, several developers wrote applications for it. However, between the limitations of the 808X computer, DOS' 640 Kbyte address space, and IBM's declining support, TopView disappeared.

DESQview, from Quarterdeck, another character-based multitasking windowing system, was introduced shortly after TopView. Although it had considerably better memory management, and is still very popular today, it lacked a bit-mapped or All-Points-Addressable (APA) display system.

The first PC-based bit-mapped windowing system besides the Macintosh to be introduced was GEM from Digital Research. Digital Research was contacted by Apple and later removed several of the look-and-feel features that it had in common with the Macintosh. The GEM interface was adopted by Ventura and a few graphics arts programs, but it never gained wide acceptance beyond that.

Windows was introduced in 1985 and was hailed as being the future for IBM PCs. It didn't turn out that way and Microsoft went through several versions trying to get it right. In 1990 Microsoft introduced version 3.0, and at last it appears that there is a viable full-featured windowing environment for the PC. The evolution of these windowing systems is shown in FIG. 3-1.

In 1988, NeXT Inc. introduced the NeXT computer with its GUI and development environment, NeXTstep. Using the Mach operating system, NeXTstep was viewed by the industry as interesting but too expensive and without sufficient applications or compatibility with industry standards to be a serious contender for the mass market.

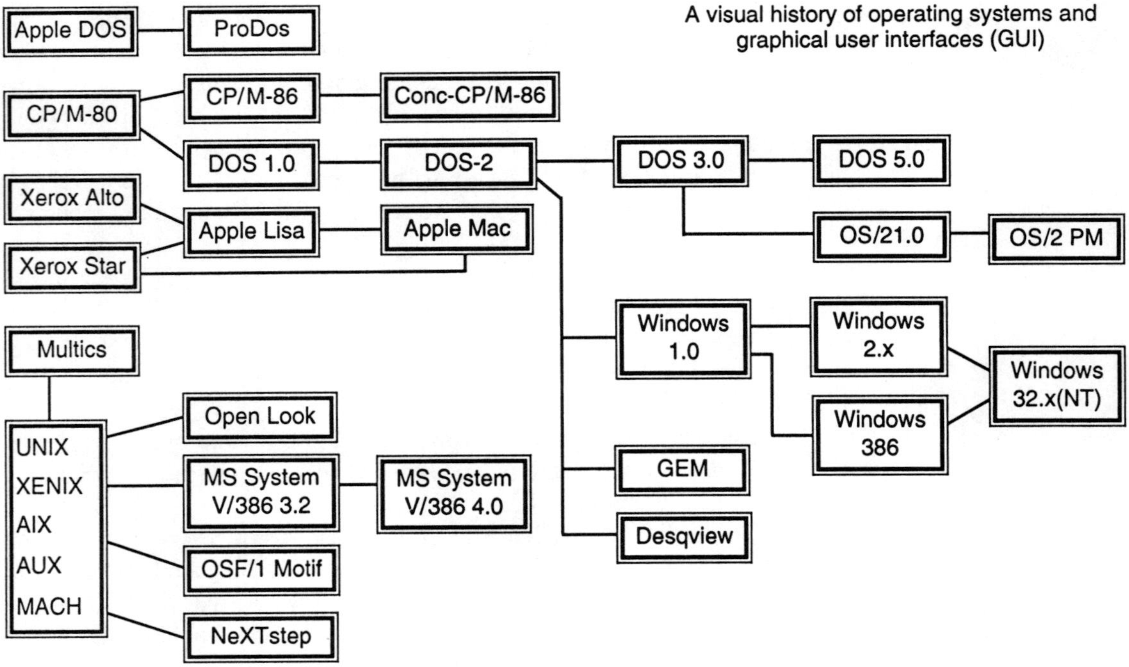

Fig. 3-1. The history of GUIs.

Interestingly, also in 1988, Tandy introduced DeskMate, a character-based environment manager and desktop metaphor.[1] It is a simple-to-use system that provides a clean and usable user interface.

When IBM introduced the OS/2 operating system and the PS/2 computer line, they also announced Presentation Manager as the windowing environment for it. Although the specifications for Presentation Manager are quite attractive, it has taken a long time for IBM, with Microsoft's help, to realize the specifications. They still aren't finished.

Several other specialized GUIs have appeared over the years. Today the industry trend is to adopt a fully overlapping windows system that treats the screen like an APA bit-mapped graphics image with soft typefonts and a mouse-driven pointer that can move around by single-pixel increments.

What is a graphical user interface?

DOS, UNIX and other command-line operating systems have long been criticized for the complexity of their user interface. This interface evolved in the late '60s and early '70s with the emergence of timesharing as the leading new computing style. Using terminals on shared minicomputers, UNIX evolved a set of applications that shared a common line-oriented interface. This interface was revolutionary in its time for its simplicity and power. UNIX introduced a concept of the *shell*, a command interpreter that read command lines from the keyboard and executed a separate process for each command. DOS, built on those same ideas, emerged in the late 70s.

Researchers at XeroxPARC, however, were doing things differently. They were experimenting with GUIs that replaced the character display and command line with a large bit-mapped display, icons, multiple windows, and a pointing device called a mouse, developed earlier at SRI. Research showed that people could learn to use applications with a graphical interface more quickly than with commands. The graphical interfaces were also easier to remember and helped users get more done quickly, besides being fun to use.

In a GUI environment, input options to many computer programs are designed as a set of *icons*, which are graphic symbols that look like the processing option they are meant to represent. Users of such programs select processing options by using a mouse or similar device to point to the appropriate icon. In the early days when fools argued that a command-line structure was faster or more efficient than a GUI, they called GUI users WIMPs—Window, Icons, Mice and Pointer users. Not many people use that expression these days.

The developers of GUIs also went to great lengths to provide the user with immediate, visual feedback about the effect of each action. In particular, think about deleting a file on a Macintosh and compare that to UNIX or DOS. On the Macintosh, the user

[1]The term metaphor should not be confused with the company named Metaphor that sells a product called Data Interpretation Systems. It is a business data analysis program, not a windowing program or GUI. The company has stated it has no plans to migrate the product to a multi user interface environment such as MOTIF, PM, NewWave, etc.

sees an icon (representing a file), then the user sees the icon deleted. With DOS or UNIX, the user types the delete command (e.g., DEL *.*) and gets nothing back in response. There is no indication of whether one or a hundred files have been deleted. For many users, that's very discomforting. A simple, consistent command language with abundant memory aids, and immediate feedback is what makes the GUI easy to use.

In his article, "So, Whose Side Are You On?" (*Esquire*, November 1990, p. 107), Donald R. Katz observed, ". . . first-time computer purchasers often felt they had to decide who they really were in order to own a computer, because the difference between a Macintosh person and an IBM person implied an entire lifestyle, attendant cultural proclivities, and which district of your brain you used. GUI programs ask me to give up the precision of language in favor of symbolization. If pictures are such wonderful ways of communicating, then why have most people spent so much time creating literature, writing letters, and building libraries?"

So the discussion of whether or not to use a GUI still goes on. However, as mentioned earlier, it is an argument born of ignorance. Aside from Mr. Katz's humorous observation of the debaters, a GUI is chosen not because it is good (as opposed to bad), or slick (as opposed to dull), or right-brained, or anything fashionable, or the latest technowonder. A GUI is purchased because it is a productivity enhancer, period. Productivity doesn't just mean getting more work done in an hour. It also means getting people (computer users) to be effective users of a computer.

Companies that sell GUIs claim that users of GUIs require 25 percent less training on specific applications during the first year, and will experience a 25 percent increase in productivity. Studies have also shown that users need less hand-holding, and they pick up the operation of an application more rapidly. That translates into thousands of dollars of savings for each GUI user in a company. A well-designed GUI will serve all users.

- A *novice* should be able to master it quickly, without training or extensive reading of manuals.
- A *casual* user, who runs several different applications daily, should find it is consistent between applications.
- A *power*, or frequent user must have accessibility to keyboard equivalents to mouse point-and-click commands.

Elements of a GUI

A GUI has to have certain features and capabilities to qualify as useful. Figure 3-2 shows the primary organization of a GUI, sometimes referred to as "the user's workspace." The concepts of desk, or user workspace, organization and icons were studied and understood at Xerox. The developers of the Xerox Star listed the five most important principles of a GUI.

1. The illusion of manipulable objects. One of the main goals of a GUI is to create the illusion of objects that can be manipulated (moved, changed, discarded, etc.) Desktop icons must be clearly displayed for selection and manipulation.

2. Visual order and user focus. This involves the balance of contrast and intensity between items and objects. Window context should have high intensity relative to the Desktop. This includes clearly showing the current status of an icon.
3. Revealed structure. The user needs the ability to see the difference between his or her intention and the actual effect (at say, the printer). Special screens can be used to tell the user about the underlying structure.
4. Consistent and appropriate graphic vocabulary. How buttons behave when activated and what their symbol is representing must be consistent. This vocabulary is one of the major elements of a user friendly interface, an interface with charm.
5. Match the medium. This calls for the graphics designer (of icons and controls) to be sensitive about the resources and/or limitations of a display system. Users and programmers should keep these concepts in mind when designing or evaluating a GUI.

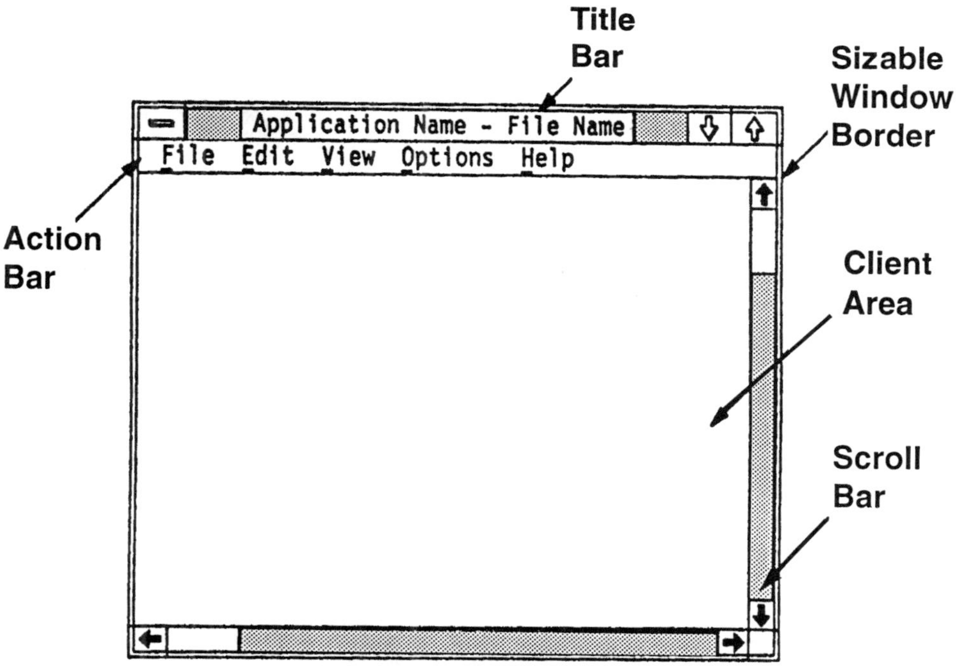

Fig. 3-2. The user's workplace.

If you glance through this book or read any of the trade journals, it becomes clear that there are dozens of GUIs today. Although there are many forms of GUIs, they all share a few basic similarities:

- A pointing device, typically a mouse.
- A bit-mapped display, with a WYSIWYG screen representation of printed output.
- Windows, which graphically display what the computer is doing.

- On-screen menus, that can appear or disappear under pointing-device control.
- Icons, which represent files, directories, applications and utilities.
- Dialog-boxes, buttons, sliders, checkboxes, and several other graphical widgets that let the user instruct the computer about what should be done. Figure 3-3 shows the elements found in a typical dialog box. This illustrates many of the concepts needed in a GUI.
- Object-action paradigm. Also know as *modeless interactivity* where the user indicates the object first and then gives the command.

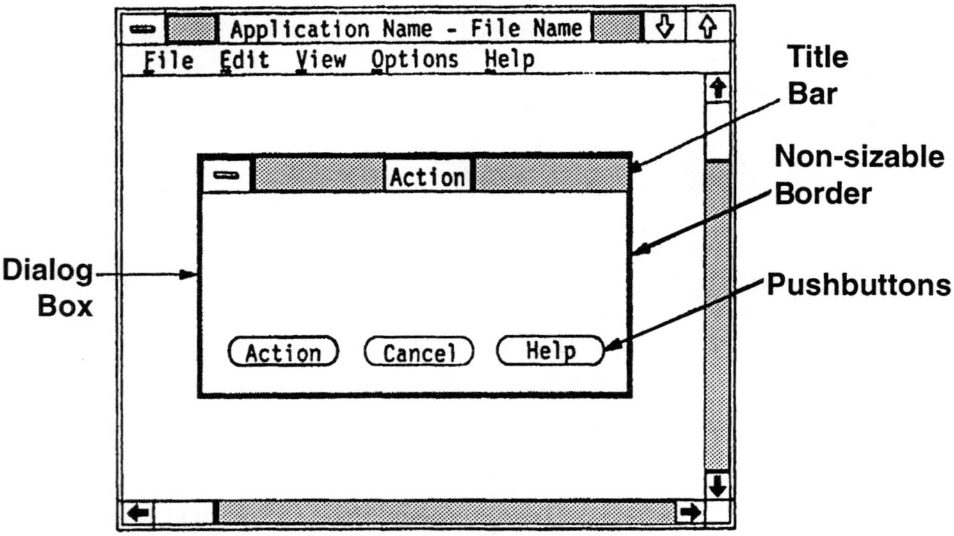

Fig. 3-3. A dialog box.

The use of a metaphor

The use of the term *metaphor* is stretched when applied to a computer. The literal definition is: a figure of speech in which a term is transferred from the object it ordinarily designates to an object it may designate only by implicit comparison or analogy. GUIs simulate the way people normally work. They have been described as an emulation of a person's desk and have been called a desktop metaphor (using the analogy concept of the definition) or paradigm. The desk contains various objects and items (books, files, etc.) that can be open at the same time. Notes are made, phone calls initiated, things are thrown in the wastebasket. These are the actions and objects icons represent. However, since almost everyone's desk is managed (or not managed) a little differently, the concept of a desktop is subjective and often controversial.

The advantage of such systems is that the icons can take up less screen space than the corresponding textual description of the functions, and they can be understood more quickly if well designed. The truly unique service provided by a windowing system is the ability to have views of multiple applications on the screen at the same time.

A single icon can contain an entire series of processes that the user need not be aware of. Figure 3-4 shows the primary visual components of a GUI with two windows on-screen and icons in the lower corner.

However, the idea of icons and a desktop representation is often misunderstood. It is not the purpose of an icon to faithfully represent some physical office item (such as a notepad or a telephone). Icons, and their actions, are designed to remind the user through recognition of the action or item. Humans have been described as being well-suited for recognizing things, but rather poor at recall.

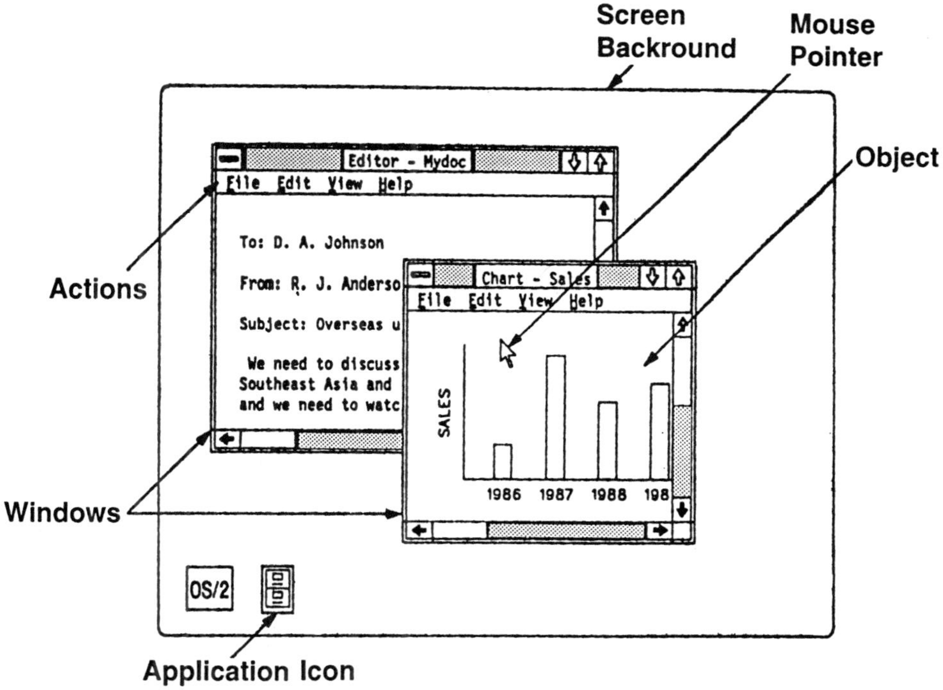

Fig. 3-4. Primary visual components of a GUI.

The meaning of an icon

The literal meaning of the word *icon* is: An image, representation; a symbol or simile. Icon is Latin from the Greek *eikōn*, likeness, image.

The use of the word in a computer environment was adopted by David Canfield Smith in 1975, while he worked at Xerox. According to Smith, he adopted the term from the Russian Orthodox Church, where an icon is more than an image, because it embodies properties of what it represents.

What an icon represents is not entirely resolved. Should they represent real objects (such as a disk or a notepad), or should they be a symbolic representation of their main use, suggesting the key point of the application? There are also cultural subtleties. In Japan, the symbolic icon is very popular. In the U.S., users seem to prefer the real-objects approach.

Because a computer has facilities and operations that are a little more complicated than icons can completely represent, the typical GUI offers command words as well as icons. These words appear on graphical *buttons*, *dialog-boxes*, and menus whenever one points (with a mouse or other pointing device) to a relevant icon or command word.

GUI capabilities

Every day, new applications and new releases of software are being designed to run under a GUI. Market-research firms and industry pundits have forecasted that, from 1995 on, all software will either be GUI-compatible or in the process of being upgraded to it. There will be only a few text-based systems.

For a GUI or its applications to be useful, it must have certain basic features and functions. The following is the set of capabilities that constitutes a robust windowing system. When considering a graphical user interface, look for these features.

- Type of output. Does the window system allow both graphics and text to be output to the same window?
- Overlapping/tiled. A tiled window system is one in which none of the windows overlap. An overlapping windowing system provides the flexibility of multiple windows on the screen with the active window in the foreground.
- Concurrent display. When there are multiple windows visible on the screen, can windows other than the topmost window be updated?
- Clipping. If output to background windows is allowed, is the output limited to the visible portion of the window? That is, does the window system allow you to (presumably accidentally) overwrite other windows?
- Obscured data. The portion of a window that is not visible is referred to as being obscured. When this portion of the window is visible again (when it is exposed), what fills in the text or graphics that belong there—the application or the window system?
- Graphics language. What graphics capability does the window system support?
- Networking. Does the window system support displaying data on a different machine, connected by a network?
- Extensibility. Does the window system allow new devices and new capabilities to be easily added?
- Old applications. Most window systems have to live in an environment where the applications were written before the window system existed. How well does the window system support these old applications?
- Databases. DBMS developers also agree on the benefits and the future of GUIs with regard to their inactivity with SQL. SQL connectivity and Client-Server computing have made database management more complex. However, the increased use of GUIs as front ends for databases has the potential to make corporate users more proficient. Furthermore, graphical databases will dramatically increase productivity over the next five years. Though such graphical applications contain underlying SQL connectivity, there will be no need for users to know SQL, no need to have complicated add-on features. SQL is not a language for end users. Simplicity and ease of use do not mean the database is a toy.

An organizational model

In this chapter an organizational layer model for GUIs will be developed. That is necessary because GUIs come in many varieties, and not everything that is called a GUI has all these features. Some GUIs don't use icons. On others, the icons are optional or available only sometimes. Some require a mouse, while others will let you work from the keyboard. Another element that is different from one GUI to another is the level of integration between the GUI and the operating system. Some GUIs are tightly bound to the operating system such as the Amiga, Macintosh and the NeXT computer. When those systems are first turned on, the GUI appears automatically. Other GUIs require the user to specifically choose the GUI (although that can be hidden with batch files at boot-up). GUIs such as Windows and most of the X Window Systems GUIs that run on UNIX are examples of the latter.

The definition of what is and isn't part of a GUI will vary from one supplier to another. The parts of a GUI that interact with each other also varies. Therefore, without imposing excruciating detail on the reader, a general model has been developed that will show which GUIs have what components. (Refer to FIG. 3-5.)

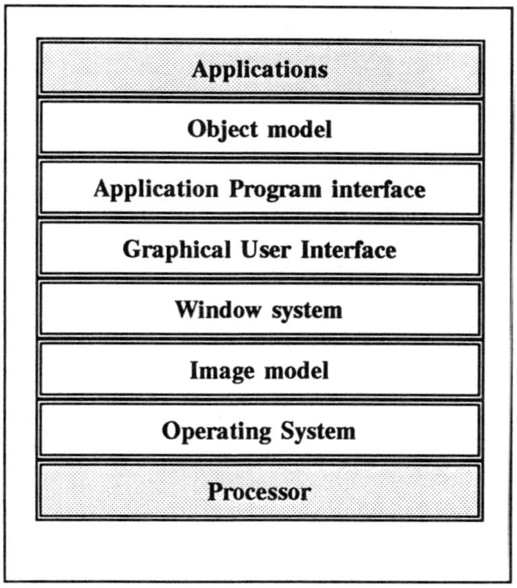

Fig. 3-5. Organizational model of a GUI.

The processor used with a given GUI will vary, as will the operating system. Therefore, one of the layers of the model contains that element. The model starts at the top with the application. This is considered the main point where the user contacts the system. However, it is also true that the user will come in contact with the elements of the GUI itself, such as the menus and icons. The layer model is not intended to be an accurate map of the functionality or the software operation. It is only used to establish a comparison between the various GUIs.

There are five basic layers to the model, plus the application, the operating system and the processor. In a few cases the operating system is an integral part of the GUI. In other situations the GUI sits on top of the operating system. Each layer is described in the following paragraphs.

Object model The way applications react with each other and themselves often involves the use of an object model. In some views Hypercards in the Macintosh can be thought of as an object model. NewWave is definitely an object model. The object model is the latest layer of the GUI scheme, and some GUIs do not yet have one. Others leave that to third-party suppliers.

Application Program Interface The Application Program Interface (API), is a set of programming-language function calls that are used by application developers to communicate with the GUI. A programmer must specify which functions (e.g., windows, menus, scroll bars, and icons) are desired and when. Both Presentation Manager and Windows have their own APIs. DECwindows uses an API called XUI for User Interface, which includes function calls for the X Window System. OPEN LOOK is the latest API for Sun Microsystems' operating system. NeXTstep uses its own API, defined by a library of objects grouped into kits, and its own windowing system, the window Server. Motif uses a combination API from Digital (XUI) and Hewlett-Packard (HP X widgets). The imaging model for Motif has not yet been selected. The API includes the toolkit that is used by the software developer to create the GUI for an application.

The GUI As mentioned elsewhere, what is and isn't part of the GUI varies from supplier to supplier. The GUI is where the screen actions and elements reside (the pop-up or pull-down menus, the scroll bars, etc.).

The window system Almost as hard to define as the GUI, the window system in a GUI is critical to its implementation and interoperability. The X Window System is only a window system and is not a GUI. Microsoft Windows, on the other hand, has both a GUI and a windowing system built in.

Image model While the X Window System doesn't have an image model, some GUIs support more than one imaging model. Sun Microsystem's NeWS is similar to the PostScript imaging model Display PostScript (DPS); however, unlike DPS, it can also turn the screen over to a complete graphics imaging system such as PHIGS or GKS for controlling a CAD program.

Figure 3-5 shows all the elements that go into making up a total GUI, from the processor to the user. As will be seen in subsequent sections and chapters, not all GUIs possess all these elements. None of the GUIs contain the application shown in light gray. If a particular GUI does not contain certain other elements (such as an Object Model), that layer is shown in dark gray.

It is very difficult to apply the kind of layered model that is described here to a variety of different systems. Each layer often has its own API, and the one most visible to application developers depends on the particular system. For example, the API provided by the X Window System is the window system API. In the case of NeXT, the visible API is the Application Kit, which is used to build the GUI.

What is meant by the GUI can be another source of confusion. If GUI refers to the look and feel of a computer's interface, then some GUIs (like NeXT's GUI) is really all of it, rather than just a particular layer.

Perhaps a more fundamental issue is that of the object model. Like an API, the object-oriented paradigm can enter in at any layer. The generic GUI model used here puts it just under the application layer. This accurately models the approach of systems such as NewWave, which are built upon nonobject-oriented platforms. ROOM's and NeXT's object-oriented paradigm are more fundamental than that. Therefore, although you can use this layered model as a vehicle for a general comparison, it should not be viewed as data-flow or architectural construction. It is a general model.

GUIs available today—an overview

There are almost as many GUIs available as there are computer models. Like computers, GUIs each have different features that may or may not be useful to a user. Also like computers, there is no best GUI.

GUIs have generally been thought of as being in one of four families: Macintosh, PCs, UNIX platforms and others that include everything else, from mainframes to Amigas. However, those lines of discrimination do not really apply, since a Macintosh is really a personal computer; after all IBM and (clone) PCs are not the only type available.

I should point out that all GUIs have the same basic purpose, which is to make using a computer easier or friendlier, to give the computer some charm. Therefore, all GUIs have similar elements, such as a desktop metaphor, the use of icons to represent functions and devices, and the use of a pointing device.

On some GUIs, the second mouse button means "display a menu." On some, it means "move the window," and on others it means "extend the selection." Clicking the Up arrow on the scroll bar displays text near the top of the document in some interfaces. It shows text near the bottom in others. Some scroll bars don't have an arrow at all.

The Macintosh's menu bar at the top of the screen is a good, reasonable approach, with a 9-inch diagonal screen and only one program at a time controlling it. With a 19-inch screen and the capability to run multiple programs simultaneously and independently in different windows, having only one control area at the top of the screen is not a good user interface design. Each process needs its own control in its own window to associate the controls with the process and to reduce "mousing around."

At the same time, an interface that can take advantage of multitasking capabilities should be able to control several windows at once. With the selection paradigm extended to the desktop, OPEN LOOK allows the user to select several windows, close them all at once, move them or zoom them to full size, or in fact do anything to the set that can be done to just one.

Briefly examined in alphabetical order, the following are a few of the more popular GUIs that are available. The rest are discussed in further detail in later chapters.

DECwindows

Although the X Window System traditionally has been associated with UNIX, there is nothing UNIX-specific or operating-system specific about the X Window Systems. As a case in point, Digital (DEC) has embraced the X Window System as the vehicle to unite under a common user interface between its VMS, Ultrix (UNIX), and MS-DOS systems, and to marry VMS and Ultrix under a common programming interface. The organization of DECwindows is shown in FIG. 3-6.

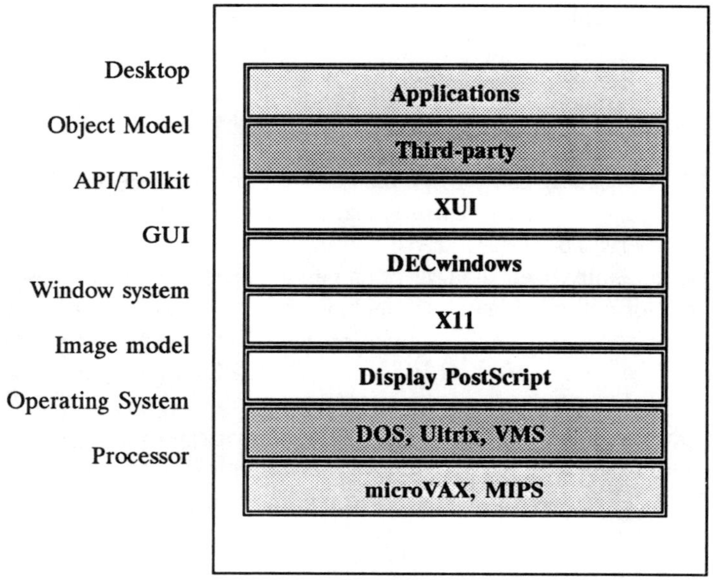

Fig. 3-6. Digital's DECwindows.

Digital has made the X Window System a major design center for new applications development. The DECwindows program (Digital's extensive implementation of the X Window System) is by far the largest single software investment the company has ever made. While DECwindows integrates Digital computers, its implementation of the X Window System architecture will enable VAX systems to communicate with all other non-Digital computers that support X.

Digital also released some numbers on DECwindows speeds that were taken from the X library tests. These are primitive graphics and window-manipulation tests. There are more than 200 individual tests; 170 are primitive tests, with 59 being window and bit-map tests. The suite is in C. How good a measure it makes is questionable. It would be useful for an implementor to test versions of their product against one another, and perhaps vendor-to-vendor to see "how we're doing," but it's not much of a real-world measurement. The results show that the DECstation 3100 is about 3.1 – 3.8 times better than a VAXstation 3100 in supporting DECwindows. They also show 1:.7 and 1:.87 ratios for DECwindows on the DECstation versus X Windows on the same machine. DECwindows is a better implementation than the X Window System standard. Digital has also announced its intention to incorporate the Macintosh in the DECwindow environment.

Macintosh

With the introduction of the Macintosh in 1984, Apple Computer put itself in a position of leadership by offering a system with a GUI. The Macintosh was a closed but complete system with a specific style guide for applications. Introduced as "the computer for the rest of us," it was embraced by a small but loyal group of users. The Macintosh is discussed further in Chapter 10. Figure 3-7 shows the organizational structure of the Macintosh system.

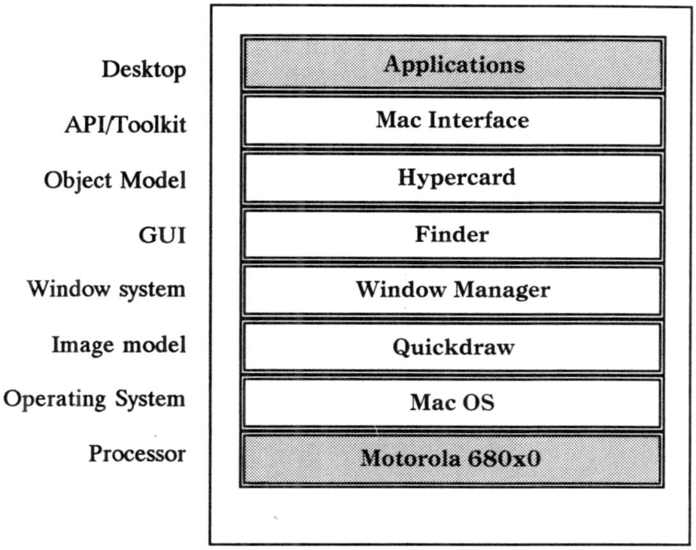

Fig. 3-7. Macintosh GUI structure.

Motif

The Open Software Foundation (OSF) GUI for the implementation of the X Window System is Motif. OSF/Motif is the standard graphical interface to computer applications being promulgated by the Open Software Foundation, a worldwide nonprofit organization dedicated to developing an open computing environment in which all hardware and software can work together more easily. The result of a 1988 solicitation of graphical user interface (GUI) technologies from the worldwide computer industry, Motif combines the best of several technologies.

The OSF's Motif is based on Digital Equipment Corporation's XUI (X User Interface) technology and Digital's UIL (User Interface Language) and toolkit, with the distinctive beveled three-dimensional appearance or look and feel of Hewlett-Packard Company's 3D windowing system (NewWave), as well as Microsoft/IBM's Presentation Manager-like behavior.

Digital has adopted an active, some would say aggressive, stance in determining the role of standards and the rules of interoperability in implementing GUIs. Digital was instrumental in coaxing OSF to adopt major portions of its DECwindows technology in the design of Motif. OSF combined Digital's XUI widgets with HP's widgets to produce the Motif widgets, resulting in a GUI that represents the best of both worlds.

For a while the divisive atmosphere that pitted Motif against Open Look loomed large and delayed some people from adopting a GUI. However, things have settled down and users are getting involved with GUIs. The battle between Motif and Open Look has also been influenced by OSF's marketing aggressiveness. OSF/Motif got off to a lead in the early days of the GUI wars because OSF formed consultative committees, inviting major vendors and representatives from Fortune 500 companies. That helped create an instant vote in favor of Motif, and an early, broad-based constituency. Figure 3-8 shows the organizational structure of Motif.

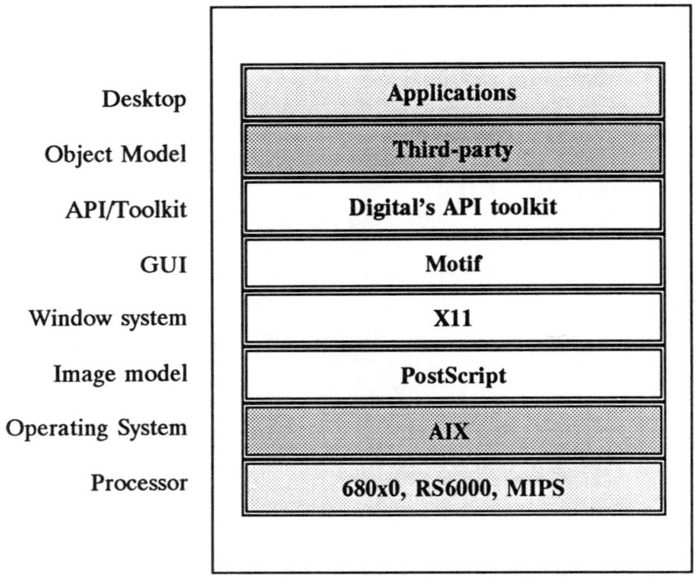

Fig. 3-8. Open Software Foundation's Motif.

UNIX International has also endorsed Motif. Motif meets the five criteria for an approved GUI for UNIX System V.4:

- It conforms to the X Window System.
- The specification is freely available.
- There are no legal encumbrances on its use.
- It is a real product (not vaporware).
- It must run on top of System 4.V.

OSF upgraded the Motif interface with version 1.1, and over 40 new features were added. Significant performance enhancements, cached gadgets, improved color coordination, and the ability to scroll through text faster are a few of the enhancements.

As Motif has gained in popularity, it has attracted add-on products and toolkits from various developers. IXI Limited has a desktop management software upgrade for Motif running under X Windows, called the X.Desktop. It has been adopted by IBM, NCR, the Santa Cruz Operation, Unisys, Dell, NEC, Uniplex, Mitsubishi, and others. It extends the "drag-and-drop" protocol to support the dragging of data objects between the desktop and other applications. Preconfigured user environments are also being included that have been tailored for different skill and experience levels to provide users with more "out-of-the-box" functionality. These levels include novice, experienced UNIX user, and systems administrator. It also supports multicolored, 3-D shaped and animated icons, as well as the capability to set various preferences such as icon size, fonts, mouse-button mapping, and directory background colors. Context-sensitive help is available through x.deskhelp, a hypertext-based online help system. Long-view and tree-view directory viewing options are also provided.

Visix Software offers Looking Glass, a desktop manager that runs on top of Motif. It allows users to execute all tasks by using the mouse, rather than typing in strings of UNIX commands as required by other UNIX interfaces. Refer to Chapter 16 for more information on these systems.

NeXTstep

In 1988, NeXT Computer, Inc. introduced its desktop computer with NeXT's Mach/UNIX operating system and its GUI NeXTstep. NeXT's window server incorporates Display Postscript from Adobe Systems for a UNIX image model across all output devices. NeXT's application kit provides a powerful set of objects for creating user interfaces. The kit does most of the work necessary for an application to present a

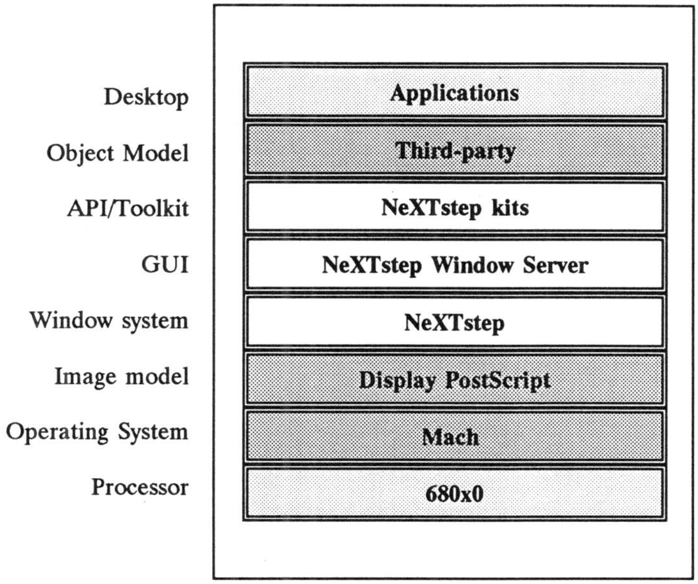

Fig. 3-9. NeXT's NeXTstep.

graphical user interface. The NeXT object model is integrated throughout the system. It is not provided by third parties. The best place to put it to make it fit the generalized model is in the toolkit, or to have two layers labeled Application Kit, as shown in FIG. 3-9.

NeXT also offers a development tool known as Interface Builder for developers and experienced users to develop a graphical user interface for applications. It uses the application kit that allows programmers to generate most of the code necessary to run the interface.

NewWave

This is a user environment from Hewlett-Packard. It is basically an environment manager that runs on top of a GUI like Windows, the X Window System or Presentation Manager, as shown in FIG. 3-10. NewWave adds two management features to the GUI: object management, task automation, and network storage and retrieval. NewWave is discussed in more detail in Chapter 13.

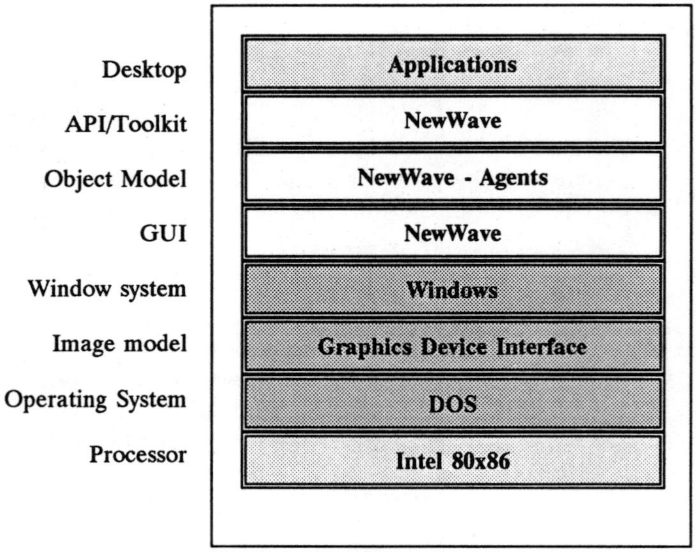

Fig. 3-10. Hewlett-Packard's NewWave.

NeWS

The Network Extensible Window System, NeWS, was an outgrowth of a research project that began at Sun Microsystems in 1984. Within NeWS, the window Server runs on the user's workstation, and the Client applications run either locally or on remote machines. Figure 3-11 shows the organizational structure of NeWS.

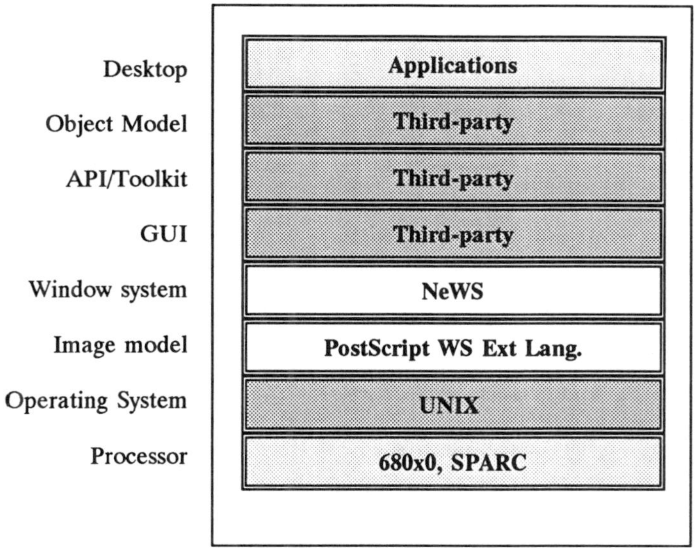

Fig. 3-11. Sun Microsystem's NeWS.

NeWS uses Adobe's Postscript window system extension language. Extensibility within a window system is an indication of the extent of flexibility that is allowed in the system. In NeWS, the user can define functions that PostScript allows. Clients can place PostScript code into the window of a Server at any time, even while the Server is running. Clients send complete PostScript programs (over the network—a potential network-clogging operation) to the Server for execution locally. The Server sets up as a viewing window in PostScript. It then interprets each Client's request based on the state of each window.

NeWS has the same Client-Server foundation as the X Window System. Its major difference is Sun Microsystem's use of paint-and-stencil models from PostScript. The NeWS Server is a PostScript interpretive programming language. It is similar to Apple's LaserWriter's language but has extensions that Sun Microsystems developed for interaction with devices, screen-oriented graphics and event handling.

Sun Microsystem's NeWS uses an object-oriented approach like Microsoft's Windows and other GUIs. However, it does not offer any toolbox for menus, icons, controls, etc. A framework is provided that Sun says allows the programmer to easily develop such items for Client applications.

Proponents of UNIX, a multitasking system with over 15 years of development, see the need to harness its power to a GUI if it is to win broader acceptance. Sun Microsystems' NeWS creates its own multitasking environment (under UNIX) by taking control of scheduling and maintenance of context information of all Client processes. They call the Client processes *threads* (some Sun Microsystems' documents refer to them as *lightweight processes*). The Server manages all of the resources that share lightweight processes or threads. It uses its own scheduling procedures for allocation of the processor's time for each thread. Lightweight processes share a common address space (whereas UNIX has information on processes' virtual address spaces). This makes it easier for lightweight processes, since the scheduler only has to save information (on registers) to allow for context switching from one thread to another.

NeWS can support multiple user interfaces without changing the application. It can impose a global user interface on applications while they are running. This allows users to choose which kind of an interface they want to apply to a particular application.

Although Sun Microsystems has optimized the Server functions, only Sun supports this GUI. However, they have decided that NeWS will have the X Window System in it, and therefore be compatible with the emerging standard. Sun's port of the X Window System is not an emulator, so there should be no degradation in performance. They have said the NeWS systems will support the proposed imaging standards of X. Therefore, applications running on a Sun workstation, using NeWS, should be able to use either NeWS or X.

OPEN LOOK

UNIX is a large, complex operating system that was originally designed for technical and scientific users with extensive computer experience. Traditionally, it has required the memorization and keying in of complicated commands, making it difficult for the novice user. However, the capabilities of UNIX are increasing demand for UNIX systems in many areas outside its original technical markets.

For this reason, Sun designed the OPEN LOOK graphical user interface, with help from AT&T and others. OPEN LOOK is an implementation of the X Window Systems. OPEN LOOK humanizes UNIX, utilizing the pull-down menus, mouse controls, and icons that have made Apple's Macintosh so user friendly. OPEN LOOK runs on top of X Windows and is based on technology licensed from Xerox Corp.

Two implementations of the OPEN LOOK Style Guide have been developed; one version, developed by AT&T, runs on top of X Windows; the second, developed by Sun, runs on top of its Network Windowing System (NeWS).

What does the Open in an Open standard really mean? For some companies it means closed; for others it means open-a-little. For practical purposes, open means nonproprietary, available from more than one vendor; and standard means widely adopted and adhered to. Nearly every design decision for OPEN LOOK was influenced by these concepts. The design had to be device-independent. A standard would have to work on platforms from a variety of vendors with different characteristics, such as screen sizes, resolutions, color or monochrome, one-, two-, or three-button mice, and square or rectangular pixels.

Sun designed OPEN LOOK in 1987, and its structure is shown in FIG. 3-12. It is not a product, but a user interface architecture defined by a specification and a style guide. It is not a piece of software. It is a book, the *OPEN LOOK Graphical User Interface Functional Specification* to be exact. The book describes what a user sees on the computer screen, and the way a user controls the computer in any applications program based on OPEN LOOK. There is also a style guide that gives designers methods of

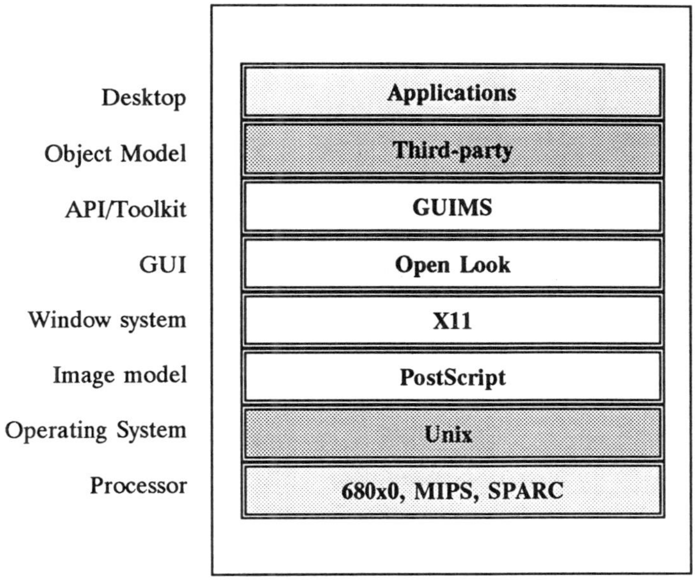

Fig. 3-12. Unix International's OPEN LOOK.

developing applications based on this GUI. A toolkit sits between the API and UI. User interfaces are usually inextricably bound to a single API, and sometimes they are bound to a single computer as well. The OPEN LOOK user interface is different. It standardizes the user interface but does not specify the API. (See FIG. 3-13.)

OpenWindows

Sun's implementation of OPEN LOOK is OpenWindows. Sun Microsystems' OpenWindows gives UNIX ease of use through an intuitive graphical user interface. It includes an X.11/NeWS windowing system that integrates the X.11 standard with a PostScript drawing engine. It also includes the development toolkit Sun calls Guide. Guide has been described as being similar to NeXT's Interface Builder. The structure of OpenWindows is shown in FIG. 3-14.

OpenWindows includes:

- OPEN LOOK, a 3D look-and-feel interface that is a part of AT&T's UNIX SVR4 and contains graphical metaphors, pop-up windows and point-and-click mouse controls.
- X11/NeWS, a high-performance window system that merges industry standard X with NeWS, featuring the PostScript imaging model.
- OpenFonts technology for displaying scalable outline fonts. It includes three pieces of licensed software: F3, an intelligent outline format; TypeMaker, a tool that enables type vendors to create outline fonts in F3 format quickly and inexpensively; and TypeScaler, which generates bitmaps in any orientation, point size, or resolution for both the screen and printer.

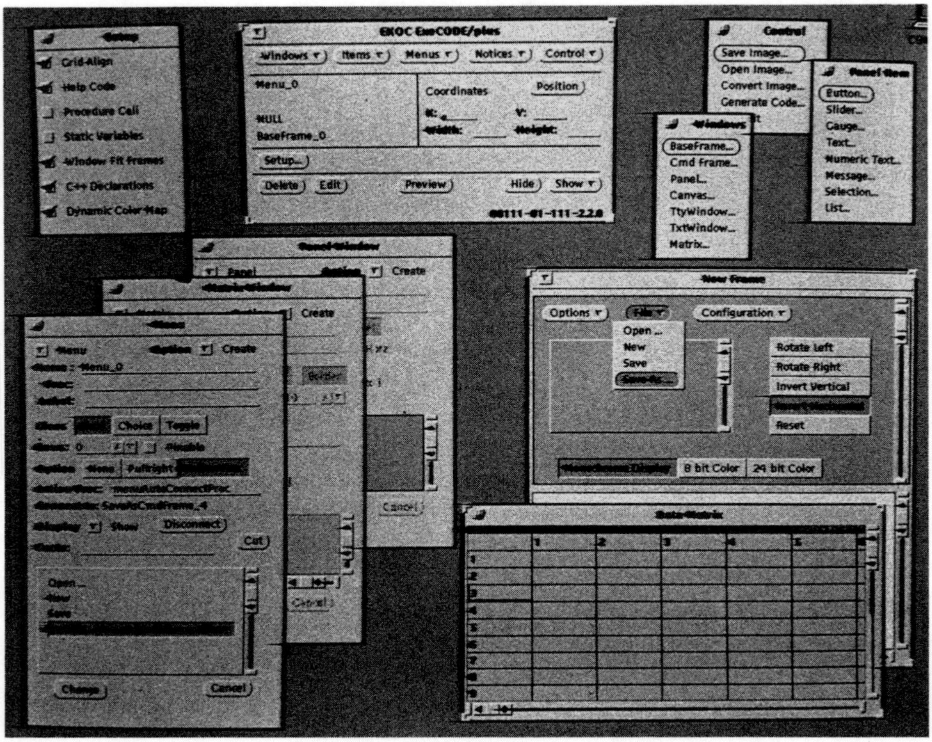

Expert Objects Corp.

Fig. 3-13. Users can create OPEN LOOK compliant windows for SUN workstations using tools like ExoCode.

OPEN LOOK

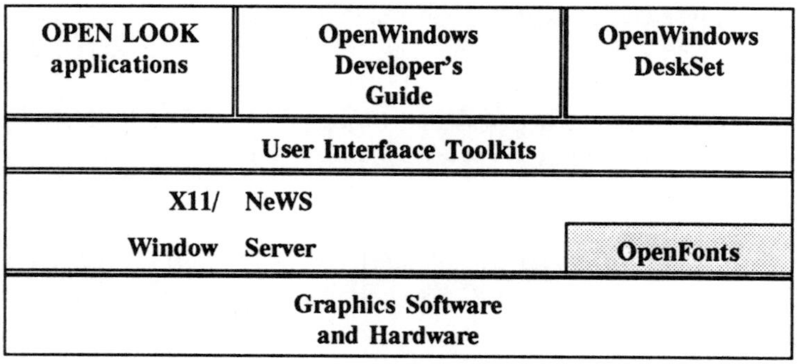

Fig. 3-14. OpenWindows architecture.

- DeskSet tools, a suite of 14 tools including a file manager, mail tool, text editor, binder, icon editor, snapshot tool, performance meters, clock, calendar manager, print tool, tape tool, and calculator.
- Toolkits, including XView, OLIT and TNT to develop OPEN LOOK applications that have a consistent look and feel.

- OpenWindows Developer's Guide is a prototyping tool from Sun that is not a part of, but complements OpenWindows. It enables developers to design the 3-D OPEN LOOK graphical user interface for their applications. It is an interactive tool and has a palette of icons that represent various objects (window control functions, scrollbars, menus). Rather than writing code, a developer can merely "drag" an icon with the mouse and "drop" it in the desired location. GUIDE automatically generates the user interface code.
- Japanese OpenWindows allows users to switch back and forth between English and Japanese within an application by simply pointing the cursor and clicking a button on a mouse.

The elements of OpenWindows are a standard part of UNIX System V,7179 Release 4, offered by AT&T.

Presentation Manager

This is the embedded GUI that comes with OS/2 from IBM and Microsoft. Cosmetically, Presentation Manager (commonly referred to as PM) resembles Microsoft's Windows (see FIG. 3-15); however, beneath it is a completely different system.

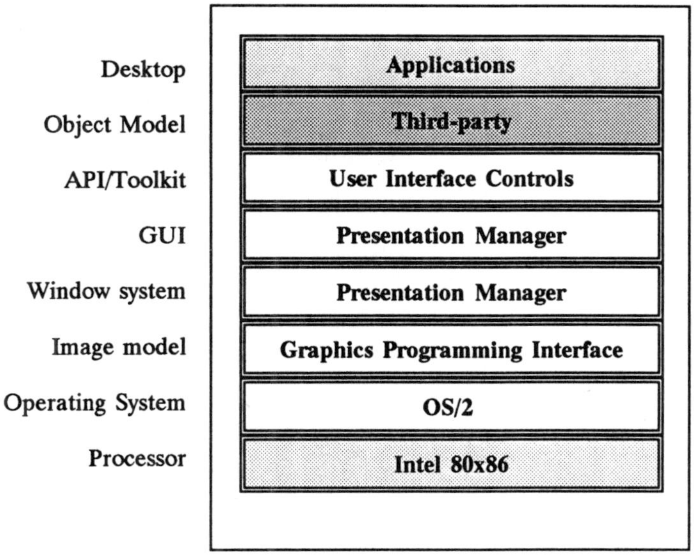

Fig. 3-15. IBM's Presentation Manager.

OS/2 is not an extension of DOS, but instead consists of a powerful multithreading, multitasking operating system with a built-in graphical user interface. Because OS/2 and Presentation Manager are so superior to DOS, OS/2 has had a slow initial growth as applications and users' understanding of it increased. However, OS/2's power will give users a future path for advanced applications that DOS can't match.

Windows

As much as Apple was influenced by Xerox, Microsoft has been influenced by the Macintosh. In 1985, within one year of the announcement of the Macintosh, Microsoft announced the first version of Windows. However, the DOS operating system and the slow 8086/8 computers of the day just weren't up to the task. Microsoft didn't give up, and as faster computers became available (80286 and then the 80386) Windows began to become usable. Version 2.1 and version 386 started to gain acceptance, fueled largely by a few popular applications like PageMaker, Excel and Pixie. When Microsoft introduced Windows version 3.0, everything was finally in place and the world took note. The organizational structure of Windows is shown in FIG. 3-16.

Windows runs on top of DOS, and gives a DOS-based personal computer a graphical user interface (GUI) somewhat similar to a Macintosh computer. Windows also provides an environment which a software developer can use to write programs that are attractive and easier to use and that can pass information to other programs more easily.

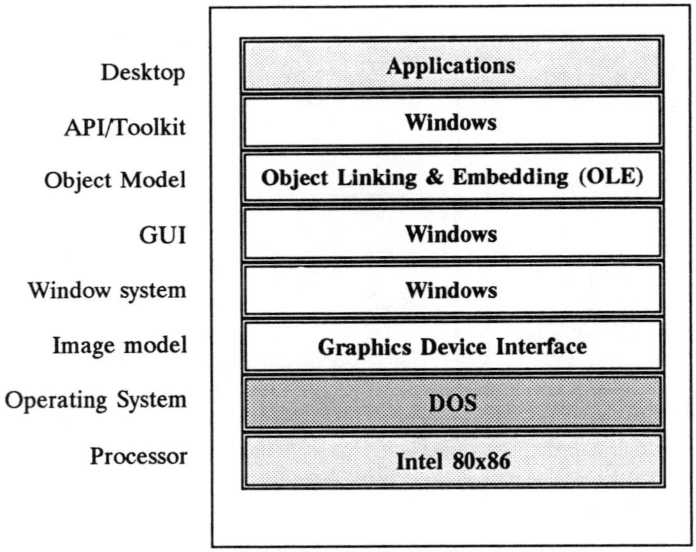

Fig. 3-16. Microsoft's Windows.

X Window System

Window interfaces have been common in engineering workstations for several years. The near-universal adoption of UNIX in that world, combined with the need to transmit data over networks, has generated more pressure for standardized interfaces. In 1988, MIT formed a consortium with most of the leading workstation manufacturers to develop the X Window System further and have it adopted as an ANSI standard. The members of the X Consortium included Apollo, Apple, AT&T, Digital, Hewlett-Packard, Sun Microsystems, IBM, Televideo, and Tektronix. The copyright for the X Window System is held by the consortium members, but permission for its use is granted to any party interested in implementing it. The X Window structure is shown in FIG. 3-17.

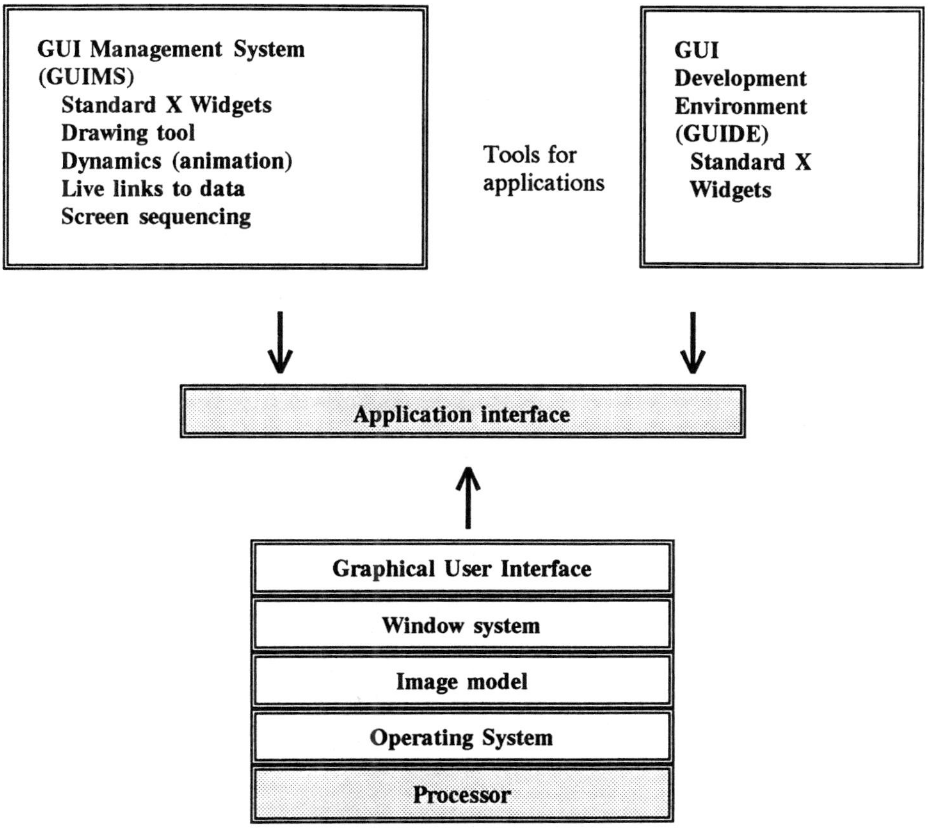

Fig. 3-17. X Windows GUI structure.

Today the majority of all graphical user interfaces run on top of the X11 Window System developed at MIT. Display PostScript is the core of Sun Microsystems' NeWS windowing system. However, Sun is adding X-windows support for NeWS. Even Microsoft and IBM explored a possible X-windows implementation of OS/2's Presentation Manager.

X11/NeWS

This window system from Sun is a high-performance engine for X applications. Sun incorporated the industry standard X Window System from MIT with its NeWS technology and created a common windowing, scheduling and input scheme. It is also based on the PostScript imaging language. X11/NeWS will work with both protocols so that X11 and NeWS applications can coexist on the same screen, along with Sun View applications, Sun's previous window system.

After resisting for a few months, Sun Microsystems decided to join the X Window System and merged NeWS with it. By merging the two, a common windowing, scheduling and input scheme was established. The organization of this system is shown in FIG. 3-18.

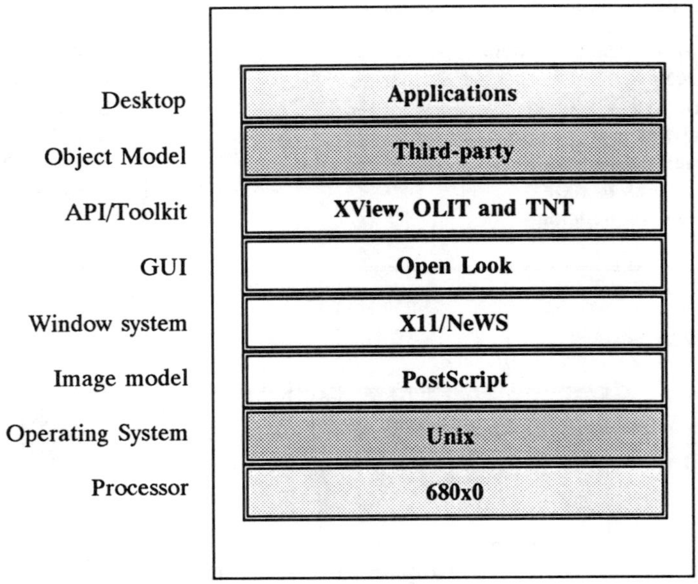

Fig. 3-18. X11/NeWS GUI structure.

An event in either window type can then be handled by a common Server. This allows users to run applications developed in either environment on the same screen.

Handwriting recognition

With handwriting-recognition GUIs, users can, for example, circle a range of text in a document or cells in a spreadsheet and send them (over a network or via a modem) to a colleague. A symbol (that the computer has been taught to recognize) such as a lightning bolt could be used to initiate the transmission.

The point of handwriting recognition is not that the user can enter data into a computer with a pen, but that the user can interact with the computer using the metaphor and style of a pen. The current method of interaction is with a mouse. That is considered disconnected. The user acts on the mouse, and the mouse communicates that action to the computer. With a pen, the user is acting directing on the computer without an intermediary. Two companies have developed programs that offer this capability: Go Corporation and Microsoft.

Microsoft's Pen Windows, formerly called Windows H and Pen Windows, is based on Windows' allowing compatibility with existing applications, but adds special Dynamic Link Libraries (DLL) that provide the extra capabilities required. However, it does not support true character recognition.

Although Go's system is graphical like Windows, it does not use the same icons, pull-down menus, or overlapping windows as Microsoft's system. Developers will have to start from scratch when designing applications for Go's non-DOS-based pen input operating system. However, Go's system is more robust and has better character recognition. For further discussion on handwriting interfaces see Chapter 16, *Specialized GUIs and Window Systems*.

Who will win?

Currently in the UNIX environment, two X Window Graphical User Interfaces are competing against each other to gain wide acceptance: OPEN LOOK and OSF's Motif. In the general-purpose desktop or PC arena, Macintosh and Windows are fighting it out.

In addition to the technical and marketing activity surrounding GUIs, there is also legal activity. Apple was being sued by Xerox for copyright infringement (in their Macintosh GUI technology) for using technology developed previously by Xerox for their Altos and Star windowing systems. Although that case has been thrown out by the courts, it does demonstrate that the big companies see the GUI market as being large enough to fight over.

Apple, on the other hand, is suing Microsoft and Hewlett-Packard over GUIs. The precedent set by the Lotus-Paperback Software case over look-and-feel made it clear that the courts will protect screen appearance and command sequences of software. Although the only remaining items to be decided in the Apple versus Microsoft/Hewlett-Packard case are the issues of overlapping windows and movable icons. Based on the Lotus judgement it appears things are now in Apple's favor. Also, a federal court has upheld the validity of Apple's copyrights on 10 separate elements (e.g., overlapping, sizable and movable windows, movable icons, icon titles, etc.), but avoided the issue of look-and-feel. If Apple does win, then Microsoft has two choices: redesign Windows (which would delay market penetration) or pay Apple a royalty (which would raise the cost of Windows and tarnish Microsoft's name).

The X Window System may infringe on a 1985 patent of AT&T's. The patent covers the Backing-store functionality of overlapping windows, maintaining and updating multiple windows in a multitasking system automatically, without special application code. It covers updating portions of windows that are obscured or covered by overlapping windows. Although software cannot be patented, some companies that are using the technology are implementing it in a mixture of hardware and software. Most GUIs (e.g., Windows, the X Window System, Macintosh, etc.) update their windows.

AT&T suggests X Window System developers license the technology from them. If anyone is using the technology, whether implemented internally or commercially, they may be in violation of the patent. However, several of the members of the X Window Consortium have already licensed the patent. MIT doesn't charge for its X Window System, which is a building block for developers. Nonetheless, AT&T's actions will not delay the progress of the X Window System.

However, despite the court battles and marketing hype, the user will determine who will win. Users will make the determination on the availability of useful applications. Before an application can be determined to be useful it has to be available. Therefore, the proponents of the major GUIs are actively soliciting ISVs and developers to write applications to their GUI.

What is the best choice?

Because of the many choices of platforms and operating systems there will not be a single best choice for quite some time. As the previous diagrams and FIG. 3-19 shows,

App										
Object Model	Third party					Patriot partner	3rd party	Hyper card	OLE & New Wave	
Toolkit	Xview	GUIMS	XUI		DEC - API		KITS	Mac IF	UIC	SDK
GUI	OPEN LOOK		Motif				Window server	Finder	Presentation manager	MS Windows
Window System	NeWS	X11 - lib.					Next step	Window Mgr.		
Image model	Display Post Script							Quick Draw	GPI	GDI
IPC	TCP/IP or OSI			DEC net	OSI		TCP	Apple talk	TCP	IPX
Op Sys	SunOS	Sys V	UNIX	VMS	AIX		Mach	Mac	OS/2	DOS
Processor	Moto, SPARC, MIPS			VAX	Various	Rs6000	Moto 680x0		Intel 80x86	
Sponsor	SUN	UNIX Int'nat	X consort	DEC	OSF	IBM	NeXT	Apple	IBM MS	MS

Fig. 3-19. Overview of GUIs.

all the GUIs share certain similarities. In the past, GUI systems have been proprietary, and each hardware platform supported one or two GUI systems. Today, GUIs that demonstrate their potential to become a hardware-independent standard are becoming available.

Currently there is a division between mainframes, minicomputers, workstations and PCs. If an organization (i.e., enterprise) tries to establish a GUI that can run in a multivendor environment, there is no simple answer. The merging of communications and applications is not possible. However, the X Window System offers great promise of becoming the common denominator needed to pull everything together. It will just take some time to get all the details worked out. In the meantime there are choices that can be made on a platform by platform basis.

In the future, users will demand interoperability. Only a few organizations will use a single computer architecture, operating system or GUI. No single GUI, operating system, computer, or network will become the standard. Rather, they will all be popular and possess the ability to communicate in an efficient manner.

References

"ABCs of GUIs." *The SUN Observer*. April, 1990. Page 23.

Bennett, James E. Technology: Windows, Graphics and UNIX. *Computer Graphics Today*, September 1988. Page 14.

Boyle, Brian and Dale Way. Battle of the networked stars. *UNIX Today!*, April 17, 1989. Page 12.

Broadhead, Steve. GUIs—Graphical User Interfaces: intuitive or not? *Datacom*, August, 1990. Page 33.

Englebart, Douglas D.C. and W.K. English. A research center for augmenting human intellect. Proceedings of the AFIPS Fall Joint Computer Conference, December, 1968, San Francisco. Pages 395 – 410.

Graphical User Interfaces now. *MIPS Magazine*, November 1989. Page 42.

Hayes, Frank and Nick Baran. A guide to GUIs, *BYTE*. July, 1989, Page 250.

Hurwitz, Judith S. Graphical User Interfaces: beyond fun and games. *ComputerWorld*, June 4, 1990, Page SR/5.

Jerome, Lawrence. GUIs: Where SUN sits now. *The SUN Observer*, April, 1990. Page 12.

Johnson, Jeff, Teresa Roberts, William Verplank, Charles H. Irby, Marian Beard, Kevin Mackey. The Xerox Star: A retrospective. *Computer*, September, 1989. Page 11.

Magnuson, Linda. Conceptual overview of the OS/2 Presentation Manager. *IBM Personal Systems Developer*. February, 1989. Page 17.

OPEN LOOK Graphical User Interface Style Guide. 1989. Sun Microsystems, Inc.

OPEN LOOK Graphical User Specification Functional Specification. 1989. Sun Microsystems, Inc.

Press, Larry. Windows, DOS, and the Mac. *Communications of the ACM*. November, 1990. Page 19.

Radding, Alan. Picture this: GUIs on every desktop system, *Digital News*. April 16, 1990. Page 31.

Reingold, Howard. GUI, The Interface of tomorrow, today, *InfoWorld*, July 10, 1989. Page 42.

Seymour, Jim. The GUI, an interface you won't outgrow, *PC Magazine*, September, 1989. Page 97.

Stern, Hal L. Comparison of window systems, *Byte Magazine*, November 1987. Page 265.

Taylor, Allen G. Serving two masters: users and programmers, *Software Magazine*. April, 1990. Page 76.

Wadland, Kenneth R. Graphical User Interfaces: A window to the future, *Computer Graphics Review*, November, 1989. Page 42.

WINDOWING—A guide to the DECwindows desktop environment. EB 32361. 1989. Digital Equipment Corporation.

4

The impact of hardware on a GUI

Beginning with Xerox's Altos system, GUIs have been largely dominated by the hardware manufacturer and not the software developer. Digital Research and Microsoft have had some influence, but they have developed for particular platforms. It is the commercial rivalry of the hardware companies that has created the problems in obtaining standardization and portability. However, in the mid to late 1980s, these companies began to listen to the users' demands for open and easier-to-use systems. This chapter discusses the response to those demands. The hardware is segregated into four categories: mainframes, minicomputers, workstations and personal computers (PCs).

Mainframes

Initially, the mainframe companies like IBM, Unisys, Bull and NCR did not give their customer base a very clear path for the incorporation of an enterprise-wide GUI, although things are improving. The mainframe in corporate America is changing from an isolated island of information to an enterprise-wide information Server on a network that can consist of mainframes, minicomputers, and desktop workstations. Two important developments are driving this change: The emergence of a new information system architecture called cooperative processing, and end-user demand for easy-to-use graphical user interfaces that allow them to integrate mainframe data with their desktop applications. The growing popularity of GUI-based PC applications is putting MIS managers under pressure to provide a graphical environment enabling them to integrate popular, easy-to-use applications, not only with each other, but also with the data retrieved from the corporate mainframe.

Cooperative processing

One of the major developments of the late 1980s and early 1990s has been the use of PC-based workstations connected to host computers through local area networks. The use of these networks has yielded greater processing efficiency at a lower cost than traditional terminal-host configurations. As a result, intelligent workstations are rapidly replacing traditional terminals as access points to mainframe hosts, and by 1992 more than 30 million workstations were connected this way.

However, the requirements of cooperative processing include complex communications protocols across many operating systems and hardware platforms and interaction among multiple users. These requirements place an even greater burden on already scarce programming resources.

Cooperative processing divides applications into *front-end* tasks that can be economically handled by the desktop workstation and *back-end* tasks more efficiently managed by the mainframe. This architecture allows the local processing power and graphical user interface common to the desktop workstation to be combined with the centralized power, control, and data storage capabilities of the mainframe host. In this way, processing loads can be distributed, greatly reducing the burden on the mainframe processor. However, if the mainframe is only served by dumb terminals the issue is moot. The following describes the approaches being taken by the leading mainframe suppliers.

IBM

IBM was one of the first companies to offer any type of an enterprise-wide computing environment. It has not been easy for the company, due to its different types of computers, operating systems and resistance to becoming an open system advocate. However, the design of its Systems Application Architecture has become a model for other companies, and an opportunity as well.

Systems Application Architecture

In 1987, IBM introduced the Systems Application Architecture (SAA) to bring together mainframes, workstations and PCs under the umbrella of cooperative processing. IBM believes SAA is the best approach to building a balanced split of enterprise-wide applications that will allow LAN-based PCs, workstations, minicomputers and mainframes to be integrated. It was designed to assure an ongoing compatibility between platforms as the base of aging 3270 (character-based) terminals is replaced by workstations and ever more powerful PCs and workstations.

SAA is a GUI and more. It is actually a whole family of end-user programming and system interfaces that IBM defined in 1987. SAA interfaces include everything from ground-level character-based terminals, PCs, high-powered graphical workstations, and minicomputers to midi-systems and multiprocessor mainframes. There are four operating systems/platforms in SAA: MVS and VM on the 390 and 370 mainframes, OS-400 on the minicomputers and OS/2 on PS/2s.

In the case of OS/2 it can be used in various situations. In a LAN a workstation with OS/2 can be the LAN Server. However, in a client-server environment, a workstation can be either. An OS/2 workstation could, for example, be the Server for an application that was using an AS400 as the Client. Alternatively, it could be the application Client for other workstations.

Although SAA specifies the user interface (via the common user access style guide (CUA) described later), it doesn't rigorously define its final design. SAA GUIs are actually a subset of SAA user interfaces, which also include user interface specifications for nonprogrammable terminals such as the 3270. An SAA user interface isn't necessarily a GUI, complete with mouse and graphics. Although supported, it doesn't depend only on a mouse. A user can do anything in an SAA GUI without a mouse, using keyboard equivalents. A characteristic of the mouse-independent nature of SAA GUIs is the menu bar, which is called the Action Bar. While other GUIs require a mouse-click to pull down a menu, it can be done in an SAA GUI by pressing a key instead. This can be very useful when working at a keyboard (in a word processor for example) and wanting to make a move or some other call without having to leave the keyboard. However, a mouse is a critical component of a GUI, and the SAA-CUA specification fully supports it. Figure 4-1 shows the general organization of the SAA environment.

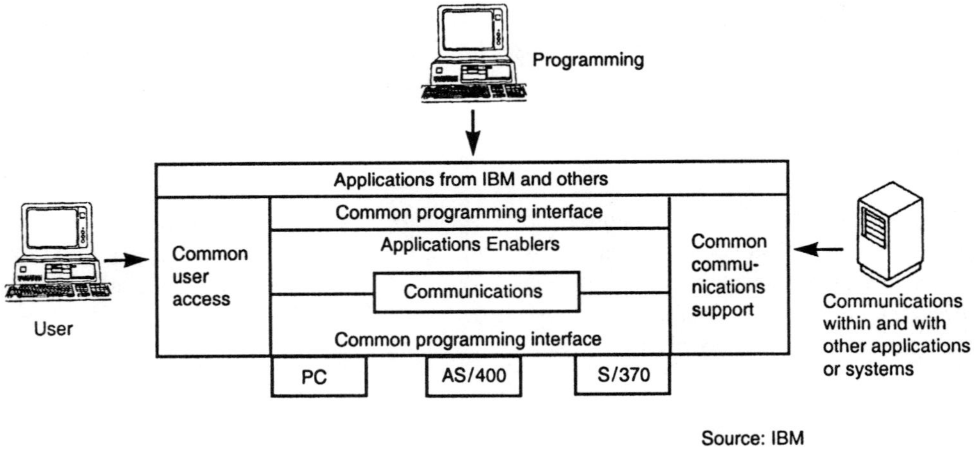

Fig. 4-1. SAA Application Interface points.

Yet, with all the freedoms in SAA, IBM has implemented Adobe's font technology across SAA platforms. This software generates consistent high-quality type across a variety of printers and displays. SAA is a complete system architecture, and as a result it goes beyond the things that relate only to user interfaces—including a standard for networking called the Systems Network Architecture (SNA), and one for database queries, the Structured Query Language, SQL. Figure 4-2 illustrates a typical SAA/CUA environment.

Key portions of SAA that have already been introduced include the OfficeVision office environment, the AD/Cycle applications development platform, and the System-View systems management platform. With such high visibility initiatives, IBM has set up high customer expectations. However, the complexities and prolonged development time frames have in some cases led to disappointment.

SAA has three major components: the Common User Access (CUA), Common Communications Support (CCS), a Common Programming Interface (CPI), and two

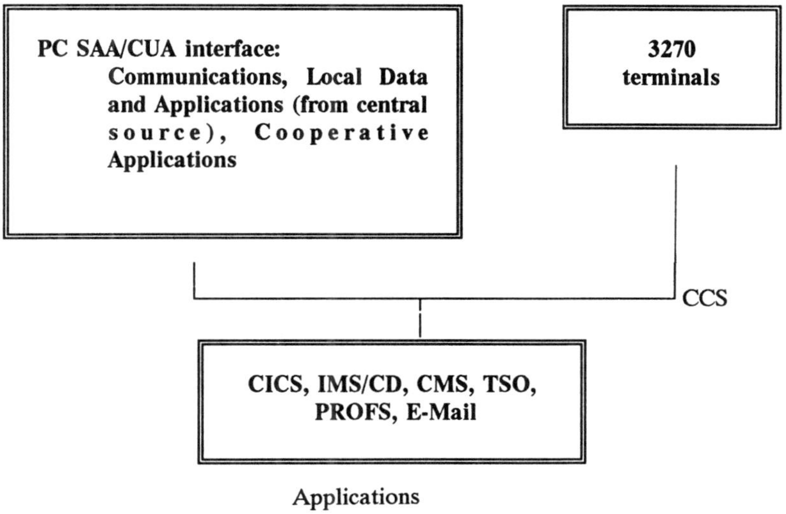

Fig. 4-2. The SAA/CUA environment.

major applications built on top of SAA: a programmer's development environment or Common Programming Interface (CPI), known as AD/Cycle and a platformwide application, OfficeVision.

Common user access

As part of the strategy, IBM established the definitions for a common user access (CUA 89), which describes how SAA-compatible applications must behave. The generation of an interface is shown in FIG. 4-3. The common user access enables usability and consistency. The CUA guidelines and protocols were developed to assure that the development of IBM computer applications will have a universal look, feel, and behavior to the user—regardless of the source of the application. This protects the skills learned by the user and eases the learning process for new applications. One of the features of the CUA is the use of a mouse-driven GUI.

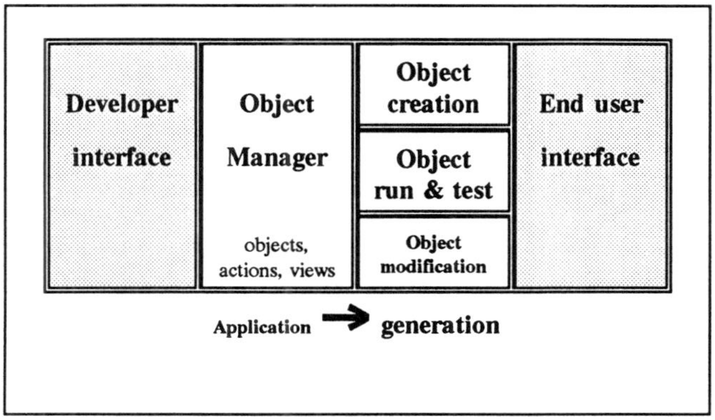

Fig. 4-3. CUA interface generation.

CUA defines rules and guidelines for designing a user interface for applications on nonprogrammable terminals and programmable workstations. The programmable workstation provides the most flexible environment for user interaction. Through the use of multiple windows on a programmable workstation, users can work with multiple applications, or different parts of the same application, at the same time. This makes it easy for the user to move information from one window to another and to integrate the user's work environment.

Common programming interface

One of the basic concepts in SAA is compatibility between platforms. This contributes to the conservation of resources and skills. The objectives of SAA are that an application written for one SAA-compatible platform must be able to be moved easily from one IBM platform to another. Developers can build on whatever platform they choose, as long as they follow the SAA guidelines; SAA is an open specification. If a program has been written in FORTRAN (for example) on an AS-400, it should be possible to recompile it and run it on a 3090 or a PS/2 (assuming adequate environmental capabilities of memory, disk and compilers). By using AD/Cycle (part of CPI), the developer has the added productivity of an integrated set of tools that provide high-level capabilities for developing applications.

IBM's goal for SAA is to provide application integration and portability across their proprietary systems, as opposed to just connecting applications between platforms from multiple vendors. Third-party developers are offered a set of specifications and guidelines that will allow them to develop compliant applications. With portability comes the transfer of programming skills. This decreases the training requirements for programmers as they move to new environments, and should lead to an increased supply of application solutions.

For example, the Database Interface, one of the CPI services, provides common access to data in a way that is largely independent of hardware and software environments and allows data to be distributed across the various processors of a distributed application. The Application Generator, one of the CPI languages, allows applications developed in one SAA environment to be executed in others by generating code that is optimized to the target environment.

Common Communications Support

Common Communications Support (CCS) designates communication architectures that provide the ability to connect SAA systems within the enterprise and with other enterprises. The architectures within CCS allow applications to exchange data and information in a consistent way. These communication architectures are the building blocks for distributed function and data. The CCS architectures provide for open communications among SAA and non-SAA systems through support for international communication standards.

OfficeVision

When IBM offered OfficeVision, it was as a set of follow-on offerings for existing IBM users. As the company developed the product, their initial view of supporting the installed base expanded. More robust features were added with the idea of picking up some additional customers. They also decided to enhance the ability of it to tie it into customer's specialized business applications. However, it also had to accommodate all the variations in its existing Office Systems product line (three different platforms: MVS, VM and OS400) and the installed base of over 4 million users. To meet that need, the company declared OS/2 as the client of choice.

What has to be realized is that IBM has a lot at stake with OfficeVision. As the first Systems Application Architecture application, OfficeVision, specifically the OS/2 version, is an indication of IBM's ability to carry out its ambitious undertakings. It is (no pun intended) a highly visible product, and IBM has to get it right. So far, over one million users are on OfficeVision. IBM, however, can't afford to lose ground to competitors such as Hewlett-Packard, Digital, AT&T, and NCR, which are moving forward with OfficeVision-like systems of their own. Many of the reasons for the delays with the system have had to do with building a multiuser, multitasking set of products that integrate smoothly with OfficeVision applications. The result of that effort has produced OfficeVision products tailored to MVS, VM, AS-400 and OS/2.

Also, there are four versions of OfficeVision, and the company will certainly add to that. The lowest level is for fixed format, character-based terminals. The next level up is the PC DOS OfficeVision. The PC version can connect to other systems via a LAN. After Windows was introduced, the company started development on a version for it and is working with customers on tailoring OfficeVision to it. OfficeVision has the capability to launch DOS applications from the OfficeVision desktop and a "send mail API." The latter feature lets users access mail directly from applications such as Microsoft's Excel.

It is the OS/2 version of OfficeVision that is the star. The company has positioned OfficeVision as the heart and soul of OS/2, and is counting on it to act as its first important LAN-based application. With OS/2 Extended Edition, all of the relational database, LAN management and communications services are integrated. Original OfficeVision only supported Token-Ring, but now it also supports Ethernet.

IBM has also had requests from users to include the Macintosh in its plans for OfficeVision. The company is exploring the potential of including Apple's Macintosh within OfficeVision, and believes it could satisfy some user complaints. The company is looking at the possibilities as a business case. IBM has demonstrated that they will respond to customers' needs and requests and accommodate products from other manufacturers.

Over a dozen software vendors have announced that they will integrate their applications with OfficeVision, and over 40 Business Partners have incorporated it into their products. IBM will continue to expand the number of APIs and also put in place a higher-level interface to accommodate the non-IBM workstations. With Windows or OS/2 as a full Client, developers working on the front-end will be connected to a Server, with part of the application on the front-end and part on the Server.

Data Interpretation System

This is a data analysis system based on a proprietary 32-bit operating system from Metaphor Computer Systems. The software uses icons and a mouse to allow users to access, analyze, manipulate and store information from IBM relational databases. It has been proposed that it should also include Windows at the PC end. When the full 32-bit version of OS/2 is available, Metaphor will replace their operating system with it. With OS/2, icons will be used to encapsulate the thought process behind various search or manipulation operations.

Patriot Partners

In late 1990, IBM formed a joint venture with Metaphor Computer Systems for the purpose of designing a combination GUI and object-oriented development environment for applications running across multiple operating systems and platforms. The cooperative arrangement was named Patriot Partners, and its charter was to create an environment to support development of object-oriented, expert systems and multimedia applications. IBM intends Patriot Partners to become an industry-wide technology and to challenge other technologies like Hewlett-Packard's NewWave object-oriented environment. Much of the specifications for Patriot Partners development environment resembles NewWave's functionality, such as its ability to run on a number of platforms and operating systems and offer imaging capabilities. Although IBM has said this new environment will be able to coexist with other GUIs such as CUA, Motif and Windows, the company expects Patriot Partners to become the prevalent GUI.

AIX

IBM's proprietary UNIX operating system, AIX, is not an integral part of SAA. However, AIX shares the same communications protocol as other SAA platforms and will share the same databases. AIX is a parallel program and is targeted at a different customer base. It has interoperability and shares a selected set of SAA functions.

In addition to OS/2 and AIX, the environment is being made available for other versions of UNIX. Theoretically, any application written for any 32-bit operating system will run in all supported environments. Also included in this environment are workstation and PC LANs.

NeXTstep

IBM positioned itself to be able to go in almost any direction. In October 1988, it licensed the NeXTstep GUI from NeXT. However, nothing much has come out of that, and there are very few applications available. When IBM licensed NeXT's object-oriented-environment NeXTstep, it was planned for use on the AIX line of computers. Then the company stopped marketing version 1.1, which was offered as AIX PS/2 GUI. After NeXT started shipping version 2.0 in 1990, IBM ported NeXTstep to its PS/2 and RS6000 computers running AIX. IBM has announced that it will offer NeXT-step release 2 on the RS6000 product line. The company has signed other licensing arrangements with companies like Digitalk (developers of Smalltalk/V), and Metaphor Computer Systems and ParcPlace for object-oriented technology.

IBM has included object-oriented technology in its AD/Cycle software development framework. Object-oriented software has caught the imagination of programmers and users. Based on reusable building blocks of information, the technology has gained recognition as a means to simplify software development and maintenance. However,

Hewlett-Packard, with its NewWave software has gained a substantial lead. IBM's Patriot Partners is viewed as the company's attempt to compete with NewWave.

ImagePlus

IBM has also integrated its ImagePlus family of image processing systems into its Systems Application Architecture. The SAA applications expand IBM's current ImagePlus offerings with new imaging features such as color and gray-scale support, as well as high-speed capture of large volumes of documents. Enhanced software programs are optimized for the MVS/ESA and the AS/400 environments.

ImagePlus Folder Application Facility version 2 for MVS/ESA organizes multiple image documents into electronic folders and into a job flow management system, prioritizing them for retrieval. Individual applications can run in the same processor, each with its own folders, users, and work flow schedules. ImagePlus Workfolder Application Facility/400 version 2 has an enhanced workfolder software program that enables users to integrate additional image processing applications into a mid-size business or large department. The program organizes and indexes image documents for storage and retrieval as folders, cases, or individual documents.

Third-party software

The trend toward cooperative processing, common user environments and the integration of multiple platform applications has created a rich opportunity for third-party developers. Even though SAA and its components (the Common User Access (CUA), Common Programming Interface (CPI) and Common Communications Support (CCS)) set the tone for cooperative processing, independent companies have introduced their own tool sets and development environments.

Most of these add-on or third-party programs result in an easy-to-use GUI. Unfortunately, easy to use does not always mean easy to build. Creating or upgrading applications with graphical user interfaces is a costly, time-consuming task, requiring specialized programming skills that COBOL programmers in the IBM mainframe environment usually do not possess. The programmer shortage already is resulting in long delays in the creation of new applications, and the time-consuming process of retrofitting existing applications with graphical user interfaces often never gets done. The result has been toolkits and programming environment products to aid developers. The following lists a few of these products.

I/F Builder Targeted at cooperative processing environments, Viewpoint Systems offers I/F Builder, a graphics design tool for developing GUIs for existing mainframe applications. The toolkit allows software developers to create GUIs that comply with IBM's SAA standards for CUA and CCS. The program runs under Windows. Unlike other graphical user interface management systems, Viewpoint's products use an intuitive, visual, Windows-based approach that essentially eliminates the writing of code, saving months of programming time, and delivering near immediate results.

Viewpoint Systems has developed a family of graphics-based software products supporting cooperative processing as defined by the SAA model. Using a visual, intuitive approach, their products offer an attractive alternative to cumbersome programming-oriented solutions that require the user to learn a completely new programming language. They allow end users as well as COBOL programmers to create SAA-compliant graphical user interfaces to existing mainframe applications while providing data integration with popular PC-based applications quickly and easily.

I/F Builder takes advantage of key Windows features, including cascading menus and Dynamic Data Exchange (DDE), allowing mainframe data to be hot-linked to desktop applications. With DDE, I/F Builder allows mainframe data to be shared dynamically with Windows-based applications by clicking on a pushbutton.

EasySAA Taking a slightly different approach, MultiSoft offers Infront/DS and EasySAA tools for the development of SAA/CUA cooperative processing applications. The toolkit allows a developer to generate an SAA/CUA graphics screen for 3270, 3101, 5250, or VT220 applications. EasySAA automatically generates the Infront development code necessary to provide a user interface that is compatible with SAA CUA 89 specifications. It supports all character-based DOS platforms.

EASEL IBM has a marketing agreement to resell EASEL from Easel Corp. It is a tool for building GUI front ends for existing databases or applications. It is designed to create GUIs on workstations that have one or more back ends residing on mainframes. The host's character-based screens are replaced with Easel's graphics screens. The existing mainframe application does not have to be modified. However, the toolkit can also be used for new applications in cooperative processing applications.

Host-to-PC connections

IBM has also made host access to Windows easier, and in late 1990, introduced a new version of Windows Connection. It is designed to integrate host sessions with desktop applications running under Microsoft's Windows. Windows Connection allows the user to jump back and forth between a host session and a Windows application while viewing both on the same screen. The program also allows easy transfer of data back and forth. With macros built into the program, a user can just click on a box and open communications with the host. Third-party software packages like Rumba (from Wall Data) and IRMA Link (from Digital Communications) offer similar capabilities.

Unisys

Formed by the merger of Burroughs and Sperry, Unisys has also acquired UNIX workstation manufacturer Convergent Technologies and resells Fujitsu's SparcStation, as well as several other computers. Although the company was part of the X Consortium and participated in the development of the X Window System, the various mergers and the company's financial difficulties have drawn its attention away from the X Window System. They have not stated a clear corporate direction with regard to the X Window System or other GUIs.

Unisys does not have a cohesive GUI environment. For the X-environment they offer the S2000 X Window System platform, which is a Sun Microsystems Sparcstation with X11R4 software running on it. This product can only be used as part of a closed environment directly, not connected to Unisys mainframes, as the mainframes cannot communicate using the TCP/IP protocol. Unisys is developing two utilities, TIC and TAC, which run on the CP2000 communications front-end processor and will allow TCP/IP communications.

The S2000s are connected to each other and must run non-Unisys software. Unisys has committed to offering TCP/IP bridge software so that applications on the mainframe can communicate with X-servers. Their plans for X-client application software are unclear.

A third-party vendor, Intercomputer Communications Corp., has a product called Intercom that will allow T27 emulation and file transfer between Unisys mainframes and Microsoft Windows. The connection is via Ethernet using TCP/IP. Intercom also supports MS-DOS file storage on A Series hosts and provides up to four terminals per PC.

Unisys has declared itself a supporter of open and standard systems. The firm unveiled a plan for wrapping its proprietary mainframes with Client-Server and open systems software approaches as the "glue" to attach these "information hubs" to each other and to hardware from other vendors. The company has opened its proprietary CTOS operating environment and offered improved interoperability with UNIX and DOS-based systems. It supports Sun Microsystems' Network File System (NFS), enabling CTOS workstations to share applications with DOS and UNIX systems. This is a result of Unisys making CTOS POSIX-compatible.

Unisys claims it has over 800,000 networked CTOS systems worldwide. With its TCP/IP based ClusterShare network, users with PCs (ATs or PS/2s) can also be connected. However, Unisys still does not have a seamless connection to its A-series mainframes.

Unisys offers multitasking of protected mode programs on 80286 and 80386 machines. They have published a set of application programming interfaces (API) for CTOS called CTOS/Open (partially based on XVT's Virtual Toolkit). The basic organization of the CTOS kernel is shown in the block diagram in FIG. 4-4.

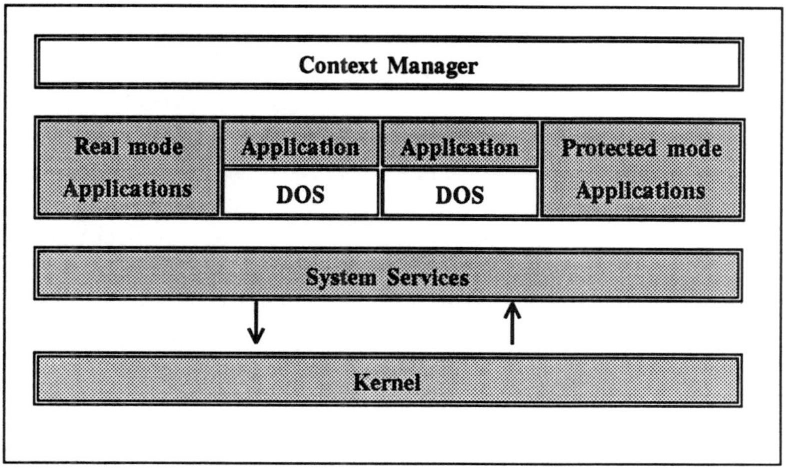

Fig. 4-4. CTOS/Open architecture.

Unisys plans to deliver more components of its distributed, cooperative architecture. The company's plan calls for mixing open, proprietary and de facto standards to unite Unisys' and other vendors' systems. CTOS and the updated CTOS/VM already have many, not most, of the current hot topics and features such as the following:

- Protected mode. Full protected-mode operation on the Intel 80286 and 80486 processor line.
- Networking. Local-Area Networking inside the operating system.
- WAN. Wide-area networking to connect several widely distributed CTOS networks, as well as Transmission Control Protocol/Internet Protocol networks.
- Multitasking. CTOS/VM will contain multitasking built-in from the beginning, not as an add-on.

By incorporating an open policy into its operating system, Unisys has positioned itself to be a contender in the GUI market. The company will add features such as demand-paged virtual memory, support for advanced GUIs and extended POSIX compliance, and eventually an object-oriented environment.

Others

The ranks of mainframe suppliers has shrunk over the past five years. What used to be the BUNCH (Burroughs, Univac, NCR, Control Data and Honeywell) has now become the BUN (Bull—which acquired Honeywell, Unisys—which acquired Burroughs, and NCR—which may be acquired). These remaining companies recognize the need for a consistent GUI strategy across their various platforms. Some of them are further along with a plan than others.

NCR

The company has made a big investment in 80486 technology and UNIX in the last few years. It has added a layer of integrating services and tools between the operating system and the application. This layer is called Cooperation and has been designed to provide an easy path for integration of data, applications and critical services between NCR and non-NCR platforms.

There are over 60 software components to Cooperation, from directory services to user interfaces. These services allow a user to access data anywhere on a network. They also allow developers to work with integrated tools to create object-oriented applications. NewWave is a key component in the company's object-oriented approach.

With the development of its X-terminal product line, the company has taken an X Window System/Motif approach. It is bundling the OSF Motif window manager in its display stations. By running OSF/Motif locally, rather than on a host, the stations do not have to continually communicate with the host.

NCR faces the same problem with Cooperation that IBM has with SAA and Unisys has with their system, the incompatibility of their older mainframes. With the adoption of the Intel 486, the company left the owners of its Tower systems (based on the Motorola 680x0) with an obsoleted system. However, because of its basic UNIX capability, Tower users can simply recompile. For its Series I users NCR has an emulator named Galaxy. But the Series V will not be able to join in Cooperation, although they will be able to share data.

Bull

If Bull can establish and identify with firms in Fortune 500, it will survive the switch from being a proprietary hardware firm to a broad-based services provider and systems integrator. To accomplish this, Bull hopes to distinguish itself in niche markets and position itself as a premier systems integrator.

The company has stepped up its efforts to wed its proprietary GCOS operating system to the world of UNIX Systems and has backed those efforts up with a $2 billion commitment to research and development. Also, in the past few years the company has made some shrewd acquisitions with the purchase of Zenith Data Systems and Honeywell Federal Systems.

Minisupers

Users of technical, single-processor minicomputers and workstations have, or want to use, applications that place greater demands on the systems than they can deliver. To satisfy their needs, power-hungry scientific and technical users have looked to minisuper computers, multiple-processor computers adept at parallel processing.

Although it has been widely predicted that mainframes will go away and users will have workstations on their desks, that is not what has happened. Instead, the Client-Server architecture has been adopted. In this environment, the minisuper or parallel processor has become a network server. In these situations and environments, UNIX and proprietary operating systems that support parallel processing are used. The role of GUIs in such a situation is then restricted to the X Window System.

Minicomputers

No particular GUI has been associated with minicomputers except for UNIX-based systems. Companies like Digital, Prime, Data General, Wang, and others with proprietary operating systems have either adopted a form of Presentation Manager or the X Window System. For systems that use some derivation of UNIX, the choice is Motif or OPEN LOOK, with Motif being the likely winner.

Digital

Not long ago, Digital's idea of user friendliness was the ubiquitous $ prompt that welcomed interactive VMS workers at dumb VTxxx terminals into DCL. During the last few years, various influences in the computer industry, including the commercial success of the Macintosh graphical user interface (GUI), have changed this. These days, in VMS circles, user-friendly is spelled DECwindows.

As with the Macintosh user interface, DECwindows is a GUI that greatly simplifies the use of VAX/VMS computer software. DECwindows-based application programs display their output through logical windows mapped onto a bit-mapped screen. As on the Macintosh, a DECwindows user is surrounded by the screen and controls the corresponding programs by pointing to displayed symbols (icons) and menus with a mouse.

DECwindows transcends Macintosh's window experience by letting the user display and manipulate windows on one computer while their corresponding application programs run on a host computer elsewhere in a network. The DECwindows software running on the display computer is referred to as a DECwindows Server, and the applications running on the host computer are called DECwindows clients.

Digital has also developed the Network Application Support (NAS) strategy for a unified application integration environment. NAS services include four categories:

- Applications Control Services (ACS), including windowing, forms, terminal and graphics.
- Communications and Control Services (CCS), including IEEE, messaging with X.400 support, electronic data interchange and application control with NCS/remote procedure call (NCS/RPC).
- Information/Resource Sharing Services (IRS), including compound document Architecture, data access, repository, file sharing and print.
- systems services, which offer Posix support.

Operating systems supported under NAS include VMS, Ultrix, OS/2, MS-DOS and Macintosh systems software. NAS also has LanWorks, services for PCs and the VAX Intersystem Data Access (VIDA) gateway product that enable users to access data from IBM's DB2.

Digital's starting point was different than IBM's. Digital didn't have the same initial challenge as IBM did in integrating applications across its platforms. However, the situation for Digital has become more complicated. Although there is some degree of interoperability with NAS through Posix and X.400, it is not the true interoperability that users have come to expect and that NAS is capable of. Digital will have to offer some more effective means of interoperability between UNIX System V Release 4, OSF/1 and NAS.

Hewlett-Packard

Hewlett-Packard offers a NewWave as a component of NewWave Office, which is their integrated office system based on Client-Server architecture (FIG. 4-5). NewWave Office is designed to operate with Windows on PCs or separately on any Hewlett-Packard platform. It also allows integration of systems and applications from multiple vendors. NewWave Office is considered by some to be IBM's OfficeVision's biggest competitor.

The Client-Server operation allows one copy of an application to be stored on the system and executed across the network. Linkages can be created across the network using hot links (refer to Chapter 2 for more information on the hot-link concept). NewWave Office incorporates existing applications while also providing a well-defined migration path from current applications to Client-Server applications. More than 60 software developers support HP NewWave Office.

The major components are:

- The HP NewWave environment, which offers a consistent graphical user interface and integration of existing and new PC applications;
- Information services, which provide easy access to a range of data sources and electronic mail across public and private networks;

- System services, for networked PC management and sharing of computer resources;
- Client-Server based management system, which allows users to manage, store, and retrieve information in a variety of forms and media.

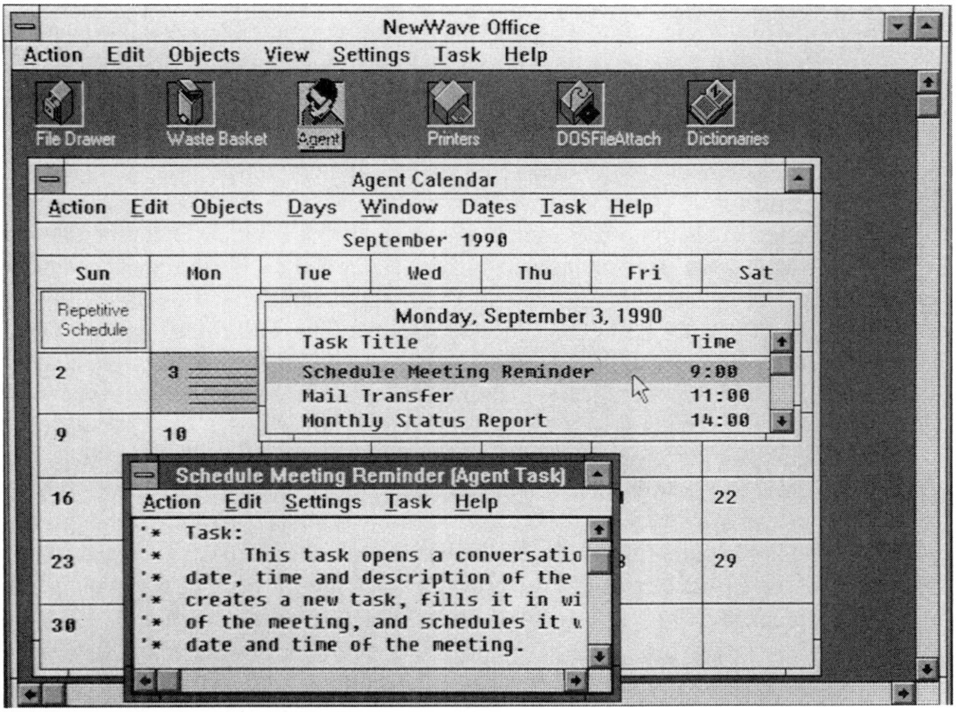

Hewlett-Packard

Fig. 4-5. HP's NewWave Office, with its 3-D effects and object-linking, is a high-level GUI.

Integral to the HP NewWave Office is an object-based integration capability, a technology developed by HP that enables information to be shared and automatically updated across applications, even if they were not designed to work together. It also includes networked object sharing, which extends HP NewWave to the workgroup by letting users store and retrieve objects on shared disks anywhere on a Local Area Network.

By supporting multiple operating systems and existing applications, HP NewWave Office should protect an organization's current investments. Users can access HP NewWave Office services across MPE, OS/2, and UNIX systems, and from 80x86-based computers, UNIX workstations, Macintoshes, or terminals.

Workstations

Two of the features separating traditional personal computers from workstations are their multiuser and multitasking capabilities, which come from the UNIX operating system. A multiuser system facilitates distributed computing, in which information and applications are shared by users linked in networks. One essential feature of these multiuser machines in multitasking, in which "windows" on the screen can run different applications simultaneously, is it appears as if several PCs were incorporated in one system.

UNIX is more complex than PC operating systems like DOS and the Macintosh OS, so its special windowing system helps facilitate distributed computing. The emerging *de facto* standard today is the X Window System. Software developers are basing their distributed applications on this window system. Workstation vendors, in order to simplify software development and thereby encourage the introduction of more third-party applications, are choosing X for their systems and creating development tools for application designers.

For workstation environments the OSF/Motif on the X Window System implementation seems to have the best potential to become an industry-wide graphical user interface standard. Organizations still have to think about which GUI to use with their workstations: AT&T OPEN LOOK or OSF/Motif. The OSF/Motif versus OPEN LOOK battle for a standard-based GUI has taken a definite shift in favor of Motif. Motif's latest coup is an endorsement from the 88open Consortium—the promoters of Motorola's 88K RISC chip.

However, sites with computers solely from Digital Equipment Corp. or Sun Microsystems Inc., will face few obstacles in implementing applications that use a GUI based on the X Window System. This is because there are still some proprietary aspects to GUIs and the implementation of the X Window System.

IBM has laid out its technology direction plans for interoperability between its AIX operating system and Systems Applications Architecture (SAA). Although it is being implemented by several groups, the Advanced Workstations Division and the Programming Systems Division are at the forefront of the work.

IBM considers SAA and AIX its strategic operating system environments. The company is addressing seven areas to achieve interoperability between the two operating environments:

- Connectivity.
- Network management.
- Distributed databases.
- Shared files.
- Presentation services.
- Common languages.
- Mail exchange.

UNIX system-function operations will be available as needed for interoperability on SAA systems. They include (or will include):

- TCP/IP.
- The X-Windows (which uses OSF/Motif as an interface).
- The Distributed Computing Environment from the Open Software Foundation.

AIX and SAA interoperability will mainly affect IBM-dominant installations. However, IBM's attention to connecting SAA and AIX technologies shows the growing importance of AIX in IBM's strategic plans. File sharing is provided between AIX and SAA through the Network File System. IBM intends to provide access to host applications and AIXwindows, its graphical user interface based on OSF/Motif, for both SAA and AIX workstations. IBM will also make AIXwindows and the X Window System available on AIX systems.

IBM's NeXTstep offering will provide AIX users with a major new application environment for enhanced business and professional productivity. NeXTstep is an application software development and user interface environment, created by NeXT and licensed to IBM. IBM will support the same application programming interfaces (APIs) as NeXTstep, providing compatibility and consistency so that developers can offer applications on both machines in order to generate a larger market for their efforts.

NeXTstep will join OSF/Motif as a GUI offering planned for the IBM PS/2 and RISC workstations running AIX. The UNIX operating system offers sophisticated features such as powerful networking and multitasking, but it may be considered by some users to be too complicated for those who are not UNIX experts. NeXTstep, which hides the complexity of the UNIX operating system under an object-oriented environment, will allow users to take advantage of the benefits of UNIX.

PCs

In the PC arena, Microsoft's Windows will probably become the dominant interface, followed by the Macintosh and Presentation Manager as the third most popular. The easy-to-use graphics approach demystifies the most complicated data entry screen. The time it takes to train a new employee to enter and retrieve data from the host can be reduced from months to hours (see FIG. 4-6). PC users requiring access to mainframe applications, as well as mainframe users or data-entry operators who find the mouse-driven interfaces easy to work with, get the maximum benefit from graphical user interfaces. Instead of struggling through an unfamiliar mainframe interface, they easily navigate through intuitive screens and windows.

X-terminals

Over a dozen companies are offering X-terminal products. Although all of them are basic X-servers, several companies such as Jupiter, NCD and NCR have introduced novel approaches to their implementation (refer to Chapter 15 for additional information on terminals and graphics hardware). Network Computing Devices for example has developed a window manager with the appearance and behavior of OSF/Motif that runs locally on its X terminals—rather than on a host computer across the network.

Conclusion

Some users feel that the last two years have been wasted by the UNIX vendor community with its wars between UI and OSF. Yet the Macintosh family of software continues

IBM

Fig. 4-6. The user is able to perform several tasks at once with a GUI.

to develop new applications, and Microsoft's Windows has introduced more applications in one year than all versions of UNIX have since their existence. The UNIX manufacturers simply have to learn that the solution set is larger than any single vendor can supply.

Only an open, coherent set of operating-system and GUI standards can produce an environment in which many vendors can produce the applications necessary to a large user base. In the case of Apple, these standards come with the operating system; in the case of Microsoft, they came with the GUI.

There really is no single GUI standard, but there are great similarities. Vendors are still trying to get product differentiation by customizing or enriching proposed standards. Some of the differences are minor but recognizable. For example, in the case of pointing devices, the Macintosh uses a one-button mouse. Windows and Presentation Manager use a two-button mouse, and X Window Systems uses from a one-button to five-button device.

The good news is that almost all hardware vendors now offer some type of a GUI and/or an X Window Systems implementation. However, if the user has a mixed hardware and operating system environment, it probably will not be possible to tie everything together and offer a common, enterprise-wide, user interface today. However, although there is not a really transparent or totally smooth way to move between operating systems, the separation is considerably less difficult through a GUI.

References

Cox, John. Users embrace interface power. *Digital News*. April 2, 1990. Page 8.

Goldberg, Adele. 1988. *A history of personal workstations*. New York: ACM Press Books.

Grochow, Jerrold M. 1991. *SAA: A guide to implementing IBM's systems application architecture*. Prentice-Hall: Englewood Cliffs, NJ.

Libutti, L. Robert. 1990. *System application architecture: The IBM SAA strategy*. TAB Books: Blue Ridge Summit, PA.

NAS Handbook: Developing applications in a multivendor environment. 1990. ECH0477. Digital Equipment Corporation.

Systems Application Architecture: Common user access panel design and user interactions. SC26-4351-0. 1987. IBM.

5

Concepts of the X Window System

The X Window System has attracted a great deal of interest and generated quite a bit of excitement in the computing industry. It offers a solution to many of the problems that have developed in networking, resource sharing, graphics and multiprocessing. A special vocabulary has developed that is partially due to the new design philosophy and the use of the letter X. The idea of Client-Server has been restructured, and the notion of distributed processing has been given real meaning.

By splitting applications at the user-interface level rather than the data level, the X Window System architecture permits mixed vendor connectivity. This interconnectivity gives the user access to the resources of the entire network, which multiplies user productivity. The Client-Server relationship enables the application program to determine (through data exchanges at log-on) the capabilities of the display being used. With new hardware, vendors only need to write a new Server driver to handle the X Window System requests. Writing such drivers requires considerably less time than porting a device to a kernel-based window system.

The computing model in the 1970s was multiple users per computer (terminals run from one large CPU), while the model in the 1980s was one user per computer (PCs), and the model for the 1990s seems to be multiple computers per user (distributed systems). The X Window System is the only mechanism where people can sit at one display device, a terminal, PC or workstation, and use software running on other machines elsewhere on a network. Users do not need to know that they're on different computers. That's why the X Window System is very important. It allows people to run software across a network without knowing they're doing it. This reduces the burden of dealing with complex remote machines and creates a user powerful environment.

History

In 1984 it became clear that students using the windowed workstations needed a hardware-independent protocol for sending graphics around the network. The X Window

System (usually referred to simply as X) originated with James Gettys, a Digital Equipment Corp. researcher assigned to MIT's Project Athena, and Robert Scheifler, a researcher with the MIT Laboratory for Computer Science. In the summer of 1984, both had been struggling with the need for a windowing system in their separate projects.

The only window software available at the time for the VS100 was some software called W, which Paul Asente and Brian Reed had worked on at Stanford University to run under the Stanford V operating system. So the project started with W, but after they had been working (hacking) on it for a few weeks, it clearly wasn't W anymore. They had to call it something, so they decided to use the next letter, and that is why X is called X.

The fundamental shift from W to X was redesigning the protocol to be an asynchronous stream-based protocol, rather than a remote-procedure-call style. Another fundamental change was removing anything but immediate graphics from the Server as well. Two years later, the Athena team made the X Window System version X10.4 available on tape at a nominal fee—in much the same way UNIX itself was distributed in its early days. The protocol was a smash success. Digital and Hewlett-Packard even designed new workstations around it.

In January 1988, MIT and most of the leading workstation manufacturers—including Apollo, Apple, AT&T, Digital, Hewlett-Packard, IBM, Sun Microsystems, Tektronix, and Televideo—formed a consortium to refine the system and to lobby the American National Standards Institute (ANSI) toward enshrining the X Window System as a standard. The X Consortium now holds the copyright to the interface but grants permission to use the X Window System to anyone who wants to implement it.

The promise of X

The X Window System was developed mainly under UNIX, but it can be implemented on top of any operating system (VAX/VMS, DOS or OS/2 for example). However, because it uses operating system calls to set up the connections between its library functions and the network, and between the network and its own Server programs, the X Window System tends to be most comfortable with multitasking operating systems that have network support.

The X Window System, also referred to as X-Windows or just plain X, is a *de facto* standard window system that provides network-based, bit-mapped graphics and window-management techniques. In addition to its graphics and windowing power, the X Window System offers other advantages to users concerning various systems applications and networks.

Heterogeneousness The X Window System achieves heterogeneous computing on networks of disparate workstations and back-end computers.

Transparency The X Window System enables workstation users to access and display, transparently, remote applications running on mainframes, minicomputers and microcomputers, and specialized computer Servers best-suited for particular programs.

Multiple applications The X Window System allows users to run, simultaneously, multiple applications displayed in overlapping windows.

Distributed applications The X Window System provides a foundation for truly distributed applications of the future, offering limitless opportunities for software vendors.

Built-in communications The X Window System allows application developers to concern themselves with application-code development. It takes care of the communication functions.

Extensibility The X Window System has been designed to accommodate future extension to support, for example, three-dimensional graphics.

Consistency The X Window System brings consistency to applications among diverse hardware systems.

Characteristics of the X Window System

The X Window System lets the user display information from two or more applications on the same screen and lets any given application use multiple windows. The windows can overlap or can hide each other completely. The interface also supports 2D graphics and text with soft fonts.

Nomenclature

In the early days of the Athena Project, the developers were quite explicit about the use of the X name. It is the X Window System. They pointed out that it was not to be called just *X*, or X-windows, or any permutation thereof. This was done so it would be clearly understood that the X Window System is not just a window manager or GUI. However, slang, acronyms and abbreviations prevail in this industry, and so the X Window System is, in spite of the efforts and wishes of its developers, commonly referred to simply as *X*.

Client-Server

To achieve device independence, the X Window System splits the job of drawing the windows into two parts. The Client program (which may be on a remote computer elsewhere in a network) asks the Server program (which runs on the individual's workstation) to handle the display portion. The X Window System uses the Client-Server model as its base. In an application process, the Client generates data to be displayed in an X-Window by the Server. The Server then runs in the X-terminal or PC-emulating X.

This nomenclature is different from the single-user Server-Client LAN arrangement where the LAN Server sends a total application program to a Client. This seems like it is the opposite of the Client-Server database model where the Server is the database engine and the Client is the user/processor making queries; however, it is not really that different.

The terminology of Client-Server has become confusing to many because of tradition, not logic. To avoid such confusion, just remember that the Client is where the application runs (the Client is not the user). In the X Window System, an application can be run on any computer connected to the network, while the graphics display system is on the Server (which is the user's display). In the X Window System the Client can be an application program or the window manager itself. For example, OSF/Motif is a Client, while the applications discussed elsewhere are all Servers. The general organization of the X Window System client-server structure is shown in FIG. 5-1.

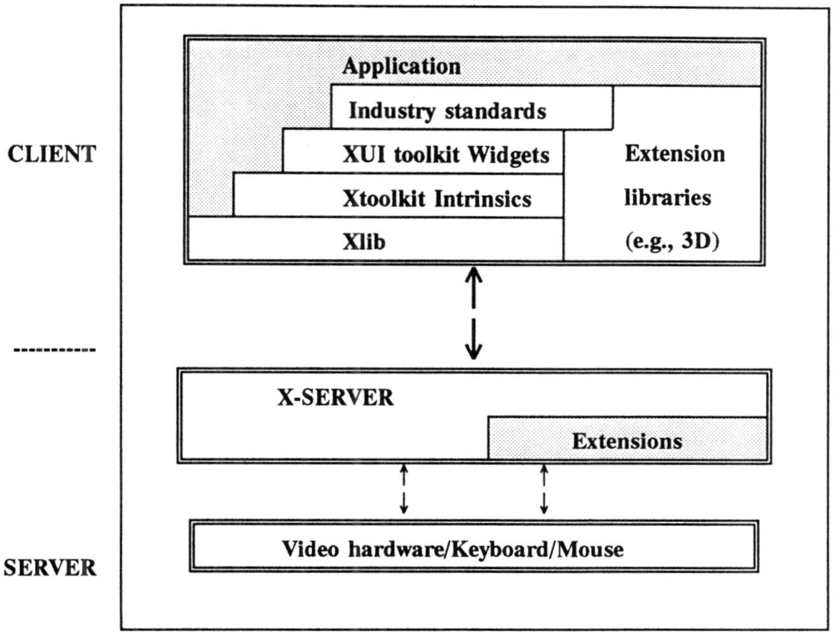

Fig. 5-1. The X Window System Client/Server architecture.

In the X Window System, the application program is replaced by the Server application, and it has complete control of the user's display screen. The application program (which is on the Client system) instructs the Server to perform the necessary screen movements, updates and other tasks. As soon as the application has sent its instructions to the X-Server, it returns to its normal operations. A response from the X-Server to the Client is not mandatory. Any application program that displays graphical output by sending instructions is designated a Client. Also note that a Server may handle the graphics output for multiple Clients concurrently (in multiple windows) and only understands X protocol requests for the generation of graphics. Figure 5-2 shows the data flow of client-server requests.

X-protocol

The X-protocol, a high-level graphics description language, carries the packets of instructions from the Client application program to the Server, which contains the hardware-independent drivers for each workstation. Both of these programs can reside on the same workstation or can be half a world away.

The Window Manager

As mentioned elsewhere, the X Window System is not a GUI, therefore, it does not have a window controller or image model. A Server can only produce output in accordance with the protocol requests it receives. It does not offer any user controls for size

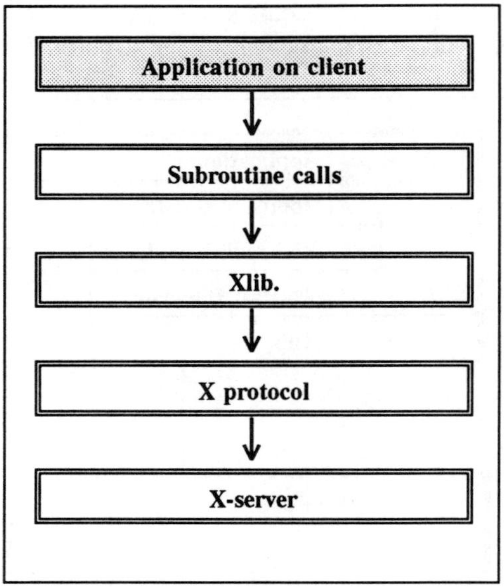

Fig. 5-2. Client-Server requests.

position or stacking order. User controls are not offered in the Client either. (If they had been offered, they would have resulted in redundant code.) Instead, each Server has a special Client program called the Window Manager.

The Window Manager has special privileges (with regard to programs). It monitors and supervises all windows that are being displayed on the Server. The Window Manager places a basic window border with a title bar around all windows that are open. There are also resizing and movement buttons.

There are several GUIs for the X Window System, such as OPEN LOOK, Motif and others. The X Window System will allow any window to be started (opened) with any manager desired (specified) by a user, without imposing any effect on the Client. Whatever a Client chooses to display in its window on a Server is independent of the Window Manager or GUI. Figure 5-3 shows the GUI's position in the structure of the X Window System.

One of the remaining arguments now is over which X-based GUI—especially OSF/ Motif or OPEN LOOK—will be or should be the standard. End users are angrily asking what is going to be done about this. It's not a trivial question and not something to be dismissed lightly, as there are literally billions of dollars of software development involved. But that's not really a technical problem; it's a political problem.

Standardization

Several industry groups have been formed to promote the standardization and promotion of X. The three major groups are X/Open, the Open Software Foundation (OSF) and the MIT X Consortium. The MIT X Consortium shapes the underlying technology of the X Window System and concerns itself with the promotion of cooperation within the computer industry in the creation of standard software interfaces at all layers in the

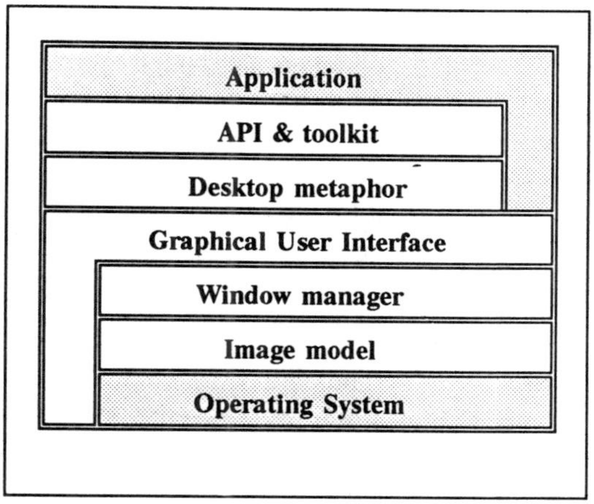

Fig. 5-3. The GUI in X.

X Window System environment. X/Open and OSF are more concerned with the commercial implementations of X-based GUIs. NIST, through FIPS, has proposed a standard based on the X Window System, and ANSI is working on one also. Figure 5-4 gives a more detailed look at the X Window System components. They will be discussed in the following paragraphs.

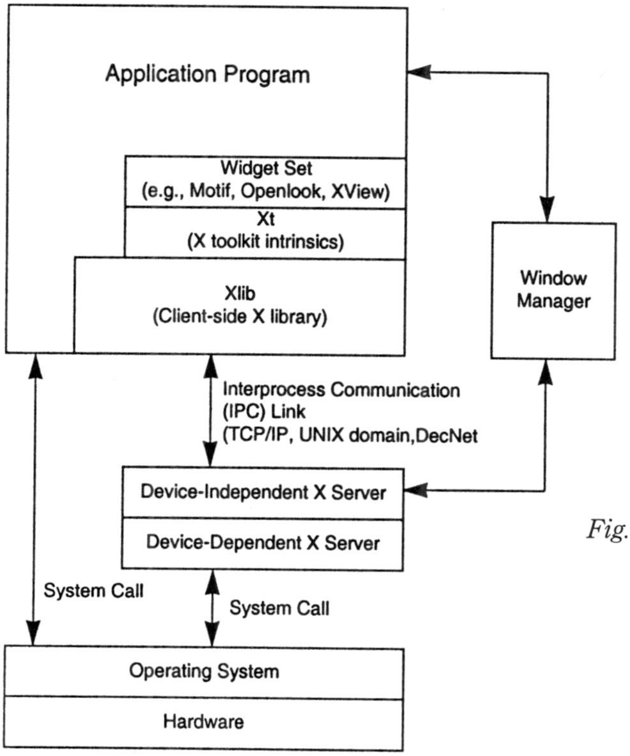

Fig. 5-4. Software layers in a typical system using X windows.

Library

The X Window System provides a library of functions that can be used to construct a windowing user interface. In order for programmers to construct the Protocol requests that allow a Client to communicate with a Server, a set of C subroutines are needed. These routines are contained in a library called Xlib. The Xlib subroutines impart none of the look and feel components to a Client. They are merely a set of requests used to create a window, draw lines or text, etc.

Toolkits

Toolkits are also available that combine library functions into composite objects called *widgets* (push buttons, radio dials or knobs, sliders, etc.). With a toolkit, an application's user interface can be built more quickly than by using just the X Window System library (Xlib). Toolkits have routines for building menus and other elements that constitute the look and feel of an application.

Programming with the X Window System can be rather difficult to get familiar with, depending on your previous programming experience. If you have not programmed with windowing or message-based systems before, it can be a little confusing. It also requires good object-oriented programming skills.

Image generation

Once a window and a context have been established, there are three steps to generating an image:

- Traversal.
- Transformation.
- Rasterization.

The first step involves traversing the Client-created data structure, also known as *the model*, to generate a stream of graphics operations. In the next step, geometric primitives are formed, transformed and clipped (to the screen's space). If required, shading operations are performed at this stage. The final step converts the primitives into pixel values and writes them to the frame buffer. Figure 5-5 shows the components used in the generation of an image.

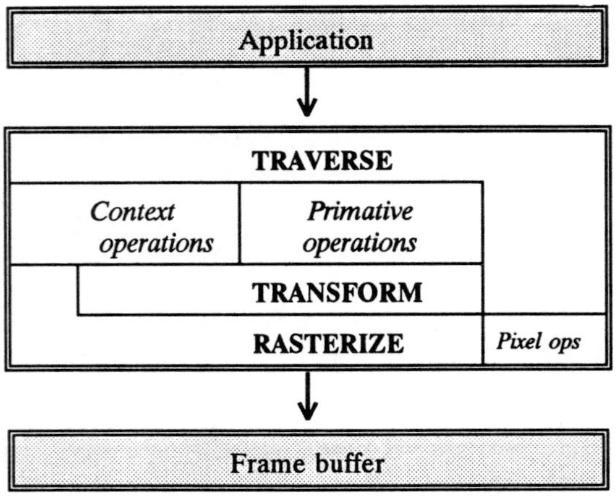

Fig. 5-5. Image generation.

Extensions

X does not currently support 3D graphics and imaging, although 3D attributes may be included in future releases or developed by independent software developers. Also, as mentioned in Chapter 1, the PHIGS Extension to X (PEX) is one of the X Window System extensions currently in consideration.

Other Extensions include:

- The MIT SHAPE extension, which allows user applications to create nonrectangular windows.
- Live video (VEX) support for additional input devices and nonrectangular windows.
- Imaging capabilities (XIE) (discussed in Chapter 1 of this book).

Vendors can add extensions to their own versions of the X Window System as well. For example, Digital has added Display PostScript compatibility in its X-based DECwindows environment.

The implementation of look and feel

Mention a user interface to five people and you will get ten definitions. Everyone has an opinion, yet no one is really an expert. It's a very poorly understood subject. The developers of the X Window System recognized this and avoided making any definitions of what a window manager should or should not be. That leaves the definition and design completely up to the application developer. That is just the opposite view of Microsoft on Windows, or Macintosh on Quickdraw.

This situation is sometimes referred to as the *freedom of design*. However, with freedom (of any type) comes responsibility. The responsibility for a comfortable user interface, one with charm, is not easy to obtain. Some of the issues effected by the freedom of design can be seen in the following sections.

Icons and the actions they represent

During the product definition phase of Hewlett-Packard's X Window System-based GUI, the designers wanted the blobs on the screen to represent useful, discernible actions. It is important that the icon, or action taken with the icon, be able to communicate to the user the effectiveness, or ineffectiveness, of the action taken. For example, if a user attempts to drag a file to a directory that is not appropriate, a *not* symbol (circle with a line through it) pops up on the screen to indicate the error. Another example is that the icon (rubber band) snaps back to its original location if an inappropriate action is taken. They also were concerned about the use of *transitory effects* in a GUI. An example of this is a door on a garbage can swinging open and closed to animate the action of deleting a file.

GUI style editors

It has been pointed out in various conferences and reports that it is important for the GUI software used to include a style editor for setting colors, fonts, backgrounds, keyboard and mouse behavior and startup environment. Typically, the style editor is run directly in the X Window System environment, and the changes take effect immediately. Some GUI implementations require that the user manipulate a text file defining these characteristics, exit the X Window System and restart it to view the changes.

Interchangeability

Applications written with the X Window System standard are supposed to run on any X Window System compliant display or host, but the actual result may not be quite as simple as the theory would suggest. There is a lot of interchangeability with systems based on the X Window System. Although a user can run a Motif application in OPEN LOOK, there may be some visual incongruities. Programmers have to exert a lot of effort resolving several issues involving fonts, operating-system calls and environmental problems to make applications written for one GUI run on the other. For example, CLOSE means one thing in Motif and a different thing in OPEN LOOK. One means "iconify" and the other means "terminate the application." A nontrivial difference. The current problems caused by incompatible APIs is not limited to OPEN LOOK and OSF/Motif, but other GUIs as well.

Networking

Currently the graphics speed of the X Window System in network applications is not very impressive or fast, but vendors are taking care of that problem by implementing graphic engines in their X-terminal hardware designs. Future developments in networking technologies will further increase the performance and graphic speed capabilities of the X Window System.

In the X Window System, the process of asynchronous event queuing should be understood by users. This is especially true when multiuser tasks from multiple applications, which may be in multiple windows and from different hosts, meet. Instead of simply starting one task and finishing it before going on to the next, the programmer (who designs Client-Server applications) must allow for input commands to be picked up and queued simultaneously while multiple requests are being handled. Therefore, one request does not have to be completed in full before another is started.

Network traffic

In testing an X-terminal, NCR made measurements of data flow across the Ethernet LAN for the basic X Window System operations. They found that the action of pushing a mouse button and holding it down for 1.5 seconds resulted in 9,072 bytes of data across the LAN. In another test, the user dragged a window diagonally across the screen from one corner to the other, resulting in over 20 Kbytes of data going across the LAN. From the results of these tests, NCR decided to design a terminal with the window manager running inside the terminal.

NCR noted that the issue with X-servers on a network is not network saturation, but GUI responsiveness. The Ethernet is able to efficiently manage the amount of data; it is the window manager that becomes congested while attempting to process incoming data and issue window commands. In the worst-case situation, one user must wait for another user to move/close a window before receiving a response to his or her request.

Bandwidth and balance

When designing applications, software developers are advised to be sure the amount of information given to a user via the GUI does not clog the bandwidth of the GUI/platform or the bandwidth of the user. The developer also needs to balance the power and efficiency of the hardware, the GUI and the system software. It is not always possible to just add more MIPS into a system.

Applications

The popularity of X Window Systems is undeniable. However, the number of actual users is difficult to gauge. In general, most users are waiting for the X Window System versions of the programs they are currently using or plan to use. Sun Microsystems officials report that 60-80 percent of their user base is still running applications under SunView rather than their X11/NeWS system. That is largely due to the number of applications available. There are less than 100 X-compatible applications available to Sun Microsystems users who are running OPEN LOOK. Contrast that with Digital's claim that the company, combined with its 416 third-party developers, offer the user over 800 X-compatible applications. However, although all those applications are available now, according to Digital officials the applications that are currently in use only comply with Digital's proprietary GUI DECwindows.

As mentioned previously, the X Window System does not currently support 3D graphics and imaging, although 3D attributes may be included in future releases or developed by independent software developers. However, that does not prevent 3D applications from being used in an X Window System environment. For example, CADKEY, Graytech Software, and others have 3D CAD packages that run on X-platforms. It should be understood that a user can run 3D graphic applications in an X-server workstation window, but cannot send the graphics between Servers and Clients. In other words, a user cannot achieve network transparency with 3D graphics in an X Window System environment, as of yet.

Not too many new applications

The X Window System right now is like a wheelbarrow. It can go over any kind of road (network), and it can go into any type of site or environment (hardware platform), but the problem is there is little for it to carry (applications). The methodology to offer commonality across platforms is available, but there are only a few applications to run under it today—although most people agree it is just a matter of time until those applications start to appear. However, users will not buy these products, be they X-terminals, X Window Systems software, or OSF/Motif toolkits, until they can actually do some useful work with them. It may be another one to two years before applications come out in any kind of volume, much the same situation that was experienced initially with Microsoft Windows.

Users should be careful and not get too caught up in the technology and its abilities because it simply does not offer a rich enough application universe across all platforms today. To get started with the X Window System, you should stay in a single-vendor environment. Also, the availability of application software, especially on non-UNIX platforms, is limited. Because Digital was one of the major sponsors of the original X Window System development, it had many years to develop application software for it, so they have a lot of enthusiasm for it. However, the other developers, such as IBM, Sun Microsystems, and Hewlett-Packard, as well as several third-party companies are rapidly developing applications for the X Window System, so it will be just a matter of time until there is a large selection to choose from.

Older applications

Because the X Window System has its roots in the UNIX world, there is a potentially large application base. Unlike the early days of UNIX, when the application software had to either be generated or ported from another environment to an entirely new environment, things are not that primitive in the X world.

One problem that affects almost all users, as well as software-support departments (IS and MIS) and companies, is the problem of converting existing character-based applications to run under a GUI. This problem is made slightly easier in the UNIX world by a utility called Xterm, which is part of the X Window System toolkit. With Xterm, character-based applications can be made to run under X-Windows. Theoretically, any existing character-based UNIX application can be run within an Xterm window. Xterm is not an eloquent method for running applications; however, it is better than nothing at all. Vendors like IXI offer programs that allow older character-based programs to run more efficiently.

Desktop managers

Convenience Plus by Softscience Corporation is a UNIX-based desktop manager, plus comprehensive Worktools, that create a powerful graphic user interface for today's X Window System environment. With it, all interaction with the operating system is visual and mouse-oriented, eliminating the need to memorize or type complicated commands. Graphic images enable the user to logically organize and effortlessly navigate the directory/file system.

This manager features programmed icons to assign a graphic image for running a system command that launches an application, or running a shell script. Intelligent controls are available to prompt for information, create a filter and/or menu, specify syntax, and more. Everyday activities are transformed into simple drag-and-drop or mouse-click operations—all user definable. Convenience Plus supports a variety of window-system environments. It neither restricts nor redefines the user interface itself. The program runs with such user interfaces as SunView, OPEN LOOK, X-window, Motif, and others.

Benchmarking X

Xbench was developed by Siemens AG in Munich and is intended to be used as a tool to assist developers in tuning X-server performance. It runs on a host and outputs a series of X-graphic tests and times for each operation. These times are used to calculate performance ratings called *Xstones*. It assumes: that the communication link has no impact on the results, that the host CPU running Xbench generates graphics requests faster than the X-terminal can process them, and that timer resolution of 1 second is adequate.

The Xstone weights were developed to reflect an application environment that is 30% text oriented, 10% scrolling, 15% lines and rectangles, 17% tiled and filled rectangles, and 10% arcs. The remainder is spread over other functions. For a different application environment, it might be better to examine the component parts of the Xstone result and evalute them individually.

However, several of the X Window System software and Server developers are warning buyers to disregard Xstone ratings. Cited as being misleading, their use by a few X-terminal manufacturers has created quite a controversy. Xstones are just one of six measurements available to evaluate the performance of X-servers and the Xlib libraries used in X-terminals. They were originally designed to help engineers tune the performance of X-products and not to measure overall performance.

Other test programs besides Xbench are X11perf from X-windows Consortium, gbench from Stanford University, graphstones from Workstation Laboratories, Xbmk from Calcomp, X Master from AT&T (measure both Server Client performance) and Suite X from Aim Technology, Inc. However, an X-terminal has far too many functions to be able to evaluate it with just a set of numbers. Usually the best thing to do is simply bring in a terminal and try it in your own environment.

Testing service

AGE established an independent testing lab for evaluation of X-window hardware and software. The service provides the personnel and equipment necessary to perform comprehensive X Window System product testing, benchmarking, and analysis. Evaluation includes utilization of the Xlib Protocol Test Suite (T7), the MIT Volume Stress Test, and the AGE Test Suite. Testing is also done using standard X-client programs and with popular commercially available X Window System applications. The benchmarks include X11perfg, Xbench, and proprietary benchmarks. The AGE Labs service is available to all vendors and is operated independently from the development teams at AGE.

Forecast

The interest and support for the X Window System standard has been tremendous. However, the development rate of applications for an X-environment has been very slow. One reason given is the newness of the technology and software development toolkits. Software always lags behind a new hardware technology. However, others forecasted a critical mass of applications emerging in 1991. Also, there has been a broad range of development environments. The X Window System is no longer limited to just a few UNIX workstations. There are several 386 and DOS developers working on the new standard.

All of the major workstation vendors have committed to the X Window System and are shipping an implementation with every system. That, combined with the X-terminals and the PC-based X-terminal and Server emulators is creating a large population of real and potential users. Although terminals and emulating PCs are popular alternatives, workstations remain the preferred device today for the X Window System users.

References

Flatten, Jim. Ins and outs of X Window. *Electronic Engineering Times*. October 30, 1989. Page 37.

Hack, Peter A. The advantages of X. *Computer Graphics World*. August, 1987. Page 57.

Heichler, Elizabeth. Developers: X standard makes DECwindows portable. (1990) *Digital News*. April 2, 1990. Page 15.

Jones, Oliver. 1989. *Introduction to the X Window System*. New York: Prentice-Hall.

McCormack, Joel, and Paul Asente. Using the X toolkit, or how to write a widget. Proceedings of the Summer, 1988 USENIX conference. Pages 1-13.

Moran, Pat. Through the X Window. *Personal Computer World*. March, 1989. Page 154.

Nye, Adrian, and Tim O'Reilly. 1990. *X toolkit intrinsics programming manual.* Sebastopol, CA: O'Reilly and Associates.

Pountain, Dick. The X Window system. *Byte Magazine*. January, 1989. Page 353.

Scheifler, Robert W., James Gettys and Ron Newman. 1990. *X Window System C library and protocol reference.* Bedford, MA: Digital Press.

Treadway, Richard. The view from DEC: The X Window System is an exceptional standard. *Digital News*. July, 1988. Page 53T.

X in a nutshell. 1990. Sebastopol, CA: O'Reilly and Associates.

6

X Windows on personal computers

This chapter will provide a detailed overview of PC-based X Window Systems Servers under DOS, Macintosh's OS, OS/2, TOS, UNIX, and other operating systems. Keep in mind that a personal computer, or PC, does not mean just IBM or compatible products. A PC is any desktop personal computer from Apple, Atari, Commodore, IBM, or Sun Microsystems.

The casual use of the X Window System may not warrant the investment in workstations or even an X-terminal. However, there are several X-server emulation packages that address the needs of PC users. With a PC operating as an X Window Systems Server, users can open multiple DOS windows within the X Window System, as well as UNIX applications running remote X Window System Clients. The number of open windows is constrained primarily by the memory available in the PC.

Screen resolution

In an X Window System there is a requirement for high-resolution screen drivers. Choosing a Microsoft Windows-based X-server places the burden of the high-resolution driver on the display-card vendor, not the GUI or X-server software supplier. All of the major high-resolution card manufacturers either have, or have committed to providing, a Windows driver. However, the choice of a Windows-based Server may require the user to make substantial investment in additional software, training and memory for his or her computer.

Overview of the X Window System

The X Window System, commonly referred to as X-Windows, or *X*, is not a GUI. It is a portable, network-transparent windowing system that acts as a foundation on which to build GUIs such as OSF/Motif and DECwindows. X-Windows provides a standard means of communicating between dissimilar machines on a network. It was developed at MIT in 1984 in conjunction with Digital Equipment Corp. for Project Athena, an MIT project addressing the problem of scale in UNIX systems. The engineers had a requirement for a windowing system, but none was available, so they developed X. The current version is X11 Release 4 (X11R4) and source code is in the public domain. The X Window System supports overlapping hierarchical subwindows and text and graphics operations on both monochrome and color displays. For additional information on the X Window System, refer to Chapter 5.

Comparison to other systems

A major advantage that the X Window System offers over other windowing systems, such as Presentation Manager or Windows, is that the X Window System can operate in a distributed environment where programs (Clients) are running on remote machines. With Presentation Manager or Windows, all programs run locally on the PC. The only remote processing possible is to make an SQL call to a database engine. In a heterogeneous networked environment, the X Window System is the only viable solution currently available.

The state of X

X today is very much a display product and environment. Contrary to what X/Open and OSF proponents might say, there are very few commercial, and even fewer mainstream, applications for X. Most of what is displayed at X-windows conferences are X-servers, both hardware and software, tools and toolkits for OSF/Motif and the X Window System, and items to make using the X Window System easier.

General personal computer issues

The PC X Window System Server is neither an X-terminal emulator nor, necessarily, a poor man's entry into the world of the X Window System, although vendors often dub their software as X-terminal emulation. Vendors do that to avoid the X Window System's reverse Client-Server terminology (X display software is the Server to a Client application executing on another system in a network).

Users have several PC X-server software vendors from which to choose. The majority of them offer X-server software at prices ranging from $400 to $600. However, if users' PCs are not on a network, they will need to hook them up. Depending on the requirements of the X applications that users want, they may need to add memory to increase performance and a high-resolution graphics monitor to achieve clarity with many windows on-screen simultaneously. Vendors' products and their prices differ based on those issues.

One of the first issues to be considered is the communications protocol. All of the X-Servers operating on PCs use TCP/IP protocol via Ethernet. Normally this is not a problem when running with a UNIX host, but is not necessarily available on non-UNIX hosts. This can be solved in the Digital environment with VMS 5.3 or higher. Ultrix TCP/IP communications software (UCX) can be obtained from Digital. It can be installed in a VMS environment and configured so that particular PC nodes on the DECnet will communicate via TCP/IP.

Another important issue is the underlying operating system (OS) of the PC. While DOS is the dominant operating system and Apple's Macintosh OS is second, the X Window System comes from the UNIX world and maintains that heritage. DOS, in its native form, does not support the multitasking environment that allows an elegant implementation of X. Vendors such as Quarterdeck and Microsoft have incorporated DOS multitasking software to overcome this issue. Apple has added A/UX, a UNIX derivative to accommodate the X Window System.

The final issue is the PC itself. The X Window System places a very heavy processing load on the PC platform. Most, if not all, of the products recommend a minimum of a 286 or a 68010 PC with 1 Mbyte of memory. It is not unreasonable to use a 386 or 68030 system as an X Window System Server.

Operation under Macintosh

Apple has made the Macintosh compatible with the X Window System with its A/UX operating system (refer to Chapter 10 for more information on Macintosh's A/UX X Window System offerings). But, Apple does not currently offer an X-terminal emulation package for the Macintosh operating system. However, like most other platforms, third-party ISVs are offering X Window System software. There are also programs available from bulletin boards.

eXodus

White Pine Software offers eXodus which functions as a display Server that links Macintosh computers to X Window Systems on a variety of host computers. The program runs under Finder as well as MultiFinder. It stays active in the background under MultiFinder. The program supports color as well as monochrome and shades of gray. Multiple user-configurable screens can be defined.

The X Window System display Server for the Macintosh operating system provides users with full-color support, multiple-screen support, and enhanced DECwindows compatibility under VMS and Ultrix. Color definitions can be customized by the user through the use of a color database and color editor built into eXodus. The program supports up to six different X screens, all of which are user-configurable. Each eXodus screen appears on a separate Macintosh window and is configured with a number of user settings, such as size and type (color/monochrome). Cut and paste capabilities allow text and graphics to be transferred from X-clients into Macintosh applications via the clipboard. Print capabilities allow color and monochrome graphics to be printed directly from the X display-Server screen or from the Macintosh clipboard or launch monitor window.

Operation under Microsoft Windows

A number of companies are offering X Window System emulations under Microsoft Windows. The market is somewhat immature at the moment, while the products are very mature in terms of development. It took a long time to educate people about the technology, but today it is no longer necessary to sell the concept of Windows.

An advantage that comes with using an X Window System-based GUI (or any other GUI) under Microsoft Windows is that the only display driver required is that for Windows. For example, this would allow a user to run Windows with a graphic card at 1024 × 768, 1280 × 1024, or 1600 × 1200 resolution, using the card manufacturer's Windows driver.

Another issue is concurrent operation of existing DOS software in the Windows environment. Non-Windows specific DOS applications can be run concurrently with Windows, although they do not run in a separate window as in DESQview. When in the Windows environment, the DOS program appears as an icon at the bottom of the Windows screen, and it is halted. The user presses specially designated keys (hot keys) or selects the icon with the mouse to switch from Windows to the DOS application. In general, the advantages that X-server programs offer include:

- Cut and paste. Graphics generated by the X-client or by Windows applications can be merged using the cut and paste utility.
- Compatibility. Most of the server programs are compatible with DOS and Windows.
- Concurrency. The program has the ability to open the X Window System on other machines while running MS-DOS and Windows applications concurrently. In most programs, up to 24 X-client sessions can be opened concurrently. The limit is set by the number of sockets available with the particular TCP/IP software being used and the amount of memory available to support X.
- Training. The retention of the investment in training that has been made to familiarize users with MS-DOS, Windows and OSF/Motif applications.
- Extended memory management. Many of the Server programs support extended memory up to 16 Mbytes. The Windows versions support virtual memory capability, which is typically not available on X-terminals. This can be very important for situations where multiple X-clients must be opened concurrently.
- Network interface. Some programs contain an integrated Telnet and FTP (File Transfer Protocol) utility for file-transfer capabilities. Others have an interface to popular network programs.

A user who is already familiar with OSF/Motif can quickly learn to use Windows or Presentation Manager, and vice versa. Since the look and feel of OSF/Motif is also based on the Microsoft Presentation Manager, user-training costs and times are therefore reduced.

Operation under DOS

Like the Windows environment for X-servers, the market is somewhat immature at the moment. However, X-server products under DOS have been available almost since the X Window System was released. It took time to educate people about the concepts of the client-server technology, but it is no longer necessary to sell the concept today.

DOS X-Terminal Solution

AT&T Computer Systems has joined the ranks of companies offering X Windows System packages for PCs and has a program named the DOS X-Terminal Solution. The company offers turnkey software solutions for the market. The DOS X-Terminal Solution program allows users to run the X Window System while providing simultaneous access to DOS applications. The package includes TCP/IP software.

X11/AT

The X11/AT program was originally written as part of an X-based artificial intelligence workstation that Integrated Inference Machines (IIM) developed. They decided to unbundle the GUI and offer it as a separate product. The program contains all the features normally found in an X-server program. In addition, it has an integrated Telnet and file transfer protocol utility and a font compiler for adding user-defined fonts to the X-font libraries.

IIM supports X11.4 and offers a package containing an Ethernet board and the X11/AT software called X/PAC. It is a proprietary board based on the Fujitsu ETHERSTAR controller chip and includes 2 Mbytes of expanded memory and mouse port. Future versions of X/PAC will include support for concurrent protocol stacks for Ethernet, Netware, and Banyan Vines. Windows is not provided in this package; it must be purchased separately.

IIM suggests that the user have a 12 MHz 286 or better for running X11/AT. Windows acts as the memory manager, so the PC can have anywhere from 1 Mbyte to 16 Mbyte for a 286 machine or up to 4 GB for a 386 machine. Under Windows, X11/AT also supports virtual memory to a local or network hard disk.

Vision Ware

XVision offers essentially the same features as the IIM product. It has the same cut and paste operations, concurrent Windows, and X-client applications. Like IIM, XVision allows a few Clients to run on a 640 Kbyte PC. It also implements virtual memory management that makes use of expanded memory, if it is available, or a hard disk. Also included is an X-font compiler for adding user-defined fonts.

XVision can be used in one of two different ways with Windows. The first is for all X-clients to appear within one XVision window. The MS Window may be positioned on the screen or as an icon in the normal Windows manner. To manage individual X-client windows within the single Microsoft Windows window, a standard X Window System window manager (such as OSF/Motif) must be used. The second method is to use XVision for each X-client to run within its own Windows window. With this method, individual X-client window management can be achieved by using the standard Windows management routines. It provides X Window System applications with a Presentation Manager look and feel to the GUI. When a Client opens a window, he supplies information such as window size, title and icon, which are converted to equivalent features of a Windows window.

VisionWare recommends a minimum of a 286 PC with 640 Kbytes of memory, Microsoft Windows 2.1 or 3.0, and a hard disk. XVision supports LIM/EMS 3.2 or 4.0 expanded memory if available. Supported network adapters include Locus TCP/IP for DOS, FTP PC/TCP and Excelan LAN Workplace. XVision can be connected simultaneously to a variety of X hosts, including UNIX and VMS over a TCP/IP network.

Vision Ware offers a number of workstation integration products and services.

Along with XVision, they offer PC-Connect, which allows PCs to act as multiwindowed workstations connected to one or more UNIX host systems.

References

Jenkins, Avery L. How X Terminal dollars make application sense, *Digital Review*. October 22, 1990. Page 27.

7

Non-MS Windows X Window System servers

The ability to run a PC as an X-server has been available for a few years—long before Windows. The software-emulating programs that offer such capability provide a viable path to an X Window System environment, while still maintaining the functionality of the PC. This chapter will review some of the most popular X-server emulation programs.

Advanced Graphics Engineering

Advanced Graphics Engineering (AGE) has developed an X-server software system, XoftWare for high-resolution TMS340X0-based graphics cards. Fast drawing speed is accomplished by executing all X-server instructions on the TMS 340x0 while the host PC is used to handle mouse, keyboard, file system and network access. Figure 7-1 shows the TIGA/DOS organizational structure.

The program's fast save-under and backing-store functions allow windows information to be stored locally for quick regeneration of covered and uncovered windows. This eliminates the need to continuously regenerate graphics information, a feature that is especially useful when working with complex images. The company has also implemented the MIT SHAPE extension.

During operation the program uses the PC's hard disk for font caching and pixmap paging. Checking functions determine if fonts and pixmaps have been recently used. If not, they are moved from system memory to disk for quick retrieval when needed. Font caching and pixmap paging result in efficient use of the available graphics accelerator memory.

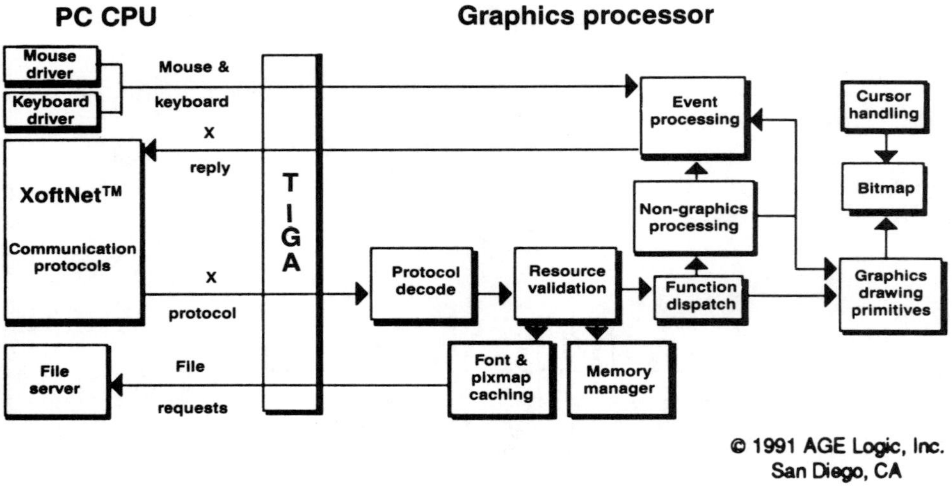

Fig. 7-1. TIGA/DOS architecture.

Quarterdeck Office Systems

DESQview/X is an X Window system for DOS-based PCs. This product is a combination of their existing DESQview multitasking DOS product and the GSS PC-Xview product discussed later in this chapter. DESQview combines DOS with the open systems attributes of UNIX through the X Window System and provides a window manager, Xlib libraries, an EGA/VGA Server, sample programs, and documentation.

The combination of DESQview and PC-XView/16 offers a powerful and sophisticated X Window System environment on PCs. It allows concurrent X Window System and DOS applications to run and offers cut and paste between them via the DESQview 3.0 Clipboard.

A great deal of effort has been invested in optimizing this product for the PC environment. For example, Quarterdeck has included remote log-in capabilities to DESQview/X so that on TCP/IP networks, DESQview/X users are able to view DOS and X Window System programs running on other DESQview/X PCs, as well as on remote UNIX and VAX systems running X. Full network support is offered, including Novell Netware and DECnet. Since it incorporates the DESQview DOS multitasking technology, multiple Client or Server programs can be operating concurrently on either a 286 or 386 platform. Full support is offered for OSF/Motif and OPEN LOOK window managers as well.

The DESQview/X user is provided with all the features of a GUI, together with the ability to run programs from other X Window Systems on his or her PC and run his or her own programs locally or on any other system on his or her X-network. Effectively, under DESQview/X, DOS programs from a PC can be displayed on any X Window System Server on the network, and provide a DOS compatibility box on any machine running the X Window System.

Since it is based on the GSS product, it has the same display limitations. The president of Quarterdeck, Therese Meyers, noted that they would like a TIGA interface for the product and are investigating how to do this.

This product offers the capability to maintain the investment in DOS software, yet have the X Window System and OSF/Motif interface available on PCs. It eliminates the issue of using Windows-based X-servers and potentially changing to Windows-based application software.

DESQview also has an X Toolkit for Sun Microsystems' implementation of AT&T's OPEN LOOK environment. It is based on Sun Microsystems' X View version of the X Window System and is Xlib-based. A version with 3-D OPEN LOOK is also available.

DESQview/X requires a 286 or 386 computer with at least 1 Mbyte of memory and hard disk. It supports EGA, VGA, EVGA, 8514/A and DGIS video displays. A network adapter for the appropriate network (Novell, Ethernet or DECnet) is also required.

Locus

PC Xsight supports up to 16 Mbytes of extended memory and allows users to run DOS applications without exiting the Server. It requires a 286 or 386 computer and supports: Locus TCP/IP for DOS Basic Services, R2.0, LAN Workplace TCP/IP Transport System from Excellan, PC/TCP Network Software for DOS by FTP Software, Inc., StarGROUP NETBIOS V3.2 from AT&T, and PC-NFS from Sun Microsystems, Inc.

PC Xsight is designed to operate with EGA or VGA controllers and does not have any capability for higher resolution graphic devices. The user can, however, create a virtual screen larger than the physical screen on graphic adapters with at least 256 Kbytes of video RAM. PC Xsight/640 is a version that runs on 640 Kbytes 808x or 80x86 machines and does not support expanded memory if available.

Unique features include the ability to switch between real and protected modes of operation in the PC, temporary suspension of the Server to execute DOS applications, and display of memory usage and availability. PC Xsight requires an 80x86 computer with 1.5 Mbytes of memory, 1 Mbyte of disk space and DOS 3.1 or higher. It can take advantage of up to 16 Mbytes of extended memory.

Graphic Software Systems

As the name suggests, Graphic Software Systems specializes in graphics-oriented software. The company offers PC-Xview/16 for converting a DOS-based PC 286 or 386 into a low-cost X Window System terminal. Currently this product is limited to displaying on IBM standard screens (EGA or VGA) or products that support DGIS.

Standard IBM displays do not offer the resolution or color availability necessary for a high-quality, legible display. DGIS is currently available on a number of high-resolution PC graphics cards, including the TI 34010-based NEC MVA 1024. PC-Xview/16 requires a 286 PC with a minimum of 640 Kbytes of memory and a hard disk. Its products include GSS DGIS and GKS, as well as graphics boards.

Hummingbird

Hummingbird offers four versions of its X-server program, eXceed: HCL-eXceed (real-mode version), HCL-eXtend (an X-client that resides on a UNIX host), HCL-eXceed Plus (protected mode version), and HCL-eXceed Plus/8514A.

Also, eXceed Plus supports an escape-to-DOS function. While in DOS, all Client applications still run on the Server. The eXceed program requires Ethernet TCP/IP communications and supports: LAN Workplace TCP/IP Transport System from Excellan (up to 16 Clients), PC/TCP Network Software for DOS by FTP Software Inc. (up to 16 Clients with eXceed and 32 Clients with eXceed Plus), WIN/TCP for DOS by the Wollongong Group (up to 10 Clients), and PC-NFS from Sun Microsystems Inc. (up to 7 Clients).

All eXceed products include an interactive utility for configuring the server's input, communication, video and color, as well as general settings. This utility also supports local viewing of fonts in a graphic rendition. An interesting feature of the eXceed products is their ability to display stored images larger than 64 Kbytes, which can be very important in image-display applications. Also included is a font compiler which compiles source-file fonts into customized HCL-eXceed run-time fonts. Users may locally modify the keyboard mapping. Also, the IBM keyboard mapping for foreign keyboards is available to the Servers.

Following is a short summary of some key features between eXceed and eXceed Plus. It should be noted that the number of simultaneous Clients is determined by the TCP/IP software, not by eXceed.

Product	Clients	Go to DOS?	Max PC memory
eXceed	16	No	1 Mbyte
eXceed Plus	32	Yes	16 Mbytes

Of the standard eXceed, eXceed Plus supports REXEC and RSH, in addition to Telnet and PASSIVE. It is intended for PCs with 640 Kbytes of RAM, while HCL-eXceed Plus can support up to 16 Mbytes of memory, allowing concurrent X-clients to run. Also, eXceed Plus supports VCPI (QEMM-386, 386MAX) and XMS EMS memory-management schemes. Users can restrict the amount of EMS memory that eXceed uses.

References

Osmundsen, Sheila. X windowing PCs provide shape of things to come. *Digital News*. September 3, 1990, Page 10.

8

Non-DOS-based X Window System servers

Since the X Window System was originally developed on UNIX platforms, the ability to run a PC in a non-DOS environment like UNIX is very important. This chapter will cover those non-DOS X-terminal emulation programs.

Advanced Graphics Engineering

Advanced Graphics Engineering (AGE) has developed X-server software for high-resolution TMS340X0-based graphics cards. Their software is often used by manufacturers of graphics cards. AGE also has a TIGA/DOS version available.

Santa Cruz Operations

Open Desktop, offered by Santa Cruz Operations (SCO), is a UNIX-based graphical operating system developed for business and technical systems. Designed for 386 or 486 PCs, it is based on OSF/Motif and can convert a PC into a departmental Server and/or dedicated workstation. Open Desktop is a GUI plus an operating environment and includes a relational database engine, a desktop manager, a networking service, a DOS service, the X Window System, the Motif GUI, and transparent file sharing. The package is targeted at the users who expect to buy shrink-wrap software as a complete load-and-run package. The package incorporates the Ingres DBMS software as an integrated database engine. It is the complete Ingres implementation minus Application By Forms (ABF).

Open Desktop conforms to the X/Open Portability Guide and POSIX. Full international libraries are also available. It uses IXI's X.desktop toolkit. However, users of Open Desktop may not know that they're actually using X.desktop (SCO doesn't mention IXI's name for the product in the documentation it supplies with the program).

X.desktop gives the user a graphical interface to the X Window System environment. Behind its operation is a distributed set of rules and specifications that govern the appearance and behavior of desktop objects. If a standard window manager such as Motif is used, the desktop surface is maintained within a separate window manager. However, it is also possible to use X.desktop's window manager, which controls the background and therefore needs no separate window to represent the desktop.

Directory windows (usually with file icons) and a desktop background are parts of the environment. The desktop consists of several features, some which are considered part of the X.desktop environment and others are not. The environment also includes menus that are attached to the icon window. Features that are not part of the X.desktop environment are non-desktop program windows (such as shell windows). Since these windows exist outside of the environment some users may get confused when trying to go from one setup to another.

The X.desktop environment is well organized and is controlled by resources and rules. Resources are those parameters that are part of the configuration of all X programs and specify such things as background colors and location of icon files and rule files. Rules are the operational parameters of X.desktop. In general, no merging of rules and resources occurs; once a resource is set, there is simply no way to change it via the dynamic operation of a rule.

Pittsburgh Power Computing

Pittsburgh Power Computing offers an X Window System for UNIX-based PCs with high-resolution 340X0-based graphics adapters. It is intended for the creation of an X Window System Server on a UNIX host under SCO UNIX or Interactive Systems 386/ix. It is a complete port of X11R3 and uses standard TCP/IP socket connections and STREAMS for local Client-Server communications. The X-Station/340, as shown in FIG. 8-1, is a version of the standard X11 Server that has been optimized to take advantage of the 340x0. This allows virtual screen capability which makes it possible for big-screen applications to run on smaller monitors.

Conclusions about X Window Systems on a PC

In an X Window System environment, there are 3 major factors driving the choice of a software vendor:

Concurrent operation The prospective user or company has to first determine how important it is to have concurrent operation of DOS applications with the X Window System Clients.

Screen resolution In an X Window System there is a requirement for high-resolution drivers.

Operating system The underlying operating system resident on the PC is a major consideration.

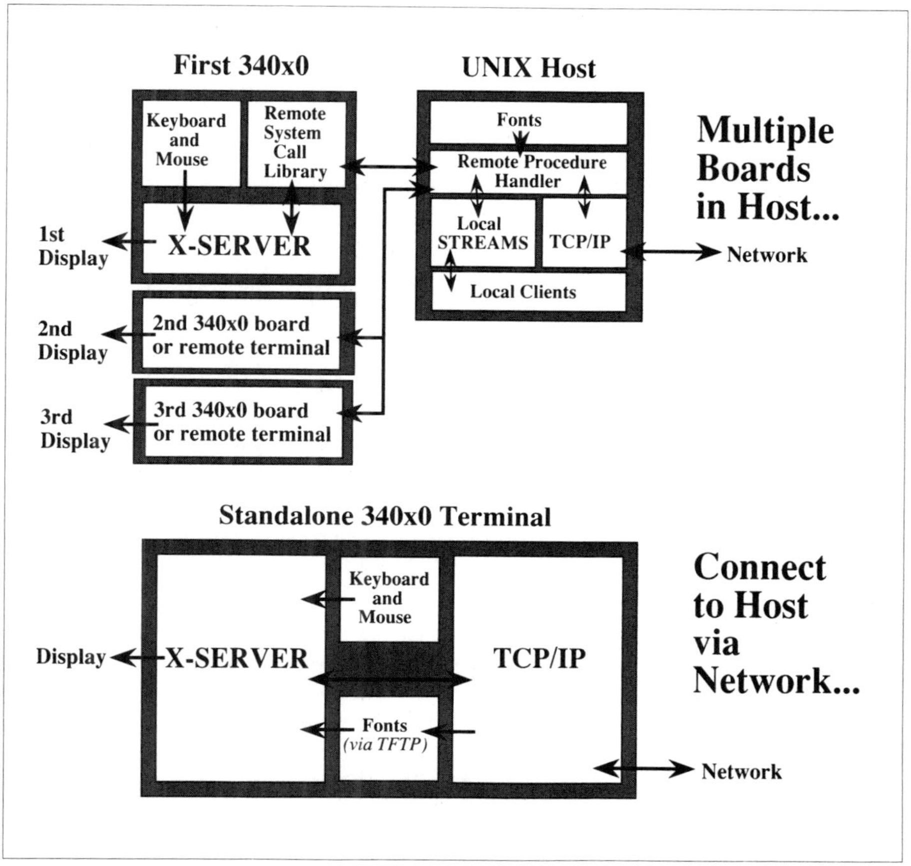

Pittsburgh Power Computing

Fig. 8-1. PC-based X-server architecture.

References

Heichler, Elizabeth. Age's X works for Unix. *Digital News*. September 3, 1990. Page 10.

9

GUIs on personal computers

This chapter provides an overview of the graphical user interfaces (GUIs) on various personal computers. It will examine some of the GUIs available for personal computers and their relationship to the underlying operating system.

Currently, only 20-25 percent of new PCs incorporate a GUI. Estimates are that by the end of 1993, GUIs will be a standard feature of most, if not all, PC systems. Contrast that market penetration against the number of PCs in use. According to statistics contained in the *1990 U.S. Statistical Abstract*, there were 25.3 million desktop computers in use in 1989. It has been estimated that there were over 30 million in 1991. That makes the ratio of keyboards to desk workers almost 1-to-1. In a few years it will be difficult to find a person who doesn't use a computer and who doesn't have a GUI.

GUIs and operating systems

The issue of a GUI is more intimately connected to the underlying operating system (OS) of the PC rather than the processor. However, the choice in one area restricts the options in the other. A company must prioritize the GUI and operating the system issues before making any choices. A common feeling among users concerning the state of the IBM PC operating system choices is that this is the optimal time for a standard operating environment to emerge. Never before have users been so confused by so many operating system options. Just look at what the industry has to contend with. DOS is not dead, OS/2 never took off, and Microsoft has improved Windows. To further complicate things, there are multiple versions of UNIX. If ever there was an operating system environment crisis, this is it.

Graphical user interfaces

Several companies have developed and offered a GUI for their personal computer. Some of the better known ones are listed here.

Amiga

The Amiga has a Macintosh-like GUI for Intuition, the operating system for the Commodore Amiga. While the Amiga's Intuition wasn't threatened with an Apple lawsuit when it first appeared, it too shared many Macintosh-like characteristics. The organizational structure of the Amiga system is shown in FIG. 9-1.

However, Intuition added a feature that Apple didn't include until several years later, the first widely used multitasking GUI. Unlike the X Window System and SAA, Intuition isn't really designed for remote applications. It is a single-user multitasking system. As Frank Hayes and Nick Baran (1989) said, "If the [Macintosh] Finder is the father of desktop computer GUIs, Intuition is arguably the father of MultiFinder."

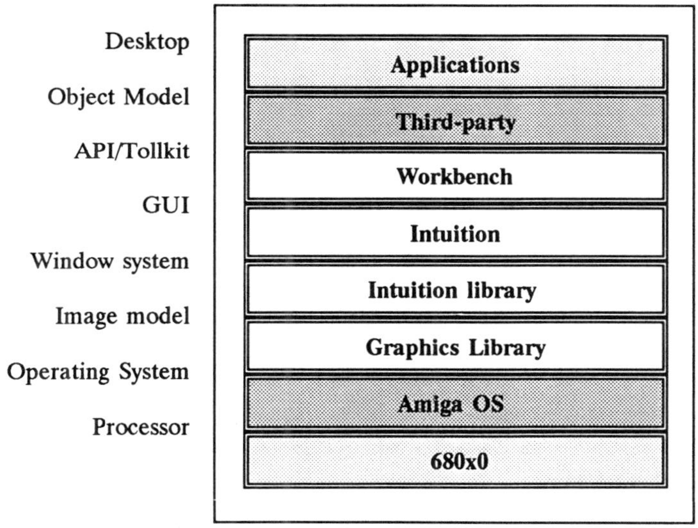

Fig. 9-1. Amiga's Intuition.

Atari

Although the Macintosh is essentially one of a kind in the GUI world, there are other Macintosh-like GUIs such as the Amiga, NeXT and Atari's. The Atari system uses the original version of GEM from Digital Research. Atari's GEM-based organizational structure is shown in FIG. 9-2.

Even though there have been disputes between Digital Research and Apple (causing Digital Research to abandon features in its GUI) the Atari ST version still has many Macintosh-like GUI features. However, the ST also lacks some of Macintosh's Desktop features such as long filenames, proportional typefaces, the ability to remove things from the trashcan, and automatic saving of the desktop.

Macintosh

The Macintosh, from Apple, is an integrated computer, operating system and GUI. The system has been the model for many other GUIs on both PCs and UNIX-based workstations. The Macintosh interface is discussed in Chapter 10.

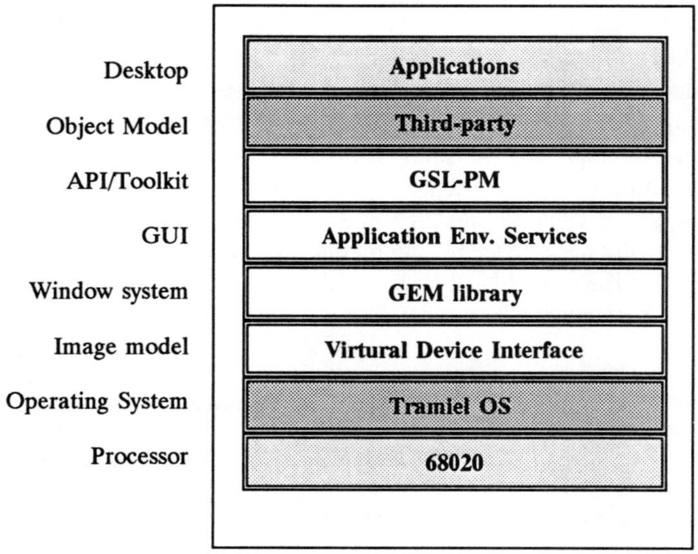

Fig. 9-2. Atari's GEM-based GUI.

NeXT

NeXTstep is the graphical user interface and associated development environment bundled with NeXT computers. It can be envisioned as an object-oriented environment sitting "between" the operating system and the application programs. It provides tools that allow programmers to construct applications in a fraction of the time traditionally required and to make the applications easy to use for even nontechnical people. NeXTstep has four components: the Window Server, Interface Builder, the Application Kit, and the Workspace.

The Window Server Taking advantage of a Display Postscript interpreter from Adobe Systems, the Window Server routes signals from the keyboard and mouse to applications, and from applications to on-screen windows. The Window Server also manages the windows. Because the Display Postscript system uses the same Postscript language that controls printed output, everything looks the same on the screen as it does when printed.

Interface Builder The Interface Builder is a tool for creating a GUI to any kind of application, with minimal programming, using objects such as those found in the Application Kit. The Workspace Manager is responsible for launching applications and utilities, managing and locating files and displaying the directory contents. It controls the workspace, which graphically displays the menus and icons that allow users to migrate through their systems.

The Application Kit The Application Kit contains preprogrammed, interacting software "objects" that embody the core functionality of applications programs' user interfaces. By picking and choosing from among these objects, modifying them as necessary and assigning how they will interact, developers can construct applications much more quickly than from scratch. The Application Kit is quite similar to the Macintosh Toolbox and Macapp (a set of tools that are used by application developers).

The NeXTstep workspace, like all other PC-based GUIs, is operating system-dependent. However, it has been complimented for having charm and an appealing visual look. NeXTstep is discussed further in Chapter 13.

Windows

Microsoft has gone through several versions of Windows in an attempt to offer a useful GUI. The current version features multiple overlapping windows, the ability to copy graphics and text from one window (i.e., application) to another, an all-points-addressable (APA) bit-mapped display system and good memory management. Windows is discussed in detail in Chapter 11.

Presentation Manager

Developed jointly by IBM and Microsoft, Presentation Manager (known as PM) has a look and feel similar to that of Windows. When the full-featured 32-bit extended edition version of Presentation Manager is released, there will be more enthusiasm for it. In the meantime it appears that Windows and possibly an intermediate version known as PM Lite, are the bridges to the future. Presentation Manager is discussed further in Chapter 12.

NewWave

When initially introduced, NewWave did not live up to its promise. Reviews of the program were not favorable because it was viewed as memory-intensive and too far removed from the open-system community. The first edition was hampered by the limitations of earlier versions of Microsoft's Windows and its poor memory management, which made NewWave look slow. The criticisms on openness proved to be unfounded when Hewlett-Packard made the specification available to everyone. In spite of the early misunderstandings, the program was successful in sparking interest in object-oriented software. Later, as Hewlett-Packard and its partners clarified their objectives, it became clear that NewWave was more than just a Windows accessory.

NewWave is the leading object-oriented program for GUIs and is being positioned by Hewlett-Packard to become a *de facto* standard. NewWave is discussed in more detail in Chapter 13.

References

Hayes, Frank, and Nick Baran. A guide to GUIs. *Byte*. July, 1989. Page 250.

Webster, Bruce. 1991. *The NeXT book, second edition*. Reading, Ma: Addison-Wesley.

10

Macintosh

The Apple Macintosh was the first popular, low-cost desktop-based personal computer with a user-friendly graphical user interface. It was introduced in 1984 after the commercially unsuccessful Lisa. The graphical user interface provided by the Macintosh is the first commercially successful GUI. Although Xerox PARC invented and introduced the GUI and use of a mouse, and sold several thousand Star systems, it was the Macintosh that really made the world aware of GUIs. The Macintosh popularized the desktop metaphor of folders for designating files and icons for mass storage devices, including a trash can for discarding things. The success of the Macintosh, even in the face of many corporate requirements of IBM PC compatibility, has shown the power of a GUI in today's marketplace.

Overview

The Macintosh system was designed with a single user in mind. It is a kernel-based system tied closely to its hardware. It is also a closed system and has not been successfully cloned. Through the use of well-defined, strict standards such as QuickDraw, the Font Manager and the file system, all applications have the same operating functions and principles. That, combined with the ability to cut and paste data from one application to another, has made the Macintosh a convenient and comfortable system to use. It has also reduced the learning process for users and allows them to reach higher levels of productivity in a much shorter time.

With an intense loyalty verging on religious zeal, the users of the Macintosh have rewarded Apple for providing this interface. The users' enthusiasm is not unwarranted, as the Macintosh has proven to be a durable and attractive environment. It is safe to say that the Macintosh is the reason Microsoft and IBM came out with a windowing system. It could also be argued that the Macintosh influenced workstation companies like Sun Microsystems, Hewlett-Packard and Digital to develop a friendly user environment.

In many GUIs, the user interface comes as an add-on to the operating system, be it DOS, UNIX, or whatever. The Apple Macintosh is an exception. In 1984, after the disappointing lack of market acceptance of the Lisa machine, Apple introduced the Macintosh. Like the Lisa, it came complete with its own graphical user interface, called the Finder operating system. It includes features unique to the Macintosh, such as the Hypercard system that lets users develop simple graphical applications at the desktop.

Unlike Windows on DOS machines, or OPEN LOOK on UNIX systems, the Finder GUI is the operating system. There is no option to get to the root of the operating system, no lower-level operating system command line. Finder is the foundation on which the Macintosh is built, which now, according to Apple, supports over 3,000 applications.

Desktop metaphor

The Macintosh brought the idea of a desktop metaphor to the public's attention. The now familiar screen is shown in FIG. 10-1, with its folders to indicate files, and icons for various computer operations such as a trash can for deleting files.

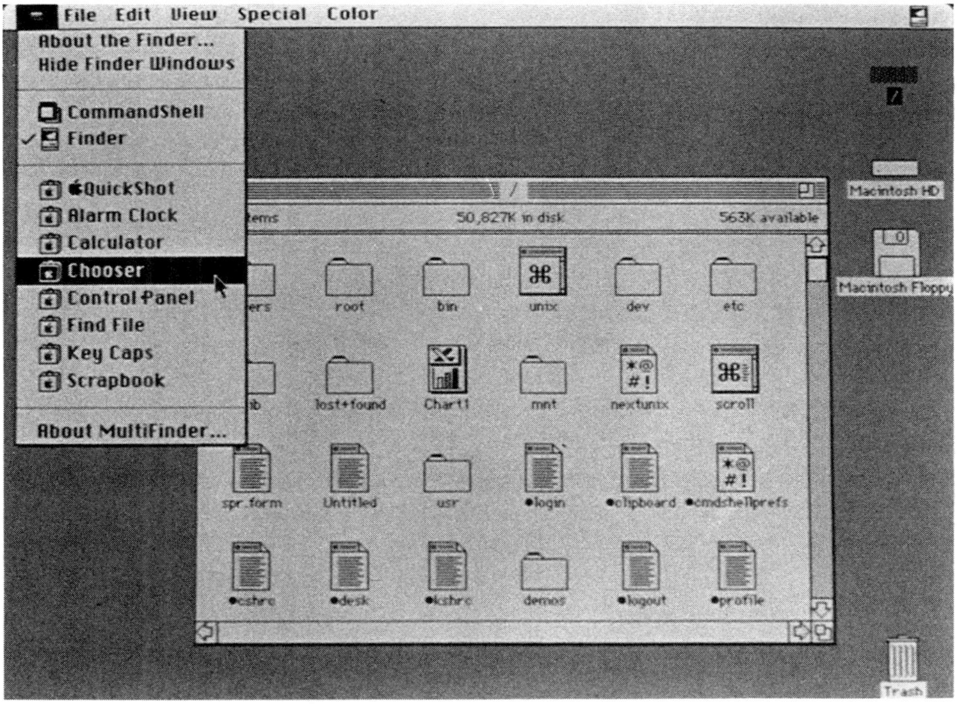

Fig. 10-1. Macintosh directory window.

Consistency

One of the major attributes of the Macintosh system has been the consistency of its desktop metaphors. They are more consistent (as of today) than any other GUI available. That consistency is sometimes criticized as limiting the richness of the environment. However, it has been given more praise than complaints.

MultiFinder

The Macintosh GUI and operating system is probably the best known for its MultiFinder because it provides a desktop-oriented view into the file system (albeit initially always at the top level). Icons are used to reflect disk folders (subdirectories), documents, and applications in rows and columns. Whenever data is produced by any application, it is given a unique icon for visual referencing. Data is easily transported from one file or application to another.

PostScript

It was PostScript software that allowed Apple to virtually invent the term desktop publishing. PostScript is a page-description language that software developers and hardware vendors can use to eliminate hardware dependencies. Apple's first laser printer, the LaserWriter, incorporated a PostScript interpreter, which understood PostScript commands produced by the early desktop publishing programs.

X Window System

Although Apple has made the Macintosh compatible with the X Window System (refer to A/UX this chapter) it does not currently offer an X-terminal emulation or X-server capabilities for the Macintosh. However, other third-party ISVs are offering X Window System software. Also, there are various programs in the public domain available from bulletin boards.

Limitations

The Macintosh enjoys a loyal following of users who staunchly defend any alleged shortcomings in the system. However, most will agree that the Filer lacks a browser or file manager. If a system has several subdirectories it is impossible to see them easily. In order to see additional subdirectories in the Macintosh, the user has to open a new window in succession to look and get at the files in the subdirectories. Users coming to Macintosh from other GUIs criticize it for its single menu bar, which displays only one menu at any time. The menu bar switches to reflect the command options for the currently open application, and therefore it is not possible to see previous menu steps.

Unlike some of the UNIX-based GUIs (e.g., NeWS, X Window System), the Macintosh window system does not permit very many changes in either the programmer or user interface. It therefore is not considered an extensible windowing system. However, despite its criticisms, Apple's main strength has been its operating system and graphical user interface. Users were not attracted to the Macintosh for its processor, screen size or its price. What distinguishes the Macintosh from all other PCs are its operating system and the ease of use and upgrade it provides, and that is essentially why people buy it.

A/UX

One of the problems with the Macintosh and Finder is that it is proprietary. Apple, however, in its effort to win corporate and government accounts, has corrected the situation to a certain extent with the release of A/UX 2.x, the latest version of Apple's UNIX derivative. With version 2.x the company has added the Macintosh desktop metaphor to UNIX. That may seem counter-intuitive; why would the friendly Macintosh take on an operating system known for its unpleasant interface? However, Apple has had a version of UNIX for the Macintosh for some time. It just didn't work very well. With the new version of A/UX it is now possible to run the Macintosh and UNIX at the same time. Rather than one environment being the guest of the other (as in the case of UNIX or OS/2 having a DOS window or box), the two are actually cohabitants.

All the elements of the Macintosh interface, point and click actions, menu bars, and similar icons, plus X Window System support, are available on A/UX. With the latest version, users can run UNIX, the X Window System and Macintosh applications concurrently. A/UX also supports text cut-and-paste between all these environments, and graphics cut-and-paste between Macintosh applications.

X Windows under A/UX

Apple Computer's implementation of X Window System for the A/UX operating system provides two distinct products: X11 and MacX. The first, X11, delivers a native X Window System environment that is well-suited for technical users and software developers. X11 provides a full development environment, including X programming libraries, the X Toolkit intrinsics, and the Athena Widget Set. The second, MacX, allows X applications to share the A/UX software Finder desktop with Macintosh and UNIX applications. With MacX, users can open frequently used X-client applications by just choosing a command from a Macintosh pull-down menu. Both X11 and MacX allow users to take advantage of the highly portable, network-transparent X Window System.

Other features of MacX include: full MultiFinder support, which allows users to switch between X-client applications and Macintosh applications from the desktop; support for multiple monitors, allowing users to view applications in a larger capacity; and a built-in window manager that allows X applications to appear in Macintosh-style windows on the desktop.

MacX software provides an X Window System display Server for the Apple Macintosh and A/UX operating systems. MacX allows X-client applications to share the desktop with Macintosh applications. With MacX, users can transparently access X applications running on a variety of computers that support the X Window System.

System 7.0

Apple Computer introduced a new operating system for the Macintosh designated System 7.0. It provides many features that demonstrate that the Macintosh interface can be updated. There is a new Finder that provides a simpler file management and access system, and updated font technology that will maintain the Macintosh superiority in desktop publishing and related applications.

Yet all these enhancements came more than a year after Windows began shipping. The real breakthroughs of interapplication communications (IAC) and the data access manager will be part of the new system, but users will have to wait for applications that take advantage of them to see any benefits. With all the interest in graphical user interfaces and multitasking, System 7.0 holds a critical role for Apple. The company must stay ahead of Windows and graphical interfaces on other platforms if it is going to continue attracting buyers to its proprietary hardware design.

While System 7.0 has retained the Macintosh look and feel, it also includes several new features. It supports virtual memory and 32-bit addressing, as well as multitasking. However, since the multitasking model is based on Macintosh's basic multitasking technique, MultiFinder, it still lacks a true preemptive scheduler. Therefore there is no easy way of assigning and changing the properties of active processes.

Nonetheless, reactions to the powerful new operating system have been positive. Because of its size, and Apple's desire to push CD-ROMs, Apple sent it out on CD-ROM to developers. The latest version of System 7.0 has a number of features not found in previous releases. These include the following.

New look A new Macintosh interface that uses color to subtly highlight interface elements such as scroll bars, window frames and menu items has been incorporated. Dimmed menu items appear in a true gray, rather than the black and white used in the original Macintosh interface. Most applications automatically take advantage of the new interface. Apple developed the new interface in response to a number of comparisons with Windows that called the Macintosh interface chunky or Tinkertoy-like when compared with Windows' colorful 3-D look.

TrueType TrueType fonts from Apple and Bitstream, Inc., as well as font-testing tools, are included. In a cooperative effort, Adobe Systems has focused its engineering on making TrueType and PostScript seamlessly compatible and interoperable. The goal with System 7.0 was to get PostScript and TrueType playing together.

Interapplication communications Two key elements, Edition Manager for live data interchange between applications, and AppleEvents, which lets programs call one another for processing are also included.

Device controls As part of Apple's long-term plan, which includes multimedia, the company will provide consistent user interfaces for media devices such as videodiscs and CD-ROMs, and for video-capture and overlay boards.

Compression Although industry standards from JPEG for compression and decompression are emerging, Apple has developed a proprietary, software-only algorithm. Therefore, only systems with the ability to compress/decompress in compliance with Apple's algorithm will be able to exchange media—a step backwards to non-open, nonstandard systems.

Video cut and paste Users are able to manipulate video as easily as text and graphics. Windows can be opened with live video in them.

Users will need help either from department support groups or outside specialists when moving to System 7. It will change the Desktop and Finder, and many users will be faced with a significant learning curve. It may also jam up already overcrowded AppleTalk networks with millions more packets, due to aliasing, FileShare, and Publish and Subscribe facilities.

User group

The Macintosh is one of the oldest systems in use. It has a loyal, some say religious, following. There are local user groups in most major cities and even with large organizations. However, users always want more from a system than most manufacturers offer, or they find weaknesses the manufacturer didn't. User groups can be helpful to a manufacturer in providing insights and information about the system. One such group is the Macintosh IS, an organization of professional and corporate users that was formed to influence Apple's development of the Macintosh.

Macintosh users

Macintosh users are loyal and feel that there is a certain something that makes their systems superior to PCs with Windows. Macintosh versus Windows is considered an issue of religion by many observers. In recent surveys of corporate information-center managers, only a handful of the Windows-buying respondents said they would adjust their Macintosh purchases in favor of Windows.

It's more than religion

In one survey after another, corporate users and information managers praise graphical user interfaces. Ease of use and simplified training and support are at the top of their lists. That means there is a huge market clamoring for the GUI and its attendant ease of use.

The experience of a publisher

A few years ago, Professional Press (publishers of *DEC Professional*) began converting its art department from the world of wax and razor blades. Now all Professional Press publications are produced on Macintoshes. The publisher runs on the edge of technology. Their color work is so advanced that there were no consultants to tell them how to do it. As a result of their efforts, they no longer need typesetters or paste-up people. Soon they will completely stop producing anything on paper other than PostScript pages.

Why do they use Macintoshes when faster and better hardware is available—including workstations from Digital? The answer is the same as before. It isn't the power. It isn't a single application. It's the Macintosh user interface and the family of software from many vendors that is bound together by the toolkit. This isn't religion, it's plain and simple technology.

Macintosh-to-DOS

Bawamba in Burbank has developed a Macintosh-to-DOS tool-kit (designated the MCP). The tool-kit allows Macintosh applications to be recompiled to run under DOS. An OS/2 version has also been completed; however, the company is not rushing into Windows. They have reservations about the performance of a recompiled application that would sit on top of Windows while Windows was sitting on top of DOS. The compiler automatically senses what type of display is in the system (CGA, EGA, or VGA—they are working on a superVGA driver) or it can be forced into one of these modes.

DOS-to-Macintosh

Although Apple arguably positioned itself as an island and showed no interest in cooperative processing or anything to do with DOS, users wanted some means of exchange. The basic problem has been file-format differences. That created an opportunity for third-party developers.

Responding to the desires of users, DataViz offers a file transfer and format-translation product that runs under Windows as well as Macintosh. Called PC DataBridge, the package includes a library of 150 format translators for word processing, database, spreadsheet and graphics files and software that allows control of the transfer process from either the Macintosh or the PC under Windows or DOS.

Macintosh and Microsoft Windows

Apple has had to make some adjustments in its strategies and has, reluctantly, recognized Windows as a viable entity and competitor. In response to this, Apple is using its Claris Corp. software division to produce applications for Microsoft Corp.'s Windows 3.x package, which it still considers a competing product that replicates the once unique screen appearance of the Macintosh personal computer.

There has been industry speculation that Apple abandoned plans to spin off Claris into a separate business unit because it feared Claris would focus on building applications for Windows. Apple Chairman John Sculley said there has always been a misconception that the company bought Claris back to prevent them from building a Windows product. However, that isn't the case, because Apple wants a Windows product. Windows development will not be Claris' primary mission, but the rapid success of Windows has made it difficult to ignore. Obviously the company no longer believes that Windows will go away.

Initial Windows development efforts were a little confused, but then focused on porting existing Claris products such as the Macwrite word processing application, Filemaker database management software and the Macdraw graphics package to Windows. Later undertakings could entail the creation of entirely new applications. Users have been enthusiastic about Claris developing for Windows and have said they would love to see a package that could span both DOS and Apple, because it would really ease the pain of integrating the two environments.

11

Microsoft Windows

Windows was a long-awaited answer to multitasking, sizable windows, and, most of all, a stable and consistent window/icon environment. Some observers feel it will have a major impact on desktop publishing and presentation graphics. The program will have a profound effect on all aspects of desktop computing during the next 10 years.

This chapter will present a review and explanation of Microsoft Windows (also referred to simply as Windows). This information is provided for two reasons. First of all, Windows is, in its own right, a GUI, albeit strictly for DOS personal computers. Secondly, Windows also serves as the basis for a number of X Window System servers.

Throughout its history, the software industry has relied on innovative products to spark its growth. This growth pattern has been remarkable. Since January 1988, software sales have increased more than 25 percent annually. And there is no slowdown in sight.

During 1990, software sales in North America expanded nearly 27 percent, while overseas sales jumped by an astonishing 61 percent. Total worldwide sales by U.S. publishers rose 34 percent. Throughout 1990, the industry experienced broad-based gains. Seven out of 10 domestic categories recorded growth rates in excess of 20 percent.

Contributing to the strength of these sales was an explosion in software purchases of Microsoft's Windows. Windows is now the third largest software format in North America, behind MS-DOS and Macintosh. In Europe, Windows has surpassed the Macintosh market. Windows' popularity also spurred broad-based gains in categories that rely on graphical interfaces. Graphics software sales have been at an all-time high in the last few years. Users already familiar with a GUI (e.g., Macintosh, GEM, Motif or NeXT) are able to use Windows applications with little or no reference to the manual.

Product overview

Windows 1.0 was introduced in late 1983 and took over six years to become a viable GUI. Windows 3.0, introduced in May, 1990, was a significant step for Microsoft. The company put a great deal of effort in avoiding a repeat of the problems with earlier releases. The product went through 17 beta versions before it was released. Windows 3.1 cleared up most of the original problems with 3.0 and added several enhancements.

As an indication of the aggressiveness of Microsoft, Windows 3.0 was rolled out simultaneously worldwide. Versions are currently available in Dutch, Spanish, French, German, Portuguese, Italian and Swedish. The fact that Windows 3.0 was released with such a rich feature set is partially due to the difficulty experienced in getting OS/2 accepted. Furthermore, it meets one of the basic requirements of a GUI: to be an environment the user wants to work in all day.

Differences from previous versions

Unlike previous versions of Windows, version 3.0 did not display file names on its start-up screen. Instead, it used a Program Manager that displayed icons to represent programs or actions. It incorporates the shadowed 3D look of OSF/Motif so that buttons seem to move in and out of the screen as they are activated.

Most activity in Windows is divided between the Program Manager and the File Manager. The Program Manager is the main desktop that contains any number of *groups*, logically associated programs and data files. For example, a user could set up an accounting group that contains spreadsheet programs and data files for various departments. Another group could be electronic mail, while another could be correspondence. Each of these groups would be configured with logically associated objects.

Windows includes additional application programming interfaces to further simplify creating Windows tools. One of the objectives for Windows was to allow users to have a one-box solution so that all they would need is a development tool and a copy of Windows. Windows is available at most computer or software stores. Although the retail price for the product is low (less than ($100), there are other costs users need to consider before going ahead with the environment.

Peripherals

The Windows user will need a mouse. A GUI user really needs a mouse for the GUI to be used effectively. Microsoft offers a mouse/Windows bundle at an attractive price. Many other companies, like Logitech, also offer a mouse that is compatible with a PC (refer to Chapter 15 for a detailed discussion on mice and other pointing devices). Also, Windows looks much better on a color monitor. VGA resolution is the minimum, an EGA monitor is an alternative if that is all that's available.

Memory needs

Although Microsoft has said Windows will run on a 286 with 1 Mbyte, it really requires a 386 with 2 to 4 Mbytes to run well. Some industry leaders think Windows should have been introduced as a 386 and above-only product. Users with a 286 will want the superior performance of standard mode. They should have at least 2 Mbytes. Most users can't see any difference in speed between a machine with 2 Mbytes and 4 Mbytes. Windows will also take up 5 to 7 Mbytes of hard disk space.

Windows will run on XT or AT class machines, but the result may be too slow for some people. Even on a fast machine, Windows programs may not be as snappy as current applications. Some companies may decide not to spend the money on the cost of upgrading to Windows. If they don't, they may find themselves at a competitive disadvantage in a year or two.

Projected users

Windows should more than meet the short-term needs of the users with a 1 to 2 Mbyte 80286 machine and above. However, experienced users who are accustomed to working from a DOS prompt may have a little difficulty getting used to the new environment. If a user has been using only one application and is not frustrated by memory limitations and/or delays in bring up other applications, there is no real incentive to install Windows.

Productivity

Generally, all GUI programs are easier to use. While this may not help an experienced user, it makes things easier for the new user. Unlike DOS programs, Windows programs (like Macintosh programs) must comply with standard interface guidelines. For example, accessing Help, opening files, and exiting an application are all done the same way in most Windows programs, regardless of what company developed the program. Many features of Windows programs are easier to find and easier to use than their DOS equivalents.

Windows allows the user to have more than one program running at once. For example, a user could leave (without exiting from the program) a word processor that was doing a mail merge, and work on a spreadsheet. Furthermore, GUI programs are generally much more attractive. While this may seem trivial to some people, GUI programs are much more inviting and usually less intimidating.

Microsoft and Zenith Data Systems sponsored a study by Temple, Barker & Sloane, Inc. designed to demonstrate that GUI-based systems are more productive than character-based systems. The study shows GUI users completed 58 percent more work in the same amount of time than non-GUI users with character-based displays. However, of the seven categories tested (for experienced and novice users), there was only a significant difference statistically in four categories for experienced users and two for novice users. The largest gains were made by experienced GUI users. They completed 35 percent more tasks and had 17 percent fewer errors than experienced users with character-based systems. In general, novice users with a GUI had only marginal improvements in speed, but they reported less frustration than novice users with a character-based system.

One aspect of productivity the consultants didn't examine is that a single icon can contain an entire series of processes that the user need not be aware of. This is the big difference between Windows and the Macintosh. (Many Macintosh functions require some user interaction with a mouse and cannot be activated with the keyboard or icons that are in different parts of the screen.)

In a typical organization, few of its applications demand multitasking to any extent other than *context switching*, moving data between two files and keeping data in separate, but not necessarily active, Windows. Windows helps by keeping programs available with a single click, which is better than exiting one program, loading another, extracting data, exiting the second program and reloading the first, and so on. Such operations may only take 15 minutes a day, but multiply that by the number of employees doing it, add in the time lost due to distraction, and for an entire year, that unproductive time becomes quite large.

Users' choices

With the introduction of Windows, DOS will remain a viable operating system (OS) for PCs, at least for the next five years. However, for users who need a more powerful operating system with networked applications, the choice between OS/2 or UNIX is still not clear. Windows only gives the perception of multitasking. In practice, only one active window is actually running. Therefore, large networked applications will not be suitable for it. DOS will never be an alternative for a multitasking environment.

However, users that have a large investment in DOS will be pleased because it helps protect their investment. Also, some users will stay in the PC/DOS/Windows environment because of fear of the unknown and/or not wanting to learn (i.e., invest in) a new system. IS and MIS administrators, on the other hand, may want to take advantage of the secret weapon in Windows, its improved MS-DOS interoperability.

Desktop organization

While every Macintosh user is familiar with desk accessories (some consider them indispensable miniature applications) Microsoft Corp. did not endow Windows with comparable features, as shown in FIG. 11-1. The Windows desktop consists of a mini-

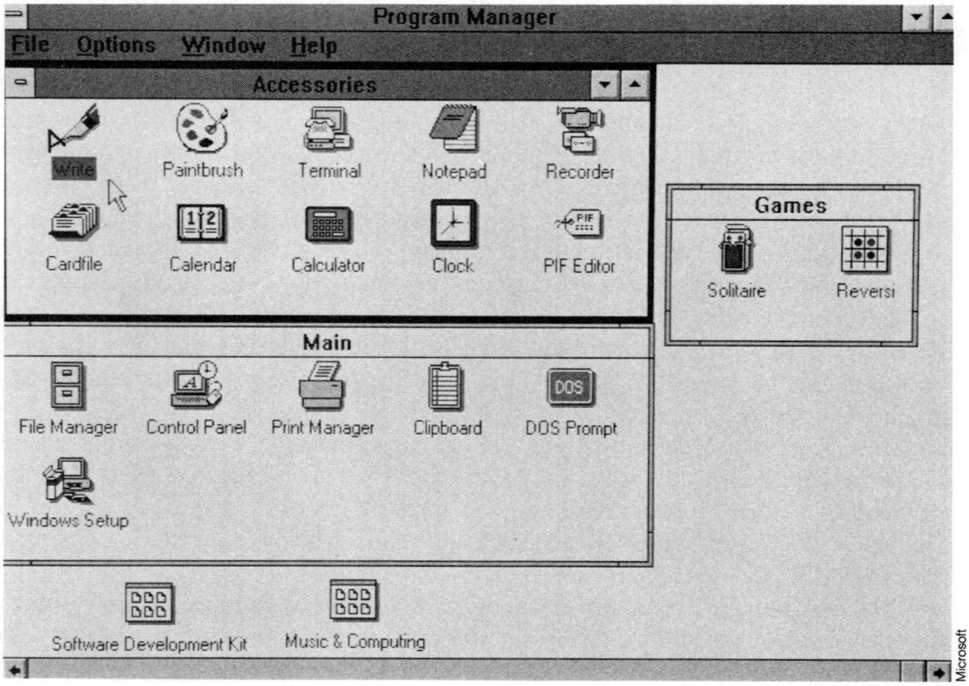

Fig. 11-1. The start-up screen for Microsoft Windows, main directory.

mum of five user and system applications: Program Manager, File Manager, Task List, Control Panel and Print Manager. Normally, the Task List is not present on the screen.

Program Manager

The Program Manager is a task organizer desktop, while the File Manager is a disk organizer.

File Manager

The File Manager operates somewhat like the popular disk management shell XTree, from the XTree Company, in that it displays the DOS tree directory structure of a particular disk. Files and directories can be moved or copied by simply moving the icon representing them to a different location on the tree. Windows does not have a file manager like OS/2's High Performance File System (HPFS). Microsoft acknowledges Windows would benefit from a HPFS. The company has indicated it may add this feature to Windows in the future. Under Windows, all older applications are displayed on a directory screen that is accessed by an icon. The icon is a miniature monitor and has the word DOS inside it.

Task List

The Task List allows the user to switch from one task to another, kill a task or rearrange windows or icons. It is invoked by double-clicking on the desktop or pressing Control-Escape.

Control Panel

The Control Panel provides a set of configuration tools. Functions that can be performed from the Control Panel include manipulating the desktop colors, installing or configuring printers and fonts, attaching to an alternate network Server, configuring communications ports, changing the video screen used and specifying multitasking settings for 386 enhanced mode. It also allows the user to view and manipulate network printer queues, selecting the appropriate queue for the desired printer. Also, local spooling can be selectively enabled and disabled, not globally as in previous versions.

The Control Panel also lets users design their own customized screen by taking advantage of more-advanced color hardware. For example, users can scan pictures or drawings from their individual screen background or choose from a set of available backgrounds called *wallpapers*.

Print Manager

The Print Manager handles both local and network queues. Local queues display only jobs printed from Windows applications, but network queues list all print jobs. By default, a network queue will not list other user's jobs, but the user can ask to see the complete list.

Technical issues

Windows 3.X is a major upgrade from the previous version 2.1 and 386. It makes greater use of icons, incorporates the 3D look of OSF/Motif and remedies the memory management problems for which the previous version of Windows was notorious. Some of its main features and reasons for existence are its use of protected mode, its own residence in extended memory, its demand-paged virtual memory, and robust multiple virtual DOS machine capability.

Major technical changes

Windows 3.X incorporates two major technical changes from previous versions. The first is the incorporation of the DOS Protected Mode Interface (DPMI) that allows Windows to address up to 16 Mbytes of RAM directly. DPMI compatibility ensures that application software shares a common Application Program Interface (API) and Application Binary Interface (ABI). Applications that meet the DPMI specification will be able to run with any DOS extender or operating system that conforms to the standard. This allows them to take advantage of the virtual memory facilities of Windows 3.X.

Windows 3.X takes advantage of the protected mode of the 286 and 386 family of processors to provide additional memory for the environment and applications running on it. This increases the number of applications that can be used concurrently and dramatically improves system use and performance.

Device independence

Standard device drivers are one of the main features of Windows, according to Microsoft. Although not new to Windows, version 3.0 finally standardized on enough display controller types to provide compatibility with CGA, EGA, VGA, plus several high-resolution controllers such as IBM's 8514/A, and cards supporting GSS' DGIS and TI's TIGA.

Some developers still criticize Windows for limitations in the Graphical Device Interface (GDI). Miscrosoft points out that there has to be a limit, and it has drawn the line at industry standards. However, developers may create their own drivers and add specialized functions. One of the positive things developers have said about Windows is that it has standardized the use of square pixels.

Memory management

The Windows program itself actually runs in extended memory and uses this memory for running Windows applications. The additional memory resources are used for loading application code and data files. Non-Windows DOS processes running as tasks under Windows have a conventional memory overhead of only 9.5 Kbytes, leaving over 550 Kbytes for application software. On 386-based systems with a minimum of 1 Mbyte of extended memory, a portion of the hard disk can be allocated as virtual memory, allowing Windows application code and data to be paged to disk.

Windows is incompatible with certain 386 memory control programs such as Quarterdeck's QEMM and Qualitas' 386Max. Under the control programs, which convert

386 extended memory into EMS memory, users could load resident DOS programs such as network drivers into *high memory*, between 640 K and 1 Mbyte. These drivers must be loaded into each individual Windows session. The control programs can be used with Windows in real mode, although real mode does not offer the large memory space that standard and enhanced mode offer.

Icons

Icons are used to represent programs and directories. Windows incorporates part of the look and feel of the X Window System and OSF/Motif in its presentation of the data and programs in a user's system. Icons can be copied by dragging them from one group window to another. Groups of icons representing associated programs and/or data files can be created.

Although it does not offer the sophistication of OSF/Motif in configuring the environment for the user, it is a great leap forward in the presentation of information to the user on a PC. The user, or system administrator, will still need to be familiar with DOS command line syntax and directory structures when opening or saving a specific file. However, the Windows desktop environment can be created by a system administrator and distributed to users, decreasing their need for DOS familiarity.

Child windows

Like Presentation Manager (PM), Windows supports *child windows* that run as windows or as icons within the boundaries of a parent window, sharing its menu bar. This technique, which IBM's Common User Access style guide defines as the Multiple Document Interface, or MDI, allows hierarchical arrangements of windows. An entire aggregation of top-level and child windows can be collapsed to a single icon, removing a lot of visual clutter from the screen. In 386 protected mode, the processes represented by the icon continue to run in the background.

Operating modes

Windows has three modes in which it can operate, dependent on the processor type and memory available.

Real mode System configurations with 640 Kbytes of conventional memory operate in *Real* mode. This mode most closely resembles version 2.1 of Windows. The user still has the benefits of a GUI, along with support for running multiple applications within conventional and expanded-memory resources. This mode is used to run existing Windows applications that have not been ported to version 3.X.

Windows selects Real mode if the computer has already been placed into protected mode by some other application or an alien memory manager such as Quarterdeck's QEMM or Qualitas' 386 Max. It does this because there can only be one memory manager at a time running. Windows can be forced into Real mode by starting the program with an "/R." This operation is required whenever pre-Windows 3.X applications are run.

Standard mode On a 286- or 386-based system, with from 1 to 16 Mbytes of memory, the default operating mode is *Standard* mode. In this mode, Windows takes advantage of the 286 protected mode to directly access extended memory. This provides excellent performance for concurrently running applications, and it facilitates data sharing and exchange between those applications.

When Windows is in Standard mode it functions like any other DOS extender and places the processor into its protected mode of operation. The problem with Standard mode is the lack of support for non-Windows DOS applications. They cannot take advantage of the virtual DOS machine or use the Multiple Virtual DOS Machine (MVDM) support provided by Windows' 386 Enhanced mode. Some analysts are referring to the Real and Standard modes as Windows' unwanted stepchildren.

Enhanced mode On a 386-based system with 2 Mbytes of memory, Windows operates in 386 Enhanced mode. In this mode, extended and virtual memory can be accessed in standard mode. Each DOS application is provided its own 8086/8088 class virtual machine. These applications can then be preemptively multitasked with other DOS applications and run as icons, in windows on the screen, or in a full-screen mode that mimics the appearance of DOS. In this mode, Windows executes from extended memory and all programs run concurrently. This mode also supports *swap files*, which are temporary files with which Windows swaps portions of programs not in use.

Multitasking is a tall order. There has been criticism that Windows forces multitasking into an operating system not designed to accommodate it. Some observers have suggested that PC users who really need to run concurrent applications may be better off with OS/2. The problem is an architectural issue and something that can't be solved with software patches. Software developers can't take something that was not developed for multitasking (i.e., DOS) and turn it into something for multitasking overnight. However, DOS 5.0 addresses a lot of these criticisms and offers a better base for Windows.

Dynamic data exchange

Windows also expands support for dynamic data exchange (DDE), which allows application software to share data. For example, a spreadsheet could be linked to a word processor document. As the data in the spreadsheet is changed, the change is reflected in the word processor document. DDE links can be either one-way or two-way. In a two-way DDE link, not only would the spreadsheet data be included in the word processor document, but changes made in the word processor document would be reflected in the spreadsheet.

To use DDE, a user must establish links between the programs that are expected to communicate, carefully defining what data contents of which application or file will be exchanged and how changes in data values will affect each application's behavior. However, there is a major difference between applications that are supplied from a single vendor and applications from multiple vendors cooperating to provide these kinds of dynamic capabilities. DDE alone is inadequate for the job. DDE is a protocol, not a specification, and therefore can be implemented in different ways. It is merely a method of passing messages from program to program and doesn't define how those messages are formatted. What was needed was a set of standards.

Compound Document Protocol

Compound Document Protocol fulfills the promise of DDE and defines application links. The Compound Document Protocol Specification (CDPS), alternatively called the Embedded Compound Document Architecture (ECDA), is a protocol specification that extends the dynamic linking technology, Dynamic Data Exchange (DDE), contained in both Windows and OS/2. CDPS eliminates use of code-heavy integrated applications and allows the application to do what it does best. Compound documents will be an important aspect of the applications of this decade and, when fully functional, will let users choose the most appropriate tool no matter where they are.

The desire (some say need) for compound document capabilities predates Windows. Projects to implement such technology were under way at least a year before the introduction of Windows 3.0. One of the first of these projects was the Pez protocol originally developed by Aldus Corp. However, before Aldus could announce it, Pez was co-opted by Microsoft, which merged it with additional technology developed by its own applications division. Meanwhile, in 1989 Lotus demonstrated a similar competing technology.

Chronology of CDPS

1989

- July. Aldus announces the Pez protocol. Microsoft application division work on linking technology is revealed.
- September. Pez becomes merged with Microsoft's effort.
- November. Lotus and WordPerfect announce hot link technology and their cooperative effort.
- December. The Linked and Embedded draft specification is released from Microsoft.

1990

- June. Powerpoint for Windows ships with CDP.
- October. Lotus/WordPerfect agree to merge their technology with Microsoft.
- December. CDPS released.

Although it is unclear which company approached the other first, shortly after Microsoft issued its draft document, the four companies agreed to merge all three efforts to create CDPS. This standard has been the result of a cooperative effort by Microsoft, Aldus, Lotus, and WordPerfect. One of the tricky aspects of making CDPS work, in fact, is getting programs to establish links with each other automatically (often referred to as *hot links*).

But CDPS is just the beginning. There are a lot of possibilities ahead. Because it works without requiring changes to DDE itself, CDPS is likely to become a technology that will allow seamless workgroup computing. Tools are already available that allow DDE to work between applications over a network.

Object linking and embedding technology

Object linking and embedding technology (OLE) applications let users perform a paste-link function and link an information object file into a compound document. If the original changes, the linked object in the compound document is automatically updated. This is similar to current DDE but is easier for users to accomplish.

In embedding, users simply paste an object, copied from another application, into a compound document. The object carries with it information on the application that created it. Users just double-click the mouse on the object—a worksheet for example—and automatically call up the application that created the object—called the *Client* application.

When a Server application is installed on a user's PC, it is identified as an *available Server* in a file called *registration services*. When a user double-clicks on an embedded or linked object within a Client application, the Client library—called the dispatcher—checks registration services to see if the particular Server is installed on the user's PC. If so, the Server application is invoked and the correct file loaded.

While there is a similarity to Client-Server network computing, OLE does not support networks. Server applications must be resident on the user's machine. However, an application can be used as both a Server and a Client application. Facilities to let OLE run on networks will be added by making changes to underlying file systems and network operating systems.

The Microsoft specification for object linking and enhancing interapplication communications in its Windows environment places the company in direct competition with Hewlett-Packard's object-oriented development environment, NewWave. IBM has a similar project, Patriot Partners, which, with Metaphor Computer Systems, Inc., is a joint development of an object-oriented environment for UNIX and OS/2. Software developers will have to choose one or the other environment for their Windows-based development projects requiring NewWave-like features.

Microsoft's object linking and embedding environment includes additions to Windows that support an object-oriented file structure, as well as add technology for linking application files together without requiring user intervention. The company has also developed a macro language for programming interapplication communications in the new environment.

However, the specifications are missing some capabilities by NewWave. For example, there is no provision for using the technology in a networked environment. Also absent are interface libraries for OS/2 and Macintosh support. Microsoft has no plans to include UNIX in the new specifications, an upcoming feature of NewWave. OLE will need more work to add remote resources. Because OLE will be an extension to Windows, meaning it will ride on top of DOS, remote links will have to wait until DOS provides the needed low-level services.

Microsoft will help Windows developers implement object linking and embedding (OLE) technology in their applications by distributing copies of code libraries. Eventually, the libraries will be shipped with Windows, but until then they are provided royalty free to developers.

Included are Server and dispatcher libraries, which provide OLE services to Server and Client applications via application programming interfaces (APIs). Once incorporated into applications, users will be able to embed or link graphics, text, spreadsheets, charts, and other information objects into *compound documents*.

Codevelopers Microsoft, Aldus, Lotus, and WordPerfect are promoting OLE as a standard technology for all Windows applications. The current version is built on top of Windows' Dynamic Data Exchange (DDE) protocol. Microsoft hopes OLE will be implemented in both OS/2 and Macintosh System 7.0.

Compatibility and upgrade path

Older Windows 2.1 applications will run in Windows 3.x in real mode. Many software developers are offering free or low cost upgrades of their application software to Windows users.

Setup

Windows has become quite complex as Microsoft has adapted it to the full range of possible system capabilities. It has a sophisticated setup program that examines the computer's hardware and selects the optimal configuration in which to run. The user can modify these setup parameters via the Control Panel or by various, somewhat poorly documented, command-line switches. During setup, Windows scans the local and network disks to find application software packages it recognizes. It then generates a Windows Applications and Non-Windows Applications desktop with these programs and Program Information Files (PIFs) that invoke them from the icon.

Training

The ease of using Windows doesn't mean IS and MIS departments should dismantle their training programs and send the instructors home. People will still need to be taught how to use the applications. When starting out with Windows, that needs to be emphasized.

Impact of DOS 5.0

DOS 5.0 accesses more memory on 286/386 and uses extended memory to hold much of the OS. Earlier testers of the operating system found up to 630 Kbytes were free, depending on CONFIG.SYS. Windows users will benefit because the memory gains are reflected in Windows' DOS virtual machines. This will reduce DOS VMs in Windows (which typically take 300 Kbytes to 400 Kbytes) to 40 Kbytes. The DOS user shell is reduced from 3.5K to 1K. All DOS 4.1 features are retained, including support for disk partitions as large as 2 Gbytes. Support for the Virtual Control Program Interface will also be included in a version of the EMM386 LIM emulator. The final version is expected to have a task switching scheduler like Quarterdeck's DESQview, according to Mark Chestnut, the product manager for DOS at Microsoft.

Future DOS

DOS 6.0, or Future DOS, as some people call it, will embody Windows in the same way OS/2 embodies Presentation Manager. It will also include built-in network functions and an interface to the Client-Server functions of the X Window System. The tighter integration of Windows and DOS will eliminate duplicate code and the criticism that Windows is just a shell sitting on DOS. Performance will also be improved. Computers could have the operating system/environment built into system ROMs. That will limit the number of upgrades possible and may at the last minute be thwarted by Microsoft because it eliminates the upgrade business. However, it may be unavoidable for laptops.

Windows and mainframes

The reality of enterprise networking today is a messy situation. Little has been done to simultaneously link PCs with multiple hosts that run different protocols. It is common to find PCs linked to IBM or Digital minicomputers or UNIX hosts. It is virtually impossible to have links to all of them at the same time. Simultaneous access to applications on different host architectures will become more critical as organization structures flatten.

Windows has the capability to be the glue that simultaneously integrates DOS-based PCs with applications on different host architectures. The key is its memory management. The memory requirements for protocol management software for just one network often prohibit running memory-intensive applications. The memory management of Windows changes this and potentially will prolong the life of DOS for many years in enterprise network environments.

Windows allows Windows and DOS applications to run in the 286 and 386 protected mode. Relatively inexpensive 286 PCs with 2 Mbytes of extended memory offer a powerful platform for this application. For example, a protocol manager supporting the Network Driver Interface Specification (NDIS) can run in one of the application program segments.

Communications

One of the problems with communicating with a mainframe has been the RAM cram of Terminate and Stay Ready programs (TSRs) needed for terminal emulations. That will subside under Windows. The memory management in Windows makes it possible for 286 and 386 computers to support IBM's LU6.2 and PU2.1 protocols, for example. That enables users to communicate directly with a host as peers, rather than through a terminal-emulation gateway.

This allows PCs with Windows to run IBM's Systems Network Architecture (SNA) sessions end-to-end (i.e., directly from the host to the PC). That capability improves throughput and fault isolation. With current terminal emulations, the host can see problems within individual PCs or workstations.

Network management

With Windows in protected mode, users can load multiple DOS sessions and have multiple DOS programs executing simultaneously. With previous versions of Windows, when one of the programs requested information from the file Server, the network physical layer protocol, such as Novell's IPX, would get confused about which session was requesting information and crash the system. To correct this, Microsoft provided network vendors with a clean design for virtual devices to which they could write drivers, placing their network protocols into high memory.

However, Windows still has some network shortcomings. Message sending and receiving are a problem across a Novell network. Printer configuration and user security are also weak areas. For example, it is possible for a user to send a document intended for a dot matrix printer to a Hewlett-Packard LaserJet II print queue. Third-party vendors, such as Automated Design Systems of Atlanta, GA, are making utilities available that augment these weak areas in Windows.

The most convenient way to install Windows is to put it and its applications on the Server. The administrator would install one version of Windows and create a directory for each user with network, mouse and video adapter drivers appropriate for that user. Windows also makes use of diskless workstations much easier. With previous versions of Windows, using diskless workstations was problematic because of the traffic it created over the network. It was also very slow because swap files were stored on the Server disk.

Third-party accessories

As Windows becomes used in more organizations, various accessory programs will be introduced. The list of third-party suppliers will be constantly growing and declining over time as developers find niches of opportunities. The following is a brief example of such programs.

Icons

Windows comes with a handful of monochrome icons. With Windows here to stay and older applications showing no signs of going away, demand for unique icons for older DOS applications has produced a flurry of offerings. Many have shown up on bulletin-boards as freeware of shareware, as well as a few bona fide products. CompuServe's service, the MSWIN forum, has thousands in its library. There are also icon design tools, PBIcon and IconDraw, available on CompuServe.

Commercial packages like Windows Express from hDC Computer, and Icon PAK I from Software Workshop are available. Add-on packages of icons have hundreds of color icons for common PC tasks such as printing, scanning, faxing, etc. The packages also have icons that can be used with applications such as Lotus 1-2-3, WordPerfect, dBASE and others.

Desktop utilities

Several accessories and desktop utilities have been introduced to enhance Windows and in some cases correct omissions. The following is a brief list of some of the most interesting ones. This list is will never be complete because developers and entrepreneurs will come up with new ideas every week.

Desktop Expander Inner Media, for example, offers Desktop Expander, which allows up to nine workspaces to be set up. It works as if the monitor is a viewport onto a much larger desktop. The user can slide the desktop around underneath the viewport.

FirstApps Offered by hDC, FirstApps includes nine accessory-like applications that perform an array of functions that the company calls MicroApps. These MicroApps run under hDC's MicroApp engine. The company has made it an open architecture so anyone can develop compatible utilities. They would like to establish MicroApp Manager as the standard platform for Windows' pop-up utilities.

deskMinder Using the concept of a desktop metaphor in its most literal sense, TechSoft Inc. has developed deskMinder, a graphical front-end for the Windows' Program Manager.

As shown in FIG. 11-2, deskMinder uses an illustration of a desk as a motif. It includes desk drawers that contain folders, a help capability, a bookshelf that contains the user's applications, and all of the other functions found in Windows. The user selects a function or application by clicking it on with a mouse. The deskMinder was developed using Asmetrix's ToolBook.

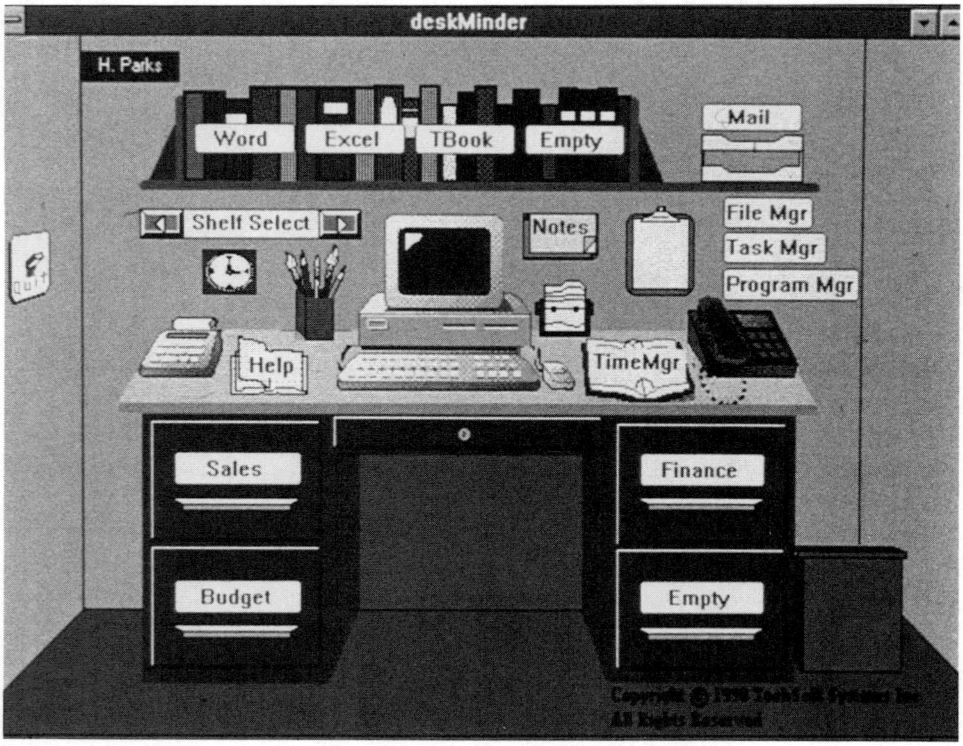

Fig. 11-2. The desktop manager deskMinder.

Application support

Windows has received a tremendous backing by the application development community. At its release, Microsoft claimed that there would be over 250 applications available by mid-year, and estimated that there would be over 1,500 applications by year-end, including Lotus 1-2-3, dBase IV, WordPerfect and Microsoft Word. The company has predicted that Windows will achieve a 25 percent to 30 percent market share in the next few years. All major application developers, including Lotus and WordPerfect, have versions of their software for Windows.

It is anticipated that many large-scale applications will move to Windows as an interim step, rather than to OS/2 or UNIX, both of which have large memory and disk requirements. The weakness of the current version of OS/2 and continual delays in delivery of version 2.0 have created a great deal of interest in Windows from application software developers.

Applications are the reason computers are sold, and computers are the reason operating systems are sold. Therefore, if a company has the world's best GUI but no applications, the GUI is not going to sell. The most popular applications on a PC are spreadsheets and word processing, and several examples of each type are now available for Windows. A report has been produced by Whitefox that lists Windows applications. Titled *The Windows Shopper's Guide*, it is a comprehensive directory of applications available for Windows.

Ami was the first WYSIWYG word processor program for Windows, introduced when only version 2.1 was available. The program was developed by Samna and considered very good, if a little slow. Recognizing the importance of the Windows environment and lacking a word processing program of their own, Lotus bought Samna. Other mergers, acquisitions and alliances will take place (such as DRI and Novell) as companies vie for market share in the Windows marketplace.

Multimedia

Multimedia has come to refer to the computer processing of audio, text, graphics, photographic images, and animation at VGA resolutions. Microsoft, IBM, Intel and other OEMs support an assortment of enabling tools, standards and specifications, and a marketing strategy for entry-level multimedia computing. This adds multimedia extensions to the Windows and OS/2 environment. These specifications are available to anyone for use on any operating system or computing platform.

A multimedia application program interface, called the Resource Interchange File Format (RIFF) has been developed. It enables audio, image, animation, and other media elements to be stored in a consistent format, regardless of platform. The multimedia specifications include data file formats common across OS/2 and Windows. The Media Control Interface (MCI) provides a consistent approach to controlling CD-ROMs, video playback units, and other such peripheral devices.

Microsoft also offers a multimedia development kit package, to be used in conjunction with a high-level authoring tool or C compiler, for creating multimedia titles and applications software for the Microsoft Windows multimedia environment. The kit consists of:

- Content and data preparation tools to assist in such tasks as audio and image manipulation.
- Software development tools, including link libraries, sample source code, and documentation.

Purposefully omitted from the current offerings, however, are advanced multimedia functions, such as full-motion video and image-data compression, although such extensions may be added later.

Development systems

Writing applications for operation under Windows is similar to any other GUI; it involves using a style guide. Microsoft's approach is that, while imposing a high degree of standardization in its Windows style guide, it also allows a substantial amount of leeway by the developer. A developer is able to control many of the visual appearances of an application by adjusting the size, location and appearance of dialog-boxes, color shading and the use of custom fonts. The Microsoft GUI also provides device-independent graphics, which means that an application doesn't have to know which input/output (I/O) device it's working with and can automatically take advantage of new I/O technology. Therefore, if a printer or display controller works with the GUI, it will work with any application that runs in Windows.

Although the concept was really established commercially by Apple with the Macintosh Quickdraw specification, Microsoft's GUI philosophy was boosted by the OSF's consideration of the Presentation Manager style guide for Motif (even though they later decided on DECwindows' X API). Microsoft's involvement in the UNIX GUI arena has been shared with Hewlett-Packard in the development of Presentation Manager for UNIX.

Although Presentation Manager for UNIX (or PM/X as it is commonly known) has been put on hold, when it is brought back to life it will coexist with the X Window System. While they were working on it, Microsoft claimed that PM/X had two key benefits over alternative UNIX GUI solutions: it would allow users familiar with Windows or Presentation Manager to work with UNIX systems running PM/X with minimal retraining, and it would allow developers to port applications more easily from OS/2 to UNIX.

An object-oriented, 4GL-like application development program called ToolBook is available from Asymetrix. It is designed for users or programmers who desire to create applications for Windows; however, it requires no programming experience to use. The program can be used to create Windows front ends for databases, user developed programs, prototypes and other specialized or niche applications. The program is a complete development system designed for power users and developers. It provides application by example, as well as a point-and-shoot environment.

When Open ToolBook, users can create Windows applications by simply creating and linking graphics and text fields. It has been described as being similar to a paint-and-draw program (in terms of ease of use). The user manipulates the software construction tools, the script recorder, buttons, graphical objects and text fields. While these actions are going on, ToolBook automatically records the actions and creates a script. It can then be played back anytime.

Languages

Object-oriented software companies are looking forward to the Windows environment for their products. Since languages like Smalltalk80 are graphic environments and interactive, the fit with Windows seems a natural. Windows could be the opportunity object-oriented software firms have been looking for. MS-DOS without Windows is well suited to procedural languages like BASIC, C and FORTRAN. However, there are no procedural languages for Windows, and object-oriented languages will have an open playing field with an advantage.

Macintosh-to-Windows

Microsoft is actively courting Macintosh developers to port their packages to Windows. Apple experienced significant problems in releasing the System 7.0 operating system for the Macintosh, which gave Microsoft additional opportunities. Later Apple brought out their low-cost machines to combat the popularity of Windows. Regardless of these events, Macintosh developers consider Windows as a relatively easy entry into the DOS world.

HyperCard, a toolbox that has given Macintosh users the ability to easily develop simple applications, has long been envied by PC users. Now, several HyperCard-like programs have been developed for Windows. One of the most popular is Asymetrix's ToolBook and Spinnaker's Plus. One of Plus' key advantages is the ability to run at least some of its applications on Macintosh, Windows, and OS/2 platforms, regardless of which environment the application was developed in.

Windows to the Macintosh

Microsoft also embraces the Macintosh with is Windows technologies. Some of the extensions to Windows included functions similar to the Interapplication Communications facilities of System 7.0, but function as an application programming interface (API) that rides on top of System 7.0. Why would Macintosh application developers use Microsoft's facilities rather than those built into System 7.0? There are two reasons: consistency across platforms, and Microsoft has a superior document linking facility (referred to as hot links).

Using Microsoft's APIs, developers are able to create universal applications that can use the same files as those on IBM PCs and compatibles, as well as write links with PC applications. Microsoft's hot links (Compound Document Protocol—CDPS, also known as the Embedded Compound Document Architecture—ECDA) automatically updates information in a linked document every time it is changed in the parent document. However, System 7.0's linking facilities are updated only when the new information is saved.

Others said they see little difference between the two approaches. Steward Alsop, editor of *InfoWorld*, has often said that Apple and Microsoft are both solving the same problems. Only Apple—in typical Apple fashion—is doing it in a way that users will understand. And Microsoft—in typical Microsoft fashion—is doing it in a way that developers and programmers will understand.

Impact on Macintosh

As mentioned here and in many other books and reports, Microsoft's release of Windows poses a real threat to Apple's dominance of the GUI user's mind and budget. Adding insult to injury, Microsoft is actively pursuing Macintosh developers. It could be an irresistible opportunity for Apple ISVs as an easier path to get into the huge PC market. There are a lot of really good programs available for the Macintosh. There are also a lot of PC users with Macintosh application envy, and this pent up demand will give instant market success to those ISVs. As good as this is for the Macintosh ISVs, it could spell big trouble for Apple. If Apple loses it hold on the GUI, as it certainly will, ISVs will make the Macintosh the second platform they develop for and therefore support. There is still the question about the level of consistency between Windows applications—especially between older updated programs and new ones that have been developed under 3.0.

Apple's market share is threatened, but it is a long way from being destroyed. Those companies who are large Macintosh users have too much invested to switch. And, of course, there will always be those die-hard Macintosh devotees who have a religious commitment to the Mac. Look for continuing comments like, "3.x is just an interface on top of DOS," and "Just because it looks pretty doesn't mean it is as functional as the Mac," etc., etc. Also, there is the issue of Windows needing to maintain compatibility with older character-based applications. That and the long-term experience Apple has with graphics support gives it more than just a fighting chance.

General comparisons

It should be pointed out, however, that Windows compares more closely to the Macintosh Finder than to the Macintosh System. Windows is a layer of code that sits between applications and DOS. The object-oriented Macintosh System has been designed around its GUI. Many consider that a major advantage over Microsoft's Windows.

Windows icons are primarily used to show what applications are available. The Macintosh uses icons primarily to indicate documents. Windows does not provide the same type of smoothness between functions as does the Macintosh. There is not a single cohesive desktop metaphor for tasks, applications, or files. This lack of consistent look and feel is why some Apple people have said that Microsoft cares the most about applications, while Apple cares most about users. Windows is still plagued by the idiosyncrasies of a system that was not designed with cohesive interface standards.

What Windows lacks

When Windows 3.0 was introduced, a comparison was made between the Macintosh System 6.0 and Windows 3.0 and a list of missing functions was generated by Macintosh users. Although both companies have introduced newer versions (7.0 for Macintosh and 3.1 for Windows) the comparisons are interesting nonetheless.

- In Setup and Installation, Windows does not: automatically do floppy disk formatting, insulate the user from command-line syntax, start up in graphical interface, or shut down from graphical interface.
- In System Configuration and Networking, Windows does not have: a complete network built-in, or an easy configuration of start-up disks and applications.
- Windows' Memory Management does not: provide compatibility with existing applications, support 24-bit linear addressing on all CPUs, provide a graphic display of memory available and in use by applications.

- Windows lacks Process Control features such as: user control of task (application) memory allocation, easy accessibility of tasks in system menu.
- The operating system is criticized because it does not have: a standard SCSI device manager, and a sound manager for digitized and synthesized sounds.
- Macintosh fans feel Windows Display Management lacks: true (nondithered) colors, photographic quality 32-bit color graphics, support for multiple video screens, and support for standard PICT graphic format.
- The User Shell is criticized for not having: consistent naming conventions for applications, files directories and file Servers; direct manipulation for file deleting, renaming and network directory access privileges; free-form arrangement of icons in any directory window; single, consistent mouse button, menu bar and system menus.

Windows can't operate applications by double-clicking. It only lists folders. The Macintosh can click and drag to load a program. Windows can't.

Other criticisms of Windows from developers and others is that the GDI does not have enough functionality. Some would like to see additional standardization added to Windows for multimedia applications. They would like support for DSP and sound functions. As these markets grow, Windows will be expanded to include such capabilities.

Windows does not have any support for 3D graphics. It is doubtful if it ever will. That will probably be left to third-party developers. Whether or not such programs can operate satisfactorily within the Windows metaphor remains to be seen.

Windows needs to give up more control of the graphics to the coprocessor for improved performance, something Microsoft improved with Windows 3.1. Microsoft plans to improve video memory management, reducing the adapter's need to make calls to system memory. The number of functions that cards can perform will also be increased.

Previously, general commentary focused on poor font display in Windows. However, Intellifont for Windows, a joint development effort between Hewlett-Packard and Agfa/Compugraphics, will be free for the asking, though it is intended primarily for use with HP's Laserjet III line of printers. Intellifont for Windows operates in the same manner as Bitstream's Facelift and Adobe Type Manager. It generates an Intellifont outline from a bit map for screen and printer rendering. All the scaling is done on the fly within Windows. True Type, the Apple/Microsoft effort will provide yet another technology for users (some say, with which users must contend).

Impact on workstations

With the introduction of Windows, some analysts predicted that the combination of a 386 or 486 DOS machine and Windows may impact the sales of some workstation products. There is no longer a clear price differential between high-end PCs and low-end workstations. As an example, Sun Microsystems offers the Sparcstation SLC at $5,000. All this makes the issue of PCs versus workstations unclear. The decision point will now move to the choice of operating systems (UNIX or DOS or OS/2) and GUI.

User group

Any popular application, computer operating system or technology usually has user groups formed around it. Windows is no different. The Windows & Presentation Manager (PMA) is a group targeted at organizations with 100 or more PCs running Windows. The organization is aimed at influencing Microsoft's development of the environment. One of the council's purposes is to encourage Microsoft's future developments of Dynamic Data Exchange and improvements to Windows File Manager. It has been compared to the Macintosh IS organization, which was formed to influence Apple's development of the Macintosh.

Improvements

The next generation of Windows will be a version of Windows for DOS that supports both the 16- and 32-bit Windows API. This release will add preemptive multitasking, multithreading, and sophisticated graphics-capabilities support with a truly object-oriented user shell. Despite reports to the contrary, Windows 3.1 does not require DOS 5.0. The update also provides greater PIF file control, such as the capability to specify a working directory and a much larger database of PIFs for third-party applications. It also includes Object Linking and Embedding (OLE) support.

Microsoft has identified four fundamental improvements that will be made in the near future, which have become known as the company's Vision:

1. Integrating information. The people at Microsoft call this change the new GUI. The implication is that making information part of the normal usage of a computer will have as big an impact on the industry as the adoption of the graphical interface.
2. Objects. A major change will be the organization of the operating system around objects instead of files. This will allow the user to focus on the relationships of the information in the system instead of the software. The benefits of object orientation are that it allows the user to eliminate the concept of files and to create a built-in way for users to program their computers without having to learn a programming language. This concept is already being implemented. The notion of a file represents an early attempt at relating a computer function with that of a real-world function—to file something away. Some people argue it is a computer concept and not a natural one. Microsoft's vision of object linking and embedding technology is also supported by several programs. The protocol, previously called the Compound Document Protocol Specification, was developed by Microsoft, Aldus Corp., Lotus Development Corp., and WordPerfect Corp. to link graphics, text, data tables, or spreadsheets embedded in a compound document to the programs that created them.
3. Seamless systems. Seamless computing. Microsoft's view includes the concepts of seamless systems to the PC Industry. Their model is a world of modeless computing where users choose functions without concern for applications, share data on transparent networks, and edit smart compound documents that know when they are changed.

4. Multimedia. Second only to GUI for the buzz-word of the decade. The logical intertwining of computer graphics, video, sound and ultimately cyberspace will be the goals of creative interface designers for years to come.

Chronology for Microsoft's "Vision"

In the development of the concept Information at your Fingertips, Microsoft has put forth a vision of coming events in the GUI/computer future.

1990

- May. Windows 3.0 ships.
- November. Microsoft's *Vision* is developed.

1991

- January. Pen Windows, SDK, OLE and multimedia extensions announced.
- Pen Windows, with name changed to PenApps, ships.
- OS/2 2.0 ships. Windows BASIC

1992

- April. Windows 3.1 ships.
- Native Windows support in OS/2 3.0.

1993

- Windows 4.0 (or Win32) ships.

1994

- OS/2 3.x ships.

With Microsoft's size, relationship with IBM, Intel and other giants, it is clearly well positioned to see future needs and dramatically influence them.

References

Cocula, John, W., and Mark Ryland. Battle of the DOS contenders. *Personal Workstation*. August, 1990. Page 34.

Gore, Andrew. The MAC vs. Windows 3.0. *Macintosh News*. June 18, 1990. Page 16.

Information At Your Fingertips. 1990. Redmond, WA: Microsoft Corporation.

Townsend, Carl. 1990. *The best book of Microsoft Windows 3.* Howard W. Sams & Company, Macmillan Computer Publishing: New York.

Temple, Barker, & Sloane, Inc. 1990. *The benefits of the graphical user interface*. Microsoft, Zenith Data Systems: Lexington, Mass.

12

OS/2 and Presentation Manager

When OS/2 was introduced in early 1987, it was positioned as the operating system of the future here today. Years later it still has not been accepted widely by the user community or widely supported by many application developers. As can be seen from the introduction of Windows in 1990, a significant shift has taken place in the marketing strategy of both IBM and Microsoft. OS/2 is now positioned as an operating system upgrade from Windows, not separate from it. OS/2 offers features such as multi-threaded operation, which Windows does not.

Chronology of OS/2

1987

- April 2. IBM and Microsoft announce OS/2, Version 1.0 (character mode) and Version 1.1 (including the Presentation Manager) and IBM's extended editions of each version. They also announce LAN Manager from Microsoft, and LAN Server from IBM.
- November. IBM ships OS/2, Version 1.0—four months early.

1988

- May. Micrografx and Aldus show the first two OS/2 Presentation Manager applications at spring Comdex.
- July. IBM ships OS/2, Version 1.0 Extended Edition.
- November. IBM and Microsoft ship OS/2 1.1—the Presentation Manager.

1989

- February. IBM and Microsoft announce Version 2.0, due in 1990.
- December. Microsoft ships initial release of OS/2 2.0 Software Developer's Kit.

1990

- March. IBM ships Version 1.2 Extended Edition, including
  a. High Performance File System.
  b. Desktop Manager.
  c. Postscript for Epson, PCL-4.
  d. Dual boot.
  e. 3-D Presentation Manager
  At the same time, IBM quietly turns nearly all of its Presentation Manager work over to Microsoft.
- April. Bugs in Microsoft's OS/2 1.2 delay LAN Manager 2.0 until at least June.
- June. OEMs begin shipping OS/2 1.21, including
  a. Improved spooler.
  b. New printer driver installer.
  c. Updated printer drivers.
- July. Microsoft ships improved SDK for OS/2 2.0.
- August. Microsoft ships LAN Manager 2.0.
- November. IBM releases OS/2 Lite. Microsoft drops its effort to port Presentation Manager's programming interface over to UNIX.

1991

- Microsoft and IBM dissolve their marketing relationship.
- IBM releases OS/2 2.0. Microsoft pushes Windows.

1992

- IBM adds multiprocessing OS/2.
- IBM releases a portable OS/2 for its RISC workstations—the RS/6000 family.

General concepts

OS/2 was designed to be a cornerstone for future growth. It was developed for 286/386/486 and above processors to remove the 640 Kbyte memory limitation of DOS. One of the characteristics of DOS is the way programs had to be organized into 64 Kbyte segments. This caused the 640 Kbyte limitation due to the smaller RAM addressing size. OS/2 1.x overcame that with flat addressing, in protected mode, for 16-bits, and OS/2 2.X expands the addressing range to 32-bits.

OS/2 was designed to operate in protected mode and exploit the capabilities of the processor by providing program isolation and the concept of sessions or logical consoles. OS/2 provides many services, including task and memory management, interprocess communications, as well as timer and I/O services. All of the services of the operating system are available through Application Programming Interfaces (APIs). API calls are handled by special device drivers so programs do not have to be concerned with the type of peripheral attached.

However, Presentation Manager, unlike the X Window System (which uses asynchronous event queuing) works synchronously, so that a return call must follow a single input before another process can be started up. Therefore, OS/2 must start a task and finish it before going on to the next. There is no provision for input (commands) to be picked up and queued (although they can be buffered).

User interface

OS/2 can look like a conventional DOS screen, a native OS/2 environment or a GUI through the Presentation Manager (PM). It can run most DOS applications in its DOS Mode session, but only one at a time. The Presentation Manager is an interface shell that provides graphical services and a GUI consistent with IBM's Common User Access (CUA) guidelines. The CUA is part of IBM's System Application Architecture (SAA). It is based on the premise that applications with a common appearance and consistent behavior will enable users to be productive and to use their PCs for more applications.

Presentation Manager

Presentation Manager is the GUI for OS/2. When OS/2 is started, the Start Programs window comes up first. This window looks like all Presentation Manager windows and has a title bar, system icons, min/max icons, an action bar and sizable borders. IBM refers to the working space of a window as the *Client area*. The Client area should be thought of as the application's workspace, where most of the display of data takes place.

The Start Programs window has menu selection for additional actions. Each item selected causes a more detailed menu to appear. When one of these items is selected, it causes a dialog-box to be displayed. A dialog-box is a special type of window. Dialog-boxes have several *buttons* that are used to provide choices for the user. Some of the buttons available are:

- Checkbox: used to monitor the state of user selections.
- Radio buttons: selection buttons from which only one choice at a time can be selected.
- Push buttons: cause the application to take immediate action.

Another type of control is the List Box. If an application has a set of selectable items that are too large to fit into the Client area, a List Box may be used to show some of the items. The List Box is scrollable.

NeXTstep

In addition to its existing features, IBM has licensed NeXTstep technology from NeXT, Inc. It has been suggested in the press that IBM will incorporate features from NeXTstep into version 2.0 of Presentation Manager.

New strategy

As an additional indication of the change in strategy. Steve Ballmer of Microsoft has noted that IBM definitely underestimated the difficulty in spurring the migration from DOS to OS/2. Peter Neupert, Senior General Manager for OS/2 at Microsoft has stated that Microsoft's goal is to make OS/2 into Windows Plus. He also clearly positioned OS/2 against UNIX, saying that its success will be not where DOS is a viable solution, but against terminals with multiuser systems. By defining OS/2 as a multiuser operating system and as a superset of Windows, Microsoft has conceded a major part of the operating system market to Windows, which it had previously portrayed as nothing more than a stepping stone to OS/2. This is especially true if Windows is teamed with multitasking DOS 5.0. The future OS/2 will allow Windows to be more integrated with it, as shown in FIG. 12-1.

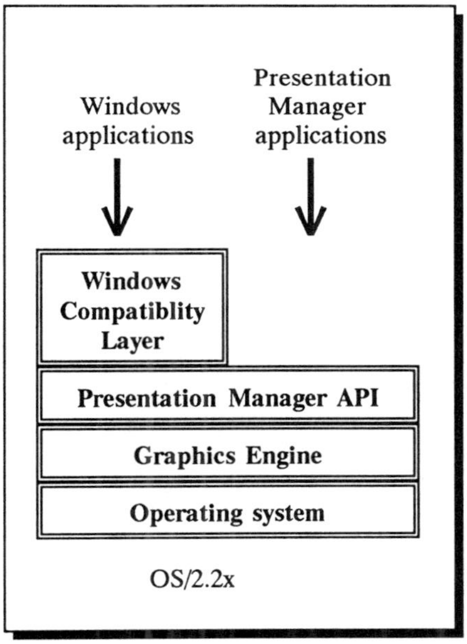

Fig. 12-1. Future of OS/2.

Version 1.2x, of OS/2, is crippled by a lack of device drivers, particularly for printers. Version 1.2x also has weak support for DOS applications, an area that is addressed by version 2.0. However, since its announcement, OS/2 has experienced significant delivery delays. Version 2.0, the 32-bit version for 80386 and 80486 computers, was not delivered until the first half of 1992. This is the version most developers and users were awaiting. This slip in delivery from the promised late 1990 date provided substantial opportunity for Windows to take the lead. One of the problems with introducing the 32-bit version is maintaining compatibility with older 64 Kbyte segmented versions of software written for DOS, Windows and OS/2 1.x. It is not an impossible feat, but it does take some careful planning to accept the older programs while still offering the advanced features of 2.0.

Version 2.0 is a full 32-bit version. It is faster and capable of running multiple virtual DOS sessions. It has additional features such as remote systems administration, which allows a central source to manage networks of OS/2 desktops. Network managers can install printer drivers and other applications remotely.

The DOS compatibility box has also been enhanced with version 2.0. In OS/2 2.0, users are able to run 16 DOS applications simultaneously, with 610K of RAM available per application. (Previously, users could only run one DOS application in the compatibility box.) Version 2.0 contains a clipboard that allows cut-and-paste between DOS applications, or between a DOS application and a Presentation Manager application. TrueType, the scalable outline fonts derived from an agreement between Apple and Microsoft, are also included in OS/2 2.0.

The role of Windows to OS/2

Steve Ballmer, senior VP for systems software at Microsoft used to believe that Windows [3.0] would demonstrate the power of graphics and would be a practical introduction for users to the potential benefits of OS/2. The question in the user community is whether the features are worth the investment and overhead in disk size, RAM memory and computer MIPS. The answer is no. Industry analysts do not expect any measurable migration to OS/2 until 1993. This timetable is underscored by the fact that there were more Windows-specific applications shipping on the day of its announcement than there are total OS/2-specific applications available today.

Windows-to-OS/2 kit

As a reflection of the change in strategy, Microsoft has the Windows-to-OS/2 Software Migration Kit (SMK), which allows current Windows applications to be ported to OS/2 by recompiling them with the Dynamic Link Libraries (DLL) supplied with the SMK. The kit, intended for use by software developers and not end users, maps Windows API calls to Presentation Manager calls, so programs can run with only minor modifications. While the SMK does not automatically take advantage of the additional functionality provided by OS/2, it does allow an easy migration from Windows to OS/2 Presentation Manager.

Some observers believe that the availability of this kit may discourage developers from creating OS/2 specific programs, although it will allow developers to easily port existing Microsoft Windows applications to OS/2 Presentation Manager. The availability of the SMK may result in turning Presentation Manager into a slower, more expensive way to run Windows applications.

Differences between Windows and OS/2

OS/2 offers sophisticated functionality that Windows does not. It utilizes a preemptive multitasking scheme, as opposed to the cooperative multitasking that Windows uses. Also, it offers true 32-bit operation on 386 and 486 computers. This feature will only become apparent in applications that have extreme data processing and number crunching requirements. The High Performance File System (HPFS) offers faster file access and longer file names, up to 32 characters, than the File Allocation Table (FAT) scheme used by DOS. Again, this performance will not affect the great bulk of PC users. Typically, it will affect only those who require extensive database searches or similar applications. OS/2 2.0 is also supposed to include an installation program that will convert DOS File Allocation Tables (FAT) hard disk partitions to HPFS partitions during installations. The gap between the look and feel of Presentation Manager and Windows has been significantly reduced with the introduction of Windows 3.0. Windows incorporates the icons and 3D look of the Presentation Manager interface.

Application support

Microsoft has committed to providing binary compatibility between Windows and OS/2 applications, but has hedged on when this will occur. Until this time, they have released the SMK to convert Windows applications to OS/2. However a third party software company, Asymetrix, has a software development tool named Author's Resource Kit (ARK) for both Windows and OS/2. They both have the same functionality, and their application files are compatible.

Presentation Manager under OS/2 2.x will eventually run Windows applications with no modifications through a binary compatibility layer (BCL) that maps Windows APIs onto Presentation Manager APIs. The Windows compatibility layer (sometimes referred to as the *Port-hole*) is a set of Dynamic Link Libraries (DLL). The problem is that anytime an extra layer of software is added, it has an impact on the application's performance. In the case of the Port-hole, Windows graphics functions must be translated (in real-time since the applications have not been recompiled) into Presentation Manager graphics functions, and then submitted to the display controller card in the system. The net result will be a certain sluggishness. The next version of OS/2, 3.x, will run Presentation Manager or Windows applications interoperably, and will not require that Windows applications use Presentation Manager. Instead of being a layer, Windows will be side-by-side. (See FIG. 12-1.)

GUI toolkit

IBM licensed EASEL, from Easel Corp., and acquired a minority equity interest in the company in order to provide developers with a toolkit for OS/2 applications. The GUI toolkit encompasses a development system, communications modules, applications templates and other components for developers. EASEL is also used to add GUI front ends on mainframe programs that use 3270s and 5250s.

Impact of Windows

Windows might be the key to greater availability of OS/2 applications. When Microsoft implements full binary compatibility with Windows applications, the OS/2 world will see an automatic increase in the number of applications that support the environment. IBM's position is that they have been a supporter of GUI for DOS from the start, but it is not a replacement for an advanced operating system like OS/2.

Improvements

After Windows was introduced, Microsoft made available a new software structure designated the Layered Device Driver (LADDR), which gives disk-drive vendors a standard way to write OS/2 device drivers. Primarily aimed at providing a standard way for writing Small Computer Systems Interface (SCSI) device drivers, it should boost the market for standard SCSI drives. However, LADDR can be used for ESDI, Macintosh or ISA devices as well. This reduces the amount of code developers have to write, which reduces the lead time for new applications and devices.

Multiuser OS/2

Citrix Corporation (Coral Springs, Fla.) has developed a multiuser version of OS/2 that could provide an alternative to UNIX. Microsoft has licensed the OS/2 source code to Citrix and is reported to be uninterested in multiuser OS/2. IBM has said it intends to provide full multiuser capabilities in OS/2. IBM is likely to license it from Citrix if the company does not come out with its own multiuser version.

OS/2 Lite

Both IBM and Microsoft are committed to developing a 16-bit version of OS/2 that fits into 2 Mbytes of memory (hence the nickname, Lite). However, it is not known when, if ever, Microsoft will release it. Late in 1990 IBM brought out its version, and named it OS/2 1.3. Some users criticized IBM for diverting resources away from the development of the more powerful 32-bit version 2.0 in order to bring out 1.3. Others suspect IBM did it to fulfill a promise to PS/2 customers that OS/2 would run on '286 platforms. Indeed, IBM has targeted the large installed base of '286 computers for OS/2. Still others see it as a competitive attack on Windows.

It's still not clear if OS/2 Lite is intended to be IBM's answer to Windows 3.0 and an entry-level path to OS/2 1.2x (or 2.0) or if it is supposed to be between Windows and OS/2 1.2x. It is called OS/2 Standard Edition 1.X (for 286 machines), incorporates Adobe Type Manager and runs in 2 MB. It also, according to Lee Reiswig (IBM's director of software strategy) runs applications 5 to 10 percent faster. Others say applications run 25 to 30 percent faster. So far, only Lotus 1-2-3/G and WP 5.1 third-party programs run with 1.X. This latest version was achieved in part by tightening the code and improving the memory management. OS/2 1.3 has demonstrably better performance than 1.2x, better file management, and uses less memory.

In an effort to overcome some of the confusion about the positions of Microsoft's Windows, OS/2 Lite and OS/2 2.x IBM and Microsoft signed an agreement in late 1990 that resulted in both sides compromising a little. Both companies now cross license all OS/2, MS-DOS and Windows products. Previously, IBM had not licensed Windows. Microsoft got IBM's smaller version of OS/2 in the deal.

As a member of the SAA platform family, OS/2 1.3 and above supports Adobe Type Manager. This software generates consistent type fonts across printers and display devices. The type will look the same on a display as it does when printed.

OS/2 3.x

Presentation Manager for UNIX, called PM/X, was described as a joint effort between Microsoft and Hewlett-Packard at a 1988 Comdex announcement. The first phase of the project, porting Presentation Manager's look and feel to UNIX, was completed and is embodied in the Open Software Foundation's (OSF) Motif user interface for its OSF/1 UNIX standard. However, OSF chose Digital Equipment Corp.'s DECwindows API on X-window over Presentation Manager's on native UNIX. In November, 1990, Microsoft dropped its effort to port Presentation Manager's programming interface over to UNIX.

Although Presentation Manager for UNIX, or PM/X, as it is commonly known, has been put on hold, when it is brought back to life it will coexist with the X Window System. While they were working on it, Microsoft claimed PM/X had two key benefits over alternative UNIX GUI solutions: it would allow users familiar with Windows or Presentation Manager to work with UNIX systems running PM/X with minimal retraining, and it would allow developers to port applications more easily from OS/2 to UNIX. The work on that project was carried over to making Windows portable to "Portable" OS/2. Portable OS/2 was renamed Version 3.X, and runs the Windows application programming interface (API) alongside Presentation Manager's. Shipments began in December, 1990.

Other

Unisys has enhanced its CTOS operating system and has adopted Presentation Manager as the standard GUI for all forthcoming CTOS applications. The significance of this is that CTOS is the third largest installed operating system (after DOS and the Macintosh), with over 740,000 systems worldwide. Also, CTOS is the first, and for now the only, non-OS/2 operating system to support the Presentation Manager user interface. CTOS is based on the Client-Server model and was developed by Convergent Technologies before Unisys acquired the company. CTOS also supports the POSIX standard.

The future of OS/2 and Windows

Microsoft has developed a new operating system structure that brings together Windows, OS/2, DOS and other operating systems such as POSIX. This new structure is known as NT (for new technology) and has also been called OS/2 3.0. In building this future operating system, Microsoft will be able to integrate its disparate efforts in OS/2 and Windows into a single 32-bit operating system.

OS/2 3.0 is a radically new product. It has a lot of new code, based on the development work of David Cutler, who also designed the VMS operating system for Digital Equipment Corp. However, Microsoft didn't start completely from scratch. It used a great deal of the code it had developed for OS/2. Fundamentally, what Microsoft did was take all the code they had developed for OS/2 and Windows 3.0, merged the two, got rid of the 16-bit code and changed all the names.

OS/2 3.0 employs an architecture that features a *micro kernel,* an operating system stripped down to its essential functions that relies on application programming interfaces (APIs) for various services. On top of the OS/2 3.0 micro kernel, known simply as NT, will sit the Windows-32 API (as well as an API for Windows-16), a DOS API, an OS/2 API that will allow for backward compatibility to applications already written for previous versions of OS/2, and a Posix API for federal government users. (Refer to FIG. 12-2.) However, by not providing binary compatibility between the APIs, unless developers want to run parallel development efforts, Microsoft forces the software community to develop for Windows first and then go to OS/2 if they so desire. The reverse migration is not supported. In 1991 the ACE consortium adapted NT.

DOS API	Windows API	OS/2 API	POSIX API
NT Kernel			

Fig. 12-2. Microsoft's new technology.

Microsoft had been calling this future system Portable OS/2. Inside Microsoft, it is known as NT, and with it the company promises that future Windows systems will run on any computer hardware. With NT, Microsoft plans to eliminate the barriers between Windows, OS/2 and UNIX applications, and to build a bridge from the Intel-based PC world to alternative hardware platforms like RISC. The company has pledged that new software will allow users for the first time to load and run these diverse applications concurrently in one PC or server.

NT has been selected as the basis for the multiplatform operating system of the Advanced Computing Environment, ACE, consortium.

UNIX Microsoft is pushing up into the UNIX world with a pledge that the new system will embrace Posix applications, giving the company a foot in the door of the open systems and government markets. The new operating system will challenge mainstream UNIX with built-in features that are just emerging in System V.4 and OSF-1, such as support for distributed computing, fault tolerance, symmetrical multiprocessing and security. Bill Gates, Chairman of Microsoft has often said that Windows has had a radical effect on every piece of software they're writing. The goal is to have a very strong platform to allow people to write distributed systems.

DOS Many of OS/2's 32-bit capabilities, such as preemptive multitasking, will be applied under DOS directly. In addition, changes will be made to DOS' Interrupt 21 calls (these are DOS calls that manage file operations) to support multiple execution threads, as well as to add direct support for named pipes and mail slots.

Windows Microsoft will introduce a 32-bit version of Windows, Win32, that may obviate the need for OS/2 for many users. Win32 is new code that enables Windows to process 32 bits of data at once, rather than 16 bits. A key issue in Win32 (which may turn out to be Windows 4.0) is compatibility with Windows 3.x applications. The company plans to make certain that 3.x applications are supported, although OS/2 Presentation Manager applications may not be. Support for a 32-bit applications programming interface (API) for Windows is also expected.

Additions will include improved graphics support in Windows' Graphics Device

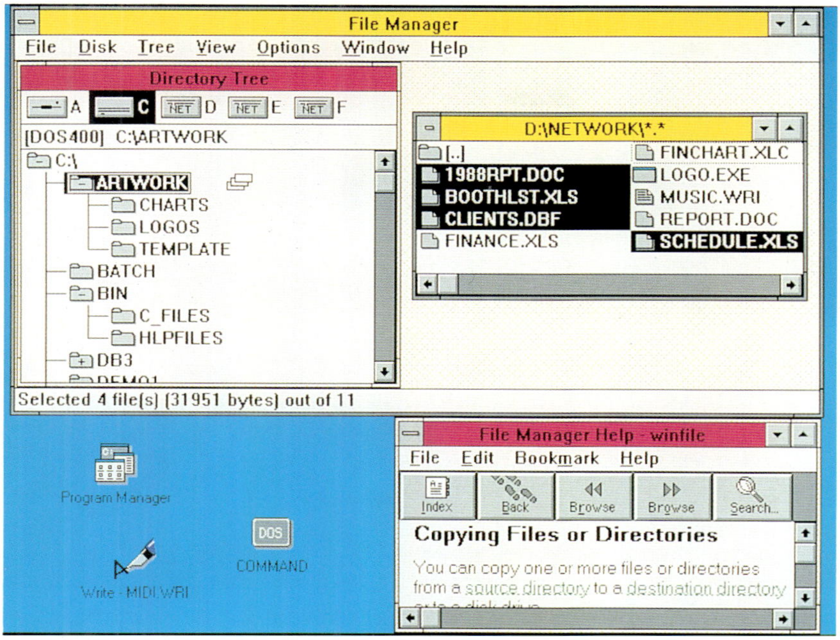

Microsoft Corp.

This illustrates the file manager in Microsoft Windows and its associated functions.

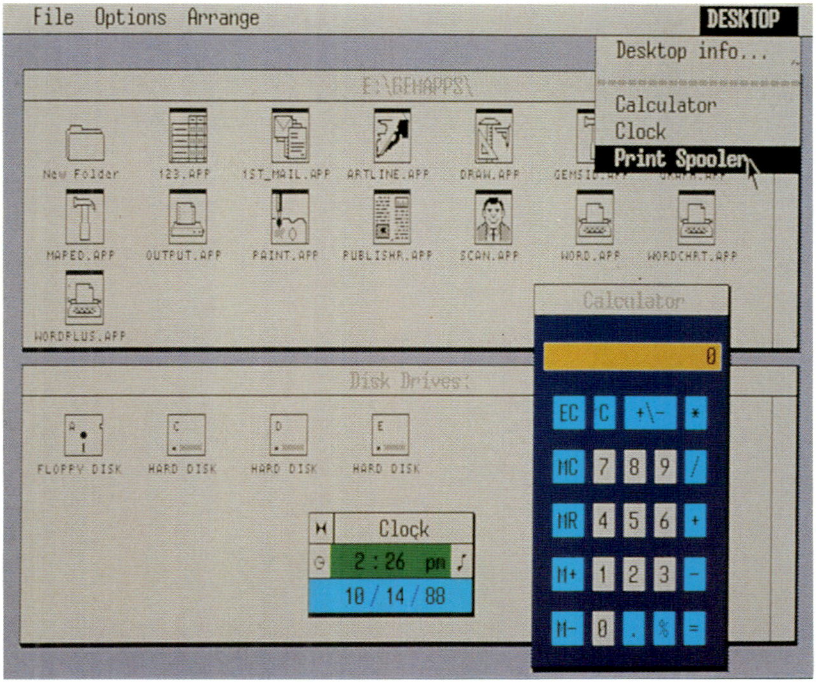

Digital Research Corp.

The initial screen for a GEM Desktop GUI.

IXI Ltd.

X.desktop 3's (Motif-based) Icon Editor can be used for producing multicolored icons.

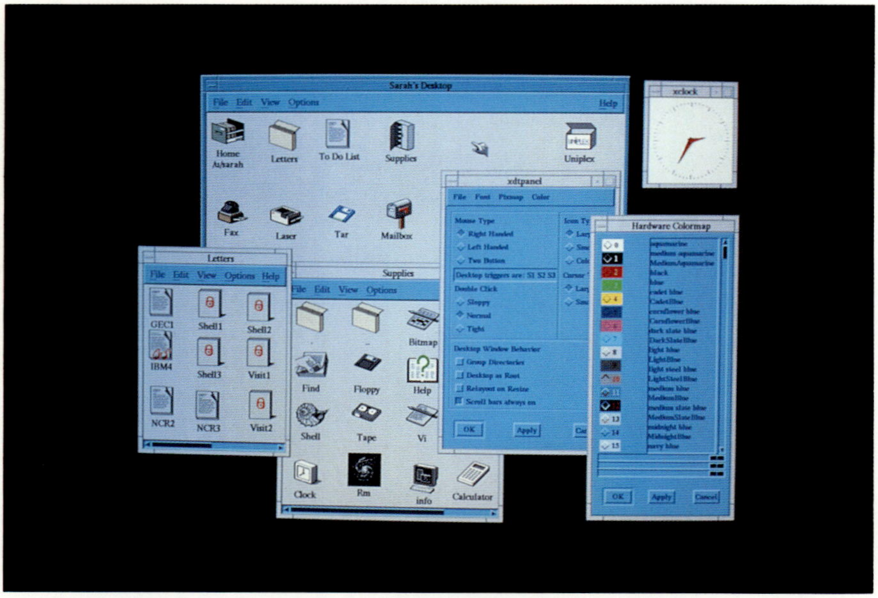

IXI Ltd.

The Interactive User Control Panel of X.desktop allows users to modify colors, icon size, fonts and mouse button mapping in Motif.

Hewlett-Packard Corp.

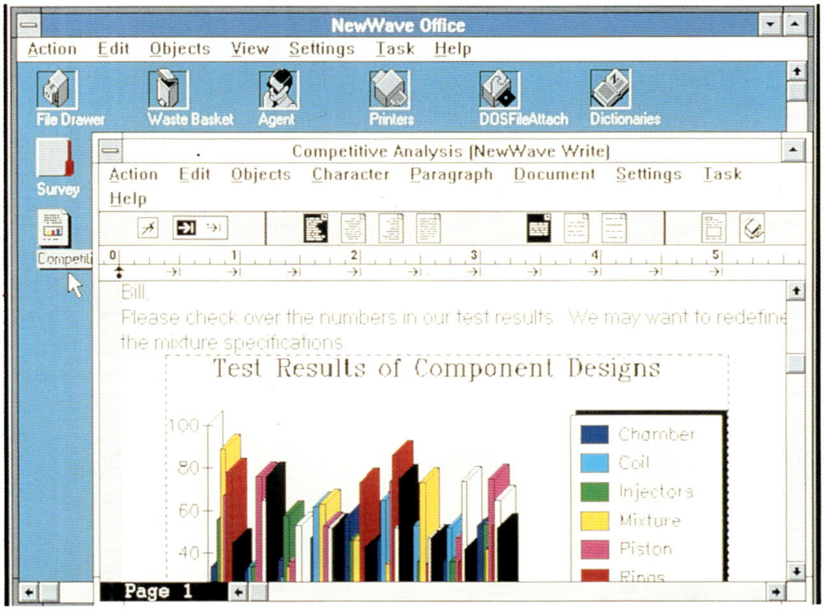

The NewWave Office Initial Screen, an application (NewWave Right) and a file (competitive analysis). Notice the 3-D shading of the icons along the top row.

Sun Microsystems

Multiple windows of OpenWindows and its use of Postscript fonts (icons in the lower left-hand corner).

Global View on a SPARC Workstation. Note the yellow highlighting of the text on the screen, and the colored icons in the background.

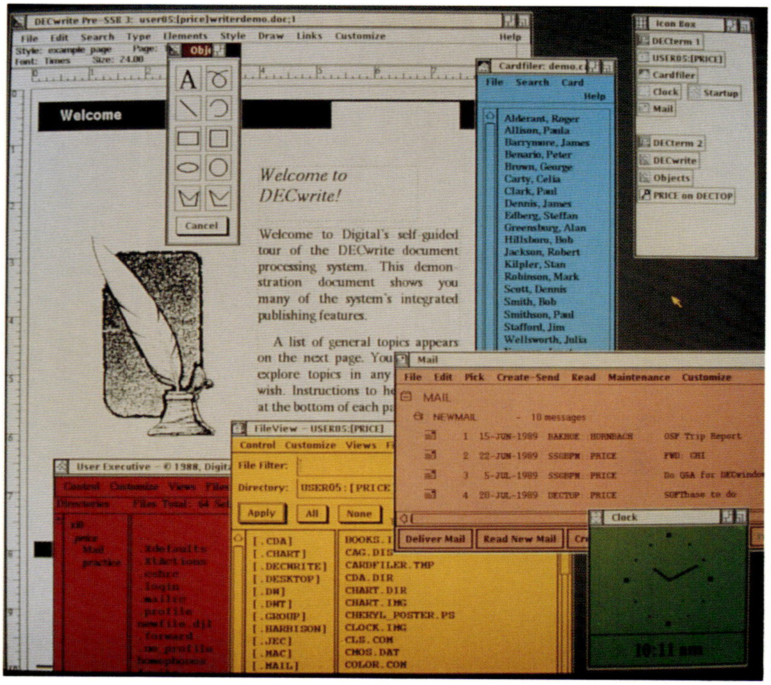

The initial workspace for DEC Windows.

Digital Equipment Corp.

IBM

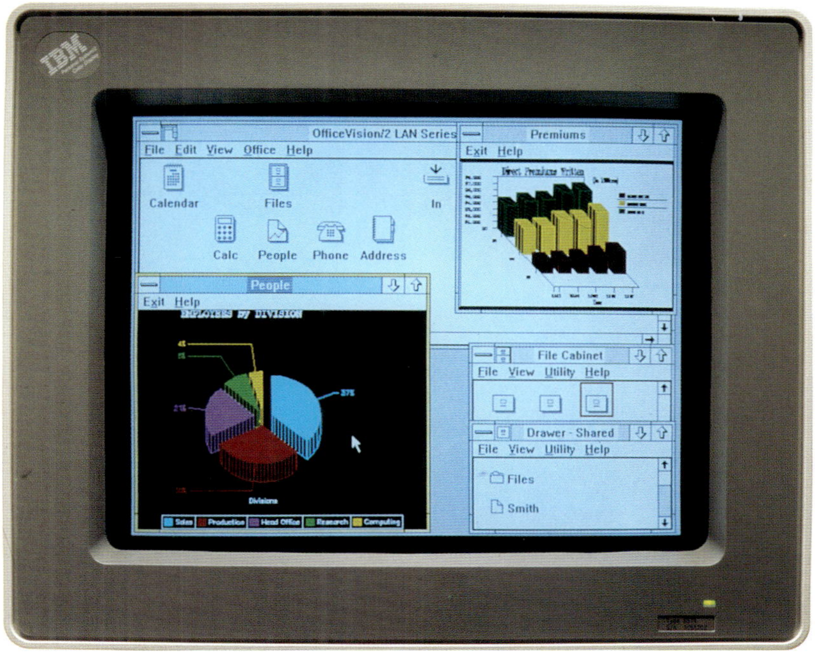

IBM's OfficeVision, an SAA/CUA compatible GUI-based application.

Digital Equipment Corp.

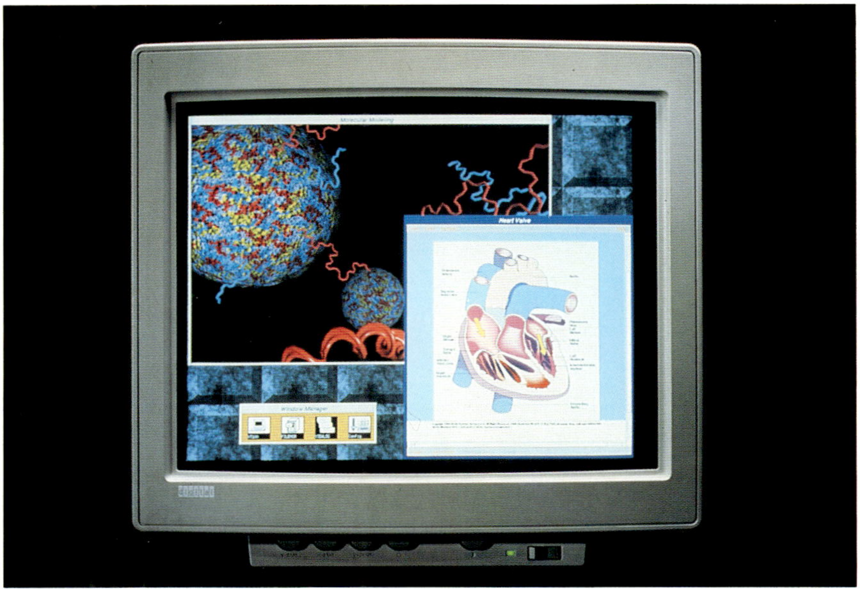

The color image capability of a Digital workstation using DEC Windows is an attractive feature of a GUI.

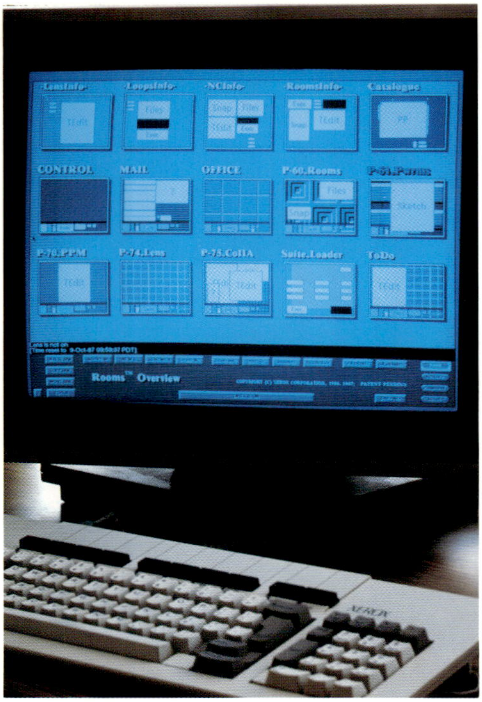

A Xerox Rooms overview screen. Each subwindow represents a room that a user can move in and out of.

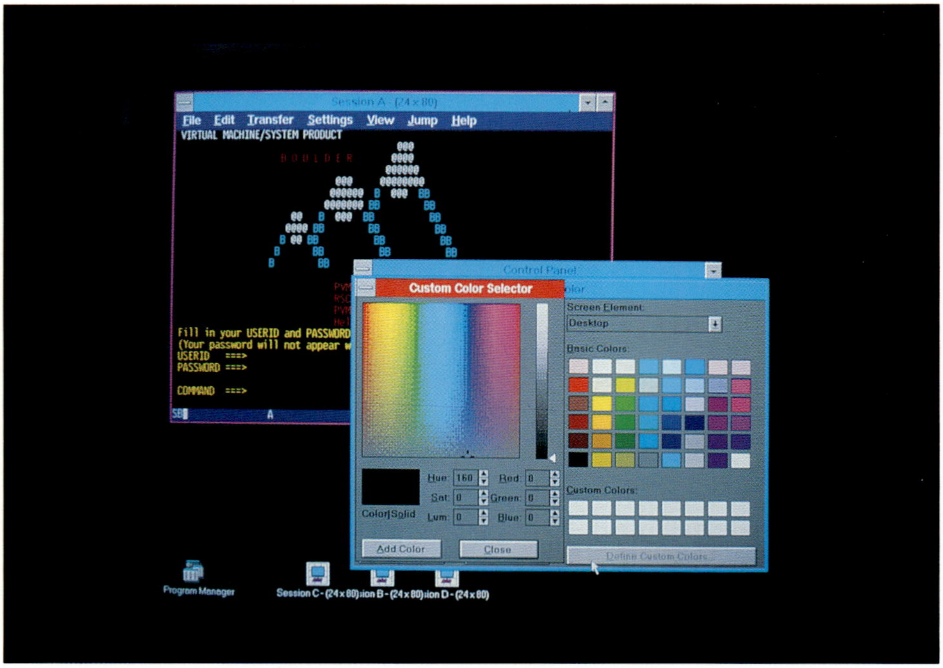

IBM

A Windows connection with SAA. Notice the session connection and screen resolution icons at the bottom of the screen.

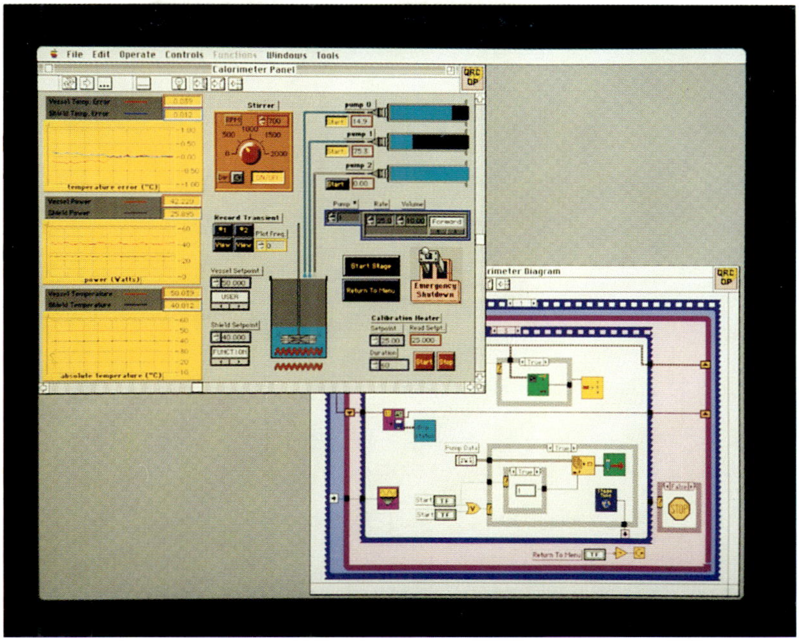

Industrial GUIs provide real-time display and event warning, and they bring flexibility.

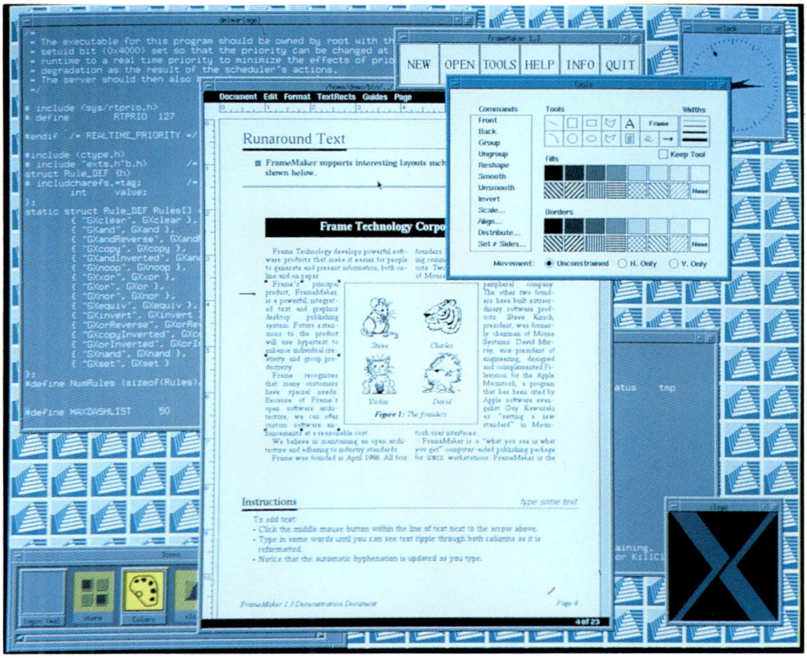

PCs can effectively be used as X Window Systems servers.

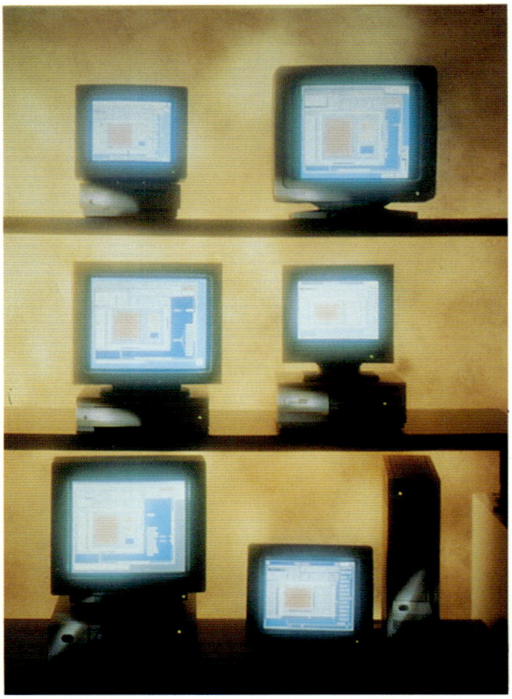

Nuron Data

Developing GUIs across multiple platforms has been a nightmare. Toolkits have been developed that make it easier.

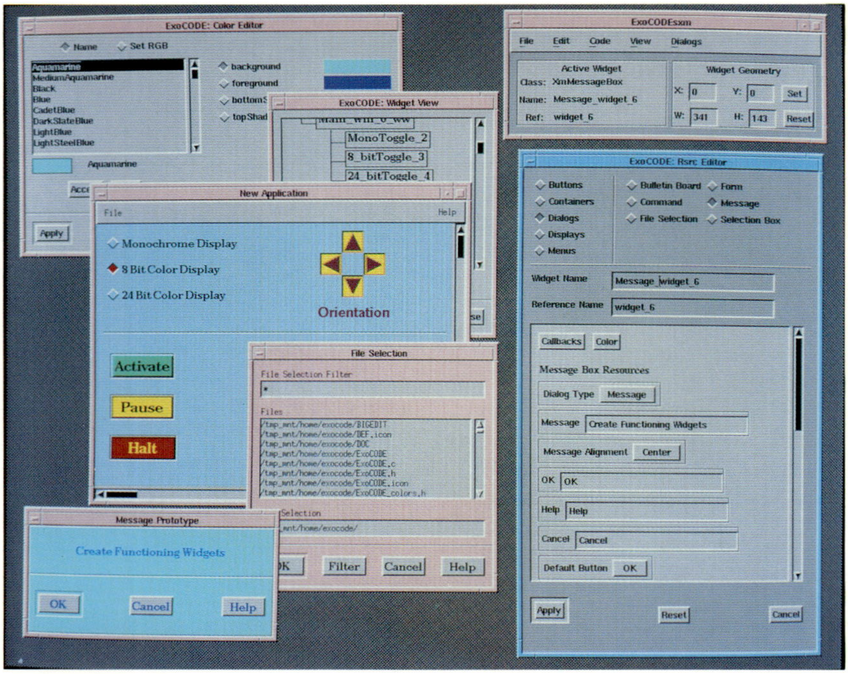

Expert Objects Corp.

Users can create Motif compliant X Window System compatible GUIs with high-level toolkits.

Interface (GDI) calls. These new functions will include Bezier curves, a transform layer to support rotation and shearing, grouping of graphics primitives for fills and other effects, and support for dithered fills. Other GDI additions under consideration include support for fractional character widths, halftones, VGA palettes, device-independent color, and rich text edit control.

The future of OS/2 and Presentation Manager Whatever happened to the total migration from DOS to OS/2, which Microsoft predicted two years ago? That migration has not materialized as IBM has hoped it would. DOS has proven to be too popular to abandon. With the path to 32-bits via NT and more than 50 million systems in use, practicality will make DOS a viable operating system for years.

Also, Microsoft never fully supported OS/2, but agreed to develop it as a concession to IBM. Now that Windows has caught on, Microsoft wants Windows applications to work with any future replacement for DOS. It may be that Presentation Manager is the big loser here, not necessarily OS/2.

However, the users who want to standardize on a Microsoft desktop can't wait until Windows has better host connectivity, as well as support for the Intel 80486 and other high-end platforms. Hence, Microsoft plans for a 32-bit Windows and a rebuilt portable platform built around the Windows interface. If that means eclipsing, absorbing or replacing OS/2 and Presentation Manager, then Microsoft will do it.

Furthermore, IBM has millions of dollars and a lot of end-user faith invested in the survival of OS/2's Presentation Manager interface. It functions as a unifying thread in Officevision and AIX, and Open Software Foundation/Motif look and feel was modeled after Presentation Manager.

OS/2 is an important platform for IBM because it is the front end for two of its most strategic initiatives: Systems Application Architecture (SAA) and Application Development/Cycle (AD/Cycle). AD/Cycle needs the functionality of OS/2, and that's not available on a graphical DOS. Nonetheless, IBM had to add a Windows client for all those would-be Officevision users who complained about the need for 8 Mbytes of OS/2 Extended Edition on every desktop.

However, even IBM admits that Presentation Manager has far to go to challenge Windows. The real issue with Presentation Manager is when it will generate a sufficient user base for software developers to make the investment in it. Nonetheless, new applications continue to come out, and volumes will follow. A significant number of companies, including Microsoft, have written code to the Presentation Manager application programming interface (API). It is reasonable to expect IBM to pledge continued evolution of its interface, no matter what Microsoft does.

OS/2 is important to users who need access to host graphics. Mainframes are not going to go away, no matter how much companies downsize in other areas. Therefore, the only way Microsoft's vision can succeed is if API changes are evolutionary, not revolutionary.

References

Cheatham, Paul, David Reich and Robert Robinson. Presentation Manager architecture. *IBM Personal Systems Developer*. February, 1989. Page 33.

13

Other PC-related window systems

Microsoft did not invent window systems, nor did the company introduce the first window system for a PC. However, Microsoft is clearly the largest company producing window systems, and it has the support of IBM (albeit, reluctantly), the largest computer company in the world. It's difficult to fight that much power. However, there are several specialized situations that cannot be satisfied by Microsoft's Windows. This chapter will list some of those window systems from other companies.

DR DOS 5.0

Digital Research has been providing an MS-DOS-compatible O/S since 1988 and boasts 35 million licenses worldwide. The company offers DR DOS 5.0, which has a graphics shell, memory management, disk caching and various other features.

The O/S comes with ViewMAX, a GUI that allows the disk layout to be viewed as icons, text or a graphical tree. It has point-and-shoot execution of programs and can be used with a mouse and/or a keyboard. The O/S has some special features such as BatteryMAX and FileLINK. BatteryMAX monitors the hardware (up to 20 times a second) and switches the hardware into low-power operation (if available). FileLINK transfers files via a serial link from one machine to another, and can install itself on the other machine even if it does not have DR DOS installed. These features are targeted at laptops and portables.

GEM

In 1984 Digital Research (DRI) became aware of a growing graphics market. The company sensed a need to provide an ease-of-use solution to people working, then, on 8086-based machines. As a result, Digital Research developed the Graphic Environment Manager (GEM) and introduced it in 1985. The GEM Desktop was provided with an attached GEM library to allow ISVs to develop graphical applications that would run under Digital Research's graphical front-end.

GEM is not a GUI, but a method whereby an application needing to use graphical features can do so, whereas MS Windows is a user interface—a difference strongly enforced by the company. While being widely perceived as a GUI, GEM is actually a library of software routines. Therefore, the GEM Desktop, which most users consider to be GEM, is simply a program based on the routines contained in the GEM library. You can't buy *GEM* (as you can Windows) and run it on a computer. However, you can buy GEM applications like Ventura. Therefore, Digital Research has never seen GEM as the GUI, but as the vehicle by which developers can use GUI features in an appropriate manner.

The routines that make up GEM are divided into two main groups: those making up the AES (application environment services) and those making up the VDI (virtual device interface). AES routines provide the programmer with a set of templates for use in developing graphic applications. VDI routines provide a standardized interface between the program and the graphics devices, screen, printer, or plotter, which the program is to drive. So programs can work with any kind of device without having to be rewritten, recompiled or otherwise modified.

GEM is a single-tasking bit-mapped environment that had the look and feel of the Macintosh, and therein lies the tale. Apple threatened to sue DRI for infringing on its copyrights. As a result, DRI agreed to remove certain features from its GUI libraries. Therefore, GEM does not have a trash can icon and does not allow the user to resize or destroy the two nonoverlapping windows of the GEM desktop. In 1990, DRI dropped the GEM name from its product line and is now concentrating on drawing packages.

Geoworks

This company first offered a GUI for the Commodore 64 and Apple II computers. It has also brought out the PC/GEOS (Graphic Environment Operating System), a multitasking GUI-based windowing environment that runs on top of DOS. Designed for XT-class computers, it is able to run with as little as 512 Kbytes of RAM and a CGA or Hercules screen. This graphics environment is targeted at all the users and machines left out of Windows or OS/2. Written entirely in machine code, it is a fast, compact (54 Kbytes) kernel. GEOS supports objects, bit-mapped and outline fonts, device-independent graphics, multitasking, multiple threads of execution in a single process and arbitrarily shaped windows. The ensemble is supplied with a suite of applications (a word processor, communications, flat-file database manager, drawing package and appliances) that use the OSF/Motif user interface. Also, a CUA/PM look is available.

Description

GEOS supports true preemptive multitasking, including: multiple threads of execution within a single process; dynamic memory management; event-driven programming; nested, overlapped, and arbitrarily-shaped windows; device-independent graphics; bit-mapped and outline fonts; and object-oriented programming. Three user interface libraries have been developed for PC/GEOS: Motif, Open Look, and CUA/Presentation Manager.

Much of the compactness and flexibility of the PC/GEOS system is the result of GeoWorks' Object Assembly system. The Assembler for PC/GEOS is a superset of the Microsoft Assembly format with Pseudo Ops for supporting class definitions. The assembler is designed to work with the object messaging system built into the operating system kernel. This approach combines the structural benefits of object-oriented programming: data and code encapsulation, inheritance, reusability, etc. with the efficiency of having object methods (the procedures that act on messages sent to an object) coded in assembly language.

PC/GEOS supports true preemptive multitasking, including: multiple threads of execution within a single process; a robust single imaging model complete with outline fonts, splines, polygons, etc. (comparable to PostScript and OS/2 GPI); dynamic memory management; and a windowing system that supports nested, overlapped, arbitrarily-shaped windows. While PC/GEOS has its own file system interface routines, these routines use MS/DOS for file access. This ensures compatibility with the wide range of disk devices used in the PC-compatible marketplace.

The program can support VGA and run under DESQview and Digital Research's DOS (DR DOS). Straight DOS applications run full-screen instead of in a resizable window like GEOS programs. GEOS runs in the 8088's real mode and simply shells out to DOS rather than act as a task manager like Windows does. Therefore, GEOS can't multitask regular DOS applications, only applications written with its kernel and libraries. The organizational structure of GEOS is shown in FIG. 13-1.

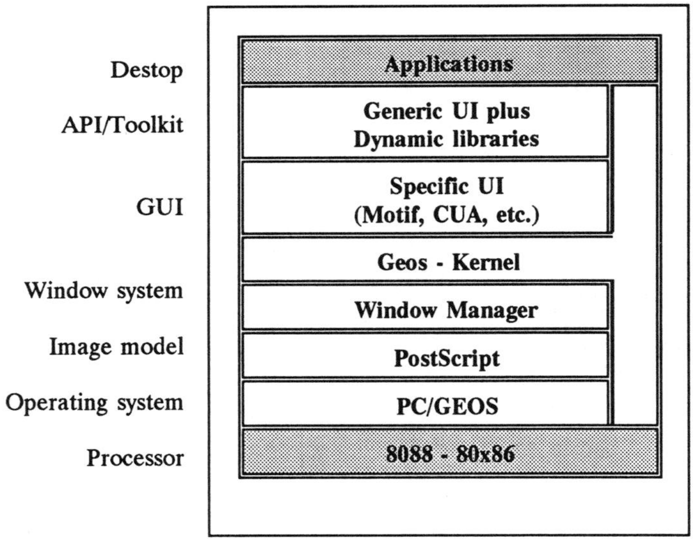

Fig. 13-1. GeoWork's PC/GEOS.

There are several layers in the PC/GEOS system architecture. The top layer is the application layer. Dynamic libraries compose the next layer. Libraries allow commonly used code to be shared among many applications. When an application is loaded, calls to library routines are automatically "linked" by the system. The kernel provides basic operating system services and communicates with the device-driver layer. Device drivers function as an interface between the kernel and physical devices. For example, applications draw graphics and text to a resolution-independent document coordinate system. Device printers are used to map these images to different screen display devices and printers.

The PC/GEOS kernel is the core of the operating system. In addition to preemptive multithreaded multitasking, it provides dynamic memory management (both global and local heaps), process management, file system access, interprocess communication, object support (instantiation, messaging, inheritance, etc.), and all of the imaging and graphics primitives. PC/GEOS is being bundled with Everex, Laser (Sears), US Integration Technology and other computers.

GlobalView

In a new effort to parlay its pioneering work in user interfaces and networking into a share of the open systems market, Xerox has struck a deal with workstation vendor Sun Microsystems. Under the deal, Xerox will resell Sun Microsystems' Sparcstation bundled with the GlobalView software environment. Xerox is betting on GlobalView, an all-encompassing, networking desktop environment with a common interface across different operating systems, similar in concept to Hewlett-Packard's NewWave. GlobalView is the result of a two-year project spanning three continents and involving four companies: Xerox, Fuji Xerox, Rank Xerox and Sun Microsystems.

Description

GlobalView has its own user interface, its own windowing system and its own file system. The GlobalView environment offers features previously unavailable or limited on desktop computers. These include:

- Portable desktop. Unlike GUIs on personal computers, the GlobalView desktop is "network-based," giving users access to their personal desktops from workstations anywhere on the network.
- Agents. GlobalView's special user-defined routines, or "agents," can be created to perform tasks for a user "on their own"—either on the workstation or across the network. GlobalView is specifically designed with workgroup collaboration and document management in mind. And, the marriage of the GlobalView GUI to distributed directory services provides global resources and a high degree of integration; applications running GlobalView share the same GUI.

X Window System calls can be made within GlobalView, and the system can share directories with Sun Microsystems' Network File System/Open Network Computing environment. Xerox pledges to follow emerging UNIX standards, but it's also taking a gamble by building so many proprietary but enhanced features into its environment. (See FIG. 13-2.)

Xerox's GlobalView environment is not limited to just UNIX workstations; it can also be used on OS/2- and DOS-based machines. GlobalView-for-the-PC, a coprocessor

Fig. 13-2. Xerox's 6520 (SPARC Workstation) with the GlobalView GUI.

package, turns DOS and OS/2 systems into multitasking, networked workstations. It consists of the coprocessor networking board (composed of a processor, video controller and 4 Mbytes of RAM, plus software, documentation, and a 19-inch monitor). Users can switch between their DOS applications running in an OS/2 compatibility box and GlobalView by using a hotkey. GlobalView for the PC may be hampered, however, by its requirement that the software run on OS/2. (See FIG. 13-3.)

Xerox provides a family of document management solutions for GlobalView. Xerox Document Search and Retrieval (DSR) integrates the Basis document retrieval software into a product that allows GlobalView users to conduct real-time searches on a database of documents on a Digital VAX. Xerox DocuTeam software for workgroup and project management incorporates an Oracle database running on a DEC VAX into a distributed network solution. Xerox DocuBuild is a fully functional SGML-based publishing system. Xerox DocuTran incorporates Systran software running a host mainframe to provide translation of compound documents between English and a number of foreign languages.

Xerox has also integrated the Basis document retrieval software into a product called Xerox Document Search and Retrieval (DSR), which allows GlobalView users to conduct real-time searches on a database of documents on a Digital VAX. The user doesn't have to give up running OS/2 and DOS applications to take advantage of the

Fig. 13-3. GlobalView for the PC Xerox.

advanced Xerox GlobalView desktop and VP applications. Both worlds can coexist on a user's PC. From the keyboard, a user can switch between the Xerox GlobalView, OS/2 and DOS environments quickly and easily.

Xerox VP Software runs within the multitasking environment of the OS/2 Task Manager. Xerox provides easy transition between the two environments, enabling VP and OS/2 applications to operate simultaneously. DOS applications are supported using the DOS compatibility session under OS/2.

In addition to SUN-based systems, Xerox offers GlobalView for the PC. The following items are components of the base product:

- VP Starter Kit Software.
- Common, fully integrated interface for over 40 VP applications and network access.
- Advanced compound document editor with full features for text, graphics, tables, and productivity tools.

- Office tools and accessories.
- Distributed network support of mail, file, print, communications, information management, and workgroup applications.

NewWave

Hewlett-Packard's NewWave is not another choice for a GUI, but rather it is an object-oriented user environment that sits on top of a GUI. As graphical user interfaces gain more acceptance, integrators are discovering that they are more than just a pretty face. A new generation of object-oriented GUIs has been developed that can tie together many different applications into a smoothly integrated system that automates a great deal of corporate work and enhances individual and group productivity.

While it expands on the basic model provided by Microsoft Windows, NewWave is not tied directly to Windows. Hewlett-Packard has said that NewWave will be available for other GUIs. Because of the Agent concept, which is different from what users trained in a character-based environment are accustomed to, retraining costs will be higher with NewWave. However, the Agent facility and the ease of use in a network environment make it an attractive product. It is unknown, though, if Hewlett-Packard will garner enough ISV support to make NewWave a viable long-term product on platforms other than Hewlett-Packard's and DOS-based machines with Windows.

Description

Hewlett-Packard's NewWave is an environment manager that runs on top of a GUI or windowing system. Currently available for Microsoft Windows, Hewlett-Packard also has an X Window System version and has committed to OS/2 Presentation Manager. The NewWave environment relies on MS-DOS and Microsoft Windows to handle operating system, memory management and GUI tasks. In addition, there are five areas in which NewWave surpasses or enhances Windows: control, communication, integration, abstraction, and ease of use.

Because NewWave controls programs and provides new methods of communication between them, users can integrate several programs to do one task easily. Furthermore, NewWave enables the users to deal with the computer at a higher level of abstraction. They can use simpler techniques to do broader, more complicated tasks. NewWave includes advanced help and computer-based training that make it simple for users to learn how best to utilize NewWave's services.

NewWave incorporates compound objects and sophisticated interprocess communications links, that Microsoft Windows does not support, and enhances the basic GUI model that Microsoft Windows provides. It is able to take advantage of the underlying system resource management that Windows provides, such as screen and printer drivers and memory management. NewWave builds on this foundation by adding two major components: the Object Management Facility (OMF) and the Application Program Interface.

NewWave is object-oriented, not file-oriented. As far as the user is concerned, there are no programs or files under NewWave. A user is not required to know DOS in order to work in the NewWave environment. An object is a combination of an application that creates and manipulates data and a specific data file that was created with it. Thus, the user does not need to know what word processor created a specific file. To create a new object, the user selects the object type (spreadsheet, word processor file, etc.) and instructs NewWave to create the object. By double clicking on the object, the appropriate application program is started, and the data file loaded into it. This capability, in a somewhat primitive form, now exists in Windows.

The program also allows a user to create compound objects, which are built from a combination of smaller objects. For example, a spreadsheet object could have several small text-note objects attached to it to explain some of the calculations. The aggregate group can be copied, printed, and moved as a single entity via the clipboard. Source objects can also be shared. A single-source object, for example, a spreadsheet, can be shared with multiple compound objects. An example of the NewWave Office window is shown in FIG. 13-4.

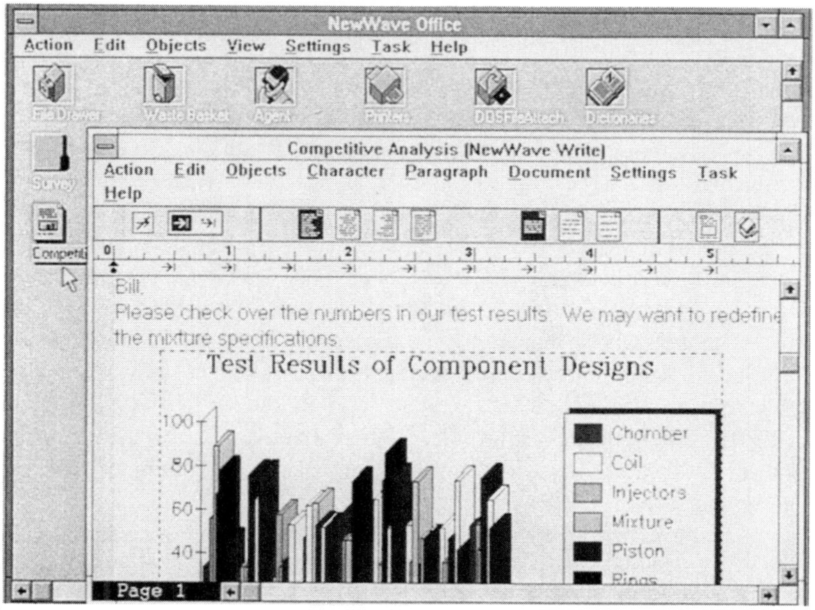

Hewlett-Packard Corp.

Fig. 13-4. NewWave Office.

As an example of the enhancements to Microsoft Windows, NewWave incorporates a wastebasket for deleting files, much like the Apple Macintosh. It also extensively uses the drag-and-drop technique for operations like copying, deleting and printing objects. Windows now includes part of this capability.

The screen and I/O data efficiency of the NewWave/Windows combination is very efficient. For example, an object can be created that includes a graphical animation sequence in motion. The sequence will move whenever it is visible, even as the document is scrolled.

One of the nicest things about NewWave to a naive user, and one of the most disturbing to a power user, is that although it does continue to use standard DOS files and directories, it manages these without input from the user. In effect, the user surrenders control over the structure of the hard disk. NewWave builds its own optimized set of subdirectories into which the OMF places all object files, which are named with numbers assigned and tracked by the OMF.

An application and its associated data file(s) appear as a single icon in the NewWave Office, which is the main window of the environment. Clicking on this icon launches the application and loads the associated file(s). Other object types include folders (which hold up to 200 other objects, and which can be nested to any depth) and various tools and system resources (the Agent task automation facility, a wastebasket for disposing of objects, the Printers icon, etc.).

At installation time, NewWave scans the system hard disk and searches for application programs such as WordPerfect and Lotus. As it finds them, it creates objects to represent them to the user. The user can then use these objects to create data objects.

Hewlett-Packard's latest version, NewWave 3.0, adds the Agent feature. An Agent is like a batch or macro file for controlling data objects, tools and other programs. It can sequence a complex series of tasks at future times within an application and reduce them to a single command.

The Agent's commands are written in an Agent task script language. An Agent can be written explicitly or recorded during a user's session. Data processing activities can be combined and automated. For example, an Agent can take data from three files, create a report on the first working day of every month and send it out to twelve people.

Because NewWave is built around the Object Management Facility (OMF) that manages the links between objects, the Agent can access this database to control the automatic flow of data between different objects. In NewWave, an object consists of data and the application program that generates and manipulates that data. The OMF is a kind of object database manager with three functions: application/data building, maintaining information links between applications, and object integration.

When a user starts up NewWave, the screen is taken up by the NewWave Office, which holds the initial objects. Subgroups of objects are in a hierarchical tree from this starting point. NewWave also incorporates numerous international character sets including Dutch, French, German and Spanish.

Because of the improved memory management and user interface features available in Windows, NewWave 3.0 requires a 286 or 386 computer with a minimum of 2 Mbytes of RAM as opposed to the 3 Mbytes it previously required. Users report that a 386 is the preferred platform for NewWave.

Another major component of the NewWave environment is the Application Program Interface, which gives NewWave applications access to system resources. These resources include the Help facility, Computer-Based Training (CBT) and the Agent Task facility. The Help facility supplies context-sensitive help for any NewWave application. Help text does not require any coding, so it can be developed by a professional writer who is independent from the programming effort.

One of the difficulties encountered in developing CBT systems is deciding whether to simulate the applications or to build a control program that actually runs the applications as part of the training process. In standard environments, both are difficult tasks. Under NewWave, the CBT facility is integrated with the actual applications, making developing a system-oriented CBT package much easier.

As part of the API services, the program has a macro-like feature called the Agent

Task facility, which can automate: the operation of individual applications, cooperating groups of applications, or the entire system. It can memorize keyboard and mouse actions to enable users to develop their own simple macros, and those simple macros can be customized by the addition of control structures for complex decision-making.

The operation of the Agent depends on the existence (in a NewWave application) of a dual control structure, which consists of the Action Processor and the Command Processor. The Action Processor interprets user actions (e.g., mouse and keyboard), as well as handling messages from the API (e.g., screen update). The Command Processor takes messages from the Action Processor or from the Agent Task facility and executes them. Thus, the particular mouse and keyboard actions used to execute are not recorded per se, only their intent (i.e., the commands they cause to be executed). The Agent Task facility is a very attractive aspect of NewWave to integrators. It can be used for a variety of system administration functions, such as automating backups (facilitated by the Agent's ability to schedule tasks for one time or repetitive execution).

Application support

Many of the major Windows application developers have NewWave-specific versions of their own software. More than 100 independent software vendors (ISVs) have indicated that they are pursuing development for NewWave, including Samna's and Da Vinci's E-mail programs. Over 150 software companies have signed up as registered developers for NewWave, and over 40 major applications are available. The Object Management Group (OMG), a collection of over eighty companies that manufacture and use computers, has adopted the technology as their object standard for future office automation programs. Computer makers AT&T, NCR, Data General, and Canon have committed to delivering NewWave systems.

WordPerfect, Lotus and Microsoft have committed to NewWave. WordPerfect uses NewWave in its Windows version of its popular word processor program. The agent feature that allows users to treat files as objects and adds macro-like functionality is beneficial to such a program.

NewWave is bundled with NewWave Write, a WYSIWYG word processor from Hewlett-Packard. In addition, any other Windows or DOS application can be used with NewWave, but to access them using the icon-based interface, users need to add a *bridge*, code that encapsulates, or registers, the application with the environment. Hewlett-Packard provides a disk with bridges for 22 popular applications, including WordPerfect 4.2/5.0 and Lotus 1-2-3 R2.01, but users can also easily develop their own bridges.

Linking applications

The real power of the NewWave environment becomes evident when the relationships that it can establish between applications is considered. In this regard, the OMF goes well beyond the capabilities of Microsoft Windows' Dynamic Data Exchange (DDE) facility, which requires that linked applications be active, and cannot maintain the links once the applications are closed. In NewWave, links established between objects (thus creating a compound object, in effect) are persistent and are even maintained when the compound object is passed to another computer via network or floppy disk (as long as the receiving computer has the same suite of applications as the sending one).

Information links NewWave supports information links, data passing links and visual links. An information link allows the same source data to be shared by many different applications. For example, a pie chart (created in a spreadsheet program) can appear in both a departmental report (created in a word processor) and the annual report (created with a DTP program) at the same time. If the pie chart is modified in any of its three locations (the spreadsheet, the word processor, or the DTP program), all other instances of the chart are automatically updated by the OMF.

Data-passing links allow one application to send data to another. For example, a spreadsheet object can be used as the source of data for a pie chart project. Each time the spreadsheet is updated, the chart is automatically updated by the OMF.

Visual links The visual link facility of the OMF is also very interesting and powerful. It allows a NewWave application to provide a view of another object's data without the need to understand the data's format. In effect, the display of visually linked information is the responsibility of the sending application. The receiving application merely furnishes a space for it.

With this facility, a user can incorporate a graphic from a NewWave business presentation package such as Charisma (from Micrographx) into a NewWave word processor such as Ami Pro (from the Samna division of Lotus) merely by dragging the icon representing the graphic into a frame in the word processor. The NewWave OMF automatically activates Charisma to display the graphic in the spot provided by Ami Pro. The user can even modify the graphic by clicking on it while working in Ami Pro; the OMF opens Charisma and turns control over to it. This has attracted several software developers. Samna identifies this ability to combine data from many different applications as one of the most attractive aspects of NewWave to a word processor developer, because the bucket that holds the data from all these applications is the word processor.

These links are possible because NewWave applications are objects that share a well-defined set of methods for sharing data, displaying themselves, printing themselves, and so forth. This enhances the productivity of software developers and system integrators. For example, an ISV developing a spreadsheet who wants it to be able to retrieve data from a host IBM mainframe does not have to develop any communications of SNA facilities. Instead, a third-party program can be used to integrate the capabilities of a communications package (such as Dynacomm, from Futuresoft Engineering Corp.). The spreadsheet can call upon Dynacomm as needed to download host data without understanding anything about synchronous communications or SNA protocols.

Integration of existing programs

NewWave also supports the integration of standard DOS or Windows applications, but such applications cannot share all the richness of the NewWave environment. There are four levels of application integration available in NewWave: DOS Programs Menu, Icon-Level Encapsulation, Advanced Encapsulation and NewWave applications. The first two levels can be accomplished by end users, the last two require advanced programming skills.

DOS programs menu The DOS programs menu is used to launch DOS or

Windows applications exactly as though NewWave were not present. No functionality beyond that furnished by the Windows environment is available.

Icon-level encapsulation By using a Bridge Object, icon-level encapsulation is accomplished and combines DOS or Windows applications with their associated data file(s) so the application can be launched and the files loaded by clicking on the assigned icon. Object titles are still limited to the DOS filename length, but data sharing is supported, and the object can be copied, mailed via network or floppy disk, and discarded through the wastebasket. A system tool called DOS File Attach allows existing files to be associated with such objects, either in their current directory (in which case they cannot be discarded via the wastebasket), or moved into the default NewWave directory assigned by the OMF (to support discarding).

Advanced encapsulation Advanced encapsulation (AE) requires the construction of a Browser shell that understands the unique data structure of the application and acts upon OMF requests accordingly. Data can be shared and linked with other AE and NewWave applications, and some context-sensitive help and Agent Task functions are supported. However, such applications are still limited to DOS filename-length names. An example of an AE application is Hewlett-Packard's own Graphics Gallery, or Lotus 1-2-3 Release 2.2.

Only NewWave applications offer the full range of this environment's capabilities, including 32-character names and full support of Agents, CBT, Help, and a completely consistent user interface. The benefits are notable, but the effort involved is proportional. Grayson, CEO of Micrographx, states that the development of NewWave Charisma took two people about nine months of work, and it still doesn't support the CBT capability.

Networks

NewWave is optimized to communicate across networks. Hewlett-Packard wants NewWave to be a communication link across networks of a range of machines running any major operating system, and to that end, it intends to port the package to its own workstation and UNIX systems. For example, objects located on different machines on the network can be associated.

Since NewWave is built around the Object Management Facility (OMF), the Agent can access the database to control the automatic flow of data between different objects. NewWave 3.0 also allows the objects to be shared across a network. A chart from a spreadsheet declared as an object and used inside a business graphic, for example, is updated automatically as the main spreadsheet application program is updated. Hewlett-Packard and Novell said they will develop a version of NewWave's application environment that supports NetWare 386.

Other

Full exploitation of the NewWave environment depends upon the existence of NewWave applications. Therefore, a system consisting of a mix of NewWave, Windows and DOS applications will probably have some confusing results sometimes, the most serious of which would be the Agent's inability to control every program to the same degree.

Rhapsody Business Orchestration environment

Some of the limitations of NewWave have been addressed in the Rhapsody Business Orchestration environment from AT&T, which is an extension of NewWave. Rhapsody offers a higher level of integration for existing applications (although in many cases this must be accomplished by AT&T programmers) and a number of enhancements to the NewWave Office. NewWave has also been adopted by Data General and NCR as part of their office automation suites, and these versions will no doubt offer other improvements. Also, UNIX versions of NewWave are now available, as is an API for network awareness that will extend the environment's support of networking beyond the mere mailing of objects to true distributed processing and linking of applications and data. OS/2 is in the works. At this point NewWave's biggest impact is in corporate systems, where the integration of disparate applications into a coherent whole is an overriding concern.

NeXTstep

NeXTstep is the graphical user interface (GUI) and associated development environment bundled with NeXT computers. This graphical system was created to solve two major problems with applications: without good user interfaces they are difficult to use, and good user interfaces are difficult to develop.

Description

The core of NeXTstep consists of 3 layers: the Workspace, Appkit and Workspace Manager. NeXT also provides an application creation tool, the Interface Builder, which significantly speeds the development of NeXTstep applications. Conceptually, NeXTstep is all of the software above the operating system but below the applications, as shown in FIG. 13-5.

The NeXTstep development environment includes a rich set of object classes in the Application Kit (AppKit) that define the appearance and functionality of the NeXTstep GUI. Examples of classes that the AppKit defines are Window, Menu, Text Field, Button, Scroll Bar, and View. Together, these and other classes in the AppKit provide developers with the building blocks needed to build a fully functional and consistent GUI for their applications. In addition, through an object-oriented concept called inheritance, a developer can modify and extend the classes in the AppKit to suit a specific need.

At the core of object-oriented programming is the same idea that led electrical engineers to use integrated circuits composed of thousands of transistors instead of individual transistors. A complex circuit board is much easier to design, build, and modify if an engineer can begin with building blocks of encapsulated functionality instead of single transistors. Object-oriented programming applies this idea to software by recognizing that a large software application is much easier to design, build, and

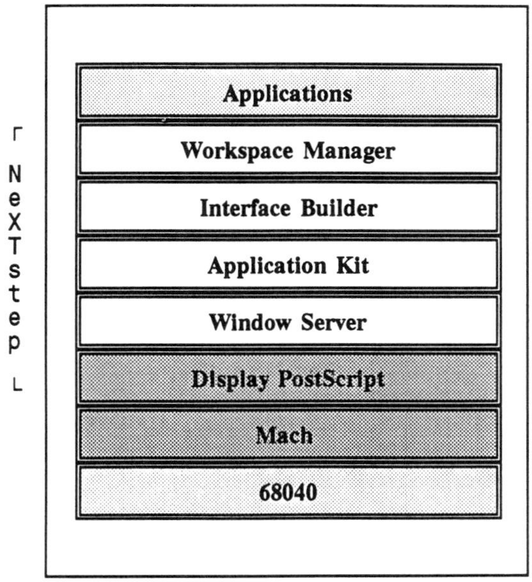

Fig. 13-5. NeXTstep architecture.

maintain when a software engineer begins with a building block larger and more functional than a single line of code. An object is exactly that building block.

Objects are capsules of functionality that have a well defined interface. The abstract description of an object and its external interface is called a *class*. An actual object in an application is called an *instance of a class*. A running application is composed of many objects, and objects work together to accomplish tasks by sending messages to each other.

Because all object interaction, and therefore all work, is accomplished through the external interface of objects, there is an encapsulation of data and functionality that allows the developer to work at a higher level than individual lines of code. Now the programmer can think in terms of objects and their interactions, rather than thinking about how to write, for example, a loop termination condition. Object-oriented programming allows the developer to take a building block approach to an application, and thus applications can be developed much more quickly and efficiently.

A core technology of all GUIs is the imaging model—the language and paradigm used to put images on the screen and the printer. The NeXTstep uses Display PostScript for a unified imaging model for the screen and the printer. By incorporating the PostScript language from Adobe, the NeXTstep Window Server unifies the imaging model for the screen and the printer. The PostScript language is an advanced graphics and page description language from Adobe that has been used on high-quality laser printers and image setters for many years. NeXT worked closely with Adobe to help bring to market a version of PostScript for the screen called Display PostScript, thus unifying both display and print graphics.

NeXT, like many other firms, looks for the possibilities of leverage from existing systems and has adopted UNIX, TCP/IP and PostScript. However, it is the view of the company that existing GUIs like the X Window System and Motif are not powerful enough to do what the company wants, therefore, they had to develop a proprietary GUI. Nonetheless, NeXT's conviction of the superiority of its proprietary systems is not preventing the company from joining the wider workstation world. NeXT has opened up to the DOS world with SoftPC from Insignia Solutions, Inc. The product allows NeXT users to run most DOS software side-by-side with NeXT applications.

NeXT recognizes the importance of the X Window System in markets such as the Fortune 500 and the education market (both of which include X capabilities on their checklist of system requirements). To meet that need, Pencom Software has developed an interface to the X Window System and to The Open Software Foundation's Motif graphical interface to NeXT. The Pencom product includes a Server based on the MIT X Consortium's X11.R4 running in NeXTstep. That will let NeXT users support X-clients or applications, and provide graphical connectivity in heterogeneous networking environments. The introduction of the product brought NeXT even further into the world at large. NeXT recognizes the importance of open systems and as a result has started to reposition the NeXT machine as a UNIX box. IBM has licensed NeXTstep from NeXT Computer for its RS6000 workstations. However, although IBM has announced systems, none have been shipped with NeXTstep.

PCSA

The DECnet Personal Computing Systems Architecture (PCSA) Client for DOS software consists of PC networking, terminal emulation, a PC mail utility, windowing software, online information and DOS utility software. Included with the DECnet PCSA Client for DOS software is the PC DECwindows Display Facility, which provides an X Window System interface. VMS Services for PCs is a DECnet application that implements PCSA and enables VAX and MicroVAX computers to act as application, data and resource Servers to large groups of personal computers.

PCSA is based on a server/client model. VMS Services for PCs, a layered VMS and DECnet application, is the Server software and runs on the host VAX or MicroVAX system. The complementary software, DECnet PCSA Client for DOS, is the Client software and runs on a DOS PC.

In this system, the DOS application software resides on the VAX or MicroVAX computer and executes on the Client PC. This allows all users to access a common base of application software and data files. The user accesses all files required from virtual devices on a Server system, located anywhere on the network. Digital was criticized for early implementations of the PCSA network because it was so memory-intensive. Running a memory-hungry GUI concurrently with it was out of the question. Digital has decided to replace the proprietary GUI of DECwindows with the OSF/Motif GUI. This move is viewed as further indication of the prominence that OSF/Motif has gained.

DECwindows will maintain its desktop utility applications and its Xlib and X11 Server software, features that are not included in the OSF/Motif specification. Applications currently written to DECwindows require some modifications and recompilation with the DECwindows Developers Kit for OSF/Motif. The integration into the DOS Environment of Motif through PCSA will probably only be with the X Window System.

Rooms

Developed by Xerox corporation, Rooms is a LISP-based window management system. It is being ported to UNIX and licensed to other manufacturers. Rooms takes a new approach to desktop management and attempts to develop a new metaphor. Several companies, including Apple, have shown a strong interest in the concepts of Rooms. Rooms is designed around the task-oriented clustering of information and provides multiple virtual workspaces (or rooms) that are furnished with windows and objects pertinent to some task.

Rooms is a result of research performed at Xerox PARC Research Center. Xerox is considering using Rooms to organize applications based on different interface technologies into a single desktop environment, most likely as part of a network. Rooms first appeared in 1986 as part of a Lisp environment project by Xerox. Xerox has held technology licensing discussions with Apple and Sun Microsystems about incorporating Rooms into their products.

Description

Rooms uses a different paradigm than current windowing systems. The main idea behind Rooms is that the screen is organized around the tasks a user is actually working on, instead of all of the applications and files in use or available, as is done on the Macintosh and Windows. In the Rooms scheme, a user typically has a number of individual Rooms on the screen, each representing a task such as a budget or report. In setting up a particular task, the user merely has to move whichever applications or tools are necessary into the Room and begin work. The architecture of Rooms is shown in FIG. 13-6.

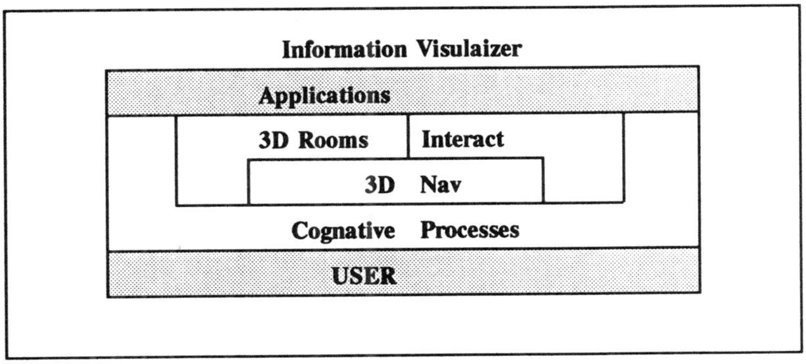

Fig. 13-6. Rooms architecture.

An important part of Rooms is that the environment keeps track of the status of the task being performed in the Room and lets the user move between related Rooms through a series of doors. If the user shifts to another task, the Room can be closed. Another important feature of Rooms is that application software can be shared among different Rooms simultaneously, rather than maintaining multiple copies of it in different groups.

Rooms helps manage information once it has been retrieved. By making it easy to switch to a new set of windows and objects, Rooms encourages the user to keep less clutter on the screen. Because users can conveniently switch from task to task, the computer anticipates their needs, more efficiently retrieving items from expensive storage (e.g., the disk or file server). The successor to Rooms, 3-D/Rooms, is a major component of the Information Visualizer, an experimental system being developed at Xerox PARC (refer to Chapter 18). The organizational structure of Rooms is shown in FIG. 13-7. Xerox has several patents pending for Rooms and may develop and market its own hardware for it, though they are focusing on third party licensees. They have had licensing discussions with Apple, but they broke off because of the legal battles over the Macintosh interface.

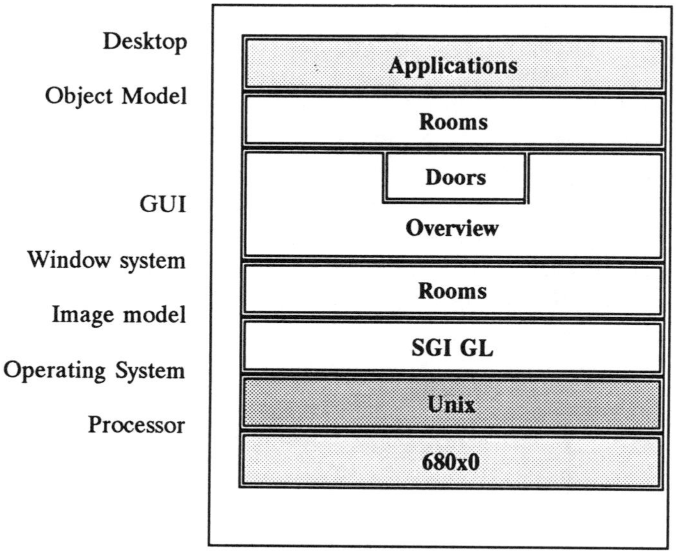

Fig. 13-7. Xerox's Rooms.

References

Card, Stuart K., and Austin D. Henderson, Jr. 1986. *Rooms: the use of multiple virtual workspaces to reduce space contention in a window-based graphical user interface*. Palo Alto, Ca.: Xerox Palo Alto Research Center.

Tello, Ernest R. Windows on a new world. *AI Expert*. October, 1988. Page 36.

14
Industrial GUIs

Historically, the user interfaces available for industrial systems and process-control applications have been difficult to use, and in some cases, intimidating. Typically they are noninteractive displays such as meters or panel lights. A few systems offer color or black-and-white graphics drawn on a low-resolution monitor with character-based graphics. Audio capabilities, if any, were usually just beeps or buzzes and other nondescriptive noises.

In the early 1980s, user interfaces such as GKS and VDI were developed. However, these emerging interfaces were designed for UNIX or IBM PCs without any consideration for real-time software requirements. Because these standards had not been integrated with a real-time operating system or kernel, factory-floor systems were largely limited to 1960s-style user interfaces. Yet, of the 50 million PCs that have been installed worldwide, five million of them are in industrial environments. Of that population, almost two million of them are in use on the plant floor. The old idea that a PC is not a real computer, or doesn't have the horsepower, or is just a pretty user interface no longer holds. Yes, the PC does offer a GUI, but more than ever, GUIs are needed in factory and industrial applications.

A complete data acquisition or instrument control system includes data presentation to convey system information. Furthermore, data presentation is often the most time-consuming and, consequently, the most frequently neglected part of an automated system. Nevertheless, an acquisition system is only as good as its data presentation. The better the data presentation, the better a user can understand the acquisition and analysis. (See FIG. 14-1.)

A process-control or an acquisition system typically displays data on a computer screen, whereas instrument-control systems display data on their front panels. Standalone instruments have a combination of a text-based interface and a graphics display on their front panels. Many instruments have digital readouts, charts, and CRT screens to display signals and other data, and front panel controls to prompt users for input.

An automated control or acquisition system could combine both the user input and graphics displays on the computer screen with a GUI. A logical and natural way to control an instrument connected to a computer is with a design that emulates the instru-

Fig. 14-1. GUIs displaying real-time manufacturing information can inform and alert operators as events dictate.

ment front panel with software using a GUI. For an automated acquisition system that consists of many instruments, a user can combine the instruments on one GUI and display only the relevant functions of each instrument, as shown in FIG. 14-2. This approach greatly simplifies complicated systems.

Graphical user interfaces make physical buttons, knobs and switches obsolete. The GUI is becoming an integral part of industrial and real-time systems as well. This is only logical, since the human interface is the most visible part of an industrial control system. Advanced systems will be able to reconfigure a plant and change control-panel layouts through a keyboard or mouse.

A GUI is also of great benefit to the system developer who is integrating into a system plug-in data acquisition boards or VXI boards, which do not have front panels. With a GUI, the developer can design the front panel in software so that the plug-in board becomes a complete, functioning instrument with a front panel. Such GUIs typically consist of graphical panels and pull-down menus, which system operators use to enter and examine data. GUIs are often mouse-driven, so operators simply point and click with a mouse-controlled cursor to enter and manipulate data.

GUIs make system information easier to interpret by displaying data in a familiar and illustrative fashion. For example, a GUI can display temperature as an analog thermometer level, and can display an ON/OFF state as a switch. As has been pointed out in the office automation and scientific areas, in the next 10 years every platform will be a graphics computer and every user will be a graphics user. The industrial area will be no different, because GUIs bring many advantages to CIM and factory automation. A

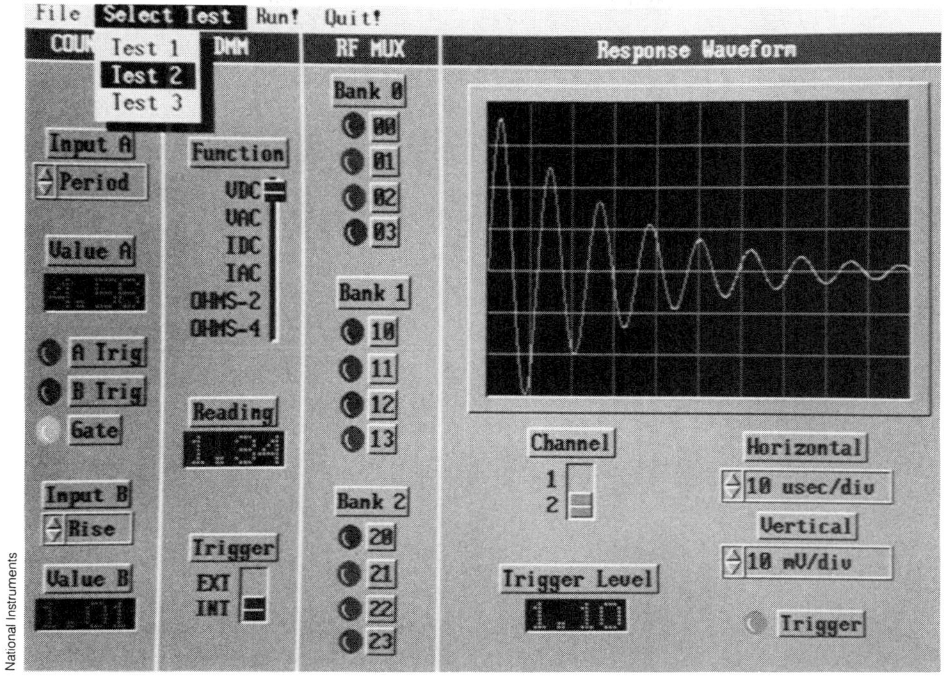

Fig. 14-2. A GUI representation of an automated control and acquisition system.

GUI provides an easily understandable view of processes to operators who may be relatively inexperienced. Processes and control functions can graphically represent the instruments and machines under control (such as vessels in a chemical plant or rollers in a steel mill).

Operators need to view data as it's being collected and be alerted to events as they happen. They may also need to interact quickly if there is a problem or a nonautomatic decision is needed. However, industrial GUIs usually have to make a compromise with the real-time requirements of a system; therefore, they are not actually real-time graphics. When a GUI is part of a real-time system, it usually gets a lower priority than interrupts from critical processes. The justification is that humans can't respond quickly enough to the requirements of a real-time system.

Complex, computerized operations in manufacturing, service, and military organizations require continuous human monitoring and control. Chemical plant technicians track the contents, temperature, and pressure in numerous reactors, and communications network administrators activate additional device nodes when system usage increases.

These activities and many others share common characteristics. Each process is monitored while or soon after it occurs, i.e., in near-real-time. Computer graphics in the form of data plots, pictures, and icons can greatly improve human response to changes in the process. Yet the operator of the system has little knowledge of or interest in the hardware required to monitor the process. The computer becomes simply another instrument or control panel.

The following is a sample of a few industrial systems (applications, application generators, toolkits and specialized programs) that have GUI capabilities. The next step in the development of industrial GUIs will be to develop an industry standard front end that represents actual controls and gauges.

CIM

In the past, most companies would develop a shop floor planning and a manufacturing resource planning (MRP) system internally. With soaring costs and late projects, MIS departments are being told to buy standard products whenever possible. Hoping to capitalize on this trend, Consilium Inc. developed a GUI-based program for manufacturing support systems. Based on Digital Equipment Corp.'s computers, the product is aimed at the computer integrated manufacturing segment (CIM). This is a critical interface that fits between business systems and plant floor systems. Using DECwindows, the interface is designed to track and control materials, equipment, personnel, work instructions and facilities. Recognizing the need for GUIs in process industries, Consilium, which is partially owned by Digital, has provided one more element in the enterprise-wide model of GUIs and interoperability.

InTouch

Wonderware Software Development Corporation has developed InTouch, a GUI application generator that lets a user or a programmer create an operator's interface for data acquisition and continuous and discrete manufacturing processes. Based on Microsoft Windows, it is DDE-compatible, which provides a path to front office systems. The program allows the creation of pen charts, alarms, and simulations. The user can design an object like a faceplate, gauge, pump or tank using on-screen controls. The user does not have to know or use any programming constructions or language.

LabWindows

LabWindows is a software development system for creating programs for data acquisition and control system applications (see FIG. 14-3). It uses QuickBASIC and C libraries for data acquisition, data analysis and data presentation. The development environment has a special interface called a function panel program that developers can use to experiment with library functions and automatically generate source code for applications. The function panels have an online help feature built into them. LabWindows is offered by National Instruments.

There are 10 libraries of functions that programmers can use to develop applications. The instrument library has 120 high-level drivers for controlling specific instruments. The user interface library has a graphical editor and various functions for creating GUIs for applications. The GUI toolkit uses a DOS extender so programs can use up to 16 Mbytes of continuous memory. The virtual memory manager (VMM) gives program access to extended and expanded memory.

The user interface library (UIL) is a set of tools for creating GUIs and seamlessly integrating them into application programs. With the libraries, programmers can create custom panels with strip charts and input-output controls. Users can create command

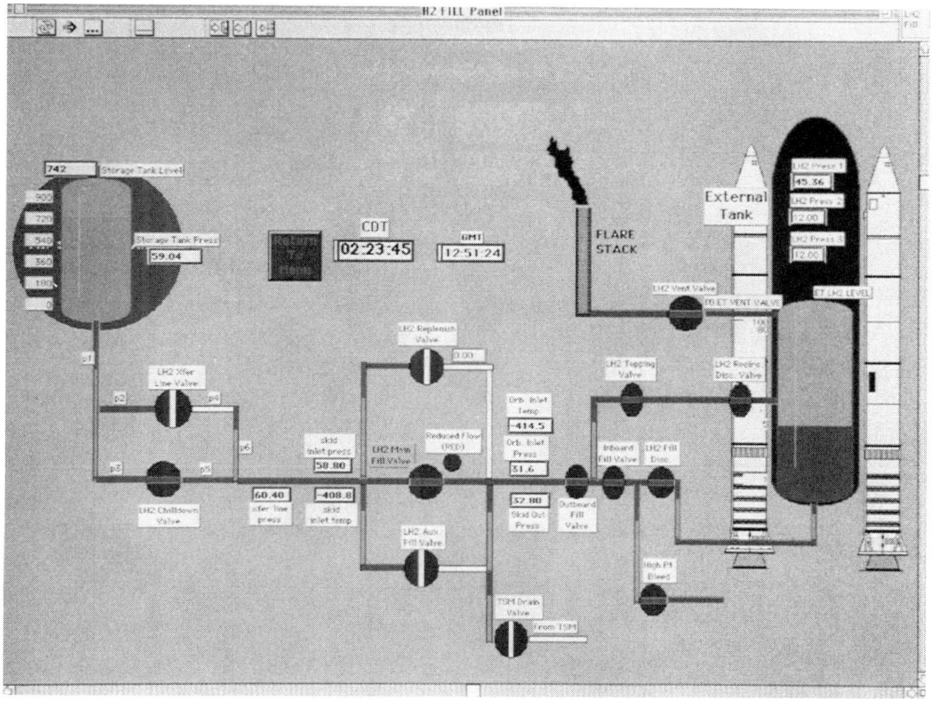

National Instruments

Fig. 14-3. GUIs can process information in a familiar and illustrative fashion.

bars, pull-down menus and pop-up dialog boxes. Each element in a control panel is created with a graphics editor so the panels can be developed and viewed without writing any code.

Rave

Microware Systems Corporation offers a Real-Time Audio/Video Environment (RAVE) that is a multimedia development tool for factory automation systems. With RAVE, designers can quickly configure realistic user interfaces and control panels using real-world sounds and images. Because the resulting user interface better represents the actual control environment, it can be manipulated and understood by nontechnical users.

Rave consists of three packages: The Graphic File Manager, Graphics Support Library, and The Presentation Editor. The Graphics File Manager (GFM) brings together all the physical resources needed for the user interface. This includes a video driver, an audio driver and drivers for the input devices. The Graphics Support Library (GSL) builds upon the GFM to create the more complex concepts needed by an application. These include controls, menus, and indicators. Controls are objects on the display that mimic the behavior of switches and slidebars. The user may interact with a control on the display to turn something on or off. A slidebar could be used to mimic something like a volume control.

Rave is directly lined to the OS-9 real-time operating system. It is part of the real-time environment, and its functions are assigned priorities under the OS-9 kernel. Rave doesn't work across a network. It's intended for embedded applications on a VME-based system.

RPCore

With factory managers and users demanding higher levels of automation, developing control systems with a GUI has become a challenge. Realtime Performance Inc., offers RPCore, a set of development tools for PCs that is capable of running the GUI and file system for control applications on a computer that is separate from the real-time modules. The C language-based development system provides manager functions for developing a real-time system. The basis of the tool is a real-time kernel: I/O controls and the user interface. The package also has a screen-editing tool, RPDraw, which contains a font editor.

The development system is available for standard DOS applications (i.e., 640K memory limitations) and for 386 protected mode applications. Included in the system is a finite state machine manager for simplifying equipment control design, an alarm manager for event-driven user prompts and a plotting/datalogging function. RPCore is a window manager and multitasker that can communicate with various sensors and controllers. The GUI supports EGA and VGA resolutions and several input devices (mouse, touch-screen, etc.)

RT-Graphics

Since specialized graphics displays are often needed for process control and other real-time applications, Farradyne Systems offers a software program that integrates graphics with such applications or processes. It is an OS/2-based program that provides the capability to develop dynamic graphics displays whose characteristics are controlled by external sources such as online databases, communications links, or integrated simulation programs.

Designed for the end user, control of color, position, scale, rotation and line styles are provided. The user can develop animated presentations in the form of histograms, dials, fluid levels and network links. Data element values can be used to change alphanumeric text in a graphics display. This allows numeric representations of sensor data to be displayed with an associated graphic symbol. Users can create and edit graphics symbols and text without any programming experience or training. The program makes it possible to create graphics for monitoring sensors, simulation programs, networks and instrumentation systems. It has an integrated communication capability that permits remote displays of animated graphics without the need for additional software. Like Dataviews and Set, which are based on VMS, RT-Graphics is a specialized program that is based on Presentation Manager. Unlike those VMS based programs, RT-Graphics is aimed at the industrial market.

SL-GMS

Recognizing the importance of providing a rapid and intuitive method of defining graphics models as part of real-time processes, SL Corporation developed SL-GMS. It is an object-oriented graphical modeling system used to develop dynamic graphic screens for real-time applications. SL-GMS offers features such as Xt widget integration, Hypercard-like screen management, and a Data Source Manager for codeless connections between screen objects and data sources. It also includes Graphical Interactive Screen Management Objects (SL-GISMOs), which are "super-widgets" capable of complex behaviors beyond Xt widgets. However, unlike many object-oriented systems, SL-GMS is hospitable to a variety of application languages around its own strict object-oriented kernel and service such as ADA, C, FORTRAN, and Pascal, for example. The system itself is written in C.

SL-GMS offers Xt event handling, which enables developers to integrate Motif, Open Look or other X toolkit widgets with custom screen objects or icons created with SL-GMS. The SL-GMS Screen Management System (SMS) allows the user to button from one screen to any other screen in the application with any degree of sequencing and nesting. In addition, SMS supports multiple overlapping windows with continuing dynamics in every window.

Screens are built in the SL-DRAW graphical editor, which in itself is constructed from the basic GL library and may be reconfigured by users. Graphical Interactive Screen Management Objects are called GISMOs to distinguish them from Xt widgets. Fully interactive with Xt widgets, GISMOs can become "superwidgets," capable of complex and compound behavior beyond Xt widgets. GISMOs can take any appearance the user wishes and can trigger any user-defined function or external program. Created with the drawing tool, GISMOs provide developers with tremendous design flexibility.

The specifications for Open Look and Motif define the basic appearance of complying applications and behavior of associated input devices such as sliders and menu buttons. At the lower level, programming interfaces specific to windowing systems such as X and SunView implement the standard. SL-GMS supports workstation layers running on top of these lower level toolkits. Thus, developers can construct a Motif specification-compliant interface using SL-DRAW and customizable GISMOs that are provided with the SL-GMS development environment. Furthermore, in SL-GMS, a user can create graphics objects by using the editor, SL-DRAW. SL-GMS is a complete system for developing dynamic interfaces to real-time process control systems.

Macintosh in the factory

National Instruments has developed a graphically oriented programming environment that's coupled with a user interface tool called Labview 2. It allows users to design graphic representations of instrument panels and analysis programs to display the data from the instruments. Users can connect a Macintosh to various instruments, typically over IEEE-488 or VXIbus, and then control them. This creates an integrated environment for instrumentation, data acquisition, analysis, and presentation.

X Window System in the factory

Some advocates believe the X Window System is the best choice for graphics interfaces for real-time process control. Because the X Window System is based on UNIX, it cannot be used for real-time applications. However, not all industrial applications are real-time. The X Window System offers the designer many options within a single user-interface environment. However, developments are underway to couple its Client-Server model very closely to real-time processes. Because the X Window System works well over a network, for monitoring a big factory, the architecture of the X Window System makes it very attractive.

FlexOS

The big complaint against UNIX and DOS for industrial systems is that they are not real-time systems. Regardless of how well either operating system does multitasking, or how popular or convenient they may be as a development environment, they will never be real-time operating systems. Digital Research has developed FlexOS for applications that need the user interface more closely coupled with the real-time environment. FlexOS is a preemptive, event-driven dispatcher-type operating system with a priority scheduler for handling real-time applications.

The graphics portion of FlexOS is logically named X/GEM (see FIG. 14-4). It is an integral part of the operating system and interfaces directly to FlexOS through a shared run-time library. Making the GUI an integral part of the operating system eliminates the performance penalty associated with layered interfaces in UNIX or DOS. This allows real-time, graphics and the file system to run on the same processor. X/GEM

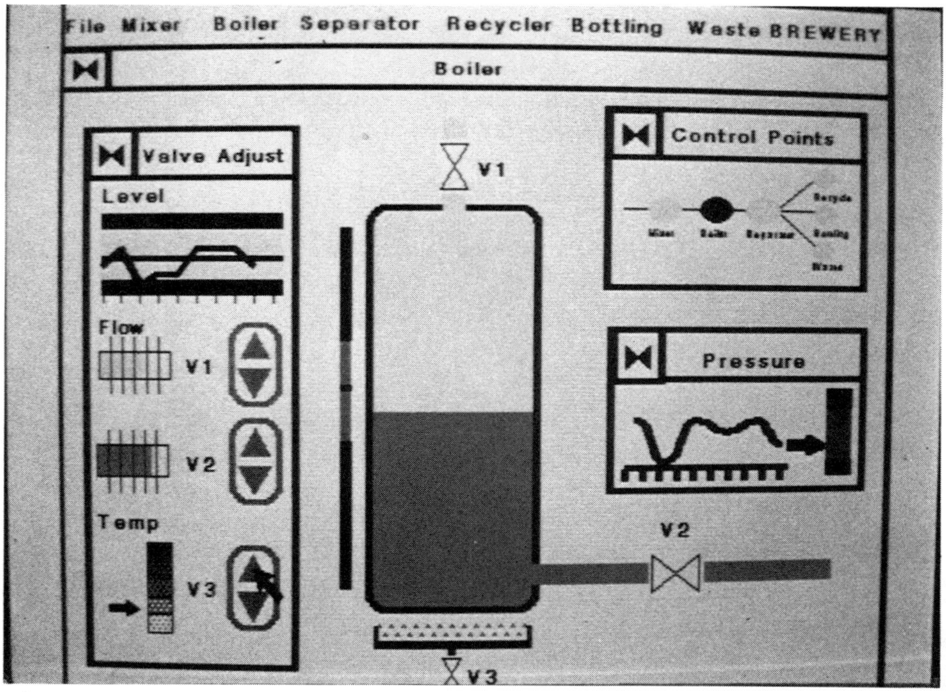

Digital Research Corp.

Fig. 14-4. A user-generated process-control monitoring panel developed with X/GEM FlexOS.

allows application prototyping via the graphics interface. Since it is based on the GEM library, applications written with GEM can be ported to this environment.

References

Shelef, D. Gary. 1990. Developing graphics in realtime, *SunTech Journal* 3 (3).

Williams, Tom. Graphical interfaces make knobs and switches obsolete. *Computer Design*. August, 1990. Page 78.

15

Graphics hardware

The very first graphic displays were of the point-plotting variety and used direct-view storage-tube technology. They did not use frame buffers, but were fed with a stream of point coordinates by the computer. Only a very limited number of points could be displayed in this fashion without creating flicker. Point-plotting displays of this kind were made obsolete by the introduction of line-drawing displays in the mid 1960s. The line-drawing display, also known as calligraphic refresh or vector display, can draw complete segments of straight lines without plotting each individual pixel on the line; it therefore has a much higher capacity than the point-plotting display for line drawing. However, as more lines are drawn on the screen the display begins to flicker.

Raster-scan technology

With the introduction of raster-scan refresh (line-drawing) displays in 1978, the ability to display dynamically changing pictures became a reality. Raster-scan technology has changed considerably throughout the years, fueled entirely by the broadcast and computer industry. Raster displays appeared first on character-based alphanumeric terminals in the early 1970s. They were expanded to include graphic displays in the late 1970s.

When IBM introduced the PC in 1981, it had a limited raster-scan text display, or a low-resolution color graphics display (CGA). Shortly thereafter, the higher resolution raster-scan workstations concept was introduced by Three River's (their PERQ) in 1982. The notion of workstations was made popular by Sun Microsystems and others. Technology has moved rapidly since 1982, and with the introduction of graphic accelerators and the addition of low-cost add-on frame buffers to workstations and PCs, affordable, high-quality graphics has finally reached the end user.

Classes of hardware devices

Complete hardware systems used to display graphic and textual information can be classified into 5 general environments.

- Alphanumeric terminals.
- Graphic terminals.
- Personal computers and entry level workstations.
- Graphic visualization workstations.
- X-terminals.

Monitors

The question of which is better for a graphics display, monochrome or color is often asked. Like all other such questions, there is no best choice. If there were a best choice, then there would be no choice and everyone would use the best. Therefore, there has to be advantages in both types.

Monochrome

The first alphanumeric terminals, PCs and workstations had monochrome or black-and-white displays. Monochrome does not mean black-and-white. It means one color. That color could be green, amber or white. Black-and-white means only two shades: black and white. Monochrome means there could be many shades, but not necessarily. When a black-and-white monitor has shades, it is usually referred to as a shades-of-gray, or gray-shade monitor. (The word grey and gray are used interchangeably.)

Monochrome monitors have a simple operation and have had decades of development of the screen's phosphors. As a result, they offer the highest quality display. In the photographic and image processing industry, resolution is measured by the number of shades that can be discerned with the naked eye. In the computer industry, resolution is measured by the number of pixels on the screen. In the area of desktop publishing, resolution is measured in terms of dots-per-inch (DPI). In the case of monochrome monitors, they have the highest ratings for all measurements of resolution. Therefore, monochrome monitors are most often used in desktop publishing (DTP) applications and other applications where the highest number DPI on the screen is needed.

Color

A color monitor uses a very fine metal screen called a *shadow mask* that is next to the phosphors (on the inside of the face-plate). Because it is very difficult to make a shadow mask with a fine pitch (*pitch* refers to the diameter of the holes in the shadow mask), it is difficult to obtain sharp images of small items on the screen (i.e., small fonts). Therefore, a color monitor is not well suited for DTP applications. However, for CAD, paint and animation, visualization and other color-dependent applications, a color monitor is a must. Color monitors typically cost more than a monochrome monitor, and so do the display controllers that are used to drive them.

Alphanumeric terminals

In the early days of batch-processing machines, the primary mode of man-machine interaction was paper, where punch cards were the computer's only input devices. The computer's output device was limited to cards and line printers. With the advent of interactive time sharing in the 1960s came alphanumeric terminals. The first of these were based on teleprinters. Later, as technology advanced, these terminals utilized CRTs as display devices. Most early video display terminals employed raster technology. The standard of 25 rows and 80 characters per line evolved primarily because it could be accommodated at television scan rates using hardware that was mass produced for the television industry.

A typical user's terminal in a time-shared mainframe environment was linked to the host computer by a low-bandwidth connection. This severely limited the speed with which the user could modify and interact with the displayed data. In an alphanumeric terminal, ASCII characters are generated on the display in a dot matrix cell just like a printer. The cell size determines the quality of the characters. Cell sizes range from a 5 × 7 pixel matrix to 10 × 10 pixel matrix or larger, and more than one may be available depending on the display device.

An example of an alphanumeric terminal is the Digital VT100, VT220 and VT320. These terminals offer text, and only text, to the user. They are low cost and hundreds of thousands of them are in use (in the form of actual Digital products, compatibles and emulators). A software package from Polestar Software (Polestar Windows) provides the functions of windowed workstations for these character-based terminals.

Graphics terminals

In the early 1960s, computer graphics developed into an important interactive medium, and a second type of terminal device developed. These early graphic terminals employed vector (stroke-written) CRT technology. These early devices were large (20 to 25 inch diameter tubes), expensive ($25,000 to $50,000), would flicker if several thousand lines were on the screen at the same time and required constant host support for updating or refreshing the image (although some systems from companies like Information Displays, Inc. had their own refresh buffer and did not need the host to refresh them).

In the mid to late 1970s, direct view storage tubes became dominant because the images that were displayed did not require refreshing from data resident on the host mainframe. Still, the problem remained of the low bandwidth of the internal bus structure of the entire computer system.

In the late 1970s and early 1980s, raster display graphic terminals were introduced. They allowed dedicated graphics to be performed at each user position. Several companies were formed to produce these devices. Then, as workstations became popular and offered their own high-resolution display capabilities, the graphics terminal companies began to lose market share. As PCs became more prevalent and also had high-resolution displays, the graphics terminal companies all but disappeared. Those who survived went into one of three markets: dedicated terminals for the military, and specialized applications like stock exchange displays; dedicated X Window Systems terminals; and add-on display cards for workstations. These products are covered in other sections when appropriate.

Personal computers and entry-level workstations

Because PCs have proliferated and become so popular, they have attracted hundreds of companies as add-on vendors. When the PC was introduced, it had a very limited character-mode black-and-white display known as a monochrome display adapter (MDA). Like alphanumeric terminals, it was specified in terms of characters per line and lines per screen. The common specification was 80 × 24.

Hercules Computer Technology introduced the first bit-mapped display for the PC in 1983, and it had a resolution of 720 × 348. That started things, and since then hundreds of companies have entered the market with add-on bit-mapped graphics controllers for PCs, XTs, ATs, PS/2s, Macintoshes and Ataris.

In a monochrome display adaptor (MDA), characters are treated as one-byte cells. They have a 1-bit or 2-bit depth for each pixel and no color palette. In all-points-addressable (APA) bit-mapped displays, they are treated as a group of pixels. Today there are dozens of resolutions available as shown in TABLE 15-1.

Table 15-1. Resolutions of displays.

Low resolution (LR), 128 x 128 to 510 x 510, which includes:	
Text-only	MDA
320 x 240	CGA, MCGA
Medium resolution (MR), 512 x 512 to 800 x 600, which includes:	
640 x 350	EGA
512 x 512	Used in most Image Processing Systems
852 x 350	Super EGA
720 x 348	Hercules
640 x 480	VGA and PGC
800 x 600	SuperVGA
High resolution (HR), 801 x 601 to 1200 x 1023, which includes:	
1024 x 768	8514/A, ExtendedVGA, most proprietary systems
1280 x 800	DTP
1024 x 1024	Advanced Image Processing Systems
1152 x 800	SUN workstations
Very high resolution (VHR), 1201 x 1024 to 2048 x 1530, which includes:	
1280 x 1024	Most workstations
1600 x 1024	Used in DTP systems
1680 x 1280	Used in full-page DTP systems
1200 x 1800	MCA (IBM's future controller)
2048 x 1530	Forecasted next DTP & CAD range
Ultra high resolution (UHR), 2049 x 1531 and above, which includes:	
3072 x 2048	UHR DTP systems
4096 x 4096	Vector displays

Graphics display controllers

There are three classes of graphics display controllers: dumb, hard-wired, and programmable.

Frame buffers

The basic display controller found in a typical workstation, a Macintosh or a PS/2 is a host-dependent *dumb* frame buffer. Basically, such devices only offer extra memory to store the image, and the timing circuitry for the monitor. If color is involved, they will also have color look-up tables and digital-to-analog converters (often called RAMDACs). A frame buffer is considered dumb because it relies on the host processor to do all the calculations for the generation of screen elements such as lines, moves, and shapes.

Fixed function

When common functions such as line drawing and bit-block-movement are built into the display controller and executed without host involvement, it is said to be *hard-wired*. Fixed function controllers offer more speed because of their immediate mode of operation and their optimized functionality.

Programmable

Graphics controllers with a programmable processor are referred to as *smart controllers*. Programmable controllers are usually found in PCs that are configured for CAD applications and in X-terminals. Programmable controllers do not contribute anything to Macintosh computers and only offer an advantage in a workstation if there is an application that has been ported to the controller.

Display drivers

In the early days of graphics on a PC, the application developers had to provide software drivers for the graphics cards it intended to use. Such graphics cards would have CGA or EGA resolution or be a specialized graphics card like Hercules, or perhaps a proprietary card from other companies like Artist Graphics or Vermont Micro Systems. When VGA came to the PC, things didn't change.

However, when Windows was introduced, the burden for writing the software driver shifted from the application developer to the manufacturer of the graphics card. With this burden also came the opportunity to provide as much resolution as possible, since the application was no longer resolution specific. On the workstation side, similar restrictions applied, and application developers wrote drivers for popular display devices or only for the display that came with a workstation. Again, with the introduction of Windowing applications, X Window Systems, etc. the freedom for software drivers was greatly improved.

Graphic visualization workstation

All visualization workstations have these common features:

- One or more powerful processors (i.e., > 6MIPS).
- Large CPU memory (i.e., > 1 Mbyte).
- Disk subsystem.
- Built-in network I/O—typically Ethernet.
- High-speed internal bus structures (≥ 32 MB/sec.).
- High-resolution (≥ 1024 × 768), color (≥ 256) display device.
- High cost (> $40,000).

There are several ways manufacturers design and market visualization workstations; they are based on the following:

- Different approaches to delivering graphics capabilities.
- Different approaches to CPU architectures that increase performance.
- Different approaches to high-speed internal bus structure.

Today's visualization workstations

Many concurrent developments in computer technology have contributed to the development of today's workstation. The most common is the decrease in the cost and size of the processing elements, memory, and mass storage capabilities. This has made it practical to decentralize computing resources. With more computer resources available at the user station, it has become possible to couple the graphic generation functions more tightly with the storage and processing functions via a high-speed internal bus structure. Today, workstations employ internal bus structures that deliver up to 320MB/sec (i.e., Stardent's Datapath) of data-bandwidth transfer between memory, processors, and I/O. Sun Microsystem's internal bus structure (the Sbus) achieves 32MB/sec, Hewlett-Packard (Apollo) achieves (the X-BUS) 150MB/sec, and Silicon Graphics achieves a sustained data-bandwidth up to 64MB/sec between memory, processors, and I/O.

These advancements in bus performance are essential in the development of visualization workstation technology today. Without a high-speed internal bus structure, graphic subsystems could not reach real-time performance rates, thus allowing interactive windowing into application programs running on general purpose processors. Examples of Graphic Visualization Workstations with high-speed internal bus architectures can be found in the high-end products from Apollo, Hewlett-Packard, IBM, Silicon Graphics, Stardent and Sun Microsystems.

Various hardware approaches

There have been many different approaches developed to deliver graphics capabilities to workstation users. Listed below are a few of the key technologies that have emerged as solutions:

- Stand-alone host CPU with display adapter.
- CPU with specialized hardware sharing common address space.
- CPU and frame buffer with display list memory.
- CPU with graphic algorithms in custom processors.

- Custom hardware system for graphics acceleration.
- Programmable high-speed bit-sliced graphic architecture.

State of the art in hardware techniques

Listed below are several techniques that utilize the cutting edge of technology to deliver high-performance graphic capabilities to the power user:

- multiprocessors with parallel processing compilers,
- high-speed internal bus structure for high-speed data and pixel transfer,
- dedicated graphic processors implemented into
  a. add-on graphic processors boards,
  b. distributed frame buffers,
  c. dedicated graphic pipelines—Geometry Engine,
  d. programmable graphic pipelines.

Performance characteristics differentiation

To differentiate performance characteristics of visualization workstations, it is necessary to separate workstation performance into computational and graphics benchmarks. Computational performance factors employed in analyzing workstations need to include MFLOPS (Million Floating Point Instructions-per-second), bus types and data-transfer rate, and I/O-transfer rate between main-memory and processors. Performance factors typically associated with graphics environments include: screen resolution, the number of 3D vectors-per-second, and the number of Gouraud Shaded Polygons-per-second.

Benchmarks

Several industry-accepted user-driven benchmarks have emerged to further validate hardware performance across all vendor platforms.

Picture Level Benchmark Graphic Performance Characterization—NCGA benchmark suite, developed by Simgraphics, Inc. The Picture Level Benchmark delivers a suite of graphic performance tests that rate the graphics capabilities of all workstations fairly. It is an industry effort to develop a standardized benchmark for measuring graphics display performance.

The software, called the Picture-Level Benchmark (PLB), gives users a consistent way to measure how fast certain graphics files derived from their own application software can be displayed on different hardware platforms. The package is available through NCGA for $300. Vendor sponsors include Alliant Computer Systems, Digital Equipment Corp., DuPont Pixel Systems, Evans & Sutherland, Hewlett-Packard, IBM, Intergraph, Megatek, Prime Computer, Silicon Graphics, Sun Microsystems, and Tektronix.

The PLB is a platform-dependent program for running graphics-display performance tests on a particular vendor's hardware. It includes three elements:

- The Benchmark Interface Format (BIF), a standardized file structure that allows users to port geometry to the PLB program, as well as actions the geometry will perform.

- The Benchmark Timing Methodology (BTM), which provides a consistent method of measuring the time it takes for hardware to display and perform requested actions on a user's application geometry.
- The Benchmark Report Format (BRP), which provides a standardized report used to measure graphics-display performance for different hardware systems.

Prior to the PLB, users had to deal with several ambiguous methods of measuring graphics performance. Now that PLB is in the public domain, hardware vendors can implement PLB software on their platforms, saving the cost of developing custom ports necessary to benchmark hardware performance for individual user applications. Users, meanwhile, will be able to convert their application geometry into BIF format. Graphics files from the user's applications can then be displayed by hardware vendors that support the PLB program, and vendors can produce reports that measure the speed with which graphics are generated. The GPC group plans to develop measurement software that addresses higher levels of capability, beyond PLB. Its ultimate goal is an application-level benchmark that would provide a standardized measure for determining how fast different machines can run specific user applications.

SPECmark Systems Performance Evaluation Cooperative. The benchmark suite released by SPEC represents a credible start in providing fair and realistic ways to measure and compare the performance of computer systems. Only a handful of systems have been measured using the SPEC suite so far, but the initial results are encouraging—and enlightening. They contradict several vendor's marketing claims in convincing ways.

The SPEC suite consists of 10 suits of C and FORTRAN programs (more will be added later). These contain over 150,000 lines of source code taken from the fields of science and engineering. Three tests target ECAD, two software engineering applications, three scientific applications, and two synthetic scientific benchmarks. Of these, four are written in C and can be considered tests of integer performance; the remaining six, which measure floating point performance, are written in FORTRAN.

The SPEC suite produces several results. These include the raw completion time for each benchmark, along with a reference time giving the run time for the test on the reference machine. The ratio of reference time to run time gives the SPECratio, the tested machine's relative performance for the individual test. Because each vendor normalizes against a single machine, SPECratios from different vendors are directly comparable. The ten tests in the suite produce ten individual SPECratios. Taking the geometric mean of these gives a single measurement of system performance, the SPECmark. The initial SPECmark tests were targeted at the implementation performance of CPU processors like the Motorola 88000, the Intel 80X86, the Motorola 68040, and IBM's RS6000. With the release of version 2, I/O capabilities, memory, multiprocessors, Servers, and multiuser performance have been included.

X-terminals

X-terminals rely on the X-Window standard to achieve a low-cost, host-dependent graphical windowing environment. For those who don't need or want desktop applications processing, X-stations are cost effective alternatives to workstations. The X-terminal is able to give people what they want on their desktops for very little cost. Connectivity options enable the X-displays to fit into heterogeneous computer environments, which include workstations, minicomputers, mainframes, and supercomputers.

The X-terminals entering the market today offer an inexpensive solution for networked diskless workstations, allowing more users access to expensive computing environments. The X-terminals' primary job is to share scarce resources available upon a networked computing environment. X-terminals are finding broad acceptance among users who do not need the performance of workstations. Many observers believe that much of the performance offered by workstations is not being fully utilized by the majority of end users. An X-terminal does offer higher performance than a PC emulating terminal. The motivation to utilize a PC emulation is to maintain the DOS application capabilities of the PC. If all applications to be run in a corporate environment are X-based, a dedicated terminal may be the most cost-effective in the long term.

X-terminals available today have from 1-8 Mbytes of internal main memory, run on powerful internal programs stored in ROM or down-loaded from a host, provide resolutions of 640 × 480, 1024 × 768 or 1280 × 1024, in monochrome, 16, 256, or true (16 million) color. The terminals attach directly to Ethernet and support TCP/IP, DECnet, and X11.3 protocols.

There are two basic architectures used for existing X Window Systems terminals. In one approach, a Motorola 68020 processor is used for running the X-server, while low-level color graphics operations are performed with a TMS34010 chip. The second approach, used in lower priced terminals, is to run both the X-server and graphics on the TMS34010. The Texas Instrument TMS340X0 appears to have become the standard graphics controller for X-terminals.

It has been said that X-terminals are somewhat of a throwback to the 1970s; they don't offer much [accessible] computing capability. That is somewhat paradoxical. A reasonable X-terminal contains a 68030 running at 25 MHz, 4 Mbytes of RAM and a 16-19 inch color monitor for about $7,000. Yet all that horsepower is necessary basically to paint a screen. It gives new meaning to the term dumb terminal!

Some vendors, such as Hewlett-Packard, are offering upgrades to their original X-terminals. Users of Hewlett-Packard's 700/X-terminals can upgrade to Hewlett-Packard 9000 diskless workstations. This allows the investment in the terminal to be protected, while allowing the hardware to expand to grow with a company's or user's needs.

X-terminals aren't the only display devices that run X Window Systems applications, however. Diskless workstations and PCs also provide GUI access and other windowing features. Deciding which desktop device type to purchase generally becomes one of determining whether the user absolutely requires the additional CPU power of a workstation or PC, or whether providing GUI access through a low-cost X Window Systems terminal will suffice.

Costs

A monochrome X-terminal sells for $2,000 to $3,000, and prices are expected to drop to the $1,000 range. Color versions are in the $5,000 to $10,000 range and may not drop as quickly as monochrome because of the smaller demand and the added cost of video memory for the color.

Drawbacks

The only drawback with X-terminals is that if they are used in extremely heavy computing-intensive, interactive, or heavy-transaction processing environments, they can severely slow down the network (if not cripple performance) due to the X-terminal (Server) constantly needing to communicate with the host (Client) CPU. X-terminals work best in applications that require normal networking capabilities. The two principal resource consuming functions in an X-terminal are the processor time for drawing and text manipulation, and screen space. An intermediary program, the window manager, manages the screen space allocations.

The X-server is responsible for scheduling work performed on behalf of the Client programs, for memory management, and for subsidiary processes such as maintaining the communications links with each Client. The Server performs all these functions by using the services of the underlying operating system. The X Window System can be used for a truly distributed system; when it opens a window on another workstation screen, it is the remote CPU (i.e., Client) that is doing the drawing.

From a structural point of view, the X-terminal consists of a device-independent layer that receives and translates server/client request messages in the X-protocol format, an operating system-dependent layer that interfaces to a particular operating system, and a device-dependent layer that is a collection of device drivers for the specific hardware supported. The current X11 version can perform two-dimensional drawing of lines, rectangles, circles, arcs, text, and arbitrary bit maps on monochrome or color displays with up to 32 bits per pixel. The X-terminal Server also loads new fonts from operating system files, stores them in memory, and makes them available for text writing.

The chain of communication in opening a window on an X-terminal under the X Window System has seven links, summarized as follows: Application → Xlib → operating system → Protocol → operating system → X Server → Screen. X-terminals create more network traffic than character-based terminals, but they impose less of a burden on a network than diskless workstations and PCs. In general, X-terminals operating in text mode require more network overhead than character-cell terminals functioning in the same mode.

In terms of protocol traffic, Xterm, which is used by X-terminals to communicate over TCP/IP, generates about the same number of network transactions as an alphanumeric terminal utilizing Telnet. However, the Xterm packet sizes tend to measure about 40 percent larger than Telnet's. For example, transferring 10 keystrokes requires only 2,628 bytes when Telnet is used, but it requires 4,468 bytes with Xterm.

Window management causes additional network traffic because the window manager for an X-terminal resides on the host. Every window movement requires the transmission of mouse position data across the network to the host-resident window manager, which then responds with a stream of window positioning commands for the X-terminal Server. To provide smooth on-screen movement, mouse position and commands are usually sent in small increments. Moving a window from the upper left-hand side of the screen to the lower right-hand side can require the transmission of more than 200 round-trip packets, amounting to 20,000 bytes of data.

In graphics-intensive applications such as CAD/CAM, however, a simple window movement would cause a large amount of data to be transferred across the network. Many users running CAD/CAM applications on X-terminals could present a substantial network burden. Diskless workstations offer their strongest challenge to X-terminals in this type of application. But for applications that don't require complex, fast-acting graphics, X-terminals are less demanding of a network than diskless workstations or PCs.

Terminals versus workstations

Choosing between an X-terminal and other machines involves other considerations that are difficult to quantify. Chief among these factors is the strategic computing direction an MIS manager takes by choosing X-terminals instead of diskless workstations or PCs. The X Window System is one of the few computer industry standards that enjoys widespread acceptance and affords true plug-and-play compatibility. Most X-terminals are interchangeable, which allows MIS managers to select X-terminal vendors according to price rather than whether or not a given device supports a given hardware and software base.

Workstations, however, require more MIS effort to obtain interoperability. UNIX versions differ significantly, so MIS managers must utilize more manpower to ensure that different workstation models can coexist. Because administration costs are generally lower for X-terminals than for diskless workstations and PCs, and because incremental costs involved in expanding an X Window System network are lower, in many cases X-terminals provide a cost-justification computing alternative that lets MIS managers exploit the productivity gains afforded by GUIs.

X-terminals may not be suitable for all graphics-intensive applications. But for the vast majority of commercial applications, as well as system and network management utilities, X-terminals generally present less of a network load and better price/performance ratios than diskless workstations and PCs. Tests have shown that windowing terminals rarely overload the network, but can drain host computer resources in some cases. Tests have found that Ethernet was absolutely not a bottleneck for the terminals; the loading seemed extremely linear. The mix or blend of CPU and graphics-intensity seems to be the single most important determining factor in terms of the kinds of resources users will need to allocate for the application. A general rule of thumb is the Client machine will need between .25 MIPS up to 1 MIPS per X-terminal user, a range that is highly dependent on the application.

Available host RAM is a key to X-terminal performance. The most critical issue is that the host must be configured with the proper amount of RAM for the number of users. When the host is equipped with optimal RAM and the LAN is not a bottleneck, the X-terminal users will have performance approaching, or comparable to, an entry-level workstation that is configured as an X-server. Furthermore, a user will get comparable interactive graphics performance. The X-terminals themselves do not require much local memory. 1 to 2 Mbytes of local RAM is usually enough for most X-terminal users. Users should not trust their initial assumptions about X network behavior and

CPU demands without testing those assumptions. A user's perception of what will be a resource-intensive application may be completely reversed in practice.

Networks

In a network control center, the thousands of cryptic messages representing the status on devices in a network can be overwhelming and confusing. Network management software with a graphical user interface can show the outlines of a network at a glance. An overview of a network can be particularly helpful in the early stages of problem hunting. Some network managers put a graphical user interface rather low on their list of concerns. While users prefer a graphical user interface over a character interface if given a choice, most are grappling with more fundamental network integration and management issues.

Traffic on the network

As in any distributed computing scenario, an application's ability to run effectively depends on the network. X-terminal implementations for graphics-intensive applications are vulnerable to performance problems because the network stands between graphics calculations and the display. A great amount of network traffic generated by diskless workstations and PCs stems from their dependence on the network as an extended disk I/O bus. Both diskless workstations and PCs must download applications code and data from the central file Server.

An X-terminal requires much less network overhead. With both data and applications residing on the host, the network ships only display-related data. The traffic differs not only in amount, but also in kind. The bursts of traffic flow typical of an X-windows environment is much more suited to a collision-detect network than are the extended file transfers that are required by diskless workstations.

A diskless workstation or PC running multiple windows and applications can easily degrade network performance. In such cases, the limited memory on a low-end diskless workstation or PC requires that the devices swap data and code across the network. For example, at a typical diskless workstation, UNIX requires about 3MB; a window manager such as the Open Software Foundation's Motif GUI adds 1.5MB; and X-window Server software eats up another 2MB. For an 8MB workstation, this leaves only 1.5MB for the application.

With such limited memory capacity, the workstation is forced to begin swapping. If other workstations on the network face the same dilemma, traffic will increase rapidly. The solution is either to add a swapping disk at each workstation or add more memory. The latter is less expensive, but both add significantly to the workstation's per-seat cost. By contrast, when an X-window terminal exceeds its memory capacity, the application it's running slows to a crawl unless extra memory is purchased for the terminal.

Network Computing Devices (NCD) has a window manager with the appearance and behavior of OSF/Motif that runs locally on its X terminals, rather than on a host computer across the network. This saves network resources and allows X terminals to be used with hosts that do not support the X Window System.

The NCDwm window manager is part of NCDware, the software for the firm's X terminal family. The X terminal-resident NCDwm window manager is identical in functionality to the OSF/Motif window manager, defining the appearance and behavior of windows (e.g., how to open and close them, their borders, icons, and menus), and managing mouse-driven events such as moving and resizing windows. However, it uses only 100 kilobytes of memory space—about one-tenth of the one megabyte consumed by OSF/Motif running on a networked host computer.

Importance of pointing devices in GUIs

It seems clear that graphical user interfaces will become commonplace on tomorrow's computers. As a result, the emphasis for input will shift from the keyboard as a pure input device, to pointing devices that are used to select screen objects and functions. Along with the maturation of PC and other hardware, which enables the use of performance-hungry graphical user interfaces, pointing devices have also matured. Pointing devices consist of the X-Y joystick, touch sensitive screens, light pens, mice and track balls.

Technology

The most popular pointing devices are mice and track balls; both use a ball. It is either rolled on a desk surface in the case of the mouse, or by the user's hand in the case of the track ball. The technology in use for most mice and track ball devices is either opto-mechanical or purely mechanical. Opto-mechanical technology is so named because, as the ball turns, it moves a wheel attached to a notched revolving disk. As the disk turns, it breaks a light beam that is produced by an LED on one side of the disk and an optical sensor on the other side. Mechanical devices use a pair of wheels that contract the ball and produce electrical currents when they are rolled (as a result of mouse movement).

Optical mice incorporate a light source, an optical sensor, and a specially designed mouse pad. As the mouse moves over the pad, the light beam is broken when lines on the pad are crossed, producing a signal representing the mouse movement. When mice were first released, they functioned primarily as cursor movement devices. Today's pointers can be used for high-resolution pixel-by-pixel movements, a significant improvement over the original pointing devices.

Resolution

The traditional mouse has also seen improvements in resolution and accuracy. The original Microsoft Mouse had a resolution of 100 dots per inch (DPI), adequate in the days of low-resolution CGA displays. The mouse that Microsoft introduced in the fall of 1987 doubled that resolution, raising it to 200 DPI—again, adequate for EGA displays and suitable for use with VGA displays. Microsoft's newest mouse, again, doubled the resolution, bringing it to 400 DPI. The proliferation of GUIs and of sophisticated drawing/design software made this increased resolution necessary. Other companies, including Logitech and Mouse Systems, also sell similar mice sporting a range of true resolutions or resolutions that can be produced by multiplying or dividing the number of points actually produced by moving the mouse.

The question of what is needed in a mouse is subject to some debate. As resolutions gradually moved up from 100 DPI to 400 true DPI, the value of the next apparent move (to 800 or 1,000 DPI) must be addressed. "If you were to have a mouse that stayed at 400 DPI at one time for text-based applications, the product would be unusable," said Tony Rodriguez, product manager at Mouse Systems Corp. "The mainstream mouse user will be satisfied [with pointer resolution] at 400," said Rich Thompson, group product manager at Microsoft's Systems, peripherals and accessories group. "The top end-user will take as much resolution as you can give them."

Other pointing devices

There are many additional pointing devices available and under development. Like everything else, there is and will be no best solution.

Data tablets

The third most popular pointing device is the data tablet. It is used primarily in CAD, paint and animation applications. A data tablet consists of a pen (with and without an umbilical cord) and a specialized pad. The pad (i.e., the tablet) can be from 10 × 10 inches to as large as 36 × 36 inches. It senses the location of the pen either by radio wave, acoustic waves, infrared waves or pressure. Data tablets have a sensitivity or resolution as small as 0.001 inch. Data tablets are also called digitizers.

Joysticks

A variation on the trackball is the joystick. Joysticks come in two models, absolute (full-swing) and incremental (stiff stick). The absolute version matches the screen to the limits of the movement of the stick. This technique has limited resolution but is very positive. The incremental version moves the cursor each time the stick is nudged or pushed.

Hands free

Mice and trackballs take up desk space. In addition, mice require extra space for the mouse to be moved around on. If GUIs are to become the interface of the masses, then an alternate pointing device is needed. One concept that has been developed is a head-mounted reflector. As the user's head is moved the screen cursor tracks that movement. The user can then activate menu functions through the keyboard.

Special keyboards

Another approach is to use pressure sensitive keyboard keys. One company offers a keyboard that allows the user to press the J key. Pressing to the right causes the cursor to move in that direction. The amount of pressure determines the speed at which the cursor moves. This technique could become popular for laptops and offices with limited desk space.

Touch screens

Elographics, a pioneer of touch screens and unique (resistive-membrane) digitizer tablets, has written a driver that makes their touch screen look like a mouse to OS/2 programs. Combining a touch screen with the 3-dimensional effects of Presentation Manager's GUI is a good idea because it makes the buttons look like they are actually depressed. Any program that uses a mouse with an OS/2 application will accept Elographics' driver (which has the dubious name, Monitomouse).

Light pens

A light pen works by means of a light sensor in its tip. An electron beam in the monitor scans the display 60 times every second and makes the phosphors glow. By sensing the time between these pulses, the pen determines its position on-screen. Pressing the pen tip against the screen functions like clicking a mouse button.

Light pens, while they may not be as versatile as mice, come closest in function and design to that most intuitive of all pointing devices, the human finger. Light pens have all but disappeared from use on a desktop, but they offer unique advantages. No other mature technology offers the light pen's immediacy of control and feedback, a contributor to a GUI's charm factor.

Although a mouse gives the advantage of using a horizontal surface, an amazing amount of connection to the application and concentration is lost when the user's job becomes that of moving a cursor to the proper location on the screen. It would be much faster and less distracting to simply touch the light pen stylus to the proper location. The light pen is a natural for specialized menu-oriented database software. Hospital record keeping, point-of-sale operations, and automotive maintenance are the biggest markets. The light pen's main drawback is that constantly holding it up can quickly tire your arm; however, in practice the user doesn't really hold the pen against the screen for extended periods of time, but rather just quickly picks points.

Studies of children have shown that pointing directly at what you want is better than moving something else (a graphic cursor) to point there for you. Although this seems obvious, the strength of the difference in interface quality is quite tangible and must be felt to be appreciated. The light pen's immediate feedback and user connection to the system can provide a superior solution for many applications and help deliver charm.

UnMouse

The UnMouse is a derivative of the touch screen technology. It was developed by MicroTouch. This device consists of a desktop pad approximately 4 × 3 inches (same aspect ratio as the monitor screen) with a grid on it. Using a finger or a pen to press any point on this surface causes the cursor (on the monitor) to relocate to that point—similar to how a mouse causes cursor movement. The user can drag his finger with slight pressure across the surface and the cursor will follow. A button to the left allows actuation of menu-selected items. A touch screen technique also has the ability to have areas of it designated for preprogrammed functions. Software is provided with the UnMouse to allow the user to set up such functionality.

Future pointing devices

The Sensor Frame Corporation, in Pittsburgh, is working on *Gesture devices*, sensors that respond to the movement of the user's hand or his arm in space. They work without physical contact and create a field of invisible IR light that is interrupted by the user's hands. The field sensors can detect several axes of movement.

The Dataglove from VPL Research is becoming more popular. Although still a little bulky and awkward to use, it has great promise.

The various ways that a computer can communicate are mismatched with current pointing devices and input techniques. Less kind observers have described the mouse as the greatest I/O impedance in the history of computing. A more appropriate view would be derived from face-to-face, human-to-human communication, emulating the conversation, not the monologue. Gestural and speech imput are examples of what is needed.

References

Teja, Ed and Laura John. 1990. *IBM PC and PS/2 graphics handbook*. Microtrend Books: San Marcas, CA.

Raster Graphics Handbook. 1980. Conrac: Covina, CA.

16

Specialized GUIs and window systems

A GUI can be in almost any form and used on any type of computer. The recent announcements of Windows, and before that, Motif, have captured the headlines and attention of the public. Recently it was Windows and NeXT, and before that it was the Macintosh. Will there be a new GUI every year or even more often? Probably not. Things seem to be settling out and standards are emerging. Nonetheless there are still several other very good, useful and often unique GUIs available and being used. This chapter will list a few of them.

One of the most popular GUIs, the Macintosh, can attribute its success to the simplicity of its interface. After working with one Macintosh application, a user learns the mouse actions and methods that drive virtually all programs for that environment. However, underneath that ease of use, the Macintosh's operating system is teeming with complexity. It has been hidden from the disinterested, and that is one of the major keys to a good operating environment. A friendly environment, one with charm, should have enough versatility to handle any job that comes along, and include a high-level layer for those who just want to run applications. That is the goal of the systems described in this chapter.

Pen-based GUIs

One of the first systems to offer intimacy between the computer and the user (i.e., the threshold of charm) was the RAND system developed at the RAND Laboratories in 1967. It was the world's first system to employ a pen-based data tablet. Later, in the mid 1970s, Alan Kay's early work with the Dyna book attempted to establish the metaphor of a pencil. He asked the question, "What would a computer be if it were like a pencil?" According to Kay, if you want people to go along with you, you have to get them involved in the same conspiracy, and a good user interface design is a conspiracy.

In the mid 1980s, the first low-cost handwriting recognition systems appeared in the market. They used opaque digitizing tablets and were often connected to low-cost

PCs. The first applications were in banks for signature verification. The early technological problems were overcome, and by the mid 1980s, handwriting recognition systems were considered a viable prospect for specialized user interfaces. In the early 1990s, improvements in handwriting recognition algorithms encouraged investors and developers to bring out systems based on such concepts. The term pen-based computing became popularized to describe small notebook-like computers with a pen-based GUI. These notebooks opened up the computer environment for a new category for users. Presumably, anyone who could write could use a pen-based computer or notebook.

The first systems have been used by professionals who must be mobile—doctors, insurance adjusters, stock brokers, reporters, sales executives, and inventory managers. The next wave of users is expected to be executives who have avoided, for one reason or another, the PC revolution. By the end of the decade, pen-based machines could become a common briefcase accessory, used for silent note taking, appointment making and monitoring, and office mail. Notebook or notepad computers with pen-based GUIs will increasingly be used for tasks that desktop machines can't accomplish, and used by people who don't touch keyboards today.

One of the keys to pen-based computer notebooks is their mobility. An unexpected side benefit users have found with them is a more personable face-to-face relationship associated with users that bring a paper notepad along to a business meeting. The pen-based system's handwriting recognition has been an enabling function that will carry it beyond even its developer's imagination.

However, although important and valuable, the significance of pen-based systems is not just using the pen or stylus as a substitute for keyboards. Although one is able to simply write directly on a tablet (that is also the display screen) and watch as the words are converted into text, there are additional capabilities that hold more promise.

The pen-based GUI is a notebook metaphor that organizes the user's work, allowing him to flip through a notebook to access an appropriate document. Meanwhile, the embedded document architecture lets the user insert documents (which can be edited) within one another and create hyperlink buttons for navigating through the notebook.

The pen thus becomes important for control and manipulation as much as it does for input. Data entry is not the major benefit because even the fastest writer can't match a typist for sheer speed when it comes to entering new material. Also, a pen can't match a mouse for revision of text and direct manipulation of images. However, the user can directly insert a word into a sentence by simply drawing a caret under the insertion point, and then writing the word above it. Some observers think that pen-based computers will teach people to use standard editor's marks in the same way that the Macintosh made users familiar with the details of typography.

Improved document control does not diminish the benefit of handwriting recognition. Yet there is still work to be done in this area. Although developers and manufacturers continue to improve the systems, they are not yet perfect (and may never be). Manufacturers brag about a 90% or greater accuracy, but even a small number of errors can mean the difference between a simple edit and a serious mistake due to misinterpretation of words (similar to the problem of a spell checker—they are not intention checkers).

Like their desktop counterparts, all pen-based computers are not the same. There are three main contenders for the pen-based notebook GUI market; Apple, Go Corp., and Microsoft. Some users will want pen-based computers based on their favorite desktop GUI and operating system. Others will offer entirely new operating systems tailored to the pen-based environment, just as Apple built the Macintosh from the ground up to leverage the unique capabilities of graphical interfaces and the mouse. In their own ways both Apple and Microsoft made it clear that they believe it is not necessary to create an entirely new operating system to implement a pen-based computing environment.

Mac Handwriter

Apple helped Communications Intelligence Corp. (CIC) introduce the Mac Handwriter, which Apple distributes in Japan. Mac Handwriter is a tablet that attaches to the Macintosh's keyboard port and can recognize all of the four forms of characters used to write in Japanese—kanji, katakana, hiragana, and roman. CIC is one of the original reseachers in the area of handwriting recognition. The Mac Handwriter has received very good reviews. Mac Handwriter is a standard peripheral to the Macintosh and therefore doesn't require any modification to the user interface or command structure of Macintosh software.

PenApps

Microsoft offers PenApps which works with standard Windows applications. It accepts characters via its handwriting recognition algorithm and enters them into programs as though they were being typed. It also takes the commands issued by the pen and translates them into the appropriate mouse or menu equivalent. Figure 16-1 shows the architecture of PenApps.

Microsoft's PenApps is aimed at the same user as GO's and Apple's pen-based system—the mobile worker. PenApps is part of the "Information at your fingertips" concept Microsoft has developed. PenApps includes a recognition context manager and a recognizer engine.

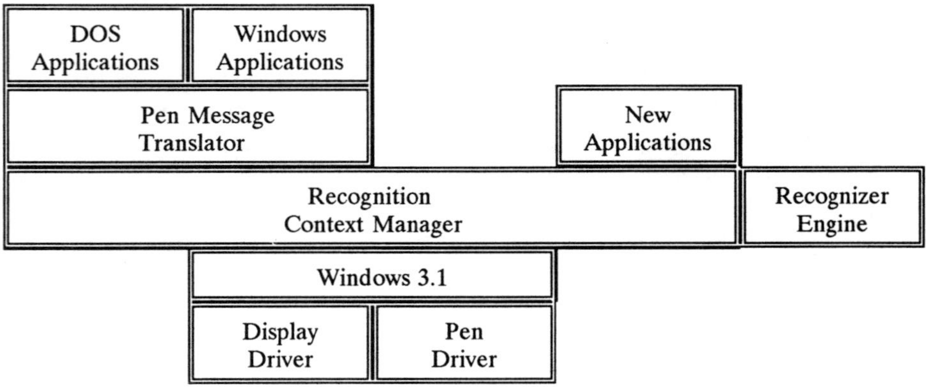

Fig. 16-1. Microsoft's PenApps architecture.

PenPoint

One of the criticisms of operating systems such as DOS, OS/2, or UNIX is that they have been designed according to principles that are fundamentally contrary to personal computing (e.g., the operating system must always be in control; it should set priorities for which task gets completed, and it should protect the machine from both software developers and users). Accomplishing that usually results in a large, complex, hard-to-understand operating system. That is more or less what users hoped to avoid when they adopted the PC, Macintosh, Commodore and other personal machines.

Go Corp. has introduced a pen-based computing system and operating system that is small, flexible, interactive, and responsive to the user. It is a GUI with an integrated operating system. It uses a flat single-tier memory model and an object-oriented file system, has a robust, speedy imaging model, can recognize handwriting and is controlled by a pen or stylus. The user interface is shown in FIG. 16-2.

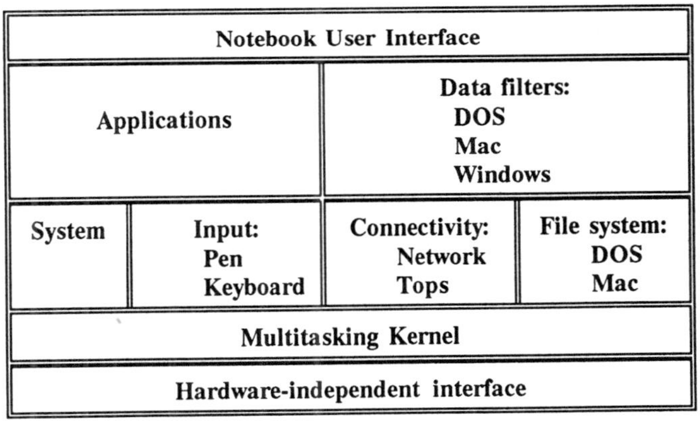

Fig. 16-2. PenPoint operating system.

The new operating system opens to an electronic "table of contents," with notebook-style tabs running vertically down the right side (refer to FIG. 16-3). Users turn to a section in the notebook by tapping a graphical tab with a pen or stylus. On a single "page," users can open multiple documents—without creating separate files or links between files—using an Embedded Document Architecture feature.

There are 11 basic gestures recognized by the notepad from the pen. The gestures are used for editing, controlling the table of contents of the notebook, or operating a drawing application. The pen or stylus is used to choose pull-down menu options, as well as to enter, cut, paste, and edit text. Go's handwriting recognition algorithm recognizes punctuation, numbers, and cursive forms of most letters, as well as uppercase and lowercase hand printing. The gestures keep the user from falling back into a character-oriented environment, which is typical of today's desktop operating systems.

In addition, the ImagePoint imaging model integrates all text operations with graphics operations, providing scaling, translation, rotation and sampled image rendering. The handwriting-recognition engine in the operating system translates printed uppercase and lowercase letters, numbers and punctuation in many handwriting styles.

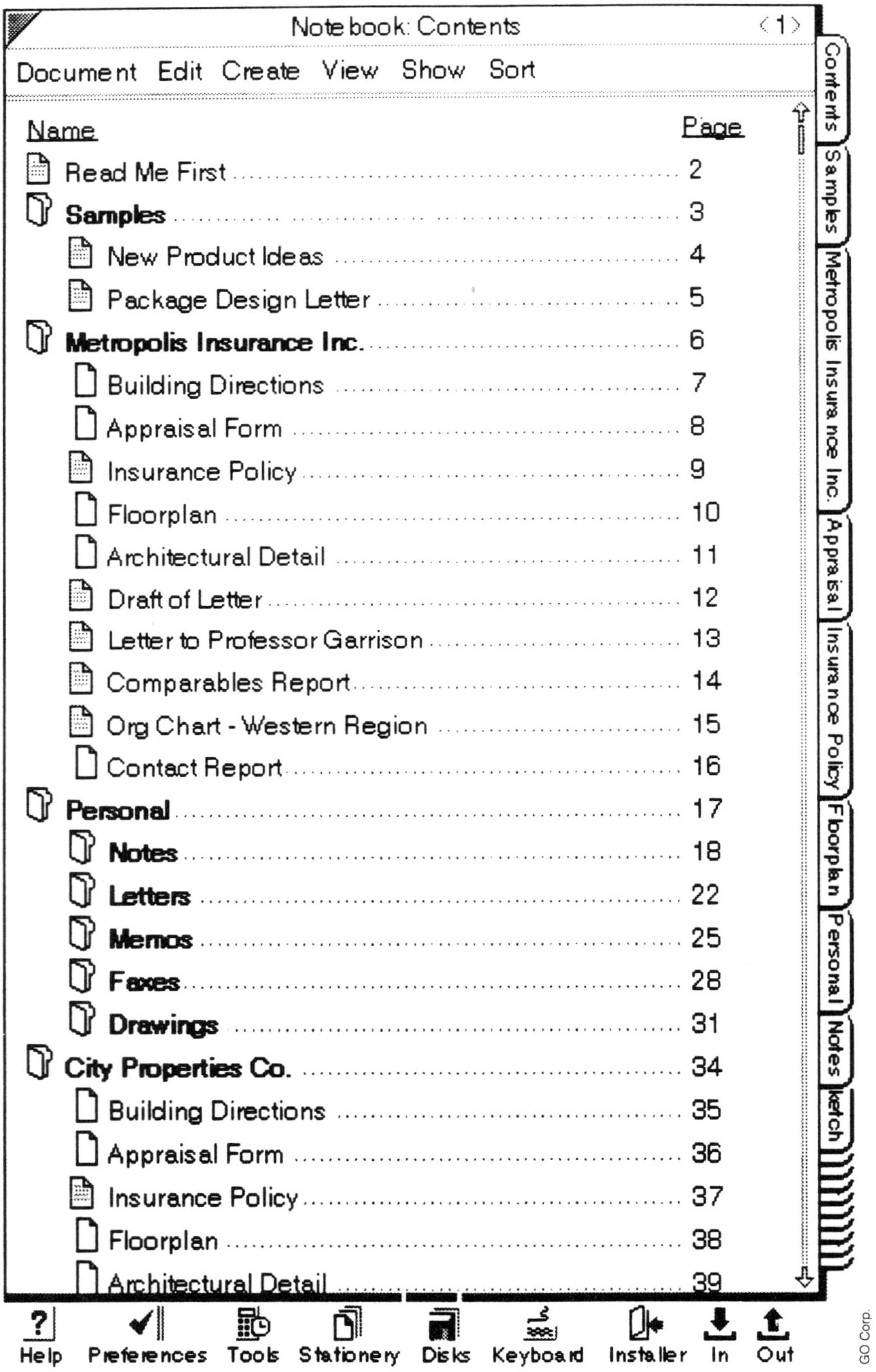

Fig. 16-3. PenPoint pen-based GUI.

The computer/desk that IBM developed for the Defense Department is based on PenPoint and uses a stylus on an LCD work surface.

Freestyle

Typically, new technology addresses the need in business to increase productivity. This is accomplished through the automation of routine processes such as order entry, payroll, purchasing, account management, etc. These are structured tasks that can be measured quantitatively.

There is another realm of the workplace, though, that is gaining increased awareness. People spend a significant portion of their work day on administrative tasks. And if new technology can more effectively address the way people actually work, a positive impact can be made on a company's bottom line. This requires an understanding of intuitive, decision-making activity that is difficult to quantify. But through improving the time and quality aspects of communicating information from one person to another, technology can produce measurable results for unstructured activities—sharing an idea, organizing multiple forms of information, clarifying meaning, gaining approvals.

The key elements here are time and quality. Up to now, time and quality in the unstructured world have not been touched by technology. Wang Laboratories feels it has broken through this barrier with the introduction of its pen-based GUI desktop, the Wang Freestyle personal computing system. (See FIG. 16-4.)

The Freestyle system provides users with a means to organize, package, and distribute information. Not just in the form of text, data, or graphics, but also personalized information—writing and speech. This allows streamlining administrative tasks and at the same time enhancing the quality of information throughout an organization.

The Wang Freestyle system is a PC-based application that allows users of industry-standard PCs to capture virtually any information on their PC screen and annotate, store, or mail the resulting Freestyle pages. The Freestyle system is a GUI in the sense that it permits direct manipulation of objects and applications. It is not a GUI toolkit for developing other applications.

The standard Freestyle system, a hardware/software combination that includes the Freestyle icon-based PC software and the electronic tablet and pencil, enables users to capture information on their PC screen in the form of an electronic piece of paper by touching the Freestyle pencil to the tablet. By writing with the pencil on the tablet, users can add a signature or notes to the resulting Freestyle page on the screen. They can also add typed notes via a keyboard. Figure 16-5 shows the Freestyle pen movements.

The Freestyle/Light package is an entry-level, software-only version that enables users to create and annotate Freestyle pages and manage the Freestyle electronic desk through their PC keyboard or an optional mouse. With the voice option, which includes a telephone-like handset, a board, and software, Freestyle and Freestyle/Light users can add spoken comments to a Freestyle page.

The Wang Freestyle system provides an electronic desktop that simulates the user's own desktop. It offers icons of such items as a stapler and printers that work the same way a real stapler and printers do. A user can select a function (such as a stapler) on the PC's screen by touching the pencil to the corresponding location on the tablet.

Wang

Fig. 16-4. The Freestyle system features an electronic tablet and pencil in lieu of a mouse.

Postage-stamp-size papers can be piled up and/or moved on the Freestyle electronic desk by touching and dragging them. Papers can be piled up and/or moved by touching and dragging them. Also, a user can create a signature file or any other handwritten image using the pencil. The Wang Freestyle system runs on the Wang PC 200/300 Series of personal computers, as well as IBM PS/2s, PC/ATs and compatibles.

Freestyle Movements

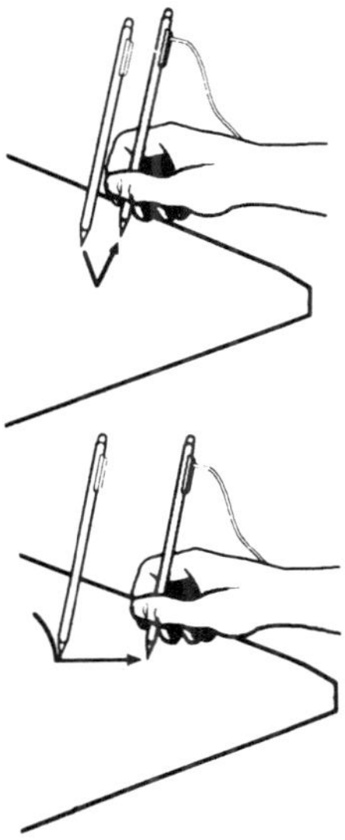

Two simple movements let you perform most Freestyle tasks: *Touch & Lift* and *Touch & Drag*.

Touch & Lift

Touch the Pencil to the Tablet so that the Pencil Point icon touches the item you want. Then lift the Pencil off the Tablet.

Touch & Drag

Touch the Pencil to the Tablet so that the Pointing Hand icon touches the item you want to move. Then, without lifting the Pencil, move the Pencil across the Tablet until the item is where you want it.

Wang

Fig. 16-5. Freestyle movements.

DataViews

DataViews is developed and distributed by Visual Intelligence Corporation of Amherst, Massachusetts. It consists of three primary software tools that provide a developer's toolkit designed for development of GUIs. DataViews includes an integrated menu-driven graphics editor and a library of subroutines to first create the graphical interface with both input and output capabilities, then link it to the user's application.

DV-Tools DV-Tools is a subroutine library that includes both input and dynamic graphic output capabilities. The user specifies the dynamic interactions of components on each screen and between screens. Adjustments can be made to processes by selecting visible components. DV-Tools allows linking of graphical objects to data, dynamic display of data as it changes, and control of displayed processes through hierarchical arrangements of screens.

DV-Draw DV-Draw is basically a drawing editor used to create 2D static or dynamic drawings (such as schematics, instrument panels, and control systems) and input objects (such as sliders and menus) without programming the application. DV-Draw includes predefined graphs, dials, meters, surface plots, and strip charts, which can be combined with drawings created with other 2D drawing tools. DV-Draw also provides vector text. The matrix compares the features and functionality between DataViews and the ANSI/ISO standards. (See TABLE 16-1.)

Table 16-1. Comparison of graphics functions.

	CORE	GKS	PHIGS	DataViews
Data Format	Flt Pt	Flt Pt	Flt Pt	Flt Pt
C Callable	Yes	Yes	Yes	Yes
Fortran Callable	Yes	Yes	Yes	Yes
Pascal Callable	Yes	Yes	Yes	Yes
Transparent Acceleration	No	Yes	Yes	Yes
Pick input Supported	Yes	Yes	Yes	Yes
2D Data	Yes	Yes	Yes	Yes
3D Data	Yes	No	Yes	No
Raster Operations	No	Yes	No	No
Modeling Transformations	Yes	No	Yes	No
View Selections	1	Multiple	Multiple	Multiple
3D Primitives	Yes	No	Yes	No
Display Vector Graphics	Yes	Yes	Yes	Text only
Viewing System	Yes	Yes	No	Yes
Modeling System	No	No	Yes	No
Segmentation	Yes	Yes	No	No
Immediate Mode	No	Yes	No	No
Linear Display List	Yes	Yes	Yes	Yes
Editable Display List	No	No	Yes	No
Hierarchical Display List	No	No	Yes	Yes
Application Data in Display List	No	No	Yes	No
Lighting	Yes	No	Yes	No
Shading	Yes	No	Yes	No
Displayable in Windowing System	Yes	Yes	Yes	Yes
File Formats	Archive CGM	GKSMet CGM	Archive Postscript	Generic MF
Comments	ANSI/ISO Standard 1979	ANSI/ISO Standard 1985	ANSI/ISO Standard 1988	Not Industry Standard Not coming

Graphical Editor The Graphical Editor Construction Kit is for programmers to create application-specific drawing editors, giving their end users the freedom to customize displays with which they interact, while enforcing constraints to maintain the integrity of the original application. The kit is a set of support routines useful for DV-Tools programmers.

ENABLE

Recognizing the need for application compatibility for character-based PCs (XTs to 346s), Enable Software introduced ENABLE, a character-based GUI emulation system with mouse access, pull-down menus and desktop tools. It runs on DOS or SCO UNIX interchangeably and can be used to bridge the DOS/UNIX transition.

Genspac

Window environments have been built for other computers besides workstations and PCs. VME, Multibus, S-bus and G-64 bus-based systems with real-time multitasking operating system-9 operating systems can use the G-Windows window manager from Genspac. The window manager allows multiple tasks to be viewed and accessed at the same time under operating system-9. The current version supports 640 × 480 displays with 256 colors.

With Genspac a window is created when a process opens a path to the device descriptors. It is done at the command line. A window may also be created from an operating system-9 shell command line if a process uses the output redirection facilities.

The G-Window system is also made available as a developer's package. The package contains the C and assembly language libraries necessary to write applications that use G-Windows and menus. The developer's kit isn't in itself a CASE environment; however, there are such environments available for operating system-9.

IXI

X.desktop, from IXI, is an application program that creates a visual working environment for users. Running on a UNIX host system, X.desktop provides an iconic representation of the files, programs, and facilities available to the user. These icons are manipulated using a mouse for running programs, managing files (deletion, copying, renaming, creation) and accessing printers and other peripherals.

IXI has developed a special function they call the *drag and drop action*. It provides a convenient way for users to initiate any process such as editing or printing a file. X.desktop replaces the error-prone text entry of cryptic UNIX commands with intuitive point and click operations and gives clear messages in the user's natural language if mistakes are made.

Users can create new icons and build an environment that matches their own working style. In addition, X.desktop's behavior and capabilities can be modified and extended, without programming knowledge, to suit any working style or to construct purpose-built UNIX shells. X.desktop does not impose any constraints or overheads on the use of the system and works alongside other UNIX shells.

X.desktop provides object management facilities including an intuitive drag and drop concept. For example, dropping the icon of a file onto another invokes the underlying program or service, such as an editor, compiler, or print server. Intelligence can be built into the desktop by linking types of files with specific programs. For example, clicking on a C source file would normally invoke the vi editor, while a click of an alternative mouse button could cause the same C source file to be compiled. Users can switch between different desktops (or rooms) by clicking on the appropriate desktop icon. A user may want to have a programming desktop and a documentation desktop, each containing programs and files relevant to the task.

Looking Glass

The big complaint against UNIX (and in some cases DOS) is that it is too hard to use. To simplify it, a layer of software has been added to UNIX by third-party organizations. Visix Software offers a proprietary desktop manager designed to allow users to execute all tasks by using a mouse, rather than typing strings of UNIX commands. Intergraph Corp. of Huntsville, Alabama, among others, has adopted this desktop manager for its UNIX workstations, and Digital is bundling it with their workstations.

Based on components from the Motif interface, Looking Glass, unlike OPEN LOOK or Motif, allows the user to perform all tasks, including file interface (similar to the Macintosh). The desktop manager has a hypertext help system, drag-and-drop protocols and multiple layouts for the desktop. Looking Glass offers the ability to determine a file's type and what applications it is associated with, which is lacking in UNIX, but necessary in GUIs. Looking Glass examines each file and compares certain characteristics to predetermined heuristics to determine type. The program offers a graphical tree view of the file system that allows users to browse by opening icons that show the contents of directories.

Looking Glass has an interesting effect that is achieved by defining transparent areas of an icon. As the icon is moved across the screen, the background or other objects on the display show through the transparent areas. Mouse selections on the transparent areas are not considered picks. User preferences such as colors and fonts can be set interactively. It also has the capability to display multiple single-colored icons in on a window.

SET 3.6

Caset Corporation, located in San Juan Capistrano, California has released their latest version of SET 3.6 (Software Engineering Toolkit). Among the numerous platforms supported, SET runs on top of DECwindows and supports the Digital VMS and ULTRIX operating systems. SET has been designed specifically for bit-mapped workstations. SET utilizes a software design philosophy that implies that 60% of software development time is devoted to how user interaction is handled. Based on that model it provides a User Interface Management System (UIMS), which consists of a run time support library and a set of window management tools.

The User Interface Management System basically converts a user interface description (specified and described or written by the user) into either C or Fortran77 source code that, without any actual user-written code, can be compiled and run. The merging of application code with the generated source or skeleton code is completely handled by the SET run time library. This User Interface Description Language (UIDL) specified by SET enables the user to develop source code that makes calls to the SET run time support system. Caset maintains portability by support versions of their run time library for many processors and device types. With the run time system, support is provided for command line input with full macro functionality, multiple forms input, 2D and 3D graphics, X-windows, icons, menus, and real-time graphical data viewing.

As a UIMS tool, SET formalizes the specification of the dialog sequences required for an application and then uses this to generate the structure of an application that matches its specification. The SET run time system consists of 5 fully integrated, modular structured run time libraries:

- graphicSET, a fast 2D and 3D graphics system that stores graphic primitives in a hierarchical display file, just like PHIGS;
- onSET, the processor and operating system-dependent layer for Sun Microsystems, Apollo, Hewlett-Packard and Digital workstations, plus their respective operating systems, UNIX, Aegis, and VMS/ULTRIX; there is also support of serial devices (i.e., VT and TEK);
- inSET, an interactive method of generating windows and menus that allow the interface designer to rapidly prototype their applications; available in C or Fortran77;
- dataSET, database creation and access facility complete with a free format data structuring capability; this can be customized to fit any data structuring, storage, or retrieval requirement;
- windowSET, provides the window management supported drives for X10 and X11, DECwindows, SunVIEW, Apollo DM, UIS/VWS, Tektronix, and VTXX0.

Differences between DataViews and SET 3.6 SET is not equipped to handle vast amounts of real-time data as well as DataViews. However, SET provides a better interactive method of prototyping graphical user interface capability than does DataViews. SET provides faster and more robust 2D and 3D capabilities than DataViews.

Numerous widgets and menu types are available with the SET toolkit, whereas DataViews only provides a small selection of previously defined icons and one menu type from which to choose. The ability to modify the look and feel of a graphical user interface is very flexible with SET.

Serial support from workstations to terminals is provided by the SET toolkit. This provides a common application interface mechanism across all hardware platforms in the user's environment. The same application interface being used on workstations can be simulated serially on VT100 terminals and TEK 4200s (only the slide bars are inactive). This provides a standard application interface on inexpensive hardware.

V-Windows

Designed for VMS-based systems, Vectus Technologies' V-Windows is a set of libraries and programs. V-Windows offers programmers a simple command-line style interface to screen management (SMG) routines and allows those routines to be used directly from Digital's command language (DCL) without any programming. V-Windows is not X-Windows or DECwindows for text-based terminals. However, because it is layered completely on SMG, an application developer can mix calls to SMG and direct calls to SMG within one application.

References

Broadbent, Carol, Vicky Hastings and Julie McHenry. 1990. Position paper on handwriting recognition technology. Go Corporation: Foster City, Ca.

Martin, Gale, James Pittman, Kent Wittenburg, Richard Cohen, and Tom Parish. Sign here, please. *BYTE*. July, 1990.

Pittman, James A. Recognizing handwritten text. *CHI'91*. May, 1991.

17

GUI development tools

It is estimated that by 1993, nearly half of all computer users will have a GUI. GUIs are popular because they make applications easier to learn and use. By standardizing the way users interact with a program and input information, errors are reduced. As a result, GUI applications not only are favored by end users, but also help save corporations both time and money by increasing productivity and ensuring accuracy.

As more users discover how time-saving and enjoyable it is to work with GUI-based applications, they will increasingly demand to use them over command-line applications. However, designing and programming for GUIs is time consuming and challenging for several reasons. A primary difficulty is the fact that development is "event-driven" rather than procedural, and requires mastering a different style of programming and design than is used to develop logic.

Developing a GUI is no longer academic; it's an important business decision. However, confusion still abounds concerning GUIs, partly because the buzzwords are used too quickly and often incorrectly and partly because the ongoing conflict within UNIX has made the GUI a popular battleground. The debates over OPEN LOOK versus Motif and Windows versus Presentation Manager have grown to a fevered pitch.

An organizational approach, however, can classify and clarify GUI issues by pinpointing the decisions to be made when planning new applications. The first decision concerns the computing environment. The next decision would be selecting the best tools available for quick creation of applications under that GUI. A bewildering array of tools has appeared to aid developers in creating application interfaces conforming to GUIs. These tools are sometimes called GUIDEs (for graphical user interface development environments). There are two classes. One class can be called widget editors, and the other class GUIMS (graphical user interface management system).

Widget editors are basically WYSIWYG (what you see is what you get) graphical editors for creating standard X widgets such as buttons, sliders, and scroll boxes used to control applications. (Examples of such widget editors are ExoCODE from Expert Object Corp. and UIMX/USEIT from UNIRAS A/S.)

GUIMS is used for creating highly interactive graphical application interfaces in fields such as manufacturing, network management, avionics, and financial trading (tools in this category include SL-GMS from SL Corp. and DataViews from VI Corp.). Such products include not only a drawing tool and dynamics, but, to one degree or another, other issues of graphics management such as the linking of screen elements to data sources, hypercard-like nesting and sequencing of screens, and the use of screen objects to control real-world processes.

A GUI such as Motif, OPEN LOOK or Digital's DECwindows is a style guide that determines what the interface is going to look like and how users will interact with it. Stressing standardization on a single GUI has been exaggerated; the various GUI styles are similar, compared with their predecessors. A Motif user would be no more dumbfounded by OPEN LOOK than a Lotus user would be by Excel.

Selecting a GUI is not the hard part. Application developers need a way to simplify the GUI development process in order to give their users the GUIs they want, without negatively impacting development schedules, without taking time away from logic development, without working in a restrictive environment, and without wasting time.

One of the problems in generating a GUI-based application is the number of procedures with which a programmer must be familiar before beginning to design an application. For example, there are more than 750 API calls that can be used to develop an OS/2 Presentation Manager application; Windows programming is nearly as complicated. Both Windows and PM require the programmer to understand how to use window resources and the script language to program them. Both require mastery of the appropriate Software Development Kit (SDK) to design dialog boxes, icons, cursors, and other interface components. And, both require learning how to write application interface code to tie into a message-oriented environment. Building an application in the X Window System using Motif, or developing one for NewWave or the Macintosh all carry a burden. All of these factors mean that adding a GUI to a character-based application, or developing a new graphically-oriented application, can add weeks or months to already tight development schedules, if the coding is done manually. How much time it will add depends on the complexity of the application and the sophistication of the user interface.

All GUI applications contain two basic parts: the user interface and the application-specific logic. The interface part of the application defines the windowing components and registers the application's windows with the environment (Windows or PM). It also defines the way messages and events are handled. The application-specific part is the logic of the program, and performs the functions and routines that the application is designed to accomplish. One way to simplify the creation of an application is to use high-level tools. Various toolkits for the different GUIs have been developed by the GUI suppliers and dozens of third-party suppliers to meet this demand. This chapter covers some of the most popular toolkits available.

Extensible Virtual Toolkit

This toolkit offered by XVT Software (formerly API Ltd.) provides a common API and libraries for five popular environments: the X Window System (both OSF/Motif and OPEN LOOK), Macintosh, Microsoft's Windows, Presentation Manager and character-based displays for CTOS, DOS, OS/2, UNIX and VMS. With the XVT toolkit, application source code can be identical across these environments.

With the Extensible Virtual Toolkit, programmers can write interactive applications that use graphics, menus, dialogs and other user-interface features and then port them to different environments. When compiled on the target system, the applications obey the appropriate user interface guidelines for each system. To achieve portability of resources across platforms, XVT is provided with a Universal Resource Language compiler/decompiler. XVT uses the abstraction approach to achieve its virtual capabilities. As good as this toolkit is, you should bear in mind that no virtual toolkit can enable every possible GUI application to be programmed, since it is necessarily limited to those features that can be virtualized for each target system.

Garnet

As has been mentioned elsewhere, user interface software can be difficult and expensive to implement. Successful, interactive interfaces are among the hardest to create, since they must handle at least two asynchronous input devices (such as a mouse and keyboard), real-time feedback, multiple windows, and elaborate, dynamic graphics. Most graphical interfaces are created using toolkits which usually contain a set of interaction techniques known as widgets or gadgets for menus, scroll bars, and buttons. Examples include the Macintosh Toolbox and Xtk for the X Window System. These toolkits are often difficult to use, since they contain from dozens to hundreds of procedures. Also, many toolkits do not help the programmer create the most important part of the application—the graphics that appear in the main application window.

Higher level tools such as interface builders (like Motif) and user interface management systems (like NewWave) have not, in the opinion of the researchers at Carnegie Mellon University, adequately addressed these problems. A conventional interface builder lets a designer graphically place user interface components in a window, thereby creating menus, palettes, and dialog boxes. Examples include NeXT's Interface Builder, Smethers Barnes' Prototyper for the Macintosh, and UIMX for X Windows.

The team at Carnegie has developed a highly interactive set of tools known as Garnet. A number of features differentiate Garnet from other user interface tools, including an emphasis on handling objects' run time behavior (how they change when the user operates on them) and on handling all visual aspects of a program's user interface, including its graphics and the contents of all application-specific windows.

The Garnet Toolkit Garnet contains a number of different components grouped into two layers. The Garnet Toolkit (the lower layer) supplies the object-oriented graphics system and constraints, a set of techniques for specifying the objects' interactive behavior in response to the input devices, and a collection of interaction techniques.

The toolkit itself is divided into several components:

- An object-oriented programming system.
- A constraint system.
- A graphical object system.

- A system for handling input.
- A collection of gadgets or widgets.

Using the X toolkit's terminology, the first four parts of the Garnet Toolkit are intrinsics (the mechanisms supporting the implementation), and the fifth is the widget set, a collection of menus, scroll bars, etc., with a prespecified look and feel. Garnet is suitable for:

- Box and arrow diagram editors, like MacProject.
- Conventional drawing programs, such as MacDraw.
- Icon manipulation programs, like the Macintosh Finder.
- Graphical programming languages in which computer programs are constructed using icons and other pictures, such as a flowchart.
- Tree and graph editing programs, including semantic networks, neural networks, and state transition diagrams.
- Board games, such as chess or Othello.
- Simulation and process monitoring programs, in which the user interface shows the status of the monitored situation or process and lets the user manipulate it, use interface construction tools (we implemented Garnet using itself), and some forms of CAD/CAM programs.

Figure 17-1 shows the organizational structure of the Garnet system.

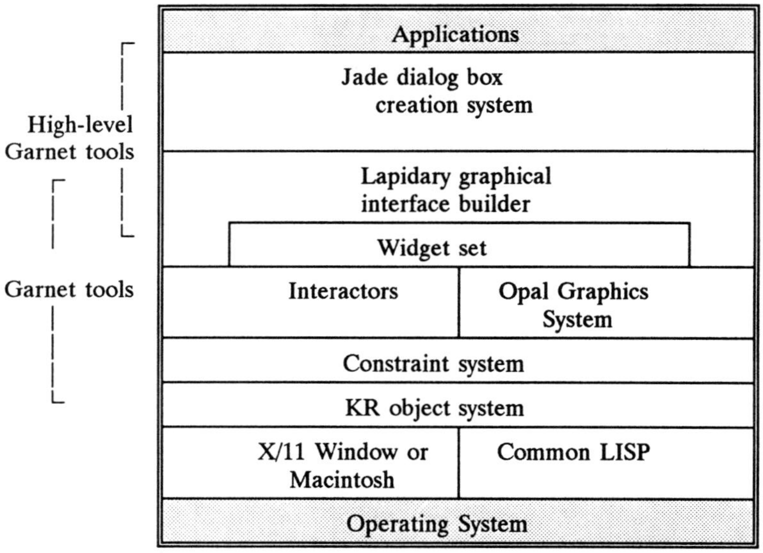

Fig. 17-1. The structure of the Garnet system.

Opal, Garnet's graphical object system, is designed to make creating and editing graphical objects easy. It provides default values for all object properties so simple objects can be drawn by specifying only the necessary parameters. Lapidary sits on top of the Garnet toolkit. It contains a number of tools for creating the user interface and provides a graphical front end. The Garnet toolkit is operational and has many local and external users. More than 80 companies have licensed it.

Open Interface

Nuron Data has developed Open Interface, a tool that lets developers design a GUI once, then recompile it to run in multiple windowing environments. These include Windows 3.0, OS/2 Presentation Manager, the Macintosh, OSF/Motif, Sun Microsystems Inc.'s Open Look and Digital Equipment Corp.'s DECwindows. Figure 17-2 shows the way applications are built across multiple platforms by Nuron's Open Interface.

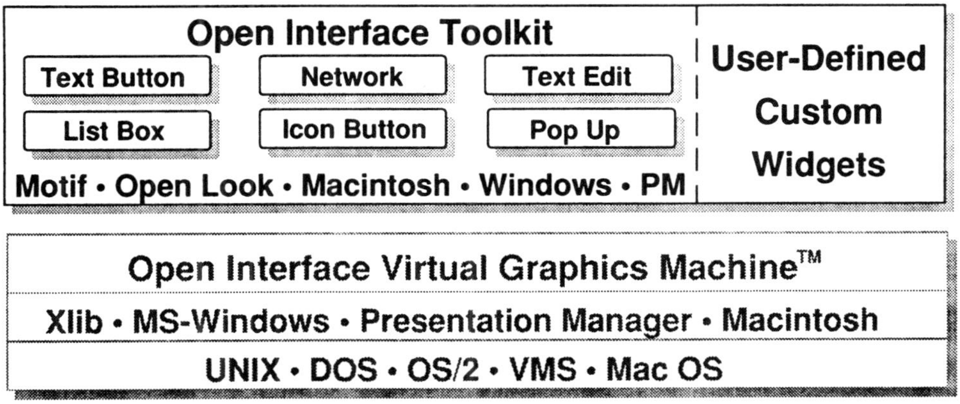

Fig. 17-2. Open Interface architecture.

Nuron Data's Open Interface is a tool that emphasizes portability across windowing environments. With this tool, developers can design their application on one platform and then, simply by recompiling and relinking on another platform, they can port their application to any of the environments supported by the product: OSF/Motif, Open Look, Microsoft Windows 3.0, OS/2 Presentation Manager, and the Macintosh.

Open Interface consists of a layout tool (Open Editor) and a set of libraries for each windowing environment. The product implements a complete toolkit and provides a superset of the widgets (windowing components such as buttons, icons, and menus) offered by the native toolkits. With Open Editor, the developer can draw interfaces in a WYSIWYG environment, drag objects to their desired locations, resize windows, and change text of labels or buttons. Open Editor consists of an object-oriented set of tools for creating and modifying all the elements that make up the user interface of an application: windows, tables, scroll boxes, text processors, pop-ups, menus, icons, custom widgets, and others. This interactive, point-and-click tool makes program development significantly easier. All editing is done graphically, and the developer can see his results as he goes, exactly as the finished windows will appear. Open Interface is extensible, and custom widgets can be created and inserted in the tool.

Open Editor goes a step further than other similar tools by outputting ANSI C program templates and makefiles along with the resource files. The C code defines a callback procedure for each widget belonging to the window. The developer then customizes the C template to add application-specific functionality. To complete the application, the code is compiled and linked to the platform-specific Open Interface libraries. Open Interface has a complete API (Application Programming Interface).

While there are a number of tools that support rapid interface prototyping, Open Interface's key benefit is the portability it provides across all of these systems (see FIG. 17-3). To accomplish the portability, the company has defined its own GUI library and resource language for writing applications with portable graphic interfaces. The libraries implement a high-level resource and event manager as the basis for portability. These libraries provide a complete API with hundreds of function calls that let the programmer control the specific behavior of a screen's objects. These function calls also implement new classes. Open Interface is extensible, allowing the addition of customized widgets and toll to an environment. It can implement widgets with its own portable resource manager and can support complex widgets such as tables across windowing environments that do not provide native support. This is abstraction-based portability and is richer than the least common denominator (LCD) approach.

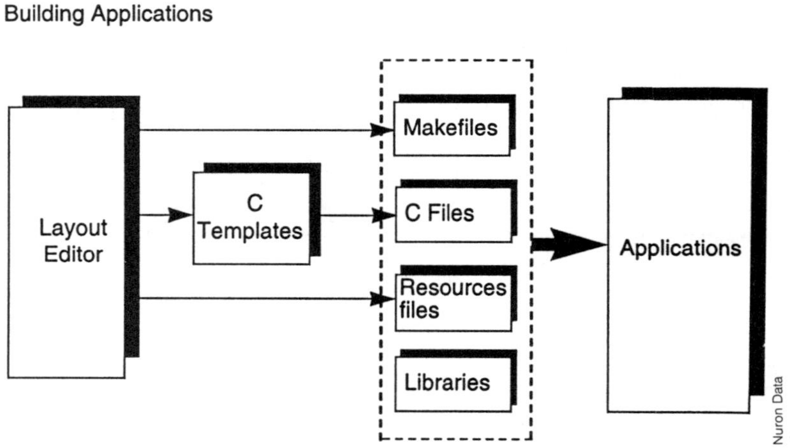

Fig. 17-3. Open Interface's libraries.

Tigre programming environment

The Tigre universal GUI builder from Tigre Objects Systems simplifies the porting of GUIs between MS Windows, the Macintosh and UNIX-based Motif and Open Look. Users can define a GUI using graphical objects on the screen. The interface is then converted into Smalltalk portable code, which can be compiled on various platforms and environments.

Tigre consists of a library of widgets (object classes), buttons, text editors, picture viewers and other commonly used objects. The programmer's selection from the library is done graphically on the screen. However, developers can create their own custom components and integrate them into the library. A multiuser object-oriented database manager, Tigris, is bundled with Tigre. Tigre runs on top of Objectworks \Smalltalk release 4 from ParcPlace Systems, which gives it portability to a wide range of platforms. Tigre is supplied with source code, and programming examples.

The toolkit supports full color graphics for text and images, and on-the-fly editing allows the developer to view and make changes on the screen.

Windows development toolkits

Microsoft admits some development tools have been lagging. However, a version of Windows' Software Developer's Kit (SDK) is available from Microsoft. Included in the package is the Codeview debugger. It runs in protected mode and is used for debugging Windows applications. It has an 1,800 page manual including information on DDE. According to the company, SDK contains a color palette manager that is combined with device-independence to shield the developer from such concerns. Microsoft widened the information available about Windows by releasing documentation on Windows' internal coding structures. The company has also added new APIs that let independent software vendors write languages and tools that do not require the Windows SDK.

Windows developers also got libraries that support multimedia and Object Linking and Embedding (OLE). Microsoft continues to work on a Binary Compatibility Layer for OS/2 2.0 that will run Windows applications on top of Presentation Manager. Windows is not the "transition" environment that Microsoft and IBM have asserted. It appears likely to be the dominant graphical platform of the 1990s. Developers without the resources to support multiple platforms will likely to forced to decide in the long run whether to write for Windows or OS/2's PM.

WILO

The Windows Libraries for OS/2 (WILO) is the Windows-to-OS/2 Software Migration Kit, which is the Windows application programming interface (API) for the portable version of OS/2—now renamed OS/2 3.X and targeted primarily to Intel processors. The libraries, which were earlier called "portholes," allow developers to move their Windows applications to OS/2 Presentation Manager with a minimum of recording. The Libraries relink Windows' code with special OS/2 Dynamic Link Libraries (DLL).

Third-party toolkits

Various types of toolkits for Windows developments are available from other third party organizations. The following is a brief list of those toolkits.

Actor The Whitewater Group offers Actor, an object-oriented programming language for developing Windows Applications. The Whitewater Resource Toolkit was designed specifically for the Windows environments. It provides programmers a visual way to create, edit and manage the look-and-feel of Windows applications.

CASE:W CASE:W is a toolkit from CASEworks Inc. for building prototype windows. Instead of touting portability, CASEworks has concentrated on a powerful feature set to attract developers to its GUI tool. It has extended code support for dialog-box controls (generating shell dialog message processors to program dialog-box functions) and variable linking. A developer can use interfaces interchangeably among all CASEworks products, across both languages and platforms. A Windows interface designed for an application written in C can be used when a PM application is generated in COBOL.

CASE:W, referred to as the Standard Edition, is aimed at developers who intend to develop applications that are not too complex. When developing a new applications, CASE:W can cut 25 to 50 percent of the development time, depending on the balance between the interface and application-specific portions of the program. It can also be used for putting a GUI face on an existing application, and involves very little application-specific coding, with most time spent on creating and linking the interface. In this instance, CASE:W or CASE:PM can reduce a significant proportion of a programmer's time.

The company also offers CASE:W Corporate Edition, an enhanced version of its CASEworks package designed for developers who create mission-critical applications for Windows. The Corporate Edition supports Microsoft Corp.'s Multiple Document Interface, a capability that lets users work with multiple documents within the main application window.

The package also contains features to ensure that the resulting application adheres to IBM's Common User Access (CUA) guidelines as defined by Systems Application Architecture. This facility can be disabled by developers who don't need to conform to CUA rules. A developer can use interfaces interchangeably among all CASEworks products, across both languages and platforms. A Windows interface designed for an application written in C can be used when a PM application is generated in COBOL.

DBfast/Windows A complete database development environment, DBfast/Windows is for dBase, Clipper and Windows developers. It was developed by Bumblebee Software.

Designer VisualSQL Solutions By Design offers Designer VisualSQL, which is a SQL front-end for graphical queries to Excel.

EASEL/Win Offered by Easel Corporation, EASEL/Win is for developers of applications for the Windows environment. It is well-suited for building cooperative processing and client/server applications. There is built-in support for front-ending existing host applications and accessing sophisticated server-oriented databases. It offers a seamless migration path to OS/2.

KnowledgePro KnowledgePro is an expert development system from Knowledge Garden.

Nexpert Object Nuron Data offers Nexpert Object, a hybrid object-based expert system that provides a Windows-based GUI. (See FIG. 17-4.)

ObjectVision A declarative visual programming object-oriented environment offered by Borland International, ObjectVision lets users develop applications by building simple decision trees on-screen. This is a whole new class of application creation tool that lets users create Windows applications. It uses 'visual programming' techniques, creates logic, links to a variety of data sources and eliminates the need to write code.

ObjectVision's declarative logic technology, which allows users to organize applications by building decision points rather than writing procedural code, has prompted Borland to file for a patent. ObjectVision's data interface will not be limited to Borland products such as Quattro Pro and Paradox, but will allow the establishment of live links to local and remote data in a multiuser environment.

SQL Windows Gupta Technologies introduced SQL Windows, an application development system that couples Windows with SQL.

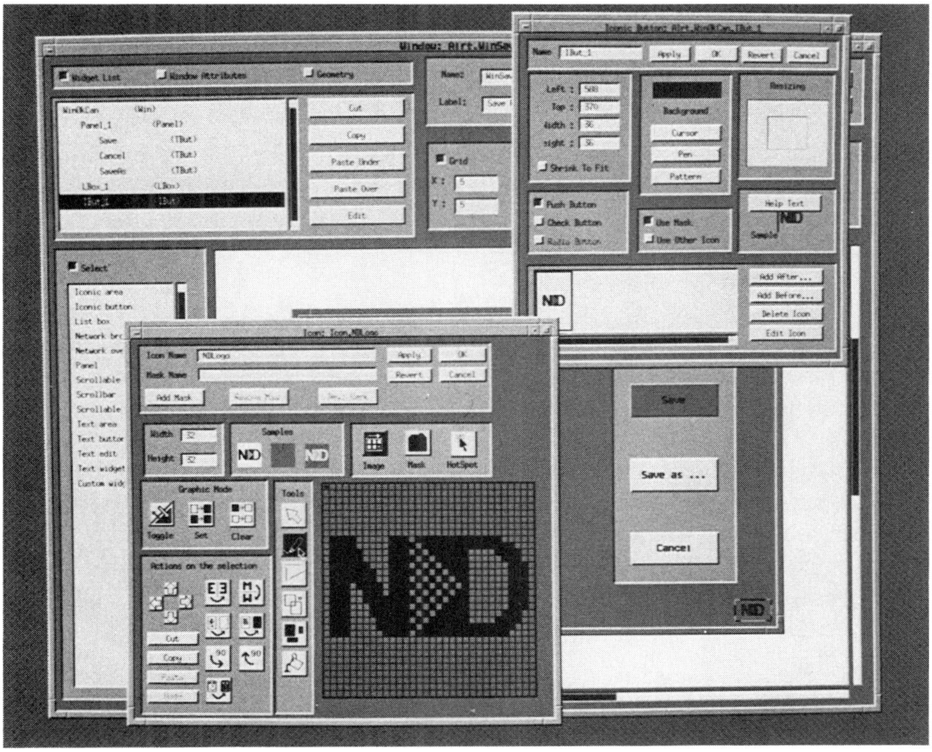

Nuron Data

Fig. 17-4. In the Open Interface toolkit, each type of object, such as a table, button or text-processing area, comes with an appropriate editor.

WindowsMaker WindowsMaker is an interactive WYSIWYG design tool for Windows applications from Candlelight Software.

Winpro2 Xian Corporation developed Winpro2 to allow the creation of skeleton code for Windows.

Tools for Windows and mainframes

Viewpoint Systems offers I/F Builder, a graphics design tool for building graphical user interfaces for existing mainframe applications. The software allows corporate developers and systems managers to create graphical user interfaces that comply with the IBM Systems Application Architecture (SAA) standards for Common User Access (CUA) and Common Communications Support (CSS). I/F Builder requires Microsoft Windows 3.x.

Extensive programming knowledge is not required to build the interface, therefore, new interfaces can be designed in a fraction of the time using I/F Builder instead of a programming language. It has the ability to consolidate data from multiple mainframe screens into one interface and offers options to set the colors and fonts on the actual interface. New panels and new fields can be created with CUA-compliant features such as check boxes, radio buttons, and pushbuttons.

Tools for SAA and CUA

Trends toward cooperative processing, consistent user environments and integrating mainframe and workstation applications have created a unique opportunity for vendors in the IBM marketplace. Users are demanding a modern, intuitive, integrated computing environment as they trade their old 3270 terminals for intelligent workstations that provide more cost-effective processing power.

There are more than 5,000 sites in the United States running MVS, IBM's mainframe operating system. 220,000 application programmers support these sites. This sizeable mainframe market continues to grow as corporations expand their use of 4GL databases to track information that is vital to their businesses.

Corporations that until now have relied on mainframe technology to handle their data processing are finding that cooperative processing—the use of PC workstations connected to host computers through local area networks—is yielding greater processing efficiency at a lower cost. Intelligent workstations are replacing traditional terminals as access points to hosts. By 1992, more than 30 million workstations will be connected this way. Naturally, an increasing demand for integrating host data with workstation applications accompanies this trend.

As users respond to the promise of cooperative processing by adding more power to their desktops, they are challenged to find a cost-effective, painless way to create new graphical interfaces for existing host applications. Not only must these interfaces comply with CUA, but they must also provide seamless integration between the host and the user's choice of workstation applications.

Most corporations have in-house developers who are responsible for the thousands of lines of code that define custom mainframe applications. These programmers are faced with the challenge of rewriting existing applications and developing new approaches to ensure that new applications comply with IBM's CUA standards. The cost could be enormous, requiring many programmers with extensive experience in user interface programming, mainframe applications, and PC-to-mainframe communications. Therefore, there is a tremendous need for high-level programming tools.

Arcadia CUA Workbench

A dialog session is an interaction between a person and a computer program using a primary window, associated pop-up windows, and help windows as the interface. Panels created with ADM/DOS serve as the primary medium through which the user can interact with the application program. ADM/DOS uses the Dialog Tage Language (DTL) to define panels and panel elements. DTL is a 4GL and is defined in the Systems Application Architecture Common Programming Interface Dialog Reference (SC26-4356-2). Programs written in DTL act as an interface between the application program and the user.

Arcadia DM for DOS (ADM/DOS) is an OS/2 Dialog Manager compatible product for the DOS world. It is designed to make SAA dialog manager applications portable across the OS/2 and DOS environments. ADM/DOS provides a DOS Dialog Manager compiler for panel definitions and panel elements, as well as run time routines to support dialog sessions for the DOS platform. The Arcadia DM for Windows (ADM/WIN) is an IBM OS/2 Dialog Manager (DM) compatible product for the Microsoft Windows world.

The Arcadia Workbench consists of a set of C functions that allow developers to implement a 100% CUA-compliant user interface for DOS, OS/2 and Windows applications. The toolkit contains a Common User Access enabling products such as a DOS Dialog Manager compiler for SAA applications, run time routines for DOS platforms, and a productivity tool for developing OS/2 SAA Dialog Manager applications. Once the developer has defined and designed the user interface panels, dialog services are used to create the application program. Then when the application is ready to run, the run time files provided with ADM/DOS are used to manage the dialog session.

Choreographer

Guidance Technologies offers an OS/2 Presentation Manager application interface. It provides a library of SAA/CUA compliant components and development tools that include: a Display Editor that creates application-specific objects by drawing them on the screen, a BitMap Editor that creates full color bit-maps, Browsers (classes, and instance), an Object Inspector that locates, inspects and edits components in the programming environment, a File Package (that loads and saves files, adds and deletes classes, instances and methods), and a Thread Manager that creates, edits, suspends and resumes OS/2 threads.

Mozart

The incorporation of GUIs into enterprise-wide systems and corporate environments in general is growing because they bring productivity. Mozart, from Mozart Systems, is a DOS-based graphical applications development environment that is used for front ends on existing mainframe applications. SAA/CUA compliant screens and ports can be generated for those applications between DOS and OS/2 without code revision. Mozart combines a development environment with a runtime environment and an integrated database facility that allows cooperative processing applications to directly read and write database files in dBASE-compatible format.

OS/2 toolkits

EASEL

Developing applications for the OS/2 Presentation Manager has been the domain of well-seasoned programmers. If programmers didn't spend considerable time and money learning C and mastering the intricacies of OS/2 and PM, they couldn't begin to decipher a Presentation Manager program, much less write one. EASEL/2 allows programmers to write Presentation Manager applications without C and PM experience.

It contains a comprehensive application development environment for the Presentation Manager. EASEL is a development tool for enhancing existing applications with graphical user interfaces and rapidly building new, highly graphical applications that operate in host-based and cooperative processing modes. The layout/CUA user interface design tool can be used to create applications that present a standardized look and feel through conformance to CUA guidelines. With this tool, developers lay out the interface in much the same way as a painting program. The tool then generates the EASEL source code required to create the working interface.

IBM has a marketing agreement for the EASEL OS/2 GUI toolkit from Easel Corp. to provide developers with a toolkit for OS/2 applications. The GUI toolkit encompasses a development system, communications modules, applications templates and other components for developers. EASEL can also be used to add GUI front ends on mainframe programs that use 3270s and 5250s.

X-windows and Motif

Perhaps one of the most popular segments for toolkits, the Motif development suites offered for the X Window System are all a little different.

Aspect

Open Inc. of Colorado Springs has an X Window System toolkit named Aspect. The toolkit editor, REd (Resource Editor) is an X-based tool that lets the user create typical GUI objects such as radio buttons, dialogs and scrolling lists with just a few mouse actions. A developer can also interactively define the layout of a window with the mouse: dragging objects to their desired locations, resizing windows and changing text. The output of REd sessions are resource files in the Aspect resource language.

Hewlett-Packard's Interface Architect

Hewlett-Packard has a software tool for developers of GUIs, called the HP Interface Architect. The product allows programmers to develop and test the complete behavior of an application's GUI. This toolkit supports the development and test of application user interfaces based on the X Window System and Motif. Interface Architect runs on the HP 9000 Series 300, 400, and 800 workstations under the HP-UX 7.0 operating system, HP's flavor of UNIX.

Designing and writing the user interface for an application is the most complex and time-consuming part of the software development process. Studies show that between 50 and 80 percent of the total code written for an application is devoted to the interface. Hewlett-Packard Interface Architect allows programmers to draw the interface on the screen (rather than writing code) by selecting interface components from menus and positioning them on the screen. The programmer then can interactively move and resize components, change resources, and add or delete components with the touch of a button.

Sammi

A slightly different approach has been taken by Kinesix Systems with their Sammi GUI for building X Window System applications. Kinesix argues that their GUI is not another GUI toolkit. Unlike GUI development toolkits, which generate code that gets embedded in an application, Sammi runs as a separate task, linked to the application through a network communication scheme. In traditional GUI toolkit architectures, one executable process is written for each display and loaded at run time. Changes to the interface necessitate changes to the display source code. Adding features and functions, therefore, requires compiling or relinking the entire application or display system environment.

By contrast, Sammi's user interface characteristics are configured using a binary data file called the "Format File" that is loaded at run time. All changes to the interface and links to the data are effected in Sammi by loading a new Format File. Sammi uses a table-driven software layer that defines the application interface; however, it does not require compiling, which eases software development. Users as well as developers can work with Sammi to define and link applications. Because of its table-driven organization, users and developers can interactively redefine the application interface at any time. When changes are made, only the underlying tables are changed; the application does not have to be recompiled.

The Sammi system consists of three parts: a run time environment (RTE), a format editor and an API. The RTE resides in the user node and controls the display, data communications and user interaction with an application. The editor, which is used to define the user interface, interactively generates the table formats that drive the Sammi run time software. The API formalizes the data requests and commands passed from the GUI/Sammi layer to the application layer, as well as the data and status passed back from the application. There are two types of API in Sammi: The client/server API for non-time-critical application engines (e.g., databases), and peer-to-peer APIs for time-dependent (e.g., critical) applications.

VMS and Motif

DECwindows is basically a superset of X.11, from the MIT Athena project (refer to Chapter 1 for more explanation of Athena). The most important aspect of DECwindows is the building toolkit which forms the API; that component was used by the Open Systems Forum for Motif, along with the Microsoft/Hewlett-Packard developed window management system, Presentation Manager. Technically, if software is developed for DECwindows, then it will run on Motif, but the window borders will look different because of the different windows manager. Several third-party organizations offer toolkits for Digital developers.

EzX

Sunrise Software Systems has EzX for VMS, a development tool designed to help programmers rapidly build GUIs based on the Open Software Foundation's Motif GUI. Along with EzX, the company supplies a free copy of Digital's Motif toolkit for VMS. EzX does not offer the complete flexibility of Motif. For example, programmers cannot change the width of borders around windows without going into Motif itself.

The toolkit includes X11R4 intrinsics for additional compliance and support for OSF/User Interface Language. It has the ability to use X Default files for compatibility with X Windows and faster modification of on-screen widgets. Style guide enhancements include convergence of OSF/Motif and CUA/PM/MS-Windows behavior, including drag model.

ExcCode

With this toolkit, users can create Motif-compliant, X-windows-compatible user interfaces for DECstation platforms by interactively drawing a prototype with a mouse and then automatically generating the C language source code. Developed by EXOC, it supports OpenWindows and extends the user's ability to generate native toolkit calls in a custom environment. Double clicking on icons loads interfaces and compiles generated code. When the Generate Code button is clicked on, ExcCode translates its internal image map of the interface into C language calls to the Motif libraries, giving the productivity of a CASE tool. The code can then be compiled or customized by the developer or user.

GUIs for terminals

GUIs top many wish lists these days, and for good reason. The ease-of-use and productivity benefits that are derived from users' access to pull-down menus, multiple display windows, dialog-boxes, scroll bars, push buttons, and the like are pronounced. For these reasons, many software developers are adding GUI features to new and existing applications alike. Programmers typically turn to GUI toolkits such as the Macintosh Toolbox or the DECwindows XUI Toolkit in order to implement a windowing environment.

For VT-compatible text terminal applications, however, there are no GUIs to support. Nevertheless, programmers can implement numerous GUI features, such as pull-down menus, dialog-boxes, and scroll bars, in applications written for text-based terminals. They just need the right tools.

Deskterm

IXI offers software tools for developers who want to move their existing character-based applications to X and build a Motif style front end onto their applications. These tools are supplied as the IXI Deskterm Developer's Kit and consist of X.deskterm and Deskterm Soft Option. (See FIG. 17-5.) Using the Deskterm approach, software can run in a mouse-driven windowing environment featuring pull-down menus, dialog boxes, scroll bars, cut & paste and multiple fonts and colors. These elements are easily added onto a basic character driven screen interface to give a user friendly graphical user interface.

Deskterm is a software tool that allows existing character-based software written in FORTRAN, COBOL, 4GL, or C to run in the X environment. Using Deskterm, software can run in a windowed, mouse-driven graphical environment featuring pull-down menus, scroll bars, dialog boxes, resizable windows, cut-and-paste and multiple fonts and colors. Deskterm is not an add-on product to IXI's other product, X.desktop (discussed in Chapter 16).

Skylight

Skylight is a windowing toolkit offered by Interactive Technology Inc. that helps programmers writing applications for text terminals provide a GUI look and feel. (See FIG. 17-6.) Skylight offers a character-based GUI and reduced API expressly designed for

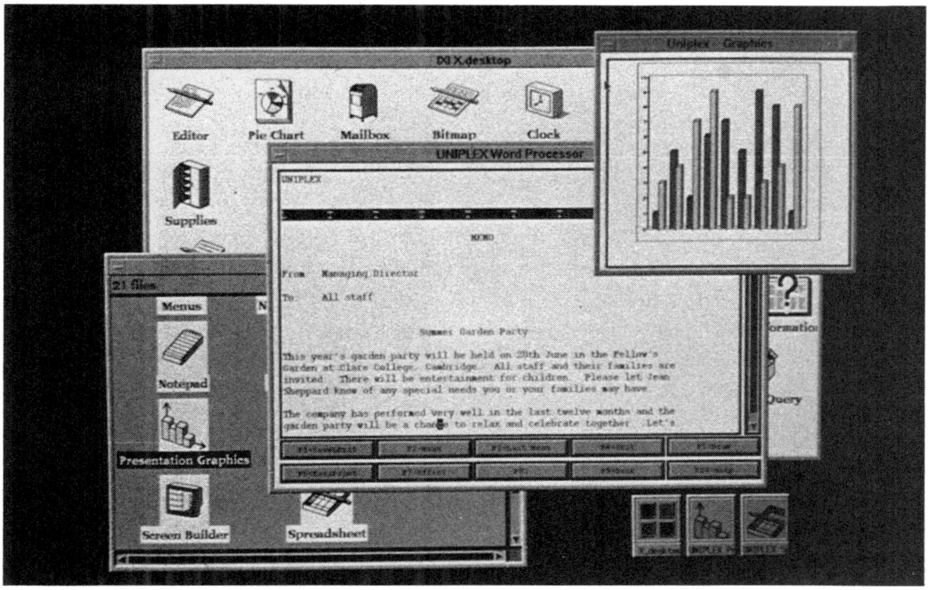

IXI Ltd

Fig. 17-5. *X.deskterm's (Motif-based) GUI with Uniplex Windows office automation software.*

Interactive Technology

Fig. 17-6. *Skylight's window programming environment for character-mode terminals.*

ordinary terminals. The toolkit includes most standard Widgets such as pull-down menus, dialog boxes, radio buttons and scroll bars, defined using ASCII characters. Figure 17-7 shows the organization of Skylight with a dumb terminal and an X Window server.

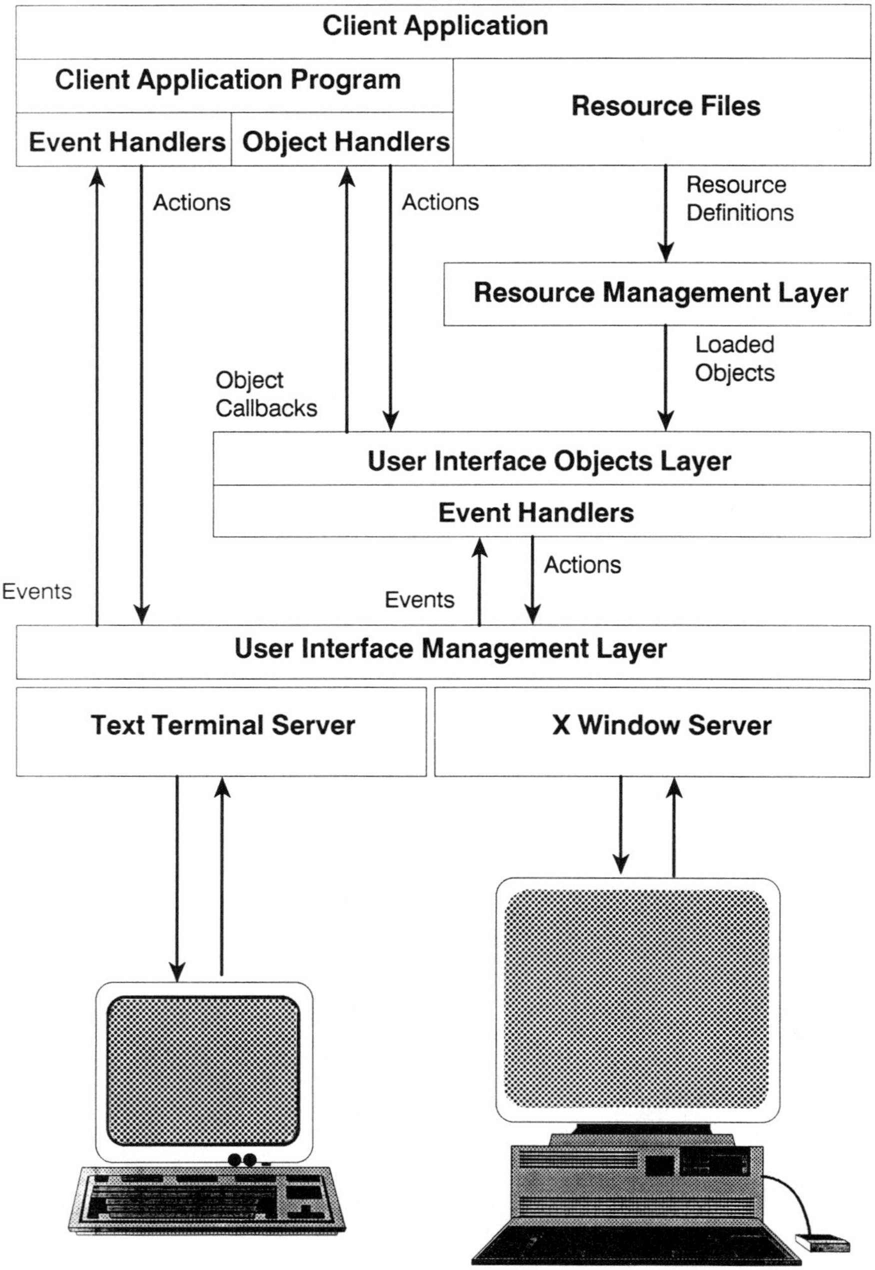

Fig. 17-7. Skylight's layered architecture.

Skylight's three-layer architecture allows programmers to maintain existing applications and user interfaces separately, and create GUI-like text displays that can be used without modification on X-terminals, workstations and character-mode terminals. This enables program migration from VT terminals to workstations with a minimum of training. Skylight supports simultaneous use of character-mode servers for terminals and the X-Server for X-terminals or workstations, from a single compiled program. It is available in AIX, HP UX, SCO UNIX, Ultrix and VMS systems.

Sun Microsystems

Sun Microsystems is giving developers the source code to the entire OpenWindows application development environment for just the cost of producing the media and documentation. With the Sun Microsystems XView OpenWindows source code package—including code for the X11/NeWS Window System, OPEN LOOK toolkits, and OpenFonts with its Typescaler technology—commercial and corporate developers can expand their Sun applications across a wide range of UNIX workstations. Along with the toolkit, Sun Microsystems also includes the OPEN LOOK Intrinsics ToolKit based on AT&T's XT + OPEN LOOK toolkit. Sun is offering developers and vendors source code for its OpenWindows interface as part of an ongoing bid to unseat Motif as the leading graphical interface for UNIX platforms.

The moves were an effort by Sun to blunt the acceptance of Motif in the UNIX marketplace. While Sun Microsystems currently has more than 80 ISVs shipping OPEN LOOK applications, a number of software vendors have developed applications that run on over 100 different platforms under Motif. OPEN LOOK is an excellent tool for creating X-window applications. Applications developers have a quick means of converting more than 2,800 SunView applications. For Sun Microsystems, the benefit is the propagation of the OPEN LOOK environment to a broader base of platforms. Motif's popularity is pressuring Sun with large corporate users and ISVs developing applications under Motif that are targeted for Sun's platforms. The OSF currently licenses Motif to 23 suppliers of Sun and SPARC-compatible workstations.

DXMconvert

Exoc (Expert Object Corp) also offers a SunView-to-Motif source code converter, for DECstations. The suite of tools are designed to enable a user to produce a working DECwindows Motif prototype from SunView source code in a few hours.

OSF/Motif

Several companies offer toolkits for developing GUIs for Motif. The following is a listing of a few of them.

Builder Xcessory

This point-and-click program provides the developer with a fast development toolkit. Its construction allows the developer to select widgets and make color selection from on-screen examples. Designed for developers who are not familiar with the details of the X Window System and Motif, it provides immediate access to the most complex aspects of Motif, including constraints, resize policies and the menu system.

Digital

Digital offers their own DECwindows developer's kit for OSF/Motif. It operates with the C language and UIL (User Interface Language) programming environments. The toolkit was specifically developed for converting DECwindows to Motif. The company also offers a Motif-compliant interface builder called VUIT (Visual User Interface Tool) for when an application is being built from the start, or being converted from another X-compliant user interface.

TeleUSE

Telesoft offers TeleUSE, a User Interface Management System (UIMS) for OSF/Motif. Its main benefits are: Object orientation, deluge management and portable code. The editor offers a graphical layout editor for painting the screen layout and a set of deluge management functions for modeling the run time behavior of the user interface. The output is C source code defining the interface.

It has a WYSIWYG editor that allows the User Interface designer to interactively create, modify, and to test the behavior of user interfaces using the OSF/Motif widgets, such as buttons, scroll-bars, menu bars and pull-down menus. The deluge manager helps to model the dynamic behavior of the UI at run time, such as states in a deluge, adding a text input to a pop-up menu and checking an input field. The deluge manager includes a compiler, an interpreter and a graphical debugger.

It is currently on the DG Aviion, DECstation 3100 and Sun workstations. There are no firm plans for a DOS version, but it will probably happen within one year. The issue is that there is the run time module that must be ported to the X-server platforms.

XBUILD

Nixdorf's XBUILD offers the same general functions as the aforementioned product. It allows a user to build widgets and design an OSF/Motif-based GUI. The output of XBUILD is either C or UIL interface code. It also offers a simulation mode that allows the GUI look-and-feel to be tested. The company offers a source code license for XBUILD. The source code allows XBUILD to be ported to a particular platform and operating system.

XBUILD uses a WYSIWYG graphical editor approach to interactively create, modify, and test the behavior of an interface that is independent of the underlying application. Since programmers build the actual interface using OSF/Motif terminology, they can design the interface with an end-user perspective. XBUILD shields them from most of the OSF/Motif toolkit's low-level construction details, and eliminates the need to learn another programming language or special tool. XBUILD has an interesting object-oriented architecture, including:

- Objects, an intelligent object base of widgets and their characteristics.
- Parent-child hierarchy, an internal programming structure based on a parent-

child tree hierarchy. This describes and manages the layout and composition of the interface.

- Editor, an interactive editor, consisting of a canvas, palette, menu bar, and settings and status lines.

The object base is a value-added implementation of the widgets defined by the X Intrinsics. It encapsulates the objects with both their key characteristics (i.e., name, class, graphical specification, display information, code information, and production rule) and the functions that act on them (i.e., store, load, code, display, copy, exit). Programmers can edit these "intelligent" objects and specify attributes using the consistent, easy-to-use object-oriented editor, eliminating code-level programming.

XView toolkit

XView is Sun's open, portable X toolkit, which offers developers an easy way to design OPEN LOOK applications, as well as to migrate 2,800 existing Sun View applications to OPEN LOOK and X. XView is mature, stable, and functional as an X toolkit because it is based on Sun View. In order to leverage the large base of Sun View applications, the XView API was designed to be compatible with that of Sun View.

XView is an object-oriented toolkit. This means developers can use building blocks such a windows, panels, icons, and other objects to construct an application. XView is extensible, so that developers can create new user interface components in order to customize their application. Software packages developed using XView are compatible with any standard implementation of X11.

The XView toolkit is included as part of the free X11, Release 4 tape. It is available for Sun workstations and Digital Equipment Corp., Hewlett-Packard, IBM, VAX/VMS and Mac A/UX platforms. As a result, application developers can standardize on a single (GUI) for UNIX workstations.

XView for workstations

Due to the popularity of Sun Microsystem workstations and their liberal source code policy with XView, more than one company has come out with a toolkit for XView on a workstation. This section is a brief list of some of those firm's products.

Exoc Expert Object Corp. claims to have released the first visual toolkit for Sun Microsystems' Open Look X Window System in October of 1989. Building on that experience, they have produced ExoCODE/plus. The toolkit allows users to create X Windows-compatible user interfaces for Sun Microsystems workstations by interactively drawing a prototype with a mouse and then automatically generating the C language source code. The toolkit makes use of Sun's XView toolkit to interactively create an interface in a WYSIWYG fashion.

UniPress UniPress Software, Inc. offers a version of Sun's XView for Digital and IBM workstations. It is a prototyping tool for developing OSF/Motif GUIs from UniPress Software. It consists of two main parts—ezXlib and ezXdraw. The tool ezXlib is a library of subroutines that provides a link between the application program and ezXfile, which stores the widgets that compose the GUI. The ezXlib tool sits on top of OSF/Motif, the X-Toolkit Intrinsics and Xlib. It performs the function calls required to access a widget.

The tool ezXdraw is a WYSIWYG graphic editor that allows the programmer to design pull-down menus and widget icons. It creates ezXfile, which contains the widget specifications for the particular GUI. Pull-down menu names and items, widget contents, colors and fonts, the icon bit-map, data entry widget parameters (including a callback to actually execute a function) and static titles are all defined from within ezXdraw. These values are then used to generate and run the menus and icons. It is a very easy system to use; it is very intuitive and logically organized.

XView for VMS

TVG offers a version of XView for Digital's VMS environment. It is compatible with VMS 5.2 or greater and provides an application architecture identical to Sun's XView.

Others

Several additional companies are offering various toolkits, test suites and other useful development tools. Some of them are listed here.

cO-Xist

The toolkit cO-Xist is the X window display system for the NeXT computer. It provides X Window System Version 11 Release 4 (X11R4) client and server support from within the NeXTstep environment. The product offering consists of three components:

- cO-Xist—a full X11R4 client and server implementation including all of the tool kits and libraries necessary to build X based applications on the NeXT machine; unlike some public domain versions of X for the NeXT machine, cO-Xist implements the X window server inside of a NeXTstep window. Unlike the X11R3 software available for NeXT Software Release 1.0, the cO-Xist X server is written using display postscript as the display engine, is a grey scale implementation, is a supported product, and runs under NeXT Software Release 2.0.
- OSF/Motif 1.1—in addition to the X11R4, the complete Motif 1.1 GUI environment is supported on the NeXT machine. This includes the Motif Window Manager (MWM), User Interface Language (UIL) and all of the tool kits and libraries necessary to build Motif based applications.
- Digital Librarian X11R4 and Motif Documentation—the company also offers a complete digital librarian version of all X11R4 and Motif documentation.

EASEL/DOS

Easel Corporation has a workstation-based development toolkit, EASEL/DOS, that provides an environment for enhancing host applications with graphical user interfaces and creating new, highly graphical cooperative processing applications. It has built-in communications facilities and other features for past prototyping. In addition, a layout tool is available for creating interfaces that conform to SAA Common User Access (CUA) rules and guidelines.

The programming language of EASEL/DOS has a range of constructs for building the workstation portion of an application. It is an event-driven, nonprocedural language with which programmers can define events and associated responses without regard for run-time execution sequence. In addition, applications can be created independently of whatever pointing device the user will select.

Xtool

XGraph Inc. has a product called Xtool that is an X-Window Server for Sun systems.

References

Grzanka, Len. Opening the XUI toolkit. *Digital News*, April 2, 1990, Page 21.

_______. Supporting two GUIs? New tools ease the headache. *Digital News*, X Windows Insert, Page 7.

Meyers, Brad A., Dario A. Guise, Roger B. Dannenberg, Brad Vander Zanden, David S. Kosbie, Edward Pervin, Andrew Mickish, and Phillippe Marchal. Garnet: comprehensive support for graphical, highly interactive user interfaces. *Computer*. November, 1990. Page 71.

Varhol, Peter. A new look at UNIX: GUnix—through the desktop looking glass, *Personal Workstation*. August, 1990. Page 37.

18

General conclusions and opinions

GUIs are being introduced to users in all industries, government and educational organizations. End users industry-wide have already begun to identify the capabilities of the computer with this type of easy-to-use interface. Application developers have begun adopting the X Window System and the look-and-feel standards defined by OSF/Motif and OPEN LOOK. It will not be long before the X Window System is accepted as an industry-wide *de facto* standard. Microsoft Windows has become popular on PCs. The world is moving toward a GUI environment.

Criticisms of GUIs

Is there a personality type associated with GUIs? A professor at the University of Delaware found an interesting relationship between users of MS DOS machines and Macintoshes. They appear to have different writing styles. The Macintosh users (according to the professor) seemed to have difficulties with the mechanics of writing, spelling, placement of commas and punctuation, but their papers were very attractive and well illustrated. There was also a difference in the style and content of essays presented by those students. Industry observers have noted that users tend to concentrate more on the appearance of a document when using a GUI than when they are working from a text-based word processor. This is not always a productive use of time, as many documents don't need fancy formatting, headers or other eye-catching doodads.

Another criticism of GUIs is that a power user on a text-based word processor can generate text much faster than a user of a GUI. This is because the user doesn't have to wait for the screen delays. All functions of word processing and spreadsheet usage (e.g., data entry, editing, formatting, etc.) can be done faster by experienced power users without the time-consuming burden of screen refreshes and other catch-up functions a GUI must perform. That problem will diminish as systems get faster, programs are better written and users become more accustomed to the use of a GUI.

Implementation

How does a user get started with a GUI? One of the first steps in implementing a GUI is making an assessment of what is available. Hopefully, this book has provided that information. Getting started typically begins with an individual in an organization who wants to experiment, to check it out. In larger organizations, the Information Systems (IS) department may establish a standard and implementation plan. There are a few basic steps an organization or individual has to consider in implementing a GUI environment. Each will be different due to its level of sophistication and operational needs. However, the following can be viewed as the basic steps.

Feasibility

The first step in most organizations is to conduct feasibility studies. One of the purposes of this book is to aid in such studies. There are various levels of a feasibility study such as technical, organizational needs (mission-critical), evaluation/testing, cost, manpower, implementation schedule and ROI.

1. Technical. As pointed out in various chapters, not only are GUIs technically possible, in some situations they may be essential. GUIs are available for almost every type of computer and operating system available. The first step in implementing a graphical user interface is making a sophisticated analysis of the GUIs available.

   Which GUI Which GUI should be chosen is a complex question. A feasibility study will show if a GUI should be adopted for each class system, or multiple GUIs for various systems. As pointed out in previous chapters, mainframes will use one type of GUI, PCs, workstations and minicomputers will use another. Also, there is the issue of the operating system.

   Organizational issues If the organization is large, it may be obliged to stay within the guidelines of an enterprise-wide system like IBM's SAA (Systems Application Architecture) for enterprise-wide connectivity. That may dictate the choice of OS/2 as a workstation standard and the use of that system's GUI, Presentation Manager, as the standard interface.

   Operating system If the organization has committed to UNIX, then the X Window System with Motif or OPEN LOOK will be the GUI chosen. If the predominant workstation in the organization is a PC with DOS, then Microsoft Windows and possibly NewWave will be chosen. If, on the other hand, the organization is a Macintosh shop, then the GUI decision has already been made.

   - File compatibility. If the operating system is changed in order to adopt a GUI the issue of file compatibility and transfer must be considered. Ultimately, it's the end function, mitigated of course by the predominant installed base, that will dictate final platform choice. Of course it is possible to mix and match. Possible, not necessarily easy.

2. Organizational needs. In determining how (or if) a GUI could aid your organization, you should determine if the organization has, or plans to have, any operations or activities that require nonambiguous, easy-to-use operator interactivity.

Other areas to consider are operations where additional productivity is desired. Also, if operators are moved from one location to another, a GUI will establish a common user interface and avoid confusion and relearning.

3. Evaluation and testing.
4. Cost. The expense of the associated hardware and software is another consideration when contemplating using graphical interfaces. GUIs have memory requirements and require graphics boards and/or terminals. There are millions of computers, workstations and terminals in use that are not powerful enough to run GUIs. Although Microsoft Windows is offered at many outlets for under \$100, many PCs now in use would require \$500 to \$1000 or more in upgrades to run it.

   The lowest cost GUI for XTs and ATs is Geoworks. Microsoft Windows for 286 and above PCs with 2 to 4 Mbytes of RAM is the next step (note: users report they cannot tell any difference in speed between a system with 2 Mbytes and one with 4 Mbytes). The next step up is a Macintosh or a NeXT computer with their proprietary GUIs. In the same price range is a PC with OS/2 and Presentation Manager. X Window System terminals start at under \$2,000. However, you must also have a Client machine somewhere. In companies that have gone to UNIX, that will not be a problem. Applications using Motif will enhance functionality. Cost therefore is a function of what you have (operating system, hardware and communications) and what needs to be added to get a functional GUI.
5. Manpower. Although in-house installation is most often done, there is an increasing role for systems integrators. Lacking the specialized skills (or just being short of manpower), large organizations will call on system integrators, VARs and other outsiders to help make the transition to a GUI environment.
6. Implementation schedule.
7. ROI. In evaluating what is possible, managers have to ask "possible at what cost?" What does it take to put together the kind of interfaces discussed in this book? Cost centers around four issues: platforms (hardware), applications (software), tools (GUIs and/or toolkits), and the expertise required by an organization to implement such systems.
8. Platforms. This is the starting point and establishes how much is already done for the user, as well as what is going to be possible. Integration, consistency and concurrency are three big issues for platforms. It should be emphasized that there is no simple, optimum solution for all applications. The requirements of each application will dictate which display platforms can coexist on the same network, each performing the applications it does best. Display platforms selection criteria can be reduced to the following:
   - Workstations (including UNIX-based PCs) are for heads-down power users.
   - Diskless nodes are for applications where disk-computer data exchanges are light.
   - DOS and OS/2 are for casual users.
   - X terminals are for general users who open many files or access great quantities of data.
9. Applications. The mission or object of an organization usually determines appli-

cations. They are the sole reason for the hardware and the systems. However, are they efficient? Are they extensible and do they use standards?

10. Tools. The GUI or toolkits determine at what level the user and/or developer has to work—C programming or 4GL point and click development. In general, tools today usually include a text editor, a compiler, and a subroutine library. Some developers feel the range of today's tools is too restricted.
11. Expertise. This is the most difficult item to evaluate. Some argue that if an organization doesn't have the necessary expertise or can't hire it, then they shouldn't embark on new developments. Others argue that if an organization doesn't invest in modern techniques and take some risks, they will be left behind and forced out of business. I personally agree with the latter.

It will be extremely difficult to apply quantitative measures for selecting and evaluating GUIs. They reach into so many aspects of an organization, from the network to the database, to the productivity of individuals, that it is almost impossible to be objective in establishing boundaries of responsibility and ROI.

Once installed, the interfaces are put to a variety of uses. At Monsanto, all employees from secretaries to executives, use the Windows application primarily to create internal and external presentations and business analysis with spreadsheets. They do not use it for routine word processing. GUIs beckon users. No one has wanted off after they got on.

Device-dependence

Older applications have been designed as device-dependent programs. Many are still being written as nonportable software, application-dependent, based on imbedded device-dependent graphic calls.

Standards will save development cost

If standards are implemented in the early planning stages of the project, it will save costly man hours, which will otherwise be required to rewrite software at a later date. Companies should be establishing standards, or plans for standards, on the following topics:

- Operating system.
- Communications.
- X-terminal client-servers.
- Graphical user interfaces.
- Development graphic libraries.
- Databases.

Standards provide the opportunity to grow with the many advancements and changes in computer hardware technology that will be faced in the future. Standards ensure that software development efforts will be processor-independent as computer hardware changes.

Problems with nonstandard software

Nonstandard products that sit on top of an operating system are often a viable solution to the visualization needs of many projects. However, if a vendor who is offering nonstandard software decides to abandon the operating system or whatever he has been using, this would severely hinder and interrupt the long-term productivity plans of a project. For example, if the product was primarily a VMS toolkit, and the vendor was purchased by a competitor who decided to phase out the VMS product line, a project using such a nonstandard interface would be in trouble. Therefore, even for specialized projects, it is strongly suggested that companies develop projects with development tools supported and supplied by a vendor whose products are based on a standard.

The need for education

Within most companies, there is a tremendous need for education about what is important and possible with the graphic standards of today. I strongly suggest that companies enlist in a Standards and Graphical User Interface training seminar for its key project planners.

X Window Systems should be put in corporate plans

Companies that have a heterogeneous environment, especially one that is networked, should be considering the X Window System. The highest level of productivity for projects and personnel can be achieved by X-terminals coupled with mainframes, minicomputers, PCs, and/or workstations.

GUIs on desktop systems

In all probability there will be more GUIs in use on PCs than on workstations and terminals. It will be the wide acceptance of such user interfaces that will push organizations to adopt a company-wide GUI policy and product.

Single user If the company has a single user environment, then a GUI like Windows, Presentation Manager or the Macintosh should be considered.

Single vendor In a networked environment with computers from either a single manufacturer or computers that are of a class (i.e., PCs and clones), a vendor-developed GUI (e.g., DECwindows, NeWS, Windows, etc.) can be used. When different classes of computers are used, an environment like IBM's SAA is the best choice.

Heterogeneous In a multivendor and/or networked environment, the X Window System is probably the best choice, with either Motif or OPEN LOOK. HP's NewWave Office should also be considered.

Modern visualization techniques

Many companies have not implemented workstation technology in their current configuration plans. Currently, each user seat typically consists of one minicomputer (e.g., MicroVAX) with two or more graphic terminals for interaction with the application and/or system. In addition, there are usually several alphanumeric terminals connected to a system for user interaction. Most project planners have not considered the enhancements that 3D visualization will bring to a project. The cost of building 3D visualization techniques into the current plans of a project would be minimal if implemented in the early stages of development.

An in-house expert needed

Most companies severely lack an in-house graphics expert. Companies need to establish a staff expert to assist all graphics plans, projects and decisions for visualization and other graphics-based projects. The cost of such an individual will prove beneficial in the long run due to the potential cost savings he or she will bring to the planning process.

If companies do not follow these suggestions, it will only be a matter of time before they encounter the costly experience of rewriting various applications and projects. Companies will have to incur this expense because they will be trying to use applications that are noncompliant with impending standards and new hardware and software systems.

Getting to charm

The closest science available for developing a system with charm is that of human factors engineering. Human factors engineering was introduced during World War II, while Air Force psychologists were looking for ways to reduce the number of flying accidents. One of their early findings was that by changing cockpit designs and the layout of instruments, pilots did not get confused or distracted during emergencies.

Since then, human factors experts have worked on everything from stereos to toothbrushes. In the computer industry, the main emphasis has been on hardware, with software generally ignored (with some notable exceptions like Xerox PARC and some DOD programs). It has only been recently that computer companies have added software to the human factors departments.

Software

Software publishers like Aldus, Ashton-Tate, Microsoft, and others have in the last few years established in-house usability departments to investigate the aspects of *human factors engineering*. Human factors engineering uses both knowledge of the human brain and a system of testing in real-world situations to try to create truly intuitive programs that work like humans. *Usability engineering* is an interdisciplinary field with roots in the more general area called ergonomics or human factors.

Human factors and usability testing has had a tremendous impact on software development. For one thing, it has shown that judicious use of color and icon design could help users distinguish software tools from data objects at a glance. Tests also showed that users preferred a single desktop over the dual file and program management strategy taken by Windows. Over 90 percent of the users tested wanted to be able to group files together by project or topics, rather than by software application. These findings resulted in two principles for the use of color and organization: first, icon colors would reflect applications capabilities (that is, only programs that actually used color would have colored icons), and second, users would be able to use color to mark files and organize information. Another aspect of the studies was the adoption of drop shadows for icons, so users could see when they had successfully selected objects (by having the drop shadows alternate on corners when an icon is selected). This gives the impression of pushing in a button.

The leading GUI software companies have adopted human factors at various times in the development of their products. Apple was one of the early adopters and launched its usability program in 1981. It was initiated to make the Lisa so intuitive that new users could be up and doing useful work in less than an hour. Hewlett-Packard's human factors group was a part of the development team for NewWave since the project began in 1985. The human factor department's objective was to use usability engineering, graphic interface design supervision, and writing interface guidelines for NewWave developers. Microsoft initiated its formal usability program in May, 1988. Given its relative newness, it is not surprising that the Microsoft usability group's contribution to Windows 3.0 was quite limited. As a result, it is possible for a user to make a mistake during a cut-and-paste command sequence and lose the text or objects they want to move. Windows users also find the file manager difficult to understand and wonder why it is separate from the program manager or why its folders lack the kind of functionality found with the Macintosh.

Location of icons

When using a GUI, logically tandem operations should be anticipated by the designers. For example, when opening a file in Windows, the user starts at the upper left hand corner of the screen. The next operation is to select a file from a list, which appears in the center of the screen. This requires the user to move the cursor and waste time hunting for the zone in the center of the screen; that is not charm. That is a distraction, a frustration and antiproductive. There are dozens of examples of mouse thrashing operations that make the user move all over the screen responding to one box after another. Future versions of GUIs will have anticipated this obstacle and will organize the operations in a smoother manner. Then we will begin to have GUIs with charm.

Hardware

A GUI's charm is not just the organization of its icons, the macros behind them or their color. It is also how smoothly and interactively the entire system works together, and that includes the hardware. If a user picks a window and drags it across the screen, does it move smoothly in a flowing manner, or does it seem to jump and skip? Does the screen flicker or redraw itself, or is it steady? These are hardware issues and mostly have to do with processor's speed. However, the way the operating system handles interrupts is also a factor. The less distracting a screen operation is, the more comfortable it will be for the user. Studies have shown that as operators get distracted or annoyed, they lose their concentration and will, to some degree, forget why they were initiating a particular operation. That reduces productivity and defeats the purpose of a GUI.

When a window or any screen element is dragged from one location to another, that operation is known as a *bit-block-move,* and more commonly referred to as a bitBLT. How well a computer handles a bitBLT is a function of its display controller. Most PCs come with a VGA display controller. There are literally hundreds of add-on display controllers for PCs. Macintoshes come with a built-in display controller, and there are over three dozen add-on display controllers for it. All workstations come with a built-in display controller. There are over four dozen add-on display controllers for the most popular workstations. All these add-on products have various ways of handling bitBLTs. In the case of dumb frame buffers (e.g., the VGA), it is left to the host processor to move the block of pixels. That is a slow and often jerky operation. Smart cards or hard-wired cards (as discussed in Chapter 15) off-load the host and offer improved bitBLT operations—for a price.

When the user moves the pointing device around, does the cursor or arrow follow immediately and smoothly? Macintoshes and Sun Microsystems workstations have a very smooth cursor, or, as they call it, mouse control. That is just another of the seemingly small, perhaps insignificant, aspects of a system that contributes to its charm. It also is an element that reflects the thoroughness of the system's designers.

And what is the best pointing device? That is a subjective question because there is no best pointing device. Some people are more comfortable with a mouse, some with a trackball and others with a light pen. A well designed system should be able to work equally well with any pointing device.

There are three major factors affecting the monitor or screen: size, resolution and colors. The size of the screen can vary from 9 to 27 inches (there are even 35-inch VGA screens). Screen size is another subjective, personal-comfort item. Although various governments are attempting to define the proper screen conditions (for radiation, height, color and glare), aside from those factors (which are just common sense) the user has to feel comfortable with the screen.

VGA resolution (640 × 480) is the minimum useful resolution for comfortable GUI work. With less than that, the icons and boxes get chunky and difficult to discern. High resolution (i.e., equal to or greater than 1024 × 768) on a small 9-inch monitor creates another problem; the letters are difficult to read. With the 0.33 mm pitch of most color monitors and VGA resolution, a minimum rectangle area with at least a 10.4-inch diagonal is required.

As a general rule, to be comfortable with a GUI the user should have at least a 14-inch monitor with VGA resolution. A 15- to 19-inch monitor will be better with high resolution. However, this is not an example where more is better. Although higher resolution (1280 × 1024 or 1600 × 1200) will be helpful, especially for computer aided design (CAD) and desktop publishing (DTP) applications, not all users can benefit from such displays. Also, a 19-inch monitor takes up a lot of desk space. Furthermore, as resolution and monitor size go up, so does cost—geometrically. The right balance of resolution and monitor size contributes significantly to the user's comfort and the charm of the overall system. That translates directly into productivity, and that increases the ROI, which is what management needs to justify the costs.

Does a user need color in a GUI? It depends on the application and general use of the system. For most applications, color is not needed. Color adds another dimension of information and aesthetics. It also adds cost. Users generally prefer to look at a color screen. However, in the case of DTP, a color monitor does not have the quality that a black-and-white display has (refer to Chapter 15 for an explanation). For paint and animation applications, or applications for generating slides, color is needed. However, the question is how many colors, 16 or 256 or 16 million? The answer is a function of the application.

In summary, a 14- to 19-inch, high-resolution display with 16 or more colors, a comfortable pointing device, a smoothly operating dragging capability and cursor movement are the contributions hardware can make to the charm of a GUI.

Environment

It has been discovered that the inability to concentrate on a book for more than 15 minutes is due to a lack of focus. What applies to books can just as easily apply to computers. Eye problems, or more specifically, vision problems, can cause a host of direct and indirect distraction.

The primary task, as far as the eye is concerned, is focusing. For the eye, using a computer can be extraordinarily complex. The eye has to deal with the flicker from the CRT, the lack of contrast on many screens, reflection and glare off the screen, a focal distance from eye to screen that may not be adjustable, the contrast of the room light versus the light on the screen, and the different focal lengths of the screen and any paper you might be reading from.

An almost subliminal distraction is the reflection of objects in the background. When you read a printed page you have only to focus on that plane. Images reflected in a computer screen are on a different plane. The eye, in trying to make sense of the scene, works to focus on both, with tiring results.

Language

Although people have used language for centuries, and there are plenty of theories about language and its ancillary attributes, there is not yet a science per se about the implications of language concerning work habits and responses to/from a computer. However, there is a group which, through careful observation, has accumulated a body of insight into the nature of language. These are the practitioners of neurolinguistic programming, or NLP.

NLP was developed 20 or so years ago by psychology researchers Richard Bandler and John Grinder. Since then, it has evolved so rapidly that it is difficult to define. NLP considers language as a tool for making behavioral changes, or shifts of understanding. NLP's insight into the power of words can benefit anyone interested in communication skills.

One of the basic tenets of NLP is that a word is always connected to an internal experience. The word file, for example, is not connected to the file a user is reading so much as it is connected to all the representations of files a person holds in memory. According to NLP theory, people make internal representations primarily in three ways:

- Through sight (visual).
- Hearing (auditory).
- Feeling (kinesthetic).

In NLP, the way functions represent things is more important than the way things really are. The mind, according to NLP is a meaning-making machine. These internal feelings and associations have more impact than any dictionary meaning of a word. The direct linkage between NLP and computers, in particular GUIs, has not been formally made. A few researchers in both fields are looking at the connections. As their efforts are published, we will see still more powerful, enjoyable, charming computer interfaces.

Conclusions

Both PC operating systems and GUIs are in a tremendous state of flux. It appears that Windows will become the dominant GUI of IBM PCs for the first half of this decade. After that, it is feasible that OS/2 will have gained enough momentum to overtake Windows in mainstream applications. The user interface of Presentation Manager will have much the same look and feel as Windows, and Microsoft has committed to binary compatibility between Windows and OS/2 applications. Over the long term, it seems that Microsoft Windows will continue to be the better choice for 286 or 386 computers with less than 4 Mbytes of memory. (See FIG. 18-1.)

X Window Systems-based GUIs appear to be the dominant GUI in heterogeneous multiuser environments. Unlike Microsoft Windows, the development of the X-based GUIs, such as OSF/Motif and OPEN LOOK, is ahead of application software. Because the X Window System is in the public domain and not specific to any platform or operating system, it stands a significant chance of becoming the *de facto* windowing system of the 1990s.

So far, it would seem that there are few drawbacks to the X Window System. Not so. Because the X Window System was designed for bit-mapped, networked graphical platforms, it can't be used with standard character-based dumb terminals. Similarly, computers based on anything less than an 80386 processor may be too slow or may not have enough memory for some of the X Window System applications. Regardless of the pros and cons, the X Window System interfaces will dominate the hardware-independent GUI market and become the industry standard of the 1990s.

Future user interfaces

A GUI offers many advancements over command-line technology. A GUI is, among other things, a means of achieving a common user interface in an enterprise-wide environment, and if done properly, it will have user friendliness, or charm. However, as mentioned earlier, the graphical user interface style of windows, icons, and mice have been around for over 15 years. The technology to support this style of interface is now maturing. An example of the effective use of the GUI is the office and programming environment. GUI developers identified problems in these domains and applied the technology to solve these problems.

For a wide range of such applications, the desktop metaphor is a tremendous improvement over the textual interface style that preceded it. Because it worked, these techniques have been applied to other domains with varying results or degrees of success. But what happens when this design is applied to applications other than "office work?" One thing that happens is that the "primitives change." The office assumes a world of "documents" composed of text, simple images, and numeric data. Applications in this domain manipulate and manage these two-dimensional, textual, and image-based objects.

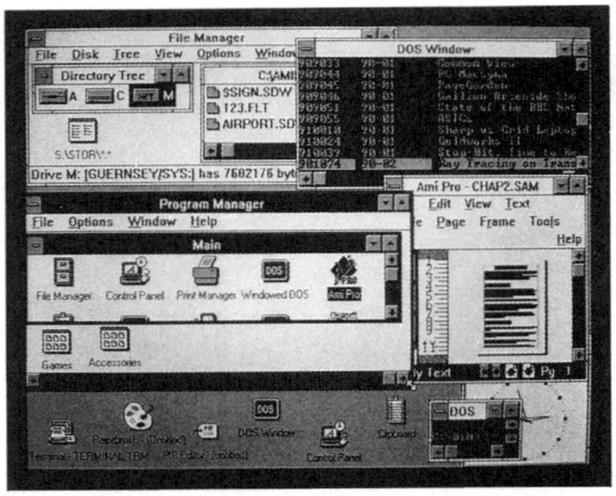

Windows 3.0

BEST POINTS
- many applications available
- runs older DOS applications and new Windows-specific programs
- in enhanced mode, can multitask DOS applications
- macro and task-automation capabilities included
- provides on-line help
- relatively inexpensive to buy (but see below)

WORST POINTS
- requires a lot of hardware and memory to take full advantage of features

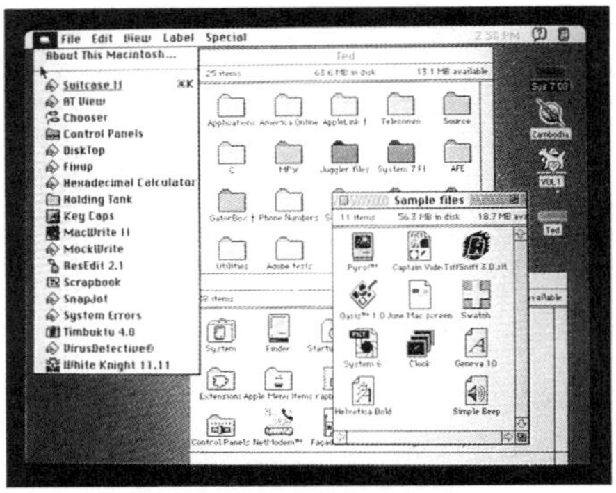

Macintosh

BEST POINTS
- system is integral to machine; easy to install
- many applications available
- applications are stable and compatible with each other
- network capability built in

WORST POINTS
- cooperative multitasking is only as good as worst-written program

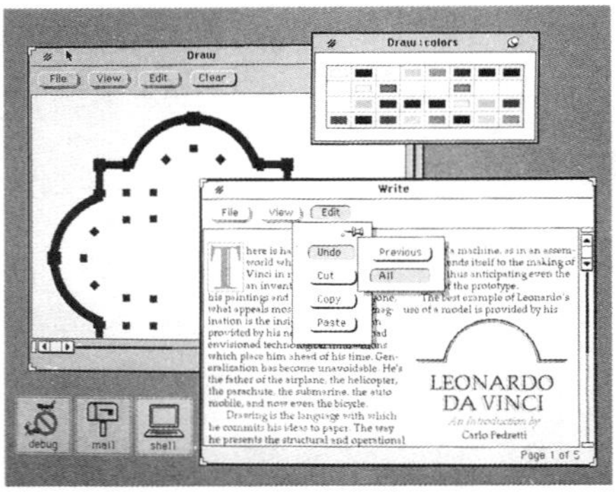

Open Look

BEST POINTS
- multitasking capabilities built in from the ground up
- network capability built in
- easy to configure for personal preferences

WORST POINTS
- no macro or task-automation features included
- developer guidelines not mandated; applications may not appear consistent

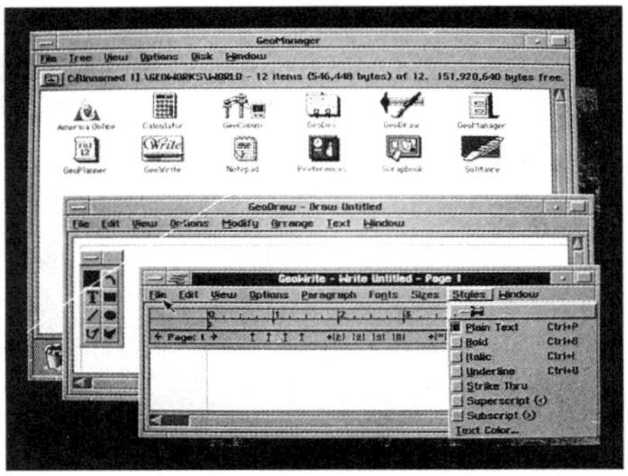

Ensemble

BEST POINTS
- inexpensive, easy-to-use package
- runs on older-model 8088 machines
- includes a number of basic applications that work well together
- multitasking capabilities built in from the ground up

WORST POINTS
- lack of "power" applications, such as database, spreadsheet, or heavy-duty word processor
- no macro or task-automation features included
- no programmer's tools
- no network capabilities included

Fig. 18-1. The best of the GUIs, the worst of the GUIs. Every graphical user interface has its good and bad points. Here, in a nutshell, are the pros and cons of the major GUIs. (Reprinted with permission from the June 1991 issue of BYTE Magazine. *© 1991 McGraw-Hill, Inc., New York, NY. All rights reserved.)*

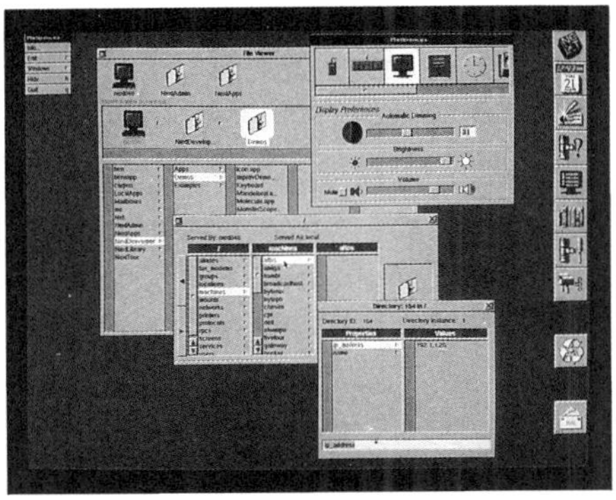

NextStep

BEST POINTS

- system is integral to machine; comes already installed
- applications are stable and compatible with each other
- multitasking capabilities built in from the ground up
- provides on-line help
- network capability built in
- good support for interprocess communication

WORST POINTS

- only available on the Next computer and the IBM RISC System/6000
- few applications available
- no macro or task-automation features included

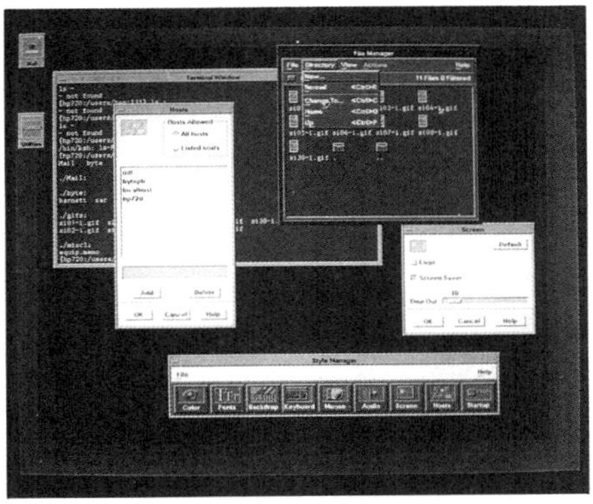

Motif

BEST POINTS

- multitasking capabilities built in from the ground up
- network capability built in

WORST POINTS

- no macro or task-automation features included
- no file manager included
- developer guidelines not mandated; applications may not appear consistent

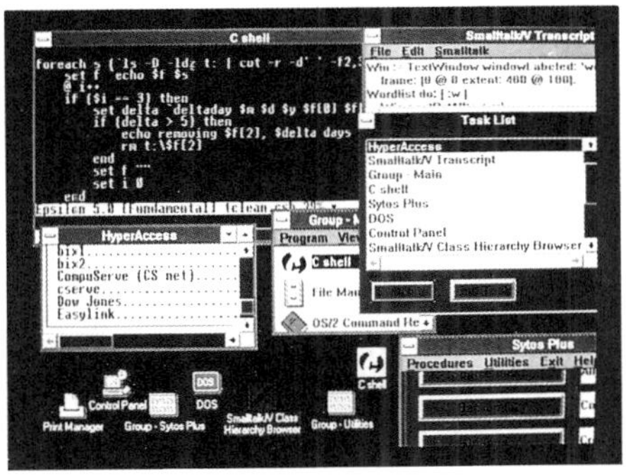

OS/2 Presentation Manager

BEST POINTS

- applications are stable and compatible with each other
- multitasking capabilities built in from the ground up
- provides on-line help
- macro and task-automation capabilities included

WORST POINTS

- sold only through IBM dealers, and many don't sell it
- few applications available

Amiga Workbench

BEST POINTS

- system is integral to machine; easy to install
- many applications available
- easy to configure for personal preferences
- multitasking capabilities built in from the ground up
- macro and task-automation capabilities included
- good support for interprocess communication

WORST POINTS

- lack of consistency across applications
- lack of 8- and 24-bit color
- no network capabilities included

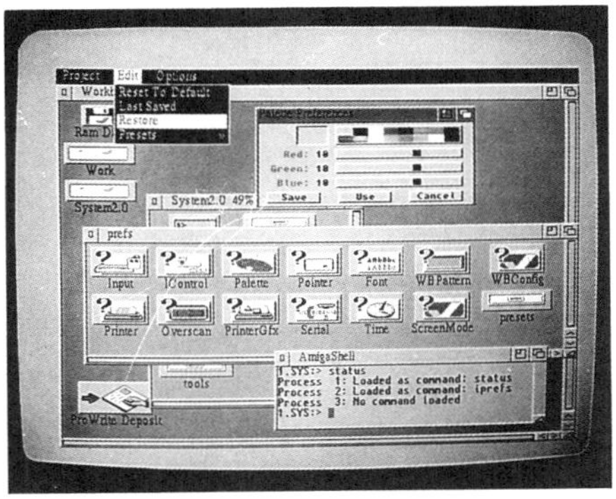

However, when looking at other application domains, the assumptions about primitive objects such as icons don't hold. Models based on physical data are often three-dimensional and dynamic. Abstract information may have relationships that don't have simple two-dimensional layouts and whose content may not lend itself to textual presentation.

That is the type of work that is being conducted at research laboratories today. For example, researchers at The Advanced Computer Technology Laboratory of the Microelectronics and Computer Technology Corporation are investigating what comes after the desktop, in particular, the limitations of current user interface technology along with the applications and technology that will take users beyond the desktop.

Researchers are discovering that it is necessary to make a distinction between the metaphor and the platform. These two are often lumped together. The ideas behind the metaphor are still good ideas that can be applied to other domains. The platforms (the underlying hardware and software) are tailored to particular kinds of interfaces. That is static, 2D, text, point and click interaction, etc. Based on continuing research into user interfaces, it seems clear that the desktop metaphor is not the final answer for all types of applications; it just doesn't scale up to complex applications. Therefore, developers are cautioned to not try to build complex applications on a desktop metaphor framework.

Multimedia, 3D, static, dynamic, still images, video and audio take advantage of having explicit models and schemas available to control the composition of the presentation and the presentations of time-based data (simulations and modeling). Media such as video and audio are more examples of time-based presentations. Given this, users should expect to see fundamental changes in the interfaces and applications of the future.

The Information Visualizer

Part of the Interactive Information Access project at Xerox PARC has been the Information Visualizer project. It is an experimental user interface with the goal of helping users better manage jobs that have large amounts of information. The Information Visualizer uses 3-D real-time animation to present information as 3-D interactive objects. The user views the Information Visualizer through a collection of 3-D (and 2-D) rooms that are filled with interactive objects such as walls and floating organizational trees. In order to understand the structure of the information that these objects represent, a user can access embedded data and examine its structure from different angles by "flying" around or through it. The interface also features other objects, such as 3-D directory trees, which can be rotated, examined, pruned, and rearranged.

These visualizations can be "animated" and are designed to shift information gathering to the user's individual perception system, freeing the conscious mind to work on larger problems. A major component of this experimental system is a compact, novel database system, called Text Database. The database system manages the storage, indexing, and search and retrieval of the information that the Information Visualizer displays. Text Database is being developed by the System Sciences Lab's Natural Language Theory and Technology group.

Limitations of visualization systems

Researchers and human factors engineers have known for some time now that the size and resolution of a computer's monitor or screen is the bottleneck in information flow. As discussed in Chapter 15, there is not much hope that monitors will increase in size much in the next ten years. However, in an interactive environment such as a GUI, all of the information from the computer is via the screen. The average computer screen is about the same size as a piece of paper.

Since the size of the screen will not change, the researchers at PARC decided to increase the effective size of the workspace it represents. In an experimental window management system called BigScreen, PARC researchers explored large virtual workspaces, something that has been used successfully in scientific and CAD visualization systems.

BigScreen distributes windows over the surface of a large virtual workspace, and the monitor is used as a sliding viewport onto that larger space. Analysis of BigScreen revealed that users tend to form clusters of windows related to particular tasks (e.g., one group of windows for reading mail and another for Lisp Programming). Rather than sliding the viewport over the workspace, users would jump directly from one cluster of windows to another as they performed various tasks. These little clusters are called locality sets, or working sets. The clustering of information is a common phenomenon. Furthermore, the elements in such working sets do not change gradually over time; rather, users tend to work with one distinct working set for a time and then shift abruptly to another.

Another way to increase the effective size of the computer screen is to increase its density (i.e., the amount of information it displays). Obvious limits exist when the information is given in the form of text or numbers, but images or a picture can yield compound results. Humans and lower animals use the method of selective omission to filter out unwanted or unneeded information. Animals with higher intelligence also use abstraction as a shorthand way of indicating information (e.g., an icon). These concepts can also be applied to a computer to simplify and organize information. Without having to deal with so many details, a computer user can process information more easily and in more universal terms.

Pictures are the obvious abstraction for the computer screen, and a 3-D representation can pack more onto a computer screen than a 2-D representation. Even 2-D structures benefit greatly from the added depth of 3-D graphics. Historically, scientific visualization has usually used objects and models that are inherently 3-D in nature. The Information Visualizer has used the power of 3-D real-time animation to show structures that are not typically thought of as 3-D objects—structures like organizational charts and calendars. Xerox also calls these representations visualizations. The prototype Information Visualizer system has visualizations for three classes of information: linear structures, hierarchical structures, and unstructured information.

Hierarchies

The Information Visualizer provides a special visualization called the Cone Tree, with which you can easily deal with large hierarchies. In Cone Trees, hierarchies are laid out in 3-D. They provide a "fish-eye" view of sorts; the closer nodes are larger and brighter than those farther away. Shadows on the floor provide another perceptual cue. They are, in effect, a 2-D projection of the 3-D structure, providing the user with another perspective.

When users select a node in one of these trees, it rotates so that the selected node and the path from the selected node to the root node are placed front and center and are highlighted. The cones rotate smoothly, like carousels, as fast as the eye can comfortably follow. As the cones turn, the human perceptual system automatically tracks the parts of the tree and their relationships. Users gain added insight into the relationships within the structure by seeing the tree from different angles as it rotates.

Visualization

The researchers at Xerox PARC feel the key to computer use in the 1990s will be the management of large quantities of information. That notion has led them to the development of the Information Visualizer interface with the goal of enabling users to deal with enormous problems by reducing the cost of using information. The Information Visualizer increases the efficiency of information exchange between the user and the application by providing highly coupled user interaction.

The use of animated 3-D visualizations makes the screen's information content much denser. Animated 3-D successfully exploits the user's perceptual system to convey information subconsciously. With an entire structure visible at once, the user can navigate through information faster and more easily. A new metaphor is being developed by Xerox, the organization that gave us the first GUI. This is just one of the many new developments that are underway in organizations around the world. The way people work together is also being revolutionized.

Distributed workforce

There will be increased shared access by multiple users allowing people to collaborate closely while being separated geographically—this is referred to as Computer Supported Cooperative Work (CSCW). Large distributed organizations will be able to rapidly bring talent together on a project, get the project done, and then move on to new jobs without having to move people around physically. Although industry is moving that way already with the phone, Voice-mail, E-mail, fax, Fed-Ex, etc., it's not good enough. These lack face-to-face contact and the resulting stimulation. More importantly, these methods make it more difficult to have the kind of chance contact that often is the catalyst for getting people to work well together. An expanded, enriched, totally charming interface is needed for this environment. Suggestions have been made for an autotracking camera (that follows the speaker's head) as part of a video-phone concept. Developments in data compression and the installation of fiberoptic and satellite links will make this possible very soon.

The user interface for such a system needs to make it easy and convenient for the participants to present information. Not just slides or personnel folders with an image of the user's face, but dynamic data that is being executed on a computer in a totally different location. This information will be presented in useful forms: for example, alternative views of information showing different aspects of the data or focusing on just the relevant information.

Pointing technologies

There are other developments in progress that will at least augment and enhance the development of the GUI, or perhaps revolutionize user interfaces in general. Gesture sensing devices that can sense motion and rotate in three axes without contact is one area that holds great promise. Galvanic contacts and sensors that can detect high-level brain waves are other areas being investigated for hands-free applications.

Synthesized reality

Moving into a synthesized world or environment known as *virtual reality* (VR) is another area being investigated. Virtual or artificial reality allows the user to walk into a computer-generated environment and react with it. Although primarily aimed at 3D simulations, its application for use in data-only situations is conceivable. Some observers and developers think it could be the ultimate user interface; others doubt it.

One of the major obstacles to VR has been in finding ways to map abstract data (i.e., a model) into visual form for the artificial reality environment. A *model* is an abstract representation of some set of data. Models are used for convenience to capture specific features of reality at the expense of others (e.g., a spreadsheet can show the cash flow of an organization, but not its morale; a synthesization of a room can show walls, but not texture or the effects of sound on them, etc.). Models come in many forms, and they range in complexity. Different models of even the same domain can have different bases of primitives. A user can move between models using transformations, if there is an explicit representation of the model. A model typically has more information than data, in that it contains structures and relationships of the data. Having an explicit model allows it to be used in different situations for different purposes.

The major obstacle in virtual reality is that even if the artificial world is perfect in detail (which at this stage of development does not seem practical), a user still exists in the real world. Except for specific domains (telepresense, video games, etc.), VR technology will probably be less a revolutionary development than what has been promised in the press.

Visualization

Although powerful hardware exists for the manipulation of data and the delivery of images, visualization is not yet a science; that is, we don't know how to derive an effective visualization from basic principles. A look at the literature for visualization hardware and software products reveals that it is a series of anecdotes relating how a visualization was applied to one specific problem or another. But there is no base of knowledge about how a user visualizes. The graphics arts industry is a little better in that there is a body of knowledge on graphic communications. However, that knowledge is more artisan skills and a set of rules of thumb and standard practice than a science.

However, in the long term, it must be the individuals with the questions who are able to produce their own visualizations if necessary, just as spreadsheets enabled a much larger population to create their own applications. Yet, today it has been suggested that a team of renaissance people are needed (data management, graphics arts, perceptual and cognitive psychologists) to obtain a visualization that accurately and quickly portrays a set of data. That means that no currently known user interface is going to help.

What the future holds

In the next century, computer systems will advance beyond just the virtual window and desktop metaphor we know today. The necessary man-machine interactions and the power required from the hardware is being investigated and developed now. Richer, more dynamic user interfaces with new levels of abstractions in the applications will empower people in ways only dreamed about today. These are not science fiction ramblings, but forecasts on the expected outcomes of today's developments. Computers will become allies, even friends, with charm.

References

Clarkson, Mark A. An easier interface. *BYTE*. February, 1991, Page 217.

Davis, Andrew S. Collective computing requires an effective user interface. *Computer Technology Review*. Winter, 1990. Page 117.

Godnig, Edward G., and John S. Hacunda. *Computers and visual stress: How to enhance visual comfort while using computers*. Seacoast Information Services: Charlestown, RI.

Laurel, Brenda. 1990. *The art of human computer interface design*. Addison-Wesley: Menlo Park, CA.

Rubin, Tony. 1988. *User interface design for computer systems*. Ellis Horwood Ltd., Halsted Press, John Wiley & Sons: Chichester, UK.

Tarlton, Mark A. 1990. *Interface design and visualization*. Frost & Sullivan Conference. Monterey, CA.

Tarlton, Mark A., and P. Nong. 1985. *Pogo: A declarative representation system for graphics*. MCC Technical Report Number ACA-HI-049-88-P.

Appendix

List of companies

ADVANCED GRAPHICS ENGINEERING (AGE)
8775 Aero Dr.
Suite 230
San Diego, CA 92123
619-565-7373

AIM TECHNOLOGY INC.
4699 Old Ironsides Dr.
Santa Clara, CA 95054
408-748-8649

APPLE COMPUTER, INC.
20525 Mariani Ave.
Cupertino, CA 95014
408-996-1010

ARCADIA TECHNOLOGIES
735 W. Duarte Road
Suite 207
Arcadia, CA 91007
818-446-6945

ASYMETRIX CORP.
110-110th Ave., NE
No. 717
Bellevue, WA 98004
800-624-8999
206-462-0501

AT&T SYSTEMS INC. (X Master)
12520 Prosperity Dr.
Silver Spring, MD 20904
301-384-1425

AT&T INFORMATION SYSTEMS
101 Southgate Parkway
Morristown, NJ 07960
800-247-1212

AUTOMATED SYSTEMS DESIGN
4782 North Inlet
Marietta, GA 30066
404-924-7331

BANYAN SYSTEMS INC.
120 Flanders Rd.
Westboro, MA 01581
508-898-1000

CADKEY INC.
4 Griffin Rd. North
Windsor, CT 06095
203-298-8888

CALCOMP
2411 West La Palma Ave.
Anaheim, CA 92801
714-821-2000

CANDLELIGHT SOFTWARE
2375 E. Tropicana Ave.
Suite 320
Las Vegas, NV 89119
702-456-6365

CANON
One Canon Plaza
Lake Success, NY 11042

CASEWORKS INC.
1 Dunwoody Park
Suite 130
Atlanta, GA 30338
800-635-1577
404-399-6236

CITRIX CORPORATION
210 University Dr.
Suite 700
Coral Springs, FL 33071
305-755-0559

COMMUNICATIONS INTELLIGENCE CORP.
333-PS 357 Ravenswood Ave.
Menlo Park, CA 94025
415-328-1311

CONSILIUM INC.
640 Clyde Court
Mountain View, CA 94043
415-691-6100

CORPORATE WINDOWS COUNCIL CM VENTURES
5720 Hollis
Emeryville, CA 94608
415-601-7842

DA VINCI SYSTEMS CORP.
PO Box 5427
Raleigh, NC 27650
919-839-2000

DATA GENERAL
4400 Computer Drive
Westboro, MA 01580
508-366-8911

DATAQUEST
1290 Ridder Park Drive
San Jose, CA 95131
408-437-8000

DATAVIZ
35 Corporate Dr.
Trumbull, CT 06611
203-268-0030

DESCRIBE INC.
4047 N. Freeway Blvd.
Sacramento, CA 95834
916-646-1111

DIGITAL EQUIPMENT CORP.
Four Results Way
Marlborough, MA 01752
508-467-7903

DIGITAL RESEARCH
70 Garden Ct., Box DRI
Monterey, CA 93940
408-649-3896

DIGITALK INC.
9841 Airport Blvd.
Los Angeles, CA 90045
213-645-1082

EASEL CORPORATION
600 West Cummings Park
Woburn, MA 01801
617-938-8440

ENABLE SOFTWARE
313 Ushers Rd. Northway 10
Ballston Lake, NY 12019
800-766-7079

ELOGRAPHICS
105 Randolph Rd.
Oakridge, TN 37830
615-482-4100

EXCELLAN
2180 Fortune Dr.
San Jose, CA 95131
408-434-2300

EXPERT OBJECT CORP.
7250 Cicero Ave.
Suite 201
Lincolnwood, IL 60646
708-676-5555

FARRADYNE SYSTEMS INC.
3206 Tower Oaks Blvd.
Rockville, MD 20852
301-468-5568

FTP SOFTWARE
PO Box 150, Kendall Sq. Branch
Boston, MA 02142
617-864-1711

FUJITSU AMERICA, INC.
3055 Orchard Dr.
San Jose, CA 95134
408-432-1300

FUTURE SOFT ENGINEERING CORP.
1001 S. Dairy Ashford
Suite 101
Houston, TX 77077
713-496-9400

GENSPAC
50 W. Hoover Ave.
Mesa, AZ 85210
602-962-5559

GO CORP.
950 Tower Lane
Foster City, CA 94404
415-345-7400

GRAPHICS SOFTWARE SYSTEMS (GSS)
9590 S.W. Gemini Drive
Beaverton, OR 97005
503-641-2200

GRAYTECH SOFTWARE INC.
2172 Menomini
Wheaton, IL 60187
708-682-4030

GUIDANCE TECHNOLOGIES
800 Vinial St.
Pittsburgh, PA 15212
412-231-1300

GUPTA TECHNOLOGIES INC.
1040 Marsh Road
Menlo Park, CA 94025
415-321-9500

hDC COMPUTER CORP.
6742 185th Ave., NE
Redmond, WA 98052
206-885-5550

HERCULES COMPUTER TECHNOLOGY INC.
921 Parker St.
Berkeley, CA 94710
800-532-0600
415-540-6000

HEWLETT-PACKARD CO.
3000 Hanover St.
Palo Alto, CA 94304-1181
800-752-0900
415-857-1501

HUMAN DESIGNED SYSTEMS INC.
421 ENABLE. Feheley St.
King of Prussia, PA 19406
800-437-1551
215-382-5000

HUMMINGBIRD COMMUNICATIONS, LTD.
2900 John St., Unit 4
Markham, Ontario, Canada L2R 563
416-470-1207

IBM CORP. (X-windows)
Old Orchard Rd.
New York, NY 10504
914-765-1900

IBM ENTRY SYSTEMS DIV. (OS/2)
100 NW 51st St.
Boca Raton, FL 33429
407-982-1975

IEEE
1730 Massachusetts Ave., NW
Washington, DC 20036
202-371-0101

IMSAL INC.
2500 Permian Tower, 2500 CityWest Blvd.
Houston, TX 77042
713-782-6060

INFORMIX SOFTWARE
4100 Bohannon Dr.
Menlo Park, CA 94025
415-926-6300

INNER MEDIA INC.
60 Plain Road
Hollis, NH 03049
603-465-3216

INTEGRATED COMPUTER SOLUTIONS INC.
201 Broadway
Cambridge, MA 02139
617-547-0510

INTEGRATED INFERENCE MACHINES
1468 East Katella Ave.
Anaheim, CA 92805

INTERGRAPH CORP.
Huntsville, AL 35894-0001
205-730-2000

INTERNATIONAL DATA CORP. (IDC)
Five Speen Street
Framingham, MA 01701
508-872-8200

IRIS ASSOCIATES
239 Littleton Road
Suite 8D
Westford, MA 01886
508-692-2800

IXI LTD.
1 Kendall Square
Suite 2200
Cambridge, MA 02138
617-494-6514

JUPITER SYSTEMS INC.
1100 Marina Village Pkwy.
Alameda, CA 94501
415-523-9000

KINESIX
1033 Richmond Ave.
Suite 1100
Houston, TX 77042
713-953-8300

KNOWLEDGE GARDEN INC.
Box 473A Malden Bridge Road
Nassau, NY 12123
518-766-3000

LOCUS COMPUTING CORP.
3330 Ocean Park Blvd.
Santa Monica, CA 90405
213-452-2435

LOCUS COMPUTING CORP.
8900 La Cienega Blvd.
Inglewood, CA 90301
213-670-6500

LOGITECH, INC.
6505 Kaiser Dr.
Fremont, CA 94555
415-795-8500

LOTUS DEVELOPMENT
55 Cambridge Parkway
Cambridge, MA 02142
617-577-8500

MCC - MICROELECTRONICS AND COMPUTER TECHNOLOGY CORP.
3500 West Balcones Center Dr.
Austin, TX 78759
512-338-3620

METAPHOR COMPUTER SYSTEMS
1965 Charleston Rd.
Mountain View, CA 94043
415-961-3600

MICROSOFT CORP.
16011 NE 36th Way
P.O. Box 97017
Redmond, WA 98052
800-426-9400

MICROGRAFX
1303 E. Arapaho Road
Richardson, TX 75081
214-234-1769

MICROWARE SYSTEMS CORPORATION
1900 N.W. 114th St.
Des Moines, IA 50325
515-224-1929

MIT SOFTWARE CENTER
Bldg. E32300, 28 Carlton St.
Cambridge, MA 02139
617-253-6966

MIT X CONSORTIUM, MIT SOFTWARE CENTER
Building E32-300
Cambridge, MA 02139
617-258-8330

MOZART SYSTEMS
1350 Bayshore Highway
Suite 630
Burlingame, CA 94010
415-340-1588

MOUSE SYSTEMS
2600 San Tomas Expressway
Santa Clara, CA 95051
408-988-0211

MULTI SOFT, INC.
Suite 207
123 Franklin Corner Rd.
Lawrenceville, NJ 08648
609-895-0072

NATIONAL INSTRUMENTS
6504 Bridge Point Parkway
Austin, TX 78730
512-794-0100

NBI INC.
3375 Mitchell Lane
Boulder, CO 80301
303-444-5710

NCD INC.
350 N. Bernado Ave.
Mountain View, CA 94043
415-694-0650

NCR CORP.
1700 S. Paterson Blvd.
Dayton, OH 45479
800-225-5627
513-445-5000

NEC INFORMATION SYSTEMS
1414 Massachusetts Ave.
Boxborough, MA 01719
800-343-4419
518-264-8000

NEC AMERICA
8 Old Sod Farm Rd.
Melville, NY 11747
513-753-7000

NEC HOME ELECTRONICS
1255 Michael Dr.
Wood Dale, IL 60191
800-323-1728
312-860-9500

NeXT INC.
900 Chesapeake Dr.
Redwood City, CA 94063
415-366-0900

NIXDORF COMPUTER CORP.
4 Cambridge Center
Cambridge, MA 02142
617-864-0066

NOVELL INC.
122 East 1700 South
Provo, UT 84601
800-453-1267

NURON DATA
156 University Ave.
Palo Alto, CA 94301
415-321-4488

OBJECT MANAGEMENT GROUP (OMG)
492 Old Connecticut Path
Framingham, MA 01701
508-820-4300

OPEN INC.
655 Softpointe Court
Suite 100
Colorado Springs, CO 80906
719-576-8967

OPEN SOFTWARE FOUNDATION
11 Cambridge Ctr.
Cambridge, MA 02142
617-621-8700

PARC PLACE SYSTEMS
1550 Plymouth St.
Mountain View, CA 94043
415-691-6700

PENCOM SYSTEMS INC.
9050 Capital of Texas Hwy N.
Austin, TX 78759
512-343-1111

PITTSBURGH POWERCOMPUTING
1501 Reedsdale Street
Pittsburgh, PA 15233
800-326-4025
412-231-3000

POLESTAR SOFTWARE
109 1/2 W. Broadway
Fairfield, IA 52556
515-472-2445

QUALITAS, INC.
8314 Thoreau Dr.
Bethesda, MD 20817
301-469-8848

QUARTERDECK OFFICE SYSTEMS
150 Pico Blvd.
Santa Monica, CA 90405
213-392-9851

REALTIME PERFORMANCE, INC.
349 Cobalt Way
Suite 304
Sunnyvale, CA 94085
408-245-6537

SAMMA CORP.
5600 Glenridge Dr., #300
Atlanta, GA 30342
800-831-9679
404-851-0007

SANTA CRUZ OPERATIONS (SCO)
400 Encinal Street
PO Box 1900
Santa Cruz, CA 95061
800-726-8649
408-425-7222

SENSOR FRAME CORPORATION
1401 Forbes Ave.
Pittsburgh, PA 15219
412-471-4071

SIEMENS A. G.
Wittelsbacherplatz 2
D-8000 Munich 2, Germany
+49-2340-0000

SL CORPORATION
Suite 110 Hunt Plaza
240 Tamal Vista Blvd.
Corte Madera, CA 94925
415-927-1725

SOFTWARE WORKSHOP
4611 Elk Ridge
Lincoln, NE 68516
800-762-9550
402-421-7969

SOLUTIONS BY DESIGN INC.
Hamilton, MA 01936

STANFORD RESEARCH INSTITUTE
333 Ravenswood Ave.
Menlo Park, CA 94025
415-326-6200

SUMMIT STRATEGIES
Box 774 Prudential Center Station
Boston, MA 02199
617-266-9050

SUN MICROSYSTEMS
2550 Garcia Ave.
Mountain View, CA 94043
415-336-1300

SUNRISE SOFTWARE SYSTEMS INC.
POB 329
Newport, RI 02840
401-847-7868

TANDY
1800 One Tandy Center
Ft. Worth, TX 76102
817-390-3700

TECSOFT SYSTEMS INC.
1375 Kemper Medow Dr.
Suite 11
Cincinnati, OH 45240
513-825-8386

TEKTRONIX INC.
P.O. Box 500
Station 50415
Beaverton, OR 97077
800-835-9433
503-627-7111

TELESOFT
5959 Cornerstone Court West
San Diego, CA 92121
619-457-2700

TEMPLE, BARKER & SLOANE, INC.
33 Hayden Ave.
Lexington, MA 02173
617-861-7580

TEXAS INSTRUMENTS
13500 North Central Expressway
PO Box 655474
Dallas, TX 75265
800-232-3200
214-995-2011

TGV INC.
603 Mission St.
Santa Cruz, CA 95060
408-427-4366

TIGRE OBJECT SYSTEMS, INC.
3004 Mission St.
Santa Cruz, CA 95060
408-427-4900

UNIPRESS SOFTWARE INC.
2025 Lincoln Hwy.
Edison, NJ 08817
201-985-8000

UNISYS
One Burroughs Place
Detroit, MI 48232
313-972-7000

USERLAND SOFTWARE, INC.
490 California Ave.
Palo Alto, CA 94306
415-325-5700

VECTUS TECHNOLOGIES INC.
28-08 Bayside Lane
Bayside, NY 11358
800-252-2304
718-767-2304

VIEWPOINT SYSTEMS
1900 South Norfolk St.
Suite 310
San Mateo, CA 94403
415-578-1591

VISIX SOFTWARE INC.
11440 Commerce Park Dr.
Reston, VA 22091
709-758-2700

VISUAL TECHNOLOGY INC.
120 Flanders Rd.
P.O. Box 5033
Westborough, MA 01581
800-847-8252
508-836-4400

VPL RESEARCH
656 Bair Island Rd.
Redwood City, CA 94063
415-361-1710

WANG
One Industrial Ave.
Lowell, MA 01851
508-459-5000

WESTERN DIGITAL CORP.
2445 McCabe Way
Irvine, CA 92714
714-863-0102

WHITE PINE SOFTWARE
94 Route 101A
P.O. Box 1108
Amherst, NH 03031
603-886-9050

WHITEFOX COMMUNICATIONS INC.
1823 N.W. 156th Ave.
Suite 100
Beaverton, OR 97006
800-669-5612

THE WOLLONGONG GROUP
1129 San Antonio Road
Palo Alto, CA 94303
415-962-7100

WONDERWARE SOFTWARE DEVELOPMENT CORPORATION
16 Technology Dr.
Suite 154
Irvine, CA 92718
714-727-3200

WORDPERFECT CORP.
1555 N. Technology Way
Orem, UT 84057
800-225-5000
801-541-5096

WORKSTATION LABORATORIES
4324 N. Beltline Rd.
Suite C211
Irvine, TX 75038
214-570-7100

THE WHITEWATER GROUP
1800 Ridge Ave.
Evanston, IL 60201
708-328-3800

WPMA (Windows & Presentation Manager)
1521 N. Glenville
Box 851385
Richardson, TX 75085-1385
214-234-8857

X-WINDOWS CONSORTIUM

XEROX
P.O. Box 1600
Stamford, CT 06904
203-329-8700

XGRAPH INC.
2855 Kifer Rd.
Suite 200
Santa Clara, CA 95050
408-492-9031

XIAN CORP.
Ridgewood, NJ

XTREE COMPANY
4330 Santa Fe Road
San Luis Obispo, CA 93401
805-541-0604

THE X USERS GROUP
163 Harvard Street
Cambridge, MA 02139

XVT SOFTWARE INC.
1800 30th Street
Box 17665
Boulder, CO 80308
303-443-4223

ZENITH DATA SYSTEMS
1000 Milwaukee Ave.
Glenview, IL 60025
312-699-4800

Glossary

ABF The Ingres Applications-By-Forms software module. This development environment offers simple menu-driven access to the Ingres 4GL.

ABI This is a general term for any Application Binary Interface. It allows executable versions of software to run directly on a platform without recompiling or modification. DOS is an example of an ABI. Standard components of the UNIX ABI definition include the following: Common object file format, memory map, entry to user process, signal handling, data types, common header file values, system calls, and required files and system installation procedure. A clear and standard ABI definition makes "shrink-wrapped software" a possibility. That is, software that can be sold off the shelf for a given hardware architecture.

action (user term) One of the defined tasks that an application performs. Actions modify the properties of an object or manipulate the object in some way.

action bar (user term) The area at the top of the primary window that contains keywords that give users access to actions available in that window. After users select a choice in the action bar, a pull-down extension appears from the action bar. The programmer term is menu bar.

active window (user term) The window that users are currently interacting with. This is the window that receives keyboard input. Contrast with inactive window.

address A unique digital code that identifies a register memory location or add-on board within a microcomputer system where information is stored. That portion of a program instruction that includes a specific memory location. The act of storing or retrieving data from a specific memory location.

AIX IBM's implementation of UNIX. The Open Software Foundation (OSF) based its first operating system (OSF/1) on AIX. The next revision of the OSF operation system (OSF/2) will also be based on AIX with a Mach kernel (Mach was developed by Carnegie Mellon University).

aliasing The undesirable distortion of a raster image by insufficient display resolution. Causes the effect commonly known as "staircasing" or "the jaggies."

Alpha channel One of four channels of information sometimes associated with each pixel of an image. The other three are Red, Green, and Blue (RGB), ordinarily used to store color information or the degree of transparency of the pixel.

Analog to Digital conversion (A/D) The process whereby an analog input signal is changed into a digital code. The digital value corresponds to the magnitude of the analog signal at the instant of acquisition.

anti-aliasing A technique or system to reduce or eliminate aliasing. In computer graphics, this frequently involves spatial frequency filtering techniques to reduce the effects of "staircasing" or "the jaggies."

API This is a general term for any Application Programming Interface. It defines a standard method of interfacing to software. Windows toolkit interface, graphics interface, network programming interface, DGIS, and TIGA are examples of an API.

application (user term) A collection of software components that users buy and install to perform specific types of work on a computer.

Application Data Application Data is a nongraphical, application specific structure element.

apply A standard pushbutton that causes the application to accept any user changes in dialogs that set properties but does not close the dialog box.

archival A mechanism for retaining and transporting graphical data. This information contains an application-independent description of one or more structures.

array A regularly ordered set. An image can be represented as a two dimensional array of numbers, each of which corresponds to the intensity (brightness) of a point in the image.

aspect ratio The proportional measurement of image size in terms of horizontal length vs vertical height. For example, an image with an aspect ratio of 4:3 has a horizontal length that is 4/3 the vertical height.

assignment In volume rendering, giving values for color, opacity, and refractive index to each volume element.

attribute An attribute is any description property that applies to an output primitive, including aspects that affect appearance, a modeling transformation, view definition, or name set. An attribute value stays in effect until another change specification supercedes it.

back plane A plane parallel to the view plane whose location is specified by a viewing coordinate space distance normal from the view reference point. When back plane clipping is enabled, portions of objects behind the back clipping plane are discarded. Clipping against the back clipping plane is controlled separately from all other clippings.

backplane The parallel circuit path that carries data and address information throughout a microcomputer system.

bandwidth The range of frequencies over which a computer subsystem will operate to within specified limits.

bit The smallest unit of information in a binary computer. A bit will have a value of "1" or "0." Eight bits make up a byte of information.

bitmap A grid pattern of bits stored in memory and used to generate the image on a raster scan display. In a bit mapped display, each bit corresponds to a dot or pixel on the raster display. A bitmap is a pixmap of depth one.

bit plane Hardware used as a storage medium for a bit map. When a pixmap or window is thought of as a stack of bitmaps, each bitmap is called a bit plane or plane.

border (user term) A visual indication of the boundaries of a window.

buffer A temporary storage area, often used to compensate for speed differences between system components.

bump mapping Similar to texture mapping. This technique creates rough surfaces, that could be difficult to render by holding in reference, a 3D texture consisting of a typical 3D section. During rendering, local points in the actual model are referred back to the bump map and deflected accordingly.

bus A communication buffer consisting of a parallel data path within the computer system that is shared by system components. Usually described by the width of the parallel data lines available, typical computer buses are 8-, 16-, or 32-bits wide.

byte Eight related "bits" of information processed as a unit. Often the smallest readily addressable unit of information.

byte order swapping For image data used in a networked environment, the server defines the byte order, and the client, with different native byte ordering, must swap bytes as necessary. For all other parts of the X11 protocol, the client defines the byte order and the server swaps bytes as necessary.

cascading pull-down A pull-down that is invoked from another pull-down.

check box (user term) A control that consists of a square box and choice text. It acts like a switch. An "X" appears in the check box to show a choice is selected. Check boxes can be used alone or grouped in related sets so users can choose one or more choices.

children The children of a window are its first-level subwindows.

click (user term) To press and release a mouse button without the mouse pointer off the choice. Compare with direct manipulation, double-click, and drag select.

client An application program connects to the window system server by some interprocess communication (IPC) path, such as a TCP connection or a shared memory buffer. This program is referred to as a client of the window system server. More precisely, the client is the IPC path itself. A program with multiple paths open to the server is viewed as multiple clients by the protocol. Resource lifetimes are controlled by connection lifetimes, not by program lifetimes.

client-server computing A system in which databases and most programming code reside on a networked microprocessor-based host (called the "server") that handles the bulk of processing. A desktop computer (called the "client") provides the user interface but does little of the processing.

client/server model The method that application software and X Window displays are based on. The client is the application software running locally or on a remote host, while the server is the software that controls the display of the information sent by the client on the user's display.

clipboard (user term) An area of storage that can hold data. Data in the clipboard is available to other applications.

clipping This process removes those parts of output primitives which lie outside a given boundary, usually a window, viewport, or view volume.

clipping region In a graphics context, a bitmap or list of rectangles can be specified to restrict output to a particular region of the window. The image defined by the bitmap or rectangles is called a clipping region.

close (user term) A choice in the system menu pull-down that removes from the screen the active window and all associated windows. Close = cancel in dialog and message boxes. Close = exit in primary windows and requires a message box if information could be lost.

colormap A colormap consists of a set of entries defining color values. The colormap associated with a window is used to display the contents of the window; each pixel value indexes the colormap to produce RGB values that drive the guns of a monitor. Depending on hardware limitations, one or more colormaps can be installed at one time so that windows associated with those maps display with true colors.

color table A workstation-dependent table, its entries define workstation values for particular colors. Colors are referenced by color index structure elements.

compound document A document composed of a variety of data types and formats. Each data type is linked to the application that created it.

cooperative processing The use of PC-based workstations connected to host computers through local area networks. Cooperative processing divides applications into front-end tasks that can be economically handled by the desktop workstation and back-end tasks more efficiently managed by the mainframe.

cursor (user term) A visual cue that shows users the current position of the keyboard input focus. The keyboard cursors are the selection cursor and the text cursor.

cut-and-paste Method of moving a portion of a document or file into another document or file, which could be in an application different from the source.

data bandwidth The amount of data, defined in bits, transferred in a single cycle to and from the image store memory.

database storage The PHIGS graphical database is, conceptually, a centralized collection of structures, PHIGS structure editing and manipulating functions act on the contents of the database.

data compression Various techniques, that reduce the data content/storage needed to represent an image.

DDE Dynamic Data Exchange of data between applications running under Microsoft Windows 3.0 or Presentation Manager. As data in one application changes, other applications which access that data are updated.

DECwindows DECwindows is a standard networked window server and toolkit shipped by the Digital Equipment Corporation. The window server is based on standard X Windows (see X Windows) from the MIT X Consortium. The toolkit implements DEC's look & feel and is based on standard MIT X intrinsics.

desktop The computer's working environment—the screen layout, the menu bar, and the program icons associated with the machine's operating environment.

desktop metaphor A desktop metaphor is the conceptual way a workstation screen area is used to emulate a user's physical desktop through graphic icon images. The icon maps directly to its real life function. For example, a trash can icon will allow a user to "throw out" a document. It gives an application a "user friendly" feel. Desktop metaphors are consistent throughout all OPEN LOOK applications.

device driver A driver is the device-dependent part of an implementation that supports a physical graphics device. The device driver generates device-dependent output and handles device-dependent interaction.

DGIS Digital Graphics Interface Standard. A standard function protocol for transferring graphic information from an application to a graphics device. In the IBM PC environment this standard has been developed by Graphics Software Systems of Oregon. This standard allows a user with a DGIS display device to use software that outputs DGIS commands, eliminating the need for a device-specific software package.

dialog box A movable window, fixed in size, in which users use controls to provide information that is required by an application so it can continue a user request. The user term is pop-up window. Compare with primary window, secondary window, and message box.

digital image An image composed of discrete pixels of digitally quantized brightness.

directory service The facility within networking software that provides information on resources available on the network, including files, users, printers, data sources, applications, and so on. The directory service provides users with easy access to resources and information on extended networks.

display device A display is a graphics device on which pictures can be represented; e.g., refresh display, storage tube display, or plotter. A display device is one component of an output or input/output workstation.

display list Sequence of display instructions that create, change, and refresh graphics displays.

distributed file systems A type of file system in which the file system itself manages and transparently locates pieces of information from remote files and distributes files across a network. It can recognize multiple servers and be accessed independently of the network location.

DLL Dynamic Link Libraries which are used in Microsoft Windows 3.0 and OS/2 Presentation Manager to configure a particular piece of software at run time.

DOS Extender A DOS Extender allows a program to run on a DOS-based 286 or 386 computer in a larger memory space than the 640 Kbytes DOS normally provides. Programs may be up to 15 Mbytes in size using this mode.

double buffer Two buffers; often where a block of data is alternatively written to one of two buffers. The advantage is that the hardware process which moves the data from the buffer to a peripheral, can be emptying the first buffer while the second buffer is being loaded by the program, giving an illusion of real-time displaying.

double-click (user term) To press and release a mouse button within a user-defined time limit without moving the mouse pointer off the choice. Compare with click, direct manipulation, and drag select.

DPMI The DOS Protected Mode Interface is the result of a committee made up of 11 PC industry leaders including Microsoft, Lotus, Borland, Intel, Locus, Phoenix Technologies and Quarterdeck. It defines a standard API interface that defines protected-mode programming under DOS. It will also allow applications to access main memory beyond 1 Mbyte and multitasking using a standard interface. This API was made available in 1990.

drag and drop The "drag and drop" definition defines how objects from one desktop application can be "dragged" out of that application, through the process of clicking on the object with a mouse, across the desktop and "dropped" on another application. For example: a file icon can be dragged from the Sun File Manager Tool and dropped on the Sun Text Edit Tool. The result will be that the Sun Text Edit Tool starts up with that file ready to be edited.

Dynamic Data Exchange (DDE) A form of interprocess communication in Microsoft Windows and OS/2. When two or more programs that support DDE are running simultaneously, they can exchange information and commands.

EEMS The Enhanced Expanded Memory Specification developed by Lotus, Intel and Microsoft. Sometimes referred to as LIM memory. This is memory that can be "substituted for" (or *mapped into*) a like-sized area of conventional memory. Unlike EMS memory, programs can be run in EEMS memory. Extended memory in 80386 computers can act like EEMS memory by use of special software such as Quarterdeck QEMM-386 or 386MAX.

electronic mail (E-mail) A system for transmitting messages or information through a communications network.

EMS The Expanded Memory Specification developed by Lotus, Intel and Microsoft. Sometimes referred to as LIM memory. This is memory that can be "substituted for" (or *mapped into*) a like-sized area of conventional memory. EMS memory is used to store data only. Programs cannot operate while in EMS memory.

enterprise network The overall networking makeup of a company. This can include a multivendor environment between a corporation's suppliers, customers, and strategic partners.

expanded memory Memory in a PC located above 1 Mbyte that can be used to run programs. In a 286 computer a special memory board must be installed, while in a 386 computer software control programs (QEMM and 386MAX) can be used to convert extended memory into expanded memory. The specification for expanded memory was originally defined by Lotus, Intel and Microsoft (LIM).

extended memory The memory space in an IBM PC computer that is located between 1 Mbyte and 16 Mbytes. Extended memory cannot be used to run programs. Typically it is used for RAM disks, print spoolers and disk caches. On 80386 machines it can act like expanded memory by using special software such as Quarterdeck QEMM-386 or 386MAX.

foundation graphics A set of graphics libraries or imaging models that form the lowest-level graphics programmer's interface. Examples: a graphics subroutine library that a program could call to draw graphics primitives like arcs, circles, rectangles, etc. Open Windows supports the Xlib and PostScript foundation libraries.

FTP A standard File Transfer Protocol defined in TCP/IP used for transferring binary files between computer systems.

Graphical User Interface (GUI) Describes both the appearance and the function of window components (frames, canvasses) and control items (buttons, pull-down menus, sliders).

gray level The brightness value assigned to a pixel. A value may range from black, through the grays, to white.

gray scale The brightness available as valid gray levels for a given image processing system. The gray scale represents the discrete gray levels defined in a system—for instance, an 8-bit system includes the values from 0 through 255.

GUI This stands for a Graphical User Interface. A GUI is a method of presenting information and system resources to a user via graphics on a CRT. Microsoft Windows 3.0 and X Windows are examples of GUIs.

handwriting recognition A system for taking handwritten notations, generated with a stylus on a computer pad or directly onto the computer screen, and converting them into machine-readable text.

hierarchical In PHIGS, hierarchy is that property of structures which permits structures to invoke other structures.

histogram The graphical representation of the gray-scale occupancy of an image. With the horizontal axis representing gray level and the vertical axis representing number of pixels, the histogram presents an easy-to-read indication of image contrast and brightness dynamic range.

hot links A methodology that references and can connect information from one document to another, regardless of the type of application used for automatic instantaneous updating.

HP-UX Hewlett-Packard's proprietary implementation of UNIX.

ICCCM The Inter Client Communications Convention Manual defines how X Windows implementations from different vendors will interoperate. For example, an application running on a server from Vendor A could display across a network on a window server from Vendor B. ICCCM was accepted as the interoperability definition by the MIT X Consortium in the fall of 1989.

icon (user term) A pictorial representation of an object or a selection choice. Icons can represent objects that users want to work on or actions that users want to perform. A unique icon also represents the application when it is minimized.

icon A graphic representation of a program, file or system resource. It can also be a shrunken window in Microsoft Windows.

image analysis Any image operation intended to numerically tabulate some aspect of the image.

image process Any method for implementing an image operation. Such processes include point, group, and frame processes.

inheritance Inheritance is the automatic passing of attribute selections from a parent structure to a child structure. The child structure need not specify all attributes explicitly to establish their values, since the inherited values act as local defaults. Attribute values are saved between structure calls, thus changes made in the child structure are not passed on to the parent.

input device This refers to a physical input device, which is part of an input or input/output workstation.

instancing Instancing is a method of defining an object once in a database and replicating it (without copying) multiple times with different positions, sizes, orientations, and other attributes. The structure network that defines the object is instanced, or referenced, by other structures and inherits its attributes from those structures.

interactive Interactivity describes the behavior of an application program in which a user may act upon the output of the application to immediately add to, change, or remove that output.

interpolation The mathematical technique used with geometric operations when the output pixel coordinates do not land exactly on a defined pixel grid point. Interpolation divides the transformed pixel's brightness and distributes portions to the four surrounding valid pixel locations.

intrinsics A component of many windows toolkits. The windows toolkit intrinsics definition has been developed by the MIT X Consortium. The intrinsics define the function of specific graphical user interface and window objects. They do not define any particular look and feel, just the function. Example: a pull-down menu intrinsic would define the function of a pull-down menu within a toolkit but not the appearance of it.

jaggies Staircasing which appears on lines, edges, and highlights in a raster display. Also referred to as aliasing.

kernel-based window system Kernel-based window systems are those in which the software application executes and displays in the same physical machine. Examples include personal computers and Macintosh. The advantage is speed. The disadvantage is that applications are closely tied to the system environment and are therefore not portable. Kernel-based window systems also do not allow users/developers to use the network as a means of sharing computer resources.

LAN A Local Area Network consisting of interface electronics and transport medium. Typically the transport medium is electrical cables, although it can be radio waves or light. Ethernet is an example of a LAN.

macro language A collection of instructions by which any kind of information in the system can be located and manipulated and by which new information types can be added to the system.

menu bar The area at the top of the primary window that contains keywords that give users access to actions available in that window. After users select a choice in the menu bar, the menu appears. The user term is action bar.

modeling transformation A modeling transformation is a structure element consisting of a general 4 × 4 matrix which can replace or be concatenated with the current composite modeling transformation matrix. The composite modeling transformation maps subsequent primitives from modeling coordinates to world coordinates.

mouse button (user term) A mechanism on a mouse used to select choices or initiate actions. For example, mouse button one is used to mark or select a choice.

NDIS Network Driver Interface Specification. A network protocol management standard that allows a maximum of four protocols to be run simultaneously on PC network adapters.

networked window system A networked window system is a protocol and a set of software services that allow an application developer to separate execution of an application from the display of that application. For example: Users would see an application displayed on the screen in front of them, but in fact, that application could either be executing locally or on some other X-compliant client across the network.

NeWS Window System The Network-extensible Window System (NeWS) was developed by Sun Microsystems. It provides all the technological benefits of a networked window system plus three key benefits: advanced office automation and electronic publishing graphics through the PostScript imaging model, the flexibility of a programmable server than can execute code that is downloaded from the client, network bandwidth advantages. The NeWS network protocol is less network-intensive than X Windows and will run applications faster when network bandwidth is limited.

NewWave NewWave is an object-oriented user environment available for personal computers from Hewlett-Packard. It includes a look & feel specification, a toolkit, and a desktop metaphor set of tools and definition. It is built upon Windows 3.0 and has been licensed to several vendors, including AT&T. A UNIX version is due out soon.

NeXTstep NeXTstep is the software development environment and GUI shipped by NeXT Computer. IBM's recently announced RISC System 6000 workstation family will support the NeXTstep environment for non-networked users. IBM has licensed the technology from NeXT.

object A software entity. An object can be a program, a data file, or a combination of a data file and its associated program.

Object-Oriented Programming (OOP) Object-Oriented is a general industry term that describes an emerging method of computer programming. Under object-oriented programming, software is assembled from discrete blocks of code called "objects." They are entirely self-sufficient and discrete from the rest of the code. The advantage of this approach is that new objects can be added modularly without disturbing existing code. Even better, new objects can be created that automatically "inherit" functions from their ancestors—the programmer has only to code what is incrementally different. This is a very powerful and flexible way of programming.

OLIT The OPEN LOOK Intrinsics Toolkit is the port of XT+ to the Sun platform.

OPEN LOOK graphical user interface The OPEN LOOK user interface specification is designed to give diverse applications a common 3-D "look and feel" through consistent, easy-to-use graphical metaphors, pop-up windows and point-and-click mouse controls—all of which greatly simplify operating a computer. OPEN LOOK is based on original work by Sun, contributions from AT&T and on technology licensed from Xerox Corporation, the originator of the concept of graphical user interfaces. OPEN LOOK was specifically designed to be the interface to today's networked, multi-user workstations.

OpenFonts technology OpenFonts is the name for the font technology that Sun bundles with the X11/NeWS Window System. OpenFonts allows for high performance scaling and rotation of fonts. This means that the X11/NeWS Window System does not have to store a copy of fonts in each type size (this consumes memory and is slow). With OpenFonts, the X11/NeWS Window Server need only store a single, hinted outline font for each face, which is scaled to size on demand. OpenFonts gives developers 627 fonts.

OpenWindows Application Environment The OpenWindows Application Environment is Sun Microsystems' networked window system software development environment. It includes the following components: DeskSet Tools, OPEN LOOK, OPEN LOOK Toolkits, X11/NeWS, and OpenFonts. The OpenWindows Application Environment is complemented by the OpenWindows Developers Guide, product, which is sold separately.

OpenWindows Developer's Guide OpenWindow Developer's Guide (or Guide) is a tool that allows Sun's OpenWindows software developers to graphically and interactively lay out their application's graphical user interface. With Guide developers can select window components and control items from a palette and "drag" them to the new application window being built. Developers can graphically lay out and simulate the operation of user interfaces in this way. When the layout process is done, the C code to implement it can be automatically generated by the tool.

OS/2 An advanced single-user operating system created by Microsoft as the successor to DOS.

OSF The Open Software Foundation, a computer industry association formed to develop and promote vendor independent software. While their major orientation is operating system software, they may develop application software. The technology they develop is offered by computer hardware and software vendors, not directly by OSF. All technology developed is available to the general industry.

OSF/Motif A GUI designed by the Open Software Foundation (OSF). It is based on the X Window specification, but adds additional features.

output primitive A primitive is a basic graphic element used to construct an object. Output primitives in PHIGS are POLYLINE, POLYMARKER, TEXT, FILL AREA SET, CELL ARRAYS, and GENERALIZED DRAWING PRIMITIVES.

palette The palette is the maximum number of colors or shades possible by all combinations of brightness levels of the three primary color (RGB) outputs. The palette size is found by taking the base 2 value of the total number of bits of the outputs. For example, if a display device has 4-bit outputs, then the palette is 2 with an exponent of 12 (4 for red, 4 for green, and 4 for blue), or 2 to the 12th which equals 4,096 colors. A device with 8-bit outputs will produce 16,777,216 colors.

pixel The fundamental picture element of a digital image. Also, the coordinate used for defining the horizontal spatial location of a pixel within an image.

pixmap A pixmap is a three-dimensional array of bits. A pixmap is normally thought of as a two-dimensional array of pixels, where each pixel can be a value from 0 to 2^n-1 ("2 to the Nth"), where N is the depth (z axis) of the pixmap. A pixmap can also be thought of as a stack of N bitmaps.

pixrects Pixrects is the primary graphics programming interface in the Sun View Window System from Sun Microsystems. It is replaced in the OpenWindows XView toolkit by the Pixwin interface, which is a thin layer on top of Xlib.

pixwin Pixwin is the primary graphics programming interface in the XView toolkit from Sun Microsystems. Pixwin is a thin layer on top of Xlib.

pointing device (user term) An instrument, such as a mouse, trackball, or joystick, used to move a pointer on the screen.

pop-up window (user term) A movable window, fixed in size, in which users use controls to provide information that is required by an application so it can continue a user request. The programmer term is dialog box.

Presentation Manager Presentation Manager is a look and feel specification and kernel-based toolkit development environment. It was developed for IBM by Microsoft with input from IBM. Presentation Manager is the standard graphical user interface and toolkit for the OS/2 operating system, which is a multitasking operating system for personal computers.

protected-mode A mode of operation of the 80286 and 80386 computers that isolates concurrent programs from one another. This mode of operation is not an integral part of DOS, but is incorporated into products such as Windows 3.0 and DESQview.

pull-down (user term) See action bar pull-down.

pushbutton (user term) A rounded-corner rectangle with text inside. Pushbuttons are used in dialog boxes for actions that occur immediately when the pushbutton is selected.

radio button (user term) A control that consists of a circle and choice text. Radio buttons are combined to show users a fixed set of choices that are mutually exclusive. These fields must contain at least two choices, one of which is usually selected. The circle is partially filled in when a choice is selected.

resolution The accuracy at which a parameter is divided into discrete levels. Pertinent resolutions in an image processing system are those of brightness, spatial, and frame rate. Also referred to as the number of rows and columns in a raster display device.

REXEC A function for Remote EXECution of programs on another computer. This feature allows a user to connect to another platform using RSH and initiate a program on that platform.

RSH The Remote Shell function allows a user to connect to another computer and operate as if he were a terminal connected directly to it.

sampling The chopping of the analog video signal into discrete pixels.

scroll bar (user term) A window component associated with a scrollable area that provides users a visual cue that more information is available and that the unseen information can be manipulated into view using the mouse. Users scroll the information in the window by interfacing with the scroll bar.

Server The Server, which is also referred to as the X Server, provides the basic windowing mechanism. It handles IPC connections from clients, demultiplexes graphics requests onto the screens, and multiplexes input back to the appropriate clients.

shell An outer layer of a program that provides the user interface, or the user's way of commanding the computer.

slider box (user term) A scroll bar component that shows users the position and size of the visible information in a window in relation to the total amount of information available.

socket A software interface, typically to a UNIX operating system module. It is a standardized method of interfacing to communications software.

stylus A pen-shaped instrument that is used to enter text, "draw" images, or point to choices on a computer desktop.

SunOS SunOS is Sun Microsystems' implementation of the UNIX operating system. It is an industry-leading merge of AT&T UNIX and Berkeley Standard UNIX (BSD UNIX) in a single operating system.

SunView SunView is Sun Microsystems' kernel-based window system. It has been shipping since the early 1980s and has more than 2,800 software applications ported to it.

TCP/IP Transmission Control Protocol/Internet Protocol. A standard communications protocol that originated in the UNIX environment. This is the standard Ethernet protocol used for X Windows and UNIX systems.

texture mapping The computer graphics equivalent of "contact paper." These maps utilize 2D images of what the surface on an object should look like. The 2D image is mapped onto a three-dimensional surface when it is rendered by the computer.

TIGA Texas Instruments Graphic Architecture. This is a standard function protocol for controlling a graphic display device based on the TI 34010 or TI 34020 graphics adapter. Unlike DGIS which is graphic device independent, TIGA is compatible with the TI graphic devices.

title bar (user term) The area at the top of each window that contains the window title and system-menu icon. When appropriate, it also contains the minimize, maximize and restore icons.

transformation pipeline A pipeline is a series of mathematical operations which act on output primitives and geometric attributes to convert them from modeling coordinates to device coordinates.

traversal This process executes the contents of a structure hierarchy to produce an image.

UI UNIX International is a consortium of computer hardware and software vendors which is interested in the development of open software standards for the UNIX industry. Prominent members include AT&T, Sun, UNISYS, and Fujitsu.

Ultrix Ultrix is Digital Equipment Corporation's proprietary implementation of the UNIX operating system. It runs on DEC's RISC-based workstations.

undersampling The sampling of an analog video signal at a rate less than that required to resolve a given spatial frequency.

VCPI The Virtual Control Program Interface is a specification by Quarterdeck and Phar Lap. It specifies the interfaces between 386 DOS extenders and 386 control programs, such as DESQview 386. It appears that it will be superceded by DPMI.

vector graphics The branch of computer graphics that deals with line drawings. Images are represented as line segments (vectors) rather than as shaded images.

view plane A 2D plane through which 3D objects are projected. The view plane is established by giving a view reference point, a view plane normal, and a view plane distance. Volumetric data can be stored in a computer as a three dimensional (3D) array, with each element containing information about the volume at some point in space.

WAN Wide Area Network. That part of a network that connects LANs.

widget An object providing a user-interface abstraction, i.e., a scrollbar widget.

widget class The general group to which a specific widget belongs, otherwise known as the type of the widget.

window (user term) 1. An area of the screen with visible boundaries through which information is displayed. A window can be smaller than or equal in size to the screen. Windows can overlap on the screen and give the appearance of one window being on top of another. 2. Window. A choice in the action bar of multiple-document interface applications.

window manager The manipulation of windows on the screen and much of the user interface is typically provided by a window manager client.

windows toolkits Windows toolkits are libraries of code that implement the graphical user interface objects that every software application uses. The toolkits save time by eliminating the need for software developers to re-implement the same user code repeatedly for each application. Toolkits also have the benefit of consistent user interface implementation across all applications that use the toolkit.

WYSIWYG This acronym, pronounced wiz-ee-wig, stands for What You See Is What You Get. It implies that the form in which data is presented on the computer screen is the same form it will appear as when printed or redisplayed. Desktop publishing using Ventura Publisher or Aldus Pagemaker is WYSIWYG. OSF/Motif form editors sometimes utilize WYSIWYG for interactive design rather than text files, which define window location, color, titles, and the like.

X Windows A GUI developed by the Massachusetts Institute of Technology and Digital Equipment Corporation in the 1980s. It is a general purpose GUI that is platform and OS independent. It has flourished in the UNIX world and is now crossing over into VMS and DOS environments. Many vendor specific products, such as DECWindows, are based on X Windows. The source code for X Windows is in the public domain and available from MIT. X Window components include the following: X11R4 - Revision 4 Window Server, Xlib - Low level programming interface, X Intrinsics - Higher level programming interface.

X11/NeWS Window System The X11/NeWS Window System is the standard window system that Sun Microsystems bundles with the OpenWindows application environment. X11/NeWS combines industry-standard X Windows with Sun's NeWS technology in a single, merged window server. X11/NeWS also includes Sun's OpenFonts technology and 57 scalable, outline fonts.

X11R3 This is the X Window specification, Release 3. It is the latest specification that all current X products are based on. MIT has recently developed Release 4 of the specification. It is expected that most vendors will add R4 functions to their client and server software.

Xlib Xlib is the lowest-level programming interface for X Windows. It was defined by the MIT X Consortium.

XMS The eXpanded Memory Specification. This defines the method of allocating and managing a 64 Kbyte block of DOS memory above 640 Kbytes.

XT+ XT+, an X Window-based toolkit, was developed by AT&T. It implements the OPEN LOOK look and feel and is based on MIT intrinsics.

XView Toolkit XView is Sun's X Windows toolkit. The XView application programming interface is based on that of Sun View. This allows for easy migration of applications from kernel-based Sun View to the network-based XView development environment. XView also implements the OPEN LOOK look and feel specification.

Z-buffer A technique used to provide hidden surface removal. It calculates the depth of a pixel, as shading or other scan conversion is taking place, and only paints it if it covers an already painted pixel.

Index

N

About the author

Jon Peddie is the president of Jon Peddie Associates, an Oakland, California-based consulting firm specializing in computer graphics. His company publishes numerous articles and reports on trends in computer graphics, including the *PC Graphics Report*, a special newletter and market service that measures market size and share, and discusses important developments in the industry.